Sovereignty or Submission

Sovereignty or Submission

Will Americans Rule Themselves or Be Ruled by Others?

John Fonte

with a Foreword by John O'Sullivan

ENCOUNTER BOOKS
NEW YORK · LONDON

First American edition published in 2011 by Encounter Books, an activity of Encounter for Culture and Education, Inc., a nonprofit, tax exempt corporation. Encounter Books website address: www.encounterbooks.com

Manufactured in the United States and printed on acid-free paper. The paper used in this publication meets the minimum requirements of ANSI/NISO Z39.48 1992 (R 1997) (*Permanence of Paper*).

FIRST AMERICAN EDITION

LIBRARY OF CONGRESS CATALOGING-IN-PUBLICATION DATA

Fonte, John.
Sovereignty or submission : will Americans rule themselves or be ruled by others? / by John Fonte.
p.   cm.
Includes bibliographical references and index.
ISBN-13: 978-1-59403-529-6 (hardcover : alk. paper)
ISBN-10: 1-59403-529-6 (hardcover : alk. paper)
1. International organization.   2. Sovereignty.   3. Self-determination, National—United States.   4. Liberalism—United States.
5. Transnationalism.   I. Title.
JZ1318.F65   2011
341.2—dc22
2010040030

For Susan

Contents

Foreword   *by John O'Sullivan*   ix

Introduction   xix

Part One: The Rise and Challenge of Global Governance

Chapter One   Durban, 2001: A Microcosm
                  of Transnational Politics   3

Chapter Two   A Perennial War of Ideas: Global
                  Governance vs. Self-Government   11

Chapter Three   Civic Nationalism and American
                  Liberal Democracy   35

Chapter Four   Liberalism under Assault   63

Chapter Five   The Rise of Transnationalism   93

Chapter Six   The European Union: A Model
                  of Global Governance   121

Chapter Seven   Ideas, Institutions, and Interests
                  of the Global Governance Party   159

Chapter Eight   Rethinking World Politics   179

Part Two: Struggle for a New World

Chapter Nine   Global Domestic Politics   201

Chapter Ten   Who Decides the Rules of War?   227

Chapter Eleven   The International Criminal Court:
                  A Supranational Judiciary   253

Chapter Twelve   Will Israel Be Allowed to Defend
                  Itself?   279

Chapter Thirteen   Assimilation of Immigrants:
                        Patriotic or Multicultural?   309

Chapter Fourteen   The Suicide of Liberal Democracy?   341

Appendix   371

Acknowledgments   377

Notes   381

Index   425

Foreword

John O'Sullivan

For some years, John Fonte has enjoyed an odd and slightly enviable reputation. He is the scholarly defender of democratic sovereignty most likely to be invited to debate the matter with his opponents in the academic school of global governance. This is partly because he is a courteous, well-informed, logical, and honest debater. That happens to be likewise true of his better antagonists, such as Peter Spiro, on the global governance side. It is not true of all, however.

Dr. Fonte is also one among very few scholarly defenders of sovereigntist ideas. In the academy, the media, the law, the foreign policy establishment, the corporate world, the wider political elite, and—almost inevitably—the bureaucracies that serve international institutions and nongovernmental organizations, the ideology of global governance is the prevailing orthodoxy. Those scholars who adopt a hostile or even skeptical attitude to its doctrines are in a distinct minority, resembling an endangered species in the academy.

Although global governance in its current form is a relatively new idea—dating roughly from the end of the Cold War—it is increasingly the basis of government decisions, bilateral agreements, and international treaties such as the Kyoto protocols or the treaty establishing the International Criminal Court. Books, op-eds, law journal articles, proceedings of international conferences, and think tank reports advocating various aspects of global governance appear almost daily in both print and electronic media. There has been little organized opposition.

Dr. Fonte's book is a major counterblast from the sovereigntist side of the debate. It is also an example of a disturbingly familiar paradox: a lone voice speaking out on behalf of multitudes. As Dr. Fonte illustrates (and as opinion polls confirm), the concept of democratic national sovereignty and the nexus of ideas and institutions built upon it reflect the beliefs of the overwhelming majority of citizens in the United States and other advanced democracies. Americans, Australians, Brits, Italians, and other free nations imagine that they are self-governing peoples who settle domestic political issues—such as the limits of free speech or an adequate level of welfare provision—by democratic debate and majority vote. Despite occasional grumbling about politics and politicians, they like it that way. All the evidence suggests that they would oppose any open attempt to replace their democracies with another political system.

"Global governance" *is* another political system or regime. It seeks to take ultimate political power from parliaments and congresses accountable to national electorates in sovereign states, and to vest it in courts, bureaucracies, NGOs, and various transnational bodies that are accountable only to themselves or to other transnational bodies. In the existing international system, legitimacy flows upward from voters in elections through sovereign governments, via treaties, to international institutions that enjoy specified and limited powers agreed in advance. Under global governance, by contrast, legitimacy flows from postnational elites in transnational institutions, via open-ended treaties, downward to postsovereign governments holding powers regulated by transnational bureaucrats and lawyers, and then finally to the voters.

Advocates of this second system argue that voters enjoy more real power as a result of "pooling" their sovereignty in transnational bodies that carry greater clout in international affairs, but they are curiously unable to describe how the voters can actually use this power. How can they amend an international law? Or vote members of the European Commission out of office? Or appeal a decision of the International Criminal Court? Or influence the diplomatic campaigns of the European Union, such as its attempt to outlaw capital punishment? The voters can do none of these things because they lack the ultimate democratic sanction: they cannot throw the (transnational) rascals out. It is not the voters but the elites running the courts, the NGOs, and the transnational bodies who exercise sovereign power in a wilderness of committees. In short, global governance is yet another attempt (the third major one since 1917 by my count) to sell elite rule in thin democratic disguise.

That's a tough sell. So it's hardly surprising that the attempt to impose it on liberal democracies has been decidedly covert. Here's how it's done: Global governance begins as the ideology of small but influential transnational elites operating outside the spotlight of national politics. Its voice is loud in academic seminars but muffled to the point of being dumb in national political debates and in the general media. Its supporters spread their ideas in the obscurity of learned journals, international conferences, and legal judgments. Then, politicians and bureaucrats travel to pleasant foreign cities to negotiate treaties and covenants that reflect the new orthodoxy. On rare occasions—as when Hillary Clinton led the U.S. delegation to the Beijing conference on women's rights—these treaties are openly crafted and fiercely debated at home. That slows the process down. So usually it is done between faceless diplomats in smokeless rooms in Geneva, watched only by lobbyists for NGOs and self-interested multinational corporations.

When they finally emerge from the long process of multilateral negotiation, these global treaties have only begun their careers. They have irreproachable titles signaling noble aspirations, such as protecting women or opposing genocide. But they are subject to extravagant reinterpretation by international courts, national courts, and even—under the rubric of the new customary international law—conferences of law professors claiming legislative force for their law review articles. The treaties themselves contain provisions that go well beyond a commonsense reading of their headlines. They incorporate monitoring and enforcement mechanisms that transfer authority from national governments to UN agencies and other transnational bodies. And they intrude into the most domestic of domestic policies—an intrusion often sought or welcomed by national courts, bureaucracies, NGOs, and other local bodies anxious to reverse a policy defeat in the nation's democratic debate. Indeed, a major impetus behind global governance is the desire of elites to insulate themselves against the possibility of such defeat.

Much of this maneuvering takes place in the political twilight inhabited by NGOs, lobbyists, and pressure groups. The wider public often learns of it only when a UN monitoring body arrives to argue that the treaty requires changes in national law or policy, or in the Constitution. Here are a few examples chosen at random from this book:

(1) The UN committee monitoring the Convention on the Elimination of All Forms of Racial Discrimination told the United States in 2001 to overturn the First Amendment of the U.S. Constitution because it was an obstacle to outlawing what the committee regarded as hate speech. (U.S. diplomats negotiating a treaty routinely insist on laying down "reservations" when they suspect that some of its provisions might be incompatible with the Constitution. This is something that greatly irks the UN and other global bodies.)

(2) In 1997, UN monitors of the Convention on the Elimination of All Forms of Discrimination against Women complained that "only 30% of Slovenia's children were in day care centers." Too many children were being raised at home by their parents because the elected Slovenian government was providing benefits to stay-at-home mothers. In the monitors' view, this policy reinforced old stereotypes and deprived children of educational and social opportunities.

(3) The UN committee monitoring the International Covenant on Civil and Political Rights complained to Australia in 2000 about its detention of illegal immigrants. It also chastised

the United States for the "increased level of militarization on the southwest border with Mexico." The committee was troubled, too, by the American federal system itself because "the states of the union retain extensive jurisdiction over . . . criminal and family law," which "may lead to a somewhat unsatisfactory application of the Covenant throughout the country."

Such intrusions into domestic politics are catnip to the tabloid press. Once it emerges that a country like Canada has agreed to submit its welfare budget for approval by a UN treaty rapporteur who is also the diplomatic representative of a notorious dictatorship, it becomes an instant political scandal. The public reacts along the lines of "What the hell is going on?" Advocates of global governance respond with variations on "Nothing to see here, folks, move along please. Just a small earthquake in theory; not many disenfranchised."

But the soft soap of global governance eventually fails to soothe. After a long period in which a revolution has been occurring largely unnoticed and unopposed, those attached to the status quo—in this case, liberal democratic governance—realize that the revolution is incompatible with their sovereign rights and established institutions. And then a genuine debate bursts forth.

Early opponents of revolutions are often disdained by their natural allies, however. In his 1968 introduction to Burke's *Reflections on the Revolution in France,* Conor Cruise O'Brien points out that his students usually assumed that Burke was writing after the Terror began. In reality, some of his most passionate philippics were written several years beforehand. Most well-informed Englishmen, including Burke's closest political friends, thought his early hostility to the French Revolution was excessive and unbalanced. They did not see the radical implications of the revolutionary ideology and therefore missed the bloody and anarchic direction in which it was leading. Burke's analysis of the revolution's early phases was profound and prescient, but only when his predictions were confirmed by events did conservative and liberal Englishmen convert to his skepticism.

Until recently, Dr. Fonte and other democratic sovereigntists have been in the same position as the early Burke. They have found it hard to persuade their fellow citizens that there is anything to worry about, partly because global governance needs a good deal of explaining. It presents itself as the fulfillment of liberalism, democracy, and internationalism, rather than their negation. It lacks the appalling frankness of Marxism or Nazism or jihadism—their willingness to state openly that their rule will brook no fundamental opposition. Instead, it describes its aims with many of the same terms used by democrats and internationalists: human rights, peace, international law. These clouds of ink deceive and pacify many.

Dr. Fonte is a pioneer in the trade of demystifying ideologies. He was the first anthropologist to classify and analyze the early primitive "transnational progressive." Accordingly, he is well equipped to extract the real meaning from the sophisticated euphemisms of global governance. (The first half of his book is a Cook's Tour of political theory over the past four hundred years— a highly readable introduction to political ideas on its own.) So he has little difficulty in demonstrating that to "pool" sovereignty is to lose it. He shows that to sign a treaty with clearly defined obligations to other nations is to exercise sovereignty, whereas to sign a treaty with a postnational entity obliging you to do whatever it demands is to surrender sovereignty. The former is internationalism; the latter is transnationalism, which first imprisons and then gradually eliminates nation-states in a euthanasia of regulations.

Dr. Fonte traces where the logic of global governance leads: to a massive, remote, undemocratic Leviathan. But why tap the thermometer when you can see the weather? In Europe, global governance advocates have already established an institution that embodies some of their fondest beliefs, namely the European Union. It provides us with a trailer of what global governance would look like in practice, as Walter Russell Mead points out:

Think of the European Union blown up to a global scale; in the Global Union nations would have their own governments and their own laws, but an increasingly dense framework of commonly agreed-upon laws and norms, and an increasingly complex and effective web of global institutions would supplement and in many cases replace the authority of national governments.

And that's putting it mildly. The current crisis of the euro demonstrates two additional dangers in such a structure: the first is that unwise and unpopular policies tend to be adopted in the absence of democratic accountability; the second is that even when they have manifestly failed, such policies tend to continue unchanged. The long-running failure of the Common Agricultural Policy—which ruins the export prospects of small Third World farmers in order to sustain high food prices for European consumers, at a cost equal to 40 percent of the EU's entire budget—shows that such folly can be maintained more or less indefinitely (or until the entire structure runs out of cash and collapses). Elites are far more unwilling to give up their fantasies than practical-minded ordinary voters, in part because elites can escape the negative aspects of utopia. The triumph of global governance would therefore risk repeating the failures of the EU on a world scale and at Brobdingnagian expense.

Global governance, however, is not an inevitable destiny, even if its advocates present it as such. In the second half of his book, Dr. Fonte examines four ideological contenders for the title of dominant political philosophy.

Democratic sovereignty, or "Philadelphian sovereignty" in Fonte-esque language, is the system that still provides the United States with its regime and that was the prevailing constitutional doctrine in Western Europe until recently. It received a marked fillip when the nations of Eastern Europe threw off communism and joined "the West," believing they were joining a structure built along liberal democratic lines. Instead, they found themselves in a halfway house to global governance, a structure that reminds them too much of both the Hapsburg empire (in more relaxed moments) and the Soviet empire (in moods of bitter despair).

Two other competitors are radical Islam and sovereign authoritarianism, such as the Chinese regime. Both can cause a great deal of damage in the world, but neither looks able to gain enough support or acquiescence to allow it to shape international relations and global institutions in its own image. Neither refutes Fukuyama's thesis that no plausible ideological alternatives would arise to challenge Western liberal democracy.

What Fukuyama did not sufficiently foresee, as Dr. Fonte points out, was that a plausible challenge might come from within. Global governance is just such a challenge. Like Marxism, it emerges from the leading social classes in Western society. It affects to solve global problems that democratic sovereign states allegedly cannot solve "on their own," or through international cooperation. It presents itself as a deeper and truer democracy than the partisan bickering of political parties. Yet it subverts democratic accountability and the consent of the governed at every turn, while it transfers ever-increasing powers from democratic institutions to global bodies and NGOs that seek to implement policies already rejected by voters and governments.

The intellectual quadrille danced by these four competitors is complicated. Day to day, the doctrines of global governance are a useful tool for Islamist sympathizers and authoritarian governments as they embark on, for instance, "lawfare" to hobble U.S. efforts to fight terrorism. But rising nation-states, whether democratic or not (China, India, Brazil, Indonesia, etc.), are particularly interested in exercising their sovereignty.

Fonte argues that it is unlikely that the forces of global governance will succeed in establishing their own utopian version of a "global rule of law." Nevertheless he warns that, assisted by transnational pragmatists, they might attain considerable influence, or even what Antonio Gramsci called "ideological hegemony," over opinion makers and statesmen in Western democracies. Though unable to achieve success on its own terms, the global governance project could essentially disable and disarm the democratic state. "If liberal democracy drinks from the cup of global governance," Fonte writes, "it will have poisoned itself."

Dr. Fonte analyzes the slow-motion suicide of the liberal democratic nation-states of western Europe as they transform themselves into subordinate states within the supranational legal regime of the European Union. Among the chief facilitators of this suicide are national judges of the various European nations. In the construction of a global legal regime, likewise, judges at the highest levels within nation-states would play a crucial role. Some comfort may be found in the growing resistance to the project of undemocratic Eurogovernance. Both at the polling booths and in the streets, European voters and taxpayers are rebelling against unaccountable power structures that deliver currency crises, high unemployment, and massive policy failures.

The forces of skepticism enjoy one potentially decisive advantage: global governance is the ideology that dare not speak its name. It has to deny on television the doctrines that it boasts about in the seminar. It has to conceal its achievements. It has to engage in verbal tricks to pass off its rules and institutions as liberal and democratic. In general, it has to dissemble constantly.

That was fine when no one was paying attention. Global governance could apparently survive anything but discussion. With the publication of this book, that qualification no longer applies. Dr. Fonte has removed the veils of circumlocution that surrounded the sovereignty issue, giving us an intellectual armory to defend our constitutional democracies against internal subversion or external attack.

He has done everything that can be done by a political writer. It is now up to his readers to do the rest.

John O'Sullivan is vice president and executive editor of Radio Free Europe/ Radio Liberty, and founder of the New Atlantic Initiative. He was a special advisor to Prime Minister Margaret Thatcher, and has been editor of *The National Interest* and *National Review,* and a senior editor at the *Daily Telegraph* and *The Times* of London. His book *The President, the Pope, and the Prime Minister: Three Who Changed the World* has been translated into several languages.

Introduction

The concept of "global governance" is very much in the air today. For many of the world's elites—who gather at places like Turtle Bay, Geneva, Davos, The Hague, and wherever the G20 meets—global governance is the big idea. Major political leaders and intellectuals tell us that today's global issues are too complex for the "obsolete" nation-state system; that "global problems require global solutions"; that sovereignty must be redefined as something that is "shared" or "pooled."

There is no doubt that as the twenty-first century progresses, global interactions in trade, people, culture, and ideas will increase, and an effective international system will be needed to deal with globalization. This book does not advocate any form of "Fortress America" isolationism or withdrawal from international obligations and responsibilities. The main argument in the future will not be whether to embrace or reject globalization, but what form it takes: Should it be international, meaning based on sovereign states, or rather transnational and supranational?

John Ruggie of the Harvard Kennedy School, a former deputy secretary general of the United Nations, explains the distinction between traditional internationalism and transnationalism (or globalism):

Simply put, postwar institutions, including the United Nations, were built for an inter-*national* world, but we have entered a *global* world. International institutions were designed to reduce *external* frictions between states; our challenge today is to devise more inclusive forms of global governance.[1]

The global governance project examined in this book is not international in the traditional sense. As Ruggie suggests, it is a grand ideological and institutional enterprise that promises to be of world-historical significance—an attempt to create new political forms above and beyond the liberal democratic nation-state. Abraham Lincoln defined the sovereign nation-state as a "political community" with no "political superior." The global governance movement aims to establish a global political community that would be "superior" to the national government of the United States and other liberal democracies.

This book suggests that the coalition of institutions and individuals that are promoting global governance will be a major competitor for power and moral authority with the democratic nation-state, and particularly with American democracy. The forces of global governance, both intellectual and material, are already significant actors on the world stage and constitute an important driver of global politics. They cannot be dismissed as hopeless dreamers, or simply denounced as shadowy conspirators; their arguments need to be taken seriously.

What do global governance and the "global rule of law" mean for American constitutional democracy, and for liberal democracy throughout the world? What happens to democratic accountability, to government by the consent of the governed? What happens to popular sovereignty and self-government? Is liberal democracy possible outside a constitutionally limited nation-state? To be sure, the advocates of global governance hope for a better world—more humane, just, and democratic; but I will argue that their proposed policies would, in fact, shrink and usurp democratic self-government.

Besides examining the worldwide conflict between liberal democracy and the forces of global governance, I will make a moral and political case for what I call "democratic sovereignty" or "Philadelphian sovereignty." It is distinct from "Westphalian sovereignty," a term often used to denote supreme political authority residing in the state itself. Historically, Americans have thought of sovereignty as belonging to "We the People of the United States," the opening words of the Constitution created in Philadelphia in 1787. The principle of Philadelphian sovereignty is also contrasted with the idea that political authority should reside in global law or supranational institutions, or be pooled among different peoples and nation-states.

Ultimately, the conflict between democratic sovereignty and global governance is a moral issue, one that concerns the oldest questions of politics: Who should govern, and why? To whom is political authority accountable? Do Americans—or Britons, Israelis, Australians, Czechs—have a moral right to self-government?

Part One of this book, "The Rise and Challenge of Global Governance," provides a historical overview of the perennial conflict between the dream of world governance and the desire for independent self-government, and then discusses how American national identity is linked to sovereign self-government. It examines the forces that are transforming American liberalism and national identity, and the increasing use of international and foreign law in the decisions of the United States Supreme Court. After looking at the European Union as a model for a new type of supranational political regime, Part One concludes with an analysis of the ideas, institutions, and interests of the coalition that is promoting global governance.

Part Two, "Struggle for a New World," describes the contemporary conflict between the global governance project and the liberal democratic nation-state on five different fronts: (1) United Nations treaties concerning human rights, social and cultural issues, (2) the laws of war, (3) the International Criminal Court, (4) the fate of Israel, (5) global migration and the assimilation of immigrants. I suggest that the internal challenge by the global government coalition may be promoting the suicide of liberal democracy, even as the liberal democratic nation-state faces serious external threats from radical Islam and a rising China in the twenty-first century.

Some may argue that the concept of a "global governance coalition" is too abstract; yet serious foreign policy practitioners, diplomats, and even military strategists often refer to something called the "international community." The European Union declares that the "international community" strongly objects to Israel's latest attempt to defend itself. The American secretary of state says that the "international community" is concerned about Iran's enrichment of uranium. The Organization of the Islamic Conference informs us that "the international community is outraged that insults to the prophet Muhammad in the Danish press go unpunished by the Danish government."

Who or what constitutes the "international community" is in the eye of the beholder. Indeed, invoking the "international community" is often just a way of legitimizing one's own policy preferences. By contrast, the forces promoting global governance are clearly identifiable and reasonably consistent in what they propose. Thus, the "global governance party" is as useful a concept as many others that are regularly employed in contemporary world politics, such as the Third World, the developed world, the global South— and more useful than the "international community."

In the coming decades, as the global governance party meets, interacts, conflicts, and wrestles with the liberal democratic nation-state, many observers maintain a hopeful vision of international harmony, transnational convergence, global cooperation, "non-zero-sum" games, and "win-win" futures. This book does not. We see contradictions that cannot be bridged. We see values that cannot be reconciled. We see core democratic principles that should never be surrendered. We see an irreconcilable conflict emerging between those people and nations that favor democratic accountability and those that seek to establish global governance—between those we call "democratic sovereigntists" and "global governancers."

In short, we see an epic ideological and political struggle that is global in scope and will last for decades, perhaps for most of the twenty-first century. The outcome of this struggle is uncertain, but one thing is for sure: like all political conflicts from time immemorial, it will not end in a fashionable non-zero-sum scenario. On the contrary, there will be winners and there will be losers. Particular institutions and individuals—nation-states, subregions, supranational organizations, multinational corporations, international lawyers, soldiers, clerics, UN officials, EU commissioners, the judges of the International Criminal Court, American citizens—will either gain more power or lose power. Liberal democracy will either expand or shrink. The idea and practice of a free society will either advance or retreat.

The struggle that we will examine in this book is existential, because it concerns whether the American nation-state and other independent nation-states will continue to govern themselves or be subordinated to a supranational authority. It concerns whether "consent of the governed" and "government of the people, by the people, for the people" will survive as living practices or be relegated to the status of antique curiosities.

A Note on Terminology

This book often contrasts the concepts of "international," "transnational," and "supranational." The term *international* is used mainly to denote relations among sovereign nation-states. Traditional international law, or what the American Founders called the "law of nations," is *inter*-national, comprising treaties and agreements to which the parties are nation-states. International politics is mostly "politics among nations," as Hans Morgenthau put it. Properly understood, internationalism does not compromise or subordinate the sovereignty of the nation-state.

On the other hand, *transnational* means "across" or "beyond" nations. In this book, the term signifies legal action and authority beyond national laws, constitutions, and officials. Transnational politics is activity directed at the internal political affairs of nation-states, undertaken by both foreign and domestic non-state actors and by foreign states. Transnational politics represents an intrusion into the domestic affairs of nation-states, including liberal democracies.

Supranational means "above" or "over" the nation-state. While advocates of transnational law are sometimes ambiguous about respect for national sovereignty, those who champion supranational law are more explicit about their aim to transfer decision-making authority (sovereign self-government) from the nation-state to global institutions, superior to any national institutions.

PART ONE

The Rise and Challenge of Global Governance

CHAPTER ONE

Durban, 2001:
A Microcosm
of Transnational Politics

A news story from the beginning of the twenty-first century offered a glimpse of world politics in the future. On October 27, 2000, Reuters reported that forty-seven prominent American human rights and civil rights activists had sent a petition labeled "A Call to Action to the United Nations" to Mary Robinson, the UN's high commissioner for human rights, in preparation for the World Conference against Racism, Racial Discrimination, Xenophobia and Related Intolerance, to be held in Durban, South Africa, the following year.[1]

The "Call to Action" declared that "although segregation has ended, persons of color in the United States of America continue to face pervasive and persistent patterns of racial discrimination and bias that threaten their livelihood, their liberty, and even their lives." It further stated that "racial discrimination in the United States is particularly pernicious" and "endemic within the US criminal justice system." The document charged that "the Government of the United States of America has not upheld its obligations" to eliminate discrimination "in all its forms," despite U.S. ratification of the UN Convention on the Elimination of All Forms of Racial Discrimination (CERD) in 1994.[2]

Therefore, the signatories declared, "We urge the United Nations and member States to: Call upon the Government of the United States of America to honor its obligations under the International Convention on the Elimination of All Forms of Racial Discrimination and other human rights treaties." The "Call to Action": (1) demanded that the United States "remove its restrictions" to the CERD treaty; (2) called upon the UN to send special rapporteurs to investigate "race bias in the US criminal justice system"; and (3) asked the UN to include the issue of "racial discrimination and race bias in the United States criminal justice system as an agenda item for the UN World Conference against Racism, Racial Discrimination, Xenophobia and Related Intolerance."[3]

Among the representatives of major NGOs (nongovernmental organizations) who signed the petition were: Kenneth Roth (executive director of Human Rights Watch), Dr. Bob Edgar (general secretary, National Council of Churches), Ira Glasser (executive director, American Civil Liberties Union), James F. Fitzpatrick (chairman, International Human Rights Law Group), Raul Yzaguirre (president, National Council of La Raza), James Zogby (president, Arab American Institute), Antonia Hernandez (president, Mexican American Legal Defense and Educational Fund), Hala Maksoud (president, Arab-American Anti-Discrimination Committee), Wade Henderson (executive director, Leadership Conference on Civil and Human Rights), Michael Posner (executive director, Lawyers Committee for Human Rights), Yolanda S. Wu (National Organization of Women, Legal Defense and Education Fund), Jesse Jackson Sr. (president, Rainbow PUSH Coalition), and Mary Frances Berry (chairman, U.S. Commission on Civil Rights).[4]

The spokesman for the NGO activists, Wade Henderson, presented Mary Robinson with the "Call to Action to the United Nations" at a press conference. Henderson explained that the NGOs had repeatedly but unsuccessfully pressed their issues with federal and state governments in the United States. "In our frustration, we now turn to the United Nations and have asked the high commissioner ... to aid us in holding the United States accountable for the intractable and persistent problems of discrimination that we, as men and women of color, face at the hands of the United States criminal justice system." Robinson responded by saying, "It is an honor for me, as high commissioner, to receive this call for action."[5]

For several years before the Durban conference, American NGOs participated in various preliminary meetings that spelled out a clear agenda for the coming event. Besides the NGOs listed in the "Call to Action," other groups including Amnesty International USA and the American Friends Service Committee were also involved. Major American foundations bankrolled the NGO initiatives related to Durban. Particularly generous financial support for the NGO activity came from the Ford Foundation, the MacArthur Foundation, the Charles Stewart Mott Foundation, and the Rockefeller Foundation.[6]

For example, the Rockefeller Foundation convened a pre-Durban strategy session for NGOs at their plush conference center in Bellagio, Italy. In 1998, three years before the conference, the Ford Foundation awarded a $300,000 grant to the International Human Rights Law Group specifically to "encourage U.S. compliance" with the UN Convention on the Elimination of All Forms of Racial Discrimination. In the four years leading up to the conference, Human Rights Watch received over $8 million from the Ford Foundation, over $8.9 million from the MacArthur Foundation, around $350,000 from the Rockefeller Foundation, and $150,000 from the Mott Foundation.[7]

The NGO agenda was spelled out in a series of reports, two of them funded by the Ford Foundation and the Charles Stewart Mott Foundation: one from a meeting of the U.S. NGO Coordination Committee on the American Hemisphere, and another from the U.S. NGO leadership meeting. In these documents, the NGOs endorsed the following positions:

Reparations. "Support the inclusion of compensatory measures" as a major subtheme of the Durban conference. "Compensatory measures" in the language of the Durban conference meant financial payments or "reparations" from Western nations to people of African descent for the historical injustice of slavery. An NGO report on the conference's regional meeting in Santiago, Chile, describes how American NGOs undermined the U.S. government's position by providing research and advocacy (with funds from American Big Philanthropy) to African nations that were promoting reparations for slavery.

Racism is systemic. "It was the unanimous view among the [NGO] participants" that statistical disparities between the races were the result of racism and racial discrimination in the United States. "Racism," the NGOs stated, "permeates every institution at every level." Thus, policies such as welfare reform and minimum mandatory sentencing are "motivated" by racism. The idea of "color blindness" is a myth that "contributes directly" to the perpetuation of racism. In addition, the NGOs insisted that "rhetoric emphasizing the progress we have made" is a form of "denial" that "ignores ... deeply imbedded racism."

Affirmative action. The NGOs recommended that the UN conference condemn opposition to affirmative action and urge "the US government and state authorities [to] reaffirm and vigorously defend ... affirmative action measures."

Adequate standard of living. The NGOs attacked the "consistent failure of the US government to recognize that an adequate standard of living is a right not a privilege." They asserted that the United States fails to protect the "economic rights" enshrined in the UN Universal Declaration of Human Rights.

Multilingualism. The NGOs characterized U.S. domestic policies that emphasize English-language acquisition for non-English speakers as "discriminatory." They recommended that "multilingualism should be encouraged and promoted, not impeded."

Anti–free market. At the NGO meetings, free-market capitalism was repeatedly criticized as "a fundamentally flawed system," and participants "expressed the conviction that it is possible to organize a more just, equitable and socially responsive system."[8]

At one level, the agenda promoted by the NGOs and funded by some of the giants of the American nonprofit world could reasonably be described as left-progressive, somewhat redistributionist, even utopian. Obviously, as citizens of American democracy, the representatives of the NGOs and philanthropic institutions have the right to promote any views they want. They are members of the American constitutional order, in which democratic decisions are made and elected officials at both the national and state levels are accountable to fellow citizens. If elected officials from either the executive or the legislative branch of government violate the constitutional rights of American citizens, there are federal and state courts to restrain them. Moreover, unlike some Western democracies, the American political system maintains a robust tradition of free speech and vigorous debate.

If we look beyond the rhetoric of the "Call to Action" and the proposals of the NGOs, however, and examine the process of implementing those proposals, we see a distinct challenge to the American democratic system. Recall that Wade Henderson, spokesman for the NGOs, said emphatically that their policy recommendations "had been repeatedly raised with federal and state officials in the United States but to little effect. . . . In our frustration, we now turn to the United Nations."[9] They had tried but failed to enact their policy agenda through our democratic institutions: the state legislatures, the state courts, the governors' offices, the U.S. Congress, the federal executive branch, or the federal courts. And so, because they didn't like the results of the decision-making process within American democracy, they were resorting to a different process, outside of American democracy and the U.S. Constitution.

The postconstitutional agenda of the human rights activists was made clear by their strenuous opposition to the reservations and restrictions that all U.S. governments have placed on international treaties. The single most significant demand of the NGOs involved in the Durban conference was that the U.S. government "ratify all international human rights treaties" and "remove all reservations" to the UN Convention on the Elimination of All Forms of Racial Discrimination and to other treaties.

For most of the past half century, the U.S. State Department has routinely qualified American ratification of international treaties with stipulations (in written "reservations, understandings, declarations," or RUDs) that the United States will not accept anything in the treaty as valid if the treaty provisions violate the U.S. Constitution. If there is a point of dispute between an international treaty and the Constitution of the United States, the Constitution trumps the international convention.

In the case of CERD, the U.S. government—specifically, the Clinton administration and the Democratic-majority U.S. Senate—ratified the treaty, but with clear reservations. The State Department memorandum in 1994 specifically noted that "the provisions in CERD restricting so-called hate speech could violate the free speech and freedom of assembly guarantees of the First Amendment to the U.S. Constitution. The United States will not accept any treaty requirement incompatible with the Constitution of the United States of America."

The NGOs and human rights activists bitterly opposed the U.S. reservations on the CERD treaty. The signatories of the "Call to Action" explicitly called on the United States to "remove its reservations" to CERD.[10]

In the days before the Durban conference, the NGOs charged that the United States was not fulfilling its obligations under the CERD treaty. On August 6, 2001, Reuters reported that the United States had presented its first explanation to a UN committee on how it was implementing the treaty; the American delegation "reiterated the US policy of condemning unequal treatment of racial and ethnic minorities."[11] But neither the UN committee nor the

American NGOs were interested in equal *treatment* for minorities; instead, they insisted on equal *results*—that is to say, statistical equality among the races in all areas of American society.

According to Nancy Chang, senior litigation attorney at the Center for Constitutional Rights, "almost every member of the [UN] committee raised the question of why there are vast disparities with respect to race in every aspect of American life, from education, housing, health, welfare, and criminal justice."[12] An attorney representing Human Rights Watch, Erika George, said that the United States had "simply restated a position which already doesn't comply with the CERD and which indicates no willingness to comply."[13]

To comply with the NGO interpretation of the CERD treaty, however, the United States would have to turn its political and economic system upside down, abandoning the free speech guarantees of the Constitution, bypassing federalism, and ignoring the very concept of majority rule, since there is little in the NGO agenda that is supported by the American people.

The Durban controversy is a case study in the future of world politics. It signaled the beginning of a new transnational politics that is "postconstitutional." Influential American interest groups appealed to transnational political institutions beyond the reach of the U.S. Constitution, and thus beyond our democratic system. Those interest groups were on the political left, but there are also groups and individuals on the center and the right of American politics that act transnationally and postconstitutionally. In so doing, they present an existential challenge to American democracy.

CHAPTER TWO

A Perennial War of Ideas: Global Governance vs. Self-Government

The Durban controversy boiled down to issues that have been debated for thousands of years: Who governs? Who has authority to make decisions, and why? Broadly speaking, two "parties" have been locked in combat over these questions since ancient times. On one side is the "party of global governance." Members of this party dream of a supranational political authority that ensures peace and solves global problems. On the other side is the "party of independent sovereignty." Members of this party aspire to self-rule and aim to curb the power of multinational and supranational empires.

For positive historical examples, the party of global governance has looked to such institutions as the Roman Empire, the empires of Alexander the Great and Charlemagne, the Holy Roman Empire, the Hapsburg and Austro-Hungarian empires, and certain aspects of Napoleon's empire and those of the Spanish, the Dutch, the French, and the British. Today this party looks favorably on the European Union, the United Nations, and supranational institutions such as the International Criminal Court.

On the other side, the party of independent self-government has identified with a competing set of historical institutions, including ancient Israel, the Athenian polis and other Greek city-states, the

Roman Republic, the Italian city-states and the free cities of northern Europe in the medieval and Renaissance era, Elizabethan England, the Dutch Republic, and the American republic of the Founders. Today this group favors liberal democratic nation-states in general, and particularly those democratic nations that exhibit a robust independent sensibility, such as the United States, Israel, and India.

The Perennial Dream of Global Governance

Since the dawn of politics, humans have envisioned a global political authority that would bring peace and harmony to the world. In the Middle Ages, Dante's *De Monarchia* advocated a world empire headed by the Holy Roman Emperor (the putative successor to the Roman emperors of the past) because he believed that a single global authority was the only way to achieve universal peace and justice. During the Enlightenment, Immanuel Kant argued for a world federation of republics that would form a "united power and the law-governed decisions of a united will" to create and maintain "perpetual peace."[1]

In the nineteenth century, Victor Hugo supported global rule, as did Alfred, Lord Tennyson, who in his famous poem "Locksley Hall" (1837) wrote:

> For I dipt into the future, far as human eye could see,
> Saw the Vision of the world, and all the wonders that would be;

> Till the war-drum throbb'd no longer, and the battle flags were furl'd
> In the Parliament of man, the Federation of the world.

> There the common sense of most shall hold a fretful realm in awe,
> And the kindly earth shall slumber, lapt in universal law.

In the twentieth century, a range of leading intellectuals advocated world government or some kind of worldwide federal system. They included H. G. Wells, Arnold Toynbee, Bertrand Russell, Albert Einstein, Robert Maynard Hutchins, William O. Douglas, Edmund O. Wilson, Carl Sagan, and Richard Dawkins, among others.

One of the most popular nonfiction books of the late 1940s was Emery Reves' *Anatomy of Peace,* published in 1945 in the immediate aftermath of the atomic bombing of Hiroshima and Nagasaki.[2] Reves, an Englishman and friend of Winston Churchill, declared that peace could be achieved only under a world government. In an "Open Letter to the American People" that accompanied the book, Reves argued that the UN Charter of 1945 was inadequate because "by maintaining the absolute sovereignties of the rival nation-states" it prevented "the creation of superior law." Instead, Reves maintained, "We must aim at a federal constitution of the world, a working world-wide legal order, if we hope to prevent an atomic World War."[3] Reves' "Open Letter" was endorsed by three U.S. senators (Fulbright, Pepper, and Thomas), Supreme Court Justice Owen Roberts, Mortimer Adler, Thomas Mann, Cord Meyer (a future top CIA official), and Albert Einstein.[4] The following year, Einstein himself wrote that "A world government must be created which is able to solve conflicts between nations by judicial decision. This government must be based on a clearcut constitution which is approved by the governments and the nations and which gives it the sole disposition of offensive weapons."[5]

Four decades later, the advocates of world government included the former CBS anchor Walter Cronkite, once touted as "the most trusted man in America." Speaking to the World Federalist Association in October 1999, Cronkite argued that national sovereignty needed to be limited for the sake of peace in the world:

> It seems to many of us that if we are to avoid the eventual catastrophic world conflict we must strengthen the United Nations as a first step toward a world government with a legislature,

executive and judiciary, and police to enforce its international laws and keep the peace. To do that, of course, we Americans will have to yield up some of our sovereignty. It would take a lot of courage, a lot of faith in the new order.... Today we must develop federal structures on a global level. We need a system of enforceable world law—a democratic federal world government—to deal with world problems.[6]

Almost no serious analyst today speaks of world government or world federalism. During the past few decades, the more sophisticated champions of a worldwide political authority have shifted their goal to a more limited concept of "global governance." It is a "less threatening concept," remarked Anne-Marie Slaughter, who was director of policy planning at the U.S. State Department under Hillary Clinton from 2009 to 2011, and previously served as dean of the Woodrow Wilson School of International and Public Affairs at Princeton University.[7]

In explaining global governance, Slaughter argues that nation-states should cede a degree of sovereignty to transnational networks in both a "horizontal" and a "vertical" sense.[8] Horizontally means that in the legal arena, for example, American judges would interact with foreign judges, quoting each other's opinions and developing joint legal doctrine—which Slaughter calls "transjudicialism." Vertically, nations would cede sovereign authority to supranational institutions, such as the International Criminal Court, in cases requiring global solutions to global problems. Slaughter maintains that such transnational networks "can perform many of the functions of a world government—legislation, administration, and adjudication—without the form," thereby creating an effective global rule of law.[9]

The main arguments for global authority—whether as a world government or some other form of global governance—have remained strikingly similar for thousands of years. To wit, world peace and global justice are universal aspirations of human beings, and they can be achieved only through a global political authority. Today's advocates of global governance emphasize "global problems that require global solutions," including war, nuclear proliferation, environmental disaster, climate change, violations of human rights, inequality, global migration from poor to rich countries, and great disparities of wealth.

One of the most influential and practical-minded advocates of global governance is Strobe Talbott, president of the Brookings Institution and former deputy secretary of state. While he was a journalist at *Time* magazine in the 1990s, Talbott published "The Birth of the Global Nation," an article that predicted and welcomed a supranational political authority in the future. "I'll bet that within the next hundred years . . . nationhood as we know it will be obsolete; all states will recognize a single global authority. A phrase briefly fashionable in the mid-20th century—'citizen of the world'—will have assumed real meaning by the end of the 21st century," Talbott wrote. In his analysis, "All countries are basically social arrangements, accommodations to changing circumstances. No matter how permanent and even sacred they may seem at any one time, in fact they are all artificial and temporary." He concluded by saying that "a devolution of power not only upwards toward supranational bodies . . . but also downward," toward "autonomous units of administration that permit distinct societies to preserve their cultural identities," would be a "basically positive phenomenon."[10]

Later, Talbott traced the historical arguments and made the contemporary case for global governance in *The Great Experiment: The Story of Ancient Empires, Modern States, and the Quest for a Global Nation.*[11] "I have qualified my forecast somewhat, but not in essence," Talbott wrote, saying that "there is reason to hope—and also to predict" that world politics will move in the direction he indicated earlier.[12] Indeed, his book is not simply predictive but normative, spelling out what he holds up as an ideal.

Talbott begins his historical review of global governance by noting that since ancient times "there has always been, and always will be, a tension between, on the one hand, the concept of an international community" and, on the other, "the appeal of a national community that thinks of itself as independent and sovereign."[13] He is sympathetic to multinational empires with global aspirations, and somewhat condescending toward independent sovereignties. Whereas Aristotle defended the Greek independent city-states, Alexander the Great had "a bigger and better idea," says Talbott: a single global political community.[14] In praising the Mongol empire, Talbott quotes Jack Weatherford's remark that the Mongols "sought not merely to conquer the world but to institute a global order based on free trade, a single international law, and a universal alphabet with which to write all languages."[15] Also portrayed mostly favorably as contributors to the cause of global governance are the Babylonian, Egyptian, and Roman empires, the Qin dynasty's empire in China, the Mauryan empire of India under Ashoka, the empires of Muhammad, Charlemagne, the Ottomans, and the Hapsburgs. The supranational European Union is presented in glowing terms as "an undertaking of great boldness and promise, a model for what is possible."[16] Talbott's tone is decidedly less positive when he examines national sovereignties. One of his "favorite definitions" of the nation comes from Julian Huxley: "a society united by a common error as to its origins and a common aversion to its neighbors."[17]

Ancient Israel as Prototype of the Sovereign Nation

The perennial conflict between transnationalists and independent sovereigntists might be said to begin in the Hebrew Bible. Talbott notes that ancient Israel in the Western imagination is the first self-governing political entity, the prototype of the sovereign nation and independent state that faced a succession of imperial foes. It broke free of various transnational empires (Babylonian, Egyptian, Hellenistic) and fought a series of conflicts with imperial forces (Greek,

Roman). It was under imperial rule for thousands of years, but was reconstituted as a democratic nation-state in the twentieth century.

Talbott's language suggests less empathy for the ancient Hebrews or for modern Israelis than for the transnational powers that have attempted to subjugate them. He portrays the ancient Hebrews as narrow and insular, saying that "in Exodus, as in Genesis, a universal, inclusive, polytheistic divine order has become a national, exclusive, monotheistic one."[18] On the one hand, he remarks that biblical law promotes tolerance for minorities, for example in the passage from Leviticus that says: "The stranger that dwelleth with you shall be unto you as one born among you." But here, "pluralism has its limits," Talbott says. "If 'the stranger' worships other gods, then his sojourn in Israel will be that of an outsider, and his graven images will, presumably, suffer the same fate as those of Israel's enemies."[19]

Talbott also emphasizes that the ancient Hebrews were rather warlike, quoting biblical passages such as this one from Deuteronomy: "[T]hou shalt smite them, and utterly destroy them; thou shalt make no covenant with them."[20] As for the "Babylonian kings and Egyptian pharaohs" who were vilified by Hebrew scribes as "tyrants," Talbott argues that they were, "in important respects, just and tolerant rulers and pioneers of the novel idea that peace was preferable to war in relations among god-kings."[21]

Similarly, Talbott sees the modern democratic nation-state of Israel as problematic, a "chronically vexing example" of "both the strength and weakness of nationhood itself." He characterizes "the fate of Israel and its Arab neighbors" in the post–World War II international system as a "nagging reminder" that while multinational imperialism had its flaws, "it also had its not quite-saving graces as a means of bringing together many nations spread over huge distances and sometimes on different continents."[22]

Talbott is a sophisticated observer, well aware of the place of Israel, both ancient and modern, in Western political thought and world history. Israel stands as a roadblock to the global governance agenda—historically, intellectually, symbolically, culturally, religiously, morally, and strategically. If the political supranational or transnational project is to advance, Israel must be taken down a peg, metaphysically as well as materially.

The struggles of ancient Israel have long provided inspiration for advocates of self-government. Israel has served as a symbol and a reminder that it is morally justified for a distinct people to establish an independent political community. This was particularly true for the founders of the American republic. The most widely read book in eighteenth-century America was the King James Bible, and so American revolutionaries were very familiar with the story of ancient Israel, the Babylonian captivity, the Exodus from Egypt, David vs. Goliath, and the book of Deuteronomy.

Clergymen and other American Whigs often described the American republic as the "new Israel." They identified with the biblical narrative, even to the point of labeling George III as Pharaoh. "The British tyrant is only acting over the same wicked and cruel part, that Pharaoh king of Egypt acted toward the children of Israel some 3,000 years ago," declared Nicholas Street, a Whig clergyman, in 1777. Another Whig leader, Dr. Banfield, said in 1783 that it was God who "raised a Joshua to lead the tribes of Israel in the field of battle; raised and formed a Washington to lead on the troops of his chosen States." Ten years after the ratification of the U.S. Constitution in 1799, in a Thanksgiving sermon, Rev. Abiel Abbot declared, "It has been often remarked that the people of the United States come nearer to a parallel with Ancient Israel, than any other nation upon the globe. Hence OUR AMERICAN ISRAEL is a term frequently used; and our common consent allows it apt and proper."[23]

Michael Novak places the "metaphysics of the Hebrew Bible" at the heart of the American revolutionaries' understanding of themselves as a people in a covenant with God, and therefore legitimately enabled to create a self-governing independent nation.[24] In his book *On Two Wings: Humble Faith and Common Sense at the American*

Founding, Novak quotes Samuel Cooper, a well-known New England divine, making "the case for liberty, independence, and republican government from biblical examples" in an address to the Massachusetts legislature in 1780. Cooper began his address "with an extended parallel between the people of Israel and 'our own circumstances' in 1780 based on the thirtieth chapter of Jeremiah which dwells on the groaning of the Israelites in captivity," Novak writes. He adds, "Not hesitating to link George III to Nebuchadnezzar, Cooper noted that the Hebrew government, 'tho' a theocracy, was yet . . . a free republic, and that the sovereignty resided in the people' and in that way he rooted republican liberty in biblical religion."[25]

From Dante to Immanuel Kant

In *The Great Experiment,* Strobe Talbott accurately depicts the medieval poet Dante Alighieri and the Enlightenment philosopher Immanuel Kant as intellectual heroes of the global governance movement. Both favored transnational governance, although in different forms: Dante, a world empire; Kant, a federation of republican states. Talbott also, with reason, presents Niccolò Machiavelli and Thomas Hobbes as competing intellectuals who took a harder-edged, more "realist" line. Certainly the two Florentines (Dante and Machiavelli) and the two Enlightenment philosophers (Kant and Hobbes) represented polar opposites on certain aspects of foreign relations, sovereignty, and human nature.

However, Talbott wrongly portrays the contrasts of Dante vs. Machiavelli and Kant vs. Hobbes as foreshadowing the division in American policy between internationalists and realists on issues of morality in international relations, national sovereignty, and the efficacy and legitimacy of transnational authority. In Talbott's view, Dante and particularly Kant "anticipated today's liberal internationalism, whose adherents imagine and seek to build a better world."

On the other hand, American "realists" who pride themselves in dealing with the world as it is, such as Henry Kissinger, "pay homage to Niccolò Machiavelli and Thomas Hobbes."[26] Talbott writes:

> In the late twentieth and early twenty-first centuries, Kant and Hobbes would be regarded as intellectual heroes by the opposing camps in the great debate over American foreign policy. For self-avowed realists, Hobbes applied to his prescription for national and international governance an acceptance of the human propensity for conflict, the frequent need for authoritarianism as an antidote to anarchy, and the indispensability of force as the arbiter of disputes, while Kant's writings provided a touchstone for liberal internationalists and their hopes for the democratic peace.[27]

For most observers of international relations (and most people), the humanitarian Kant is more attractive than the gloomy Hobbes, with his talk of life in the state of nature being "nasty, brutish, and short."[28] By presenting a Kant vs. Hobbes dichotomy, Talbott stacks the deck for the party of global governance. He stakes out the moral high ground for his preferred ideological position. But the Enlightenment thinker who deserves to carry the intellectual banner for the party of independent self-government is not Thomas Hobbes; it is another Englishman, John Locke, who deeply influenced America's founding generation of leaders. To understand the conflict between global governance and independent self-government, we should review the fault lines dividing the thought of Immanuel Kant and John Locke.

Kant is rightly recognized as the intellectual father of the modern global governance project. He is also seen as a founding father of modern liberal internationalism, although in the final analysis his ideas support transnationalism. Strobe Talbott describes his legacy as follows:

Kant's concept [perpetual world peace through a league of democratic states] anticipates some of the major, if still unfulfilled, features of the United Nations system: international (or what Kant called "cosmopolitan") law, open covenants openly arrived at, nonintervention and nonaggression, the international regulation of national defenses (i.e., disarmament and arms control), decolonization, self-determination, democratization, the punishment of war crimes, and a universal code of civil and human rights.

As Talbott puts it, "Kant constructs a grand syllogism in support of liberal principles as the basis for global governance."[29]

For Kant, the purpose of global governance was to secure "perpetual peace." He rejected the concept of a universal monarchy (Dante's idea for world peace) because it would likely become a tyranny, "a soulless despotism." Kant opposed autocracy and favored government based on the consent of the citizens, which he called "republican" or "constitutional" government. His "First Definitive Article for Perpetual Peace" states: "The Civil Constitution of Every State Should Be Republican."[30] Today this is usually understood as support of liberal democratic states.

"The republican constitution," argues Kant, "besides the purity of its origin . . . also gives a favorable prospect for the desired consequences, i.e., perpetual peace." Free states are less likely to go to war with each other because, "if the consent of the citizens is required in order to decide that war should be declared . . . nothing is more natural than that they would be very cautious in commencing such a poor game, decreeing for themselves all the calamities of war."[31]

The "positive idea of a world republic," according to Kant, is "correct in theory" and would be the most rational form of government that would lead to world peace. But given the complexities of human nature, a single world state is not realistic. What is possible is "only the negative surrogate of an alliance which averts war,

endures, spreads, and holds back the stream of those hostile incli-
nations which fear the law." This "negative surrogate" would be a
federation of republican states, or a "league of peace" *(foedus paci-
ficum)*. This federation of free states, sometimes called a "League
of Nations," would first be formed in Europe, but would "ultimately
include all the nations of the world."[32] It would not interfere in the
domestic affairs of the member republics, but would decide matters
of war and peace.

Kant attacks the traditional concept of the "law of nations," and
criticizes the established fathers of international law by name. "Hugo
Grotius, Pufendorf, Vattel and many other irritating comforters
have been cited in justification of war," he writes. Under their theories of international law, war is still possible because "states as such
do not stand under a common external power." There is "no
supreme legislative power" to restrain states. What is needed, Kant
maintains, is a federation of free states under a world constitution.[33]
He explains:

> In a league of nations, even the smallest state could expect secu-
> rity and justice, not from its own power and by its own decrees,
> but only from this great league of nations ... from a united power
> acting according to decisions reached under the laws of their
> united will. However fantastical this idea may seem ... the nec-
> essary outcome of the destitution to which each man is brought
> by his fellows is to force the states to the same decision (hard
> though it be for them) that savage man also was reluctantly
> forced to take, namely, to give up their brutish freedom and to
> seek quiet and security under a lawful [global] constitution.[34]

Because of evils such as the devastation of war, Kant insists, "our
race is forced to find, above the (in itself healthy) opposition of
states which is a consequence of their freedom, a law of equilibrium
and a united power to give it effect. Thus it is forced to institute a
cosmopolitan condition to secure the external safety of each state."[35]

Kant's vision thus moves from the international, meaning relations between sovereign states, to the transnational, meaning relations that reach above sovereign nation-states. Independent self-governing entities, even liberal democratic nation-states, are to be subordinate to a supranational authority. They are not the final decision makers. They are not sovereign in the traditional sense of nation-state sovereignty.

In this book, sovereignty is understood as Abraham Lincoln defined it in a message to a special session of Congress on July 4, 1861: as "a political community, without a political superior."[36] In the United States, Lincoln noted, the state governments were subordinate to the American federal union. In Kant's scheme, similarly, nation-states would be subordinate to the federation. A supranational "sovereignty" would thus be a "political superior" to liberal democratic nation-states.

In *Law Without Nations: Why Constitutional Government Requires Sovereign States,* Jeremy Rabkin, a professor of constitutional law at George Mason University, challenges Kant's main premises and points to ambiguities in his thinking. For example, Kant says that all governments should be constitutional republics because peace, in the end, depends upon free self-government. Rabkin asks, "How is republican government in each state consistent with ultimate control in the federation?"[37] True, Kant tries to address this dilemma by limiting the federation's power to issues of war and peace. But, of course, decisions about going to war are among the most important that a self-governing people could possibly make for themselves.

Rabkin notes that Kant himself "acknowledges that a peacekeeping federation must unite force with law. It is not enough to sign treaties or conventions against war. It is necessary to put force at the disposal of the peacekeepers. Hence, there must be a federation of states which has more force at its disposal than any one member."[38] Rabkin comments on a basic contradiction: "Not the least of the utopian elements in Kant's vision is the notion that an international federation can be endowed with sufficient power to ensure peace but then somehow be constrained from interfering in the internal affairs of member states."[39]

Most significantly, Rabkin argues that Kant's vision was in crucial respects at odds with the views of America's Founders. Although they shared some Enlightenment values and could "see the appeal of a project for universal peace," the Founders clearly rejected the idea that "power outside of American society" could ensure republican principles within American society. Paraphrasing James Madison in *The Federalist* No. 51, Rabkin comments that "If Americans cannot devise a constitutional scheme of their own to ensure republican government, they cannot trust to outside power to assure it for them."[40] The Founders believed that "in the last resort, independent republics cannot trust to others to determine their rights without forfeiting their independence," and therefore, as Madison remarked, "universal and perpetual peace ... will never exist but in the imagination of visionary philosophers, or in the breasts of benevolent enthusiasts."[41]

John Locke and the American Tradition

The phrase "one entire, free, independent society" rings clearly throughout John Locke's famous *Second Treatise on Civil Government*. The philosophical basis of the Declaration of Independence owes much to Locke's defense of self-government. When Alexander Hamilton visited his home, Thomas Jefferson pointed to portraits of Sir Francis Bacon, Sir Isaac Newton, and John Locke, saying, "They are my trinity of the three greatest men the world has ever produced." But more than simply national independence, Locke advocated what we could call "democratic sovereignty," arguing that authority was legitimate only with the consent of the governed. If the government became a tyranny, the people had the right of revolution.

Locke explicitly rejected the Kantian notion that it would be legitimate for an independent democratic state to cede some of its sovereignty to a transnational or foreign political authority:

> The delivery also of the people into the subjection of foreign power, either by the prince, or by the legislative, is certainly a change of the legislative, and so a dissolution of the government. For the end why people entered into society being to be preserved one entire, free, independent society, to be governed by its own laws, this is lost whenever they are given up into the power of another.[42]

If the "legislative" (or the democratic political process) transfers sovereign authority to an outside power, the nature of the "free, independent society" itself is changed, amounting to a "dissolution of government." The political community would no longer be governed by its own laws. By Lincoln's definition of sovereignty, the formerly independent state would have a "political superior" and would no longer be sovereign.

Americans are primarily Lockean rather than Hobbesian, argues Marc Plattner in *Democracy Without Borders? Global Challenges to Liberal Democracy.*[43] Plattner, who is vice president of the National Endowment for Democracy and co-editor of the *Journal of Democracy,* notes that Americans combine the particular and the universal along the lines found in Locke's *Second Treatise on Government.* Americans believe in universal principles, such as "all men are created equal" and "they are endowed by their Creator with certain unalienable Rights." But Americans also believe, as did Locke, that "universal human rights" can be realized "only within particular commonwealths" whose governments are based on "popular consent and respect for individual rights."[44] The implementation of universal principles "should be the business of democratically elected and accountable national governments," not transnational authorities.[45]

We could think of four major intellectual influences on the formation of American self-government: (1) natural law theory and

Enlightenment tradition, particularly the ideas of John Locke and Montesquieu; (2) the biblical narrative, with a strong emphasis on the story of ancient Israel; (3) the classical narrative of ancient Greece and Rome; and (4) the oppositionist literature of the English Whig republican "country party" in the seventeenth and eighteenth centuries. All four of these influences support independent sovereignty, in opposition to transnational authorities. We have discussed the influence of John Locke and natural rights theory, as well as the biblical narrative; let us now examine the other two major intellectual influences on the American revolutionaries.

Classical Republicanism

The Founders studied and identified with the republican heroes of classical Greece and Rome. "The more widely read Romans were Cicero, Livy, and Tacitus; among the Greeks, Demosthenes, Aristotle, and Polybius," notes the historian Forrest McDonald. But the most-read ancient book was Plutarch's *Parallel Lives of Noble Greeks and Romans,* which provided examples of good and bad statesmanship.[46]

In Plutarch's *Lives,* the American Founders discovered heroes to emulate and villains to decry. In their political writing, they took pseudonyms directly from Plutarch (along with Livy and other classical writers): Cato, Brutus, Cincinnatus, Phocion, Camilus, Horatius, Agrippa, Aristides, Fabius, Helvidius, and many more. Alexander Hamilton, James Madison, and John Jay chose to write *The Federalist Papers* under the pseudonym "Publius," after Publius Valerius Publicola, described by Plutarch as a statesman who wrote the laws that established the legal foundation of the Roman Republic after the overthrow of the last king in 509 B.C. *The Federalist Papers* were intended to explain and defend the proposed Constitution of 1787, which would establish foundational law in the new American republic after the power of the British king was thrown off.

Professor Carl Richard, in *The Founders and the Classics,* says that Greek and Roman writers provided models of positive statesmanship and "anti-models" of tyranny, self-aggrandizement, corruption, and demagoguery.[47] The most commonly cited positive models were the defenders of the Roman Republic and the independent Greek city-states against imperial rule, particularly Cato the Younger, Cicero, Brutus, Cassius, and Demosthenes.[48] The anti-models were either the emperors, dictators, and tyrants who attempted to crush liberty, or the demagogues who instigated the mob rule that undermined republican government. The major anti-models, Professor Richard tells us, were Julius Caesar and Alexander the Great, who destroyed independent republics and sought to create global empires.[49] In addition, demagogues like Catiline in Rome and Alcibiades in Athens were often cited as negative models.[50]

All of the Founders portrayed Julius Caesar as essentially a negative model, and often attempted to tag their political opponents as "Caesar." Thus, while Jefferson and Adams accused Hamilton of admiring and being like Caesar, Hamilton responded in kind, attacking the Jeffersonian Party as "the Catilines and Caesars of the community."[51] A leading Hamilton biographer, Ron Chernow, remarks that "Hamilton's collected papers are teeming with pejorative references to Julius Caesar."[52]

An earlier American historian, Thomas P. Govan, examined Hamilton's correspondence and found that all references to Julius Caesar were negative except for one neutral mention of his military skill. George Washington was initially attracted to Caesar's *Commentaries* and studied his military strategy in preparation for and during his army command. But Washington rejected Caesar as a political model and embraced the opposite political image of Cincinnatus, the republican hero who relinquished power and returned to private life.

Professor Richard states that the Founders saw themselves as involved in the perennial conflict between republican liberty and imperial tyranny:

The founders were thrilled by the belief that they were beginning anew the work of the ancient republicans, only this time with an unprecedented chance of success. Cato and Cicero had lost the first round of combat against the tyranny of Caesar and Augustus, but the founders, starting afresh in a virgin country with limitless resources, could pack the punch that would win the second and decisive round.[53]

Whig "Country Party" Republican Opposition

In 1967, Professor Bernard Bailyn of Harvard published a book titled *The Ideological Origins of the American Revolution,* which had a powerful impact on rethinking of the ideas that motivated America's revolutionary generation. As Professor Bailyn put it, "We shall not understand why there was a revolution until we suspend disbelief and listen with care to what the Revolutionaries themselves said was the reason there was a revolution."[54]

With abundant citations from leaders like George Washington, John Adams, Thomas Jefferson, John Dickenson, and many others including midlevel revolutionaries, Bailyn argued that the American colonists believed there was a deliberate design by British authorities to subvert liberty in America (and even in Britain itself). They viewed the Stamp Act, the Townshend Duties, the Boston Massacre, the Coercive Acts, and other events of the 1760s and 1770s as elements of an organized assault on liberty by corrupt and power-hungry officials.[55] And they saw it all as falling into the pattern of a perennial conflict between liberty and arbitrary power. "Britain, it was said, was following Greece, Rome, France, Venice, Denmark, Sweden ... from the liberty of a free constitution into autocracy, and the colonies ... were in the van," writes Bailyn.[56]

The idea that there was a never-ending conflict between liberty and arbitrary power permeated British political culture from the seventeenth to the late eighteenth century. This concept was essentially the worldview of what has been called the "country party": the Whig, republican, commonwealth (and sometimes radical Tory) opposition to the ruling "court party." Leading thinkers that Bailyn and other scholars have placed in the British "country party" include James Harrington, John Milton, Algernon Sidney, Bolingbroke, and particularly John Trenchard and Thomas Gordon, authors of *Cato's Letters.* The great writers of the age—Swift, Defoe, Pope, Fielding, Addison—and a host of lesser journalists contributed to this "opposition" sensibility with their attacks on centralized power and abusive government.[57]

The American colonists were an integral part of this British political culture. Most significantly, Bailyn says, the Americans "soaked up" the opposition literature and put it at the center of their worldview.[58] Eighteenth-century British subjects at home and in the colonies considered Britain the freest nation on earth. Other Europeans agreed. In 1731, Montesquieu called England "the freest country that exists in the world." His countryman Voltaire also praised British freedom. Mozart's *Abduction from the Seraglio* has a character declare, *"Ich bin eine Engländerin, zur Freiheit geborn"* (I am an Englishwoman, born to freedom).[59] British liberty was seen as the product of a sound constitution in which power was mixed among monarchical, aristocratic, and popular elements, in the Crown, Lords, and Commons. The American revolutionaries were impressed by Montesquieu's *Spirit of the Laws* (1748) and Blackstone's *Commentaries on the Laws of England* (1765), with their emphasis on the separation of executive, legislative, and judicial powers as a means to limit governmental authority and preserve liberty.

Bailyn posits that Cato—through Trenchard and Gordon's highly influential *Cato's Letters* and Joseph Addison's popular play *Cato*—came to personify opposition thought in the perennial struggle of liberty against despotism.[60] Addison's *Cato* was George Washington's favorite play, and he directed that it be performed for his troops to inspire them in their fight for liberty. Thus, "The opposition vision of English politics ... was determinative of the political understanding of 18th century Americans," Bailyn remarks. "The colonists universally agreed that man was by nature lustful, that he was utterly untrustworthy in power, unable to control his passion for domination. The antinomy of power and liberty was accepted as the central fact of politics," and thus "the duty of free men was to protect the latter and constrain the former."[61]

Different Influences on the American Founders

Bernard Bailyn is the foremost representative of what has come to be called the neo-Whig school of American historians. They have not persuaded all scholars. For example, Forrest McDonald has written that while he admires much in the work of the historians who emphasize the influence of the "country party" opposition literature, he nevertheless sees "shortcomings" in this approach.[62]

Professor McDonald says that the "opposition" historians downplay the influence of Locke and the natural rights school, as well as the Scottish intellectual influence of David Hume and Adam Smith among others. McDonald characterizes the Founders as "multilingual" in the sense that "they could speak in the language of Bolingbroke, Montesquieu, Locke, the classical republicans, Hume, and many others, whichever seemed rhetorically appropriate to the particular argument at hand."[63] They also referred to the Bible narrative numerous times in their arguments with the Crown.

Before deciding to break with Britain, American colonists emphasized the British common law, particularly the writings of Blackstone, in claiming "the rights of Englishmen." At the same time, the practical experience of day-to-day politics in the colonial legislatures, crafting legislation and sometimes fighting the executive power of the royal governors, made a great impression on American thinking. To most American patriots, writes McDonald, republicanism meant "government of the sort to which they were accustomed," in the colonial legislatures, "but without royal or proprietary officials"; or it meant "the absence of hereditary status."[64]

Professor Donald Lutz and Professor Charles Hyneman studied the intellectual influences on the American founding by reviewing about 15,000 items—including books, pamphlets, and newspaper articles—written by delegates to the Constitutional Convention. Rating the material for the most "significant and coherent theoretical content," Lutz and Hyneman narrowed their sample to 916 items, which "represents approximately one-third of all public political writings longer than 2,000 words published between 1760 and 1805."[65] In these writings, they identified over 3,154 references to other sources. Of all the citations, 34 percent were from the Bible, particularly the book of Deuteronomy; 22 percent referred to Enlightenment thinkers, especially Montesquieu, Locke, Hume (his histories, not his philosophy), and Pufendorf; 18 percent were from Whig opposition literature, particularly *Cato's Letters* (Trenchard and Gordon), Bolingbroke, Milton, and Algernon Sidney; 11 percent were from the British common law, particularly Blackstone; and 8 percent were from the classics, most often Plutarch's *Lives of Noble Greeks and Romans,* although Cicero, Plato, and Aristotle were also cited.[66]

Professor Lutz concluded that "there was no one European writer, or one tradition of writers, that dominated American political thought" during the late 1700s.[67] That said, it could certainly be argued that all the influences discussed above contributed to placing the Founders emphatically on the side of independent sovereignty and in opposition to transnational governance. The favored choice was always clear whether it was David over Goliath, the ancient Israelites over their imperial foes, Cato over Caesar, the Roman Republic over the Roman Empire, the English republican Algernon Sidney over the Stuart kings, the British Parliament over the British monarch, or American self-government over an autocratic power abroad.

The American Founders and the Law of Nations

"The doctrine of national sovereignty is an American birthright—literally," writes Professor Jeremy Rabkin. He notes that the Declaration of Independence endorses both "unalienable rights" for individuals and "separate and equal station ... among the powers of the earth" for nations or "independent states."[68] Thus, national sovereignty is afforded the same "moral claim" as individual rights.

The American revolutionaries made their argument for independent sovereignty on the basis of their interpretation of natural law, hence the explicit appeal to "the Laws of Nature and Nature's God." They believed that there could be "no ultimate or reliable intermediary between an independent nation and the 'Supreme Judge of the world.'"[69] Thus, decisions involving the proper interpretation of natural law were made, not in negotiations with other states or in consultation with transnational judicial authorities, but unilaterally by the Continental Congress, which claimed the right to speak for the American people. The revolutionaries showed "a decent respect for the opinions of mankind" by presenting a reasoned case for independence to the world, but the decision to rebel was made by the Americans alone.

The leading theorists of traditional international law, or the "law of nations," at the time of the American founding were Hugo Grotius, Samuel Pufendorf, and Emmerich de Vattel. American leaders were well read in their writings. Donald Lutz places the three on his list of the thirty-six European thinkers most read and quoted by the founding generation, along with Locke, Montesquieu, Plutarch, and Blackstone, among others. It is not surprising that the Founders embraced international law or the law of nations as defined by Grotius (1625), Pufendorf (1672), and Vattel (1758). All emphasized state sovereignty and the equality of nations. Grotius argued that sovereign states answer to no transnational authority; they "are not subject to the legal control of another, so that they cannot be rendered [legally void] by the operation of another human will." He explicitly rejected the political legitimacy of a universal empire.

Grotius and Pufendorf framed their concepts of international law in terms of the "rights" of states. That is to say, states as sovereign entities would possess certain rights that other states should respect. The law of nations meant that sovereign states would respect the rights of other sovereign states in waging war, protecting private property, assuring freedom of the seas, ensuring the safety of ambassadors, and the like. These rights are based on more or less universal agreement and state practice, and constitute a logical "natural justice." Since there is no supranational authority, sovereign states are the final arbiters of what constitutes "natural rights" in the particular circumstances in which they find themselves.

This outlook was clearly consistent with the Founders' views on the rights of independent states. It was particularly relevant for Americans who believed in the rights of a self-governing people to make their own decisions on war and peace, commerce, domestic justice, and everything else.

The Swiss diplomat Emmerich de Vattel was a near contemporary of the American Founders, publishing his most important work, *The Law of Nations* (*Le droit des gens*) in 1758. Like Grotius and Pufendorf, Vattel emphasized sovereignty and the equality of nations; in argument and language he is close to Locke. "Nations are composed of men who are by nature free and independent," he wrote. And these "nations or sovereign States must be regarded as free persons living together in a state of nature. It follows that nations are by nature equal and hold from nature the same obligations and rights.... [A] small Republic is no less a sovereign State than the most powerful Kingdom." Like Locke, Vattel rejected transnational authority in favor of national sovereignty, saying, "Each independent state claims to be and actually is independent of all others." Vattel's theory posited a natural law that included obligations to other nations and peoples, but the interpretation of those obligations remained within the decision-making process of the nation-state. "It is for each Nation to decide what its conscience demands of it, what it can or cannot do," he wrote, ". . . and therefore it is for each Nation to consider and determine what duties it can fulfill towards others without failing in its duty towards itself."[70]

As we noted earlier, Kant attacked Vattel, Grotius, and Pufendorf by name for arguing that because there should be no transnational authority over sovereign states, decisions on war and peace should rest in the hands of nation-states. On this crucial question, the Founding Fathers of the American republic stood clearly with Vattel, Grotius, and Pufendorf—and against Kant. The Founders created a constitutional system of government by "the consent of the governed," in which decisions on war and peace, among other matters, would be made by elected representatives of the people, not by transnational or international authorities and institutions. Today, it is Congress and the president, not the United Nations or a world court, that decide whether America in particular circumstances will be at peace or war. National sovereignty is indeed at the heart of the American political regime.

CHAPTER THREE

Civic Nationalism and American Liberal Democracy

There are different types of sovereign states, some democratic and others not. The liberal democratic nation-state is a product of the modern age that emerged during the Enlightenment. As the political theorist James W. Ceaser explains, it is a compound regime consisting of two different political strands: liberalism and democracy.[1] Liberal democracy goes by a variety of other names: constitutional democracy, representative democracy, constitutional republic, democratic republic, liberal republic, and the like. We will use the terms "liberal democracy" and "constitutional democracy" interchangeably.

Liberalism (in the traditional sense), *constitutionalism,* or *constitutional liberalism* means an emphasis on individual rights including free speech, freedom of the press, freedom of association, freedom of religion, and limited government in which the power of the rulers is restrained by a constitution and a just legal order. Traditionally, liberalism has meant support for free enterprise, private property, and the rule of law. Constitutionalism has also meant checks and balances on governmental power and the separation of power into different branches of government.

Democracy means rule by the *demos,* the people or political community, and thus majority rule in some form. A full democratic society would include equality of citizenship in political participation, including the right to vote. In modern times, democracy means government by the consent of the governed, in which citizens choose their representatives through regular elections and are able replace them in like manner. Modern democratic politics includes independent political parties that represent the different viewpoints of the people.

Together, these two political ideas compose *liberal democracy* or *constitutional democracy*. The political regime is a democratic government based on "consent" and majority rule, but the majority is restrained by a constitution, the rule of law, and individual rights. In essence, the people agree to put restrictions on themselves in order to possess greater individual freedom.

Westphalian Sovereignty and Philadelphian Sovereignty

In this book I distinguish the sovereignty of a self-governing free people from sovereignty in general, as possessed by any nation-state, including undemocratic ones like North Korea and Burma. I will make a moral and political case for what I call "democratic sovereignty" or "Philadelphian sovereignty," as distinct from what many Western scholars and diplomats refer to as "Westphalian sovereignty."

Modern state sovereignty emerged with the Treaty of Westphalia in 1648. The treaty brought an end to the Thirty Years War, which involved religious disputes between Catholics and Protestants, along with political disputes among the Hapsburg Empire, national monarchies, and lesser principalities. To curb religious strife and restrain imperial authority, the treaty makers at Westphalia developed an international system where supreme political authority would reside in the sovereign (the monarch or prince) of a nation or principality, rather than in emperors or clergy with supranational authority, or in feudal lords. Later, sovereignty was seen as being located in the state or nation-state itself. The resulting European system of sovereign states is often called the "Westphalian system," and Europeans today usually think of sovereignty in Westphalian terms.

Americans, on the other hand, think of sovereignty in "Philadelphian" terms, as expressed in the U.S. Constitution, written in Philadelphia in 1787 and beginning: "We the People of the United States . . . do ordain and establish this Constitution for the United States of America." The Founders viewed sovereignty as something that resided in the people themselves, rather than the government or the nation-state. It is the citizens who hold ultimate political authority. In this book, "Philadelphian sovereignty" is synonymous with "democratic sovereignty," meaning that the people of a specific nation-state rule themselves through a representative democracy.

In the last chapter, we noted that the American Founders absorbed the classics and identified with the republican heroes who fought tyranny in the ancient world, such as Cato, Brutus, and Demosthenes. But they also acknowledged and acted upon the differences between the ancients and themselves.

First, a small number of residents in the ancient republics were entitled to citizenship, while a large part of the population consisted of resident aliens, foreigners, and slaves. In Athenian democracy, a limited group of citizens ruled directly, not through representatives. The citizens all assembled in the agora (the main square) and voted on issues of war and peace as well as domestic policy. Office holders were usually chosen by lot.

The ancient republics also lacked any concept of a natural equality of all human beings, an idea that lies at the heart of the American Declaration of Independence. They did not have any notion of individual rights; they were not in any sense "liberal." In fact, writes Marc Plattner of the National Endowment for Democracy, "The democracies of ancient Greece . . . were genuinely and wholeheartedly illiberal."[2]

The American revolutionaries were cognizant of these differences; they were consciously constructing a modern republican regime, not recreating the ancient republic. One of the authors of *The Federalist Papers*, Alexander Hamilton, characterized the new American government as a representative democracy, as distinct from a direct democracy. The other main author of *The Federalist Papers*, James Madison, makes a clear distinction in *Federalist* No. 10 and elsewhere between the American representative constitutional republic and the direct democracy of antiquity. Madison, Hamilton, and the other Founders agreed that the ancient model did not preserve either liberty or republican government. Indeed, the purpose of the U.S. Constitution was to create a durable republican regime that would avoid the failures and mistakes of the ancient republics.

For the greater part of human history, most people lived under undemocratic rulers: emperors, kings, feudal lords, clerical authorities, aristocratic princes, and tyrants of various sorts. As early as the Magna Carta in 1215, however, constitutional limits were placed on the power of the English monarch. During the seventeenth century, England witnessed a long struggle by the Parliament to restrict the executive power of the king. This conflict culminated in the institution of a limited monarchy with the Glorious Revolution of 1688–89 and the enactment of the English Bill of Rights, which established such liberal principles as judicial independence from royal interference, freedom to petition the Crown, freedom to elect members of Parliament without royal interference, freedom of speech within Parliament, and freedom from cruel and unusual punishment.

It was around this time that John Locke advanced the case for locating sovereignty in the people, who therefore could replace a king or a parliament that violated their trust. While Locke was a liberal rather than a democrat, Marc Plattner notes that the principle of sovereignty belonging to the people in a legitimate regime is a characteristic of both liberalism and democracy.[3]

Throughout the Western world, constitutional liberalism was established before the full advent of democracy. Britain and the United States both had a bill of rights, trial by jury, and a rule-of-law system long before the working class, women, and all minority citizens in those countries could vote. On the European continent as well, liberalism preceded full democratic participation. For example, the Austro-Hungarian monarchy that ruled a good part of central Europe from 1857 to 1918 was, as Fareed Zakaria put it, "a classic liberal autocracy," a government that provided the rights of constitutional liberalism but could not be characterized as democratic.[4]

National Identity and Liberal Democracy

How is liberal democracy strengthened, improved, maintained, and perpetuated? For many academics in political science and history, this question is mainly an issue of process, of ensuring the proper mix of individual liberty and majority rule through legal and constitutional mechanisms. Many others, however, believe that this procedural approach is inadequate and that there must be an emphasis on responsible citizenship.

Textbooks and curricula in American schools are filled with references to "democratic citizenship" and "citizenship for a democratic society." But rarely do they use terms like "American democratic citizenship" or "citizenship for American constitutional democracy." For decades there has been a reluctance to delve too deeply into questions of the relationship between national identity, patriotism or civic nationalism on the one hand, and the perpetuation of American liberal democracy on the other hand.

Can a constitutional democratic nation-state be sustained in the long run without a strong national identity? Natan Sharansky, the former Soviet human rights activist and current Israeli statesman, probes the connection between national identity and liberal democracy in *Defending Identity: Its Indispensable Role in Protecting Democracy.* Sharansky decries the loss of national and religious identities among Western elites:

In *Imagine,* his ode to such a utopia, John Lennon conceives of a world without heaven and hell, religion, or nation-states, where there will be "nothing to kill or die for, a brotherhood of man." But a brotherhood without actual brothers, with no one committed to anyone else or to a way of life, is nothing but empty air.[5]

Without a robust national identity and attachment to a "particular way of life," says Sharansky, "democracy," meaning the democratic state, cannot defend itself:

Democracy offers a vision of opportunity, self-determination, and peace. But without a particular way of life and a set of commitments to live for, the democratic vision inevitably loses force, becoming empty and abstract ... incapable of defending even the values it holds most dear.[6]

Sharansky distinguishes between negative and positive kinds of national identity. An identity that opposes democracy and freedom—like Nazism, communism, or radical Islam—is negative. An identity (whether national, religious, or ethnic) that reinforces democracy and freedom is positive. Thus,

Saudi Arabia and Iran are threats to peace not because their subjects have strong identities but rather because their regimes permit no democracy. In contrast, the strong identity of the Japanese people endangers no one because of a robust Japanese democracy.[7]

What is necessary, Sharansky asserts, is "that identity be framed by democracy and that democracy be anchored by identity. Identity without democracy can become fundamentalist and totalitarian. Democracy without identity can become superficial and meaningless."[8]

Sharansky gives the example of the United States and argues that its democracy is strengthened by robust identities. That includes, first, *national* identity, or American patriotism. Second is *religious* identity; Sharansky agrees with Tocqueville that in America, unlike traditional Europe, religion and liberty are allies. Regarding *ethnic* identity, Sharansky agrees with the historian John Higham that hyphenated Americanism (Irish-Americans, Italian-Americans, etc.) helped the assimilation of immigrants by providing a bridge to the American mainstream.

"Nationalism," Sharansky reminds us, "has been a powerful weapon in defending the free world against aggression." During the Second World War, "Roosevelt, Churchill, and De Gaulle ... gave their peoples hope and strength by appealing to history, tradition, and national values. They each drew on their nations' unique past to help secure its future."[9]

Like Sharansky, the British-born philosopher Roger Scruton argues that a strong national identity and nation-state are requisites for both liberalism and democracy. A "national idea," he says, is necessary for liberalism and democracy to function at all. Scruton notes that when British politicians address the electorate in parliamentary elections, "they ask a definite question: what do *we* want?" The "we" in the question is "a perfect instance of the national idea ... the idea of a moral unity between people, based on territory, language, association, history and culture, and so bound up with the self-consciousness of those who are joined by it."[10]

Scruton argues that five crucial points constitute the core of the "we," or the national identity that forms the main bulwark of the liberal democratic nation-state:

A bounded territory. "Until territory is *ours,* there is no real 'mine' or 'thine.' "[11]

A shared language. "There is no more dramatic mark of the stranger than his inability to speak my language. My language is not only mine. It is public and shared.... My language is always our language; the first thing that I inherit from my forefathers.... Attachment to language is the root of national culture."[12]

Shared associations. "Settled people," as opposed to nomads, "can meet not only in family, festival, team and army, but also in places given to membership: churches, clubs, schools, localities of work and leisure. They have an opportunity for institution-building, and for attaching their institutions to the land.... We can see a nation as partly constituted by the long-standing associations which are formed and inherited within it."[13]

Shared history. "People united by language, association and territory triumph and suffer together. They have common friends and common enemies." And they have a "historical *narrative.*"[14]

A common culture. A nation is "formed through a conception of itself," writes Scruton. "This self-consciousness of a nation is part of its moral character. It endows nations with a life of their own, a destiny, even a personality. People who think of themselves as a collective 'we' understand their successes and failures as 'ours.' "[15]

Scruton identifies the United States as "the most stable liberal polity in the modern world," with "all the characteristics of nationhood" listed above. It has a concept of "we." To wit: "America is first of all a territory." It also "has a common language, common habits of association, common customs, and a common Judaeo-Christian culture." Moreover, there is "a strong religious dimension to the American idea." American national loyalty "has its own historical myths, its own 'dreams,' its own sense of mission, its own powerful self-image, in which the American land is the last refuge of the dispossessed, and also the birthplace of a new and unfettered enterprise and will."[16]

Natan Sharansky and Roger Scruton agree on crucial points. Both maintain that a purely rational liberal democratic polity needs nonrational elements—emotional attachment, a robust national identity—in order to survive. Both explicitly embrace Edmund Burke's concept that a legitimate regime is one that envisions itself as connected to past and future generations. "History becomes as Burke described it: a pact between the dead, the living, and the yet unborn," Sharansky writes.[17] Scruton notes that Burke "was right to suspect that without loyalty to the dead ... the whole project of liberal politics is endangered. For a liberal state to be secure, the citizens must understand the *national* interest as something other than the interest of the *state*. Only the first can evoke in them the sacrificial spirit upon which the second depends."[18]

American National Identity

America is a compound political regime built of two distinct elements: liberalism or constitutionalism, and democracy or republicanism. Both are laid out in the second paragraph of the Declaration of Independence. *First,* "Governments are instituted among men" in order to "secure" "certain unalienable rights." *Second,* these governments derive "their just powers from the consent of the governed." In other words, "natural rights" and "consent of the governed" are the twin pillars of the American political system.

From "natural rights" come the principles that we associate with traditional liberalism: individual rights, free speech, freedom of the press, freedom of religion, freedom of association, property rights, and the rule of law. Governments are not allowed to violate "unalienable natural rights"; therefore governments should be limited. Individuals are "created equal" and possess equal natural rights.

From "consent of the governed" come the principles that we associate with democracy, such as the right of a self-designated people to govern themselves, majority rule, regular and fair elections, and equality of citizenship. The American people exercise self-government, while accepting the constraints of a constitution and the rule of law.

Obviously, the ideal of American liberal democracy has not always been realized in practice, as slavery, segregation, racism, discrimination against minorities and women, restricted voting, unequal and unfair justice have been part of America's story. At the same time, many Americans—including John Quincy Adams, Abraham Lincoln, Frederick Douglass, Susan B. Anthony, and Martin Luther King—have employed that ideal, particularly as expressed in the

Declaration of Independence and the Constitution, as a means of improving the practice of our constitutional democracy and strengthening the moral basis of the American regime.

Creed and Culture

America is often described as a "proposition nation," founded on a set of universal political principles, as Abraham Lincoln declared in his Gettysburg Address when he said that "our Fathers brought forth a new nation conceived in liberty and dedicated to the proposition that all men are created equal." The central argument is that America is built on ideas, unlike most other countries, which grew around a common ethnicity, religion, language, and culture.★ To be an American, in this view, is to believe in the principles set forth in the Declaration of Independence and the Constitution. In theory, anyone can become an American by accepting the "American Creed."

It is at least partly true that America is a proposition or creedal nation. From the beginning, the American regime has had a robust ideological component. In 1776, the American Patriots who supported the War of Independence and the American Tories who opposed it were, for the most part, from the same ethnic stock, held the same religious beliefs, spoke the same language, belonged to the same general culture. What drove them into war with each other was a clash of political ideas. The same is true of the American Civil War.

It would be more accurate, however, to say that the United States is a "proposition-plus" nation: both a creedal and a cultural nation. America is more than a proposition, and being an American is more

---

★During the Cold War it was noted that the Soviet Union was also a regime based on political ideas, and thus the major global conflict of the later twentieth century was between two powerful but very different ideological nations.

than adhering to a set of abstract universal ideas. There is a powerful homogenizing culture that includes an attachment to a historical narrative, not just adherence to certain political ideas. On the other hand, there have been major periods in American history—such as the Civil War and the civil rights era—when the founding creed has in fact dominated and altered the culture.

We could think of an American national identity in the sense that Roger Scruton discussed in his formulation of the "national idea." That is to say, there is a sense of the national "we" that comes from living in a bounded territory with a common language, shared culture, and shared history. This would also apply, I will argue, to immigrants who have "patriotically integrated" into this "we" and who have "adopted" the American Creed, American history, and civic culture as "their" creed, history, and civic culture.

Since America is not a nation based on ethnicity, race, or religion, American patriotism is consistent with that of a multiethnic civic nation based on political principles, a civic culture, and a multiethnic historical narrative. Here we will employ the term "civic nationalism" as it is used by social scientists, to distinguish the character of American nationalism from the ethnic or racial nationalism prevalent in many countries.

A Realistic View of Human Nature

In their understanding of humanity, the American Founders were neither overly optimistic like Rousseau, who believed that man was inherently good but institutions made him bad, nor pessimistic like some of their Calvinist forefathers who believed man to be intrinsically wicked. Instead, they believed that human nature was a mix of positive and negative characteristics, and that any successful republican government would have to be based on a realistic view of human nature. James Madison said it best in an often quoted paragraph of *Federalist* No. 51:

Ambition must be made to counteract ambition. . . . It may be a reflection on human nature, that such devices should be necessary to control the abuses of government. But what is government itself but the greatest of all reflections on human nature? If men were angels, no government would be necessary. If angels were to govern men, neither external nor internal controls on government would be necessary. In framing a government which is to be administered by men over men, the great difficulty lies in this: you must first enable the government to control the governed; and in the next place oblige it to control itself.[19]

A leading historian of the "Whig oppositionist" school, Bernard Bailyn, noted that both the supporters of the Constitution (George Washington, John Marshall, Alexander Hamilton, James Madison) and their opponents (Patrick Henry, George Mason, Richard Henry Lee) adhered to a realistic concept of human nature. Bailyn wrote that "the antifederalists, no less than the federalists, had a thoroughly realistic sense of human nature, and never deluded themselves that any people could be entirely virtuous or that any political population could be principally animated by public spirit."[20]

While rejecting Rousseau's doctrine that man is naturally good, the Founders believed that citizens could develop good character, use reason to positive effect, and possess sufficient public virtue or patriotism. Indeed, without the existence of these qualities in some measure, republican (democratic) government would not be possible. Madison writes in *Federalist* No. 55, "As there is a degree of depravity in mankind which requires a certain degree of circumspection and distrust, so there are other qualities in human nature which justify a certain portion of esteem and confidence. Republican government presupposes the existence of these qualities in a higher degree than any other form."[21]

A republican form of government that can be preserved and perpetuated would have to be built in a manner consistent with human nature. Furthermore, its citizens would need to possess a greater degree of public-spiritedness than the citizens or subjects of other forms of government. The Founders believed that sustaining a republican government required a well-ordered constitution, along with civic and moral education provided mostly by the institutions of civil society.

How to Preserve the Liberal Democratic Regime

In *Liberal Democracy and Political Science,* Professor James Ceaser argues that Alexis de Tocqueville is "the political thinker of our age, of our regime, and even of our nation" because he, more than any other thinker, seriously and systematically addressed the crucial question of how to preserve and perpetuate the liberal democratic nation-state.[22]

Professor Ceaser points out that Tocqueville, like Aristotle and Montesquieu, took a "traditional" approach to political science, focusing on types of regimes. The term "regime" would include not only the type of government (democratic, aristocratic, etc.), but also the intellectual, moral, cultural, religious, economic, material, and geographic aspects of a nation. Put another way, the elements of the "regime" in the traditional sense are both *political* (the constitution, laws, governmental institutions) and *cultural* (customs, attitudes, ethics, religious beliefs, habits, and economic practices). As Ceaser comments, "Liberal democracy depends upon a certain political culture, which is a product not just of law, but of philosophic and religious views, of habits and sentiments."[23]

In a section of *Democracy in America* titled "On the Principal Causes Tending to Maintain a Democratic Republic in the United States," Tocqueville first discusses physical factors, such as a favorable geographic position. Second, he looks at political institutions, particularly federalism, the importance of local government, and the positive influence of the judiciary, dominated by Federalist Party adherents. Tocqueville puts the greatest emphasis, however, on the moral-cultural framework of the American regime, saying, "I consider mores to be one of the great general causes to which the maintenance of a democratic republic in the United States can be attributed." Tocqueville adds, "I would say that physical causes contribute less than laws, and laws less than mores."[24]

Tocqueville, writes Ceaser, defined mores broadly as "the sum of the moral and intellectual dispositions of men in society ... the habits of heart ... [and] the sum of ideas that shape mental habits."[25] Tocqueville examined the roles of religion and patriotism in American life. Unlike the situation in France in the nineteenth century, religion and freedom were friends not enemies in the United States. Tocqueville believed that religious institutions strengthened the American political system, that "Americans so completely confuse Christianity and freedom in their minds that it is almost impossible to have them conceive of the one without the other."[26]

Maintaining and perpetuating a democratic regime does not mean preserving the status quo. A regime is often preserved and perpetuated by political change. For example, the American regime was sustained, and its legitimacy was strengthened, by political actions that altered the social structure, such as ending slavery in the nineteenth century, and enacting civil rights legislation in the twentieth century.

The Founders, being well acquainted with Montesquieu and conversant with Aristotle's *Politics,* were in a sense proto-Tocquevillians in their approach to sustaining both the political institutions and the cultural mores that undergirded the American constitutional system.

First, starting from a realistic view of human nature, the Founders sought to create and to perpetuate a constitutional republic based on the twin pillars of natural rights and the consent of the governed. They knew that previous republics had failed because of the weaknesses of human nature. The historical record of ancient republican government was often a sorry one of disorder disintegrating into anarchy, followed by a tyrant who restored order at the expense of liberty. As the Founders explained in *The Federalist Papers* and numerous other writings, the danger was that republics could become either too weak, and thus unable to secure liberty and establish effective government, or too strong, and thus tyrannical and unjust.

The answer to this problem, the Founders believed, was the establishment of the Constitution of the United States, which is at the heart of the "political" half (law, institutions) of the Tocquevillian concept of regime. By establishing a system with separation of powers, checks and balances, representation, federalism, and limited government, the U.S. Constitution created the political framework for an independent sovereign nation-state that was neither too strong nor too weak, and that fostered consensual government and protected individual liberty.

Second, the Founders understood that political institutions alone were not enough to sustain the republic. There was the question of "mores," or what Montesquieu called the "genus of a people." As Charles Kesler of the Claremont Institute put it, the Founders realized that the American Union needed "its own culture" to sustain its particular regime. Therefore, they repeatedly called for encouraging public and private virtue, religion, education, good character, civic-mindedness, love of freedom, patriotism, and a sense of nationhood, which were all viewed as complementary. Creed and culture "may be combined to shape a national identity and a common good."[27] A healthy sense of civic nationalism was necessary to sustain the liberal democratic nation-state.

The Founders believed that it was important to cultivate those qualities in human nature that would sustain and strengthen the American regime. In several official documents they declared the desirability of promoting morality and religion for this purpose. Most notably, George Washington in his Farewell Address of 1796 said that the cultivation of religion and morality was necessary to sustain popular government:

Of all the dispositions and habits which lead to political prosperity, Religion and morality are indispensable supports. In vain would that man claim the tribute of Patriotism, who should labour to subvert these great Pillars of human happiness, these firmest props of the duties of Men and citizens. The mere Politician, equally with the pious man ought to respect and to cherish them.... And let us with caution indulge the supposition, that morality can be maintained without religion. Whatever may be conceded to the influence of refined education on minds of peculiar structure—reason and experience both forbid us to expect that National morality can prevail in exclusion of religious principle. 'Tis substantially true that virtue or morality is a necessary spring of popular government.[28]

The Founders repeatedly referred to "morality, religion, and education" as a conceptual whole, and necessary to sustain free government. Thus, while the Constitution was being written in Philadelphia, the Continental Congress in July 1787 passed the Northwest Ordinance to establish policies for the territories northwest of the Ohio River that would later form ten new states. Article 3 of the Ordinance said: "Religion, Morality, and knowledge being necessary to good government and the happiness of mankind, Schools and the means of education shall forever be encouraged."

In advocating civic education for American citizenship, John Adams set forth a broad concept of the mores necessary to strengthen American political culture:

The instruction of the people, in every kind of knowledge that can be of use to them in the practice of their moral duties, as men, citizens, and Christians, and of their political and civic duties, as members of society and freemen, ought to be the care of the public, and of all who have any share in the conduct of its affairs, in a manner that never yet has been practiced in any age or nation. The education here intended is not merely that of the children of the rich and noble, but of every rank and class of people, down to the lowest and the poorest. It is not too much to say, that schools for the education of all should be placed at convenient distances, and maintained at the public expense.[29]

More specifically, Adams held that "Children should be educated and instructed in the principles of freedom," in keeping with Aristotle's view that "the instruction of youth should be accommodated to that form of government under which they live; forasmuch as it makes exceedingly for the preservation of the present government, whatsoever it be." In contrast with Immanuel Kant's argument that "a nation of devils" could survive if properly organized,[30] John Adams once stated: "Our constitution was made only for a moral and religious people. It is wholly inadequate for the government of any other."

Patriotism and Emotional Attachment

The American Founders emphasized that for an independent, sovereign American constitutional democracy to be improved, maintained, and bequeathed to future generations, it was vital that citizens possess a clear sense of patriotism and national identity, and an emotional as well as rational attachment to the American republic.

In *Federalist* No. 49, James Madison wrote that the American republic required "that veneration which time bestows on everything, and without which perhaps the wisest and freest governments would not possess the requisite stability."[31] Rational adherence must be fortified with emotional attachment:

> The reason of man, like man himself, is timid and cautious when left alone, and acquires firmness and confidence in proportion to the number with which it is associated. When the examples which fortify opinion are *ancient* as well as *numerous,* they are

known to have a double effect. In a nation of philosophers, this consideration ought to be disregarded. A reverence for the laws would be sufficiently inculcated by the voice of an enlightened reason. But a nation of philosophers is as little to be expected as the philosophical race of kings wished for by Plato. And in every other nation, the most rational government will not find it a superfluous advantage to have the prejudices of the community on its side.[32]

In *Federalist* No. 55, Madison argues that there is "sufficient virtue among men for self-government." As the political philosopher Walter Berns points out, Madison is using "virtue" in the sense that Montesquieu used the word, meaning "love of country," public-mindedness, or patriotism. Montesquieu characterized patriotism as something that is "felt," and as the most important quality among the citizens of a republic; thus, patriotism is to be the principle business of education in a republic. The Founders absorbed Montesquieu's teaching about education for patriotism, while rejecting his notion that republics could exist only in a small territory.[33]

Both James Madison and John Jay called on the memory of the shared sacrifice of the Revolutionary War to perpetuate the American democratic republic and national independence. In words prefiguring Lincoln's Gettysburg Address, Madison wrote in *Federalist* No. 14 that "the mingled blood which they have shed in defense of their sacred rights, consecrate their Union, and excite horror at the idea of their becoming aliens, rivals, enemies. . . . They formed the design of a great confederacy, which it is incumbent on their successors to improve and perpetuate."[34] In *Federalist* No. 2, Jay declared that "Providence has been pleased to give this one connected country, to one united people . . . who, by their joint counsels, arms, and efforts, fighting side by side throughout a long and bloody war, have nobly established their general Liberty and Independence."[35]

The two giants of American history, George Washington and Abraham Lincoln, through words and deeds were major sculptors of a powerful American civic nationalism that continues to this day. In Washington's Farewell Address and Lincoln's major speeches, including the Lyceum Address of 1838, the first and second inaugurals, and the Gettysburg Address, they sounded common themes at the heart of American civic nationalism that their statesmanship put into practice.

Both emphasized the *unum* over the *pluribus,* setting national unity above diversity. Washington in his Farewell Address and Lincoln in the Gettysburg Address argued that unity was essential to the survival of liberty and self-government in America. In *A Sacred Union of Citizens,* Matthew Spalding and Patrick Garrity suggest that the Gettysburg Address is "foreshadowed" in the Farewell Address, where Washington tells the nation that "your Union ought to be considered as a main prop of your liberty, and that the love of one ought to endear to you the preservation of the other." If American unity is destroyed, liberty will not be preserved.

Both used the language of civic nationalism in promoting American identity and patriotism. In the Farewell Address, Washington described patriotic attachment as akin to a moral duty:

> Citizens by birth or choice, of a common country, that country has a right to concentrate your affections. The name of American, which belongs to you, in your national capacity, must always exalt the just pride of Patriotism, more than any appellation derived from local discriminations. With slight shades of difference, you have the same Religion, Manners, Habits, and political Principles. You have in a common cause fought and triumphed together—the independence and liberty you possess are the work of joint councils, and joint efforts—of common dangers, sufferings and successes.[36]

Similarly, in his Address before the Young Men's Lyceum of Springfield, Illinois, Lincoln exhorted his audience to identify with the patriotic dedication of the Founders:

> As the patriots of seventy-six did to the support of the Declaration of Independence, so to the support of the Constitution and Laws, let every American pledge his life, his property, and his sacred honor;—let every man remember that to violate the law, is to trample on the blood of his father, and to tear the charter of his own, and his children's liberty.[37]

Washington and Lincoln both placed religion visibly in the public square. Washington characterized religion and morality as "indispensable supports" to political prosperity.[38] In his second inaugural address, Lincoln spoke about the will of God in the ongoing Civil War. While Americans prayed for an end to war, he said, "if God wills that it continue until all the wealth piled by the bond-man's two hundred and fifty years of unrequited toil shall be sunk, and until every drop of blood drawn with the lash, shall be paid by another drawn with the sword, as was said three thousand years ago, so still it must be said 'the judgments of the Lord, are true and righteous altogether.'"[39]

Washington and Lincoln believed that American liberty and independence would have universal historical significance by providing the world with a successful example of popular constitutional government. Both were concerned to bequeath an independent constitutional republic to future generations. Washington voiced this aim in his Farewell Address, where he said: "I shall carry it with me to my grave, as a strong incitement to unceasing vows that Heaven may continue to you the choicest tokens of its beneficence— that your Union & brotherly affection may be perpetual—that the free constitution, which is the work of your hands, may be sacredly maintained."[40]

Throughout his career, Lincoln returned again and again to the theme of maintaining the American regime, which would offer the

world an example of free government. The Lyceum Address was
titled "The Perpetuation of Our Political Institutions." On the way
to the city of Washington to assume the presidency in 1861, Lincoln
addressed the New Jersey State Senate in Trenton and said:

> I am exceedingly anxious that this Union, the Constitution, and
> the liberties of the people shall be perpetuated in accordance
> with the original idea for which that struggle was made, and I
> shall be most happy indeed if I shall be an humble instrument
> in the hands of the Almighty, and of this, his almost chosen peo-
> ple, for perpetuating the object of that great struggle.[41]

In his first inaugural address, Lincoln declared that the American
union is "perpetual," and the Gettysburg Address famously ended
with the hope "that government of the people, by the people, for
the people, shall not perish from the earth."

The Founders promoted education to help develop the mores
required to sustain a free society. John Adams, for example, argued
that all Americans rich and poor, as citizens of a republic, would
need civic and moral education.

Matthew Spalding and Patrick Garrity write that George Washington believed education to be important not only for its own sake,
but also for the "political task of uniting" the new nation.[42] In his
eighth annual message to Congress, Washington advocated the
establishment of a national university to bring together students
from all across the country, from Massachusetts to Georgia, to promote friendships and connections among the nation's future leaders.
"The Youth, or young men from different parts of the United States
would be assembled together, & would by degrees discover that
there was not cause for those jealousies & prejudices which one
part of the Union had imbibed against another part," he said.[43] In
his Farewell Address, Washington remarked that fostering education
was particularly important in a free society influenced by public
opinion: "In proportion as the structure of a government gives force
to public opinion, it is essential that public opinion should be

enlightened." Therefore, promoting "Institutions for the general diffusion of knowledge" was a matter of primary importance.[44]

Thomas Jefferson too emphasized the importance of education for American citizenship. Like Washington, he preferred that young Americans study at home rather than in Europe, where they were more likely to imbibe antidemocratic principles. Jefferson founded the University of Virginia and developed ideas for public schools in his home state, putting the study of history at the center of this effort. If students were acquainted with "Graecian, Roman, European and American history," he wrote, they could understand "the experience of other times and other nations," and thus be able to "know ambition under every disguise it may assume; and knowing it, to defeat its views."[45]

In a similar vein, James Madison thought that good civic education would help future citizens understand the designs of unlimited power. "Learned institutions ought to be the favorite objects with every free people," he said. "They throw that light over the public mind which is the best security against crafty and dangerous encroachments on the public liberty."[46]

One of the American republic's first educators, Noah Webster, called for citizenship education for the young: "Every child in America should be acquainted with his own country," its geography, history, political principles, and "those illustrious heroes and statesmen." The purpose of civic education was to "call home the minds of youth and fix them upon the interests of their own country," and to "assist in forming attachments to it, as well as in enlarging the understanding."[47] Webster developed a very popular book of readings that went through seventy-five editions over a period of fifty years and included patriotic and moral stories, orations, the Declaration of Independence, Washington's farewell to the Continental Army, excerpts from Shakespeare, Addison's *Cato,* and the like. On the first page of Webster's reader was this epigraph: "Begin with the infant in the cradle; let the first word he lisps be Washington."

Patriotic Assimilation of Immigrants

The Founders did not use the term "Americanization," but their civic nationalist approach to assimilating immigrants into the American "we" was similar to the views that inspired the "Americanization" movement in the early twentieth century, including those of Theodore Roosevelt, Woodrow Wilson, and Louis Brandeis.

George Washington believed that "the bosom of America is open to receive not only the Opulent and respectable Stranger, but the oppressed and persecuted of all Nations and Religions."[48] He also believed that immigration policy should primarily serve American national interests, and that immigrants should leave old habits behind and join the American people by accepting American "customs, measures, laws." In 1794, President Washington sent a letter to Vice President Adams on the issues of immigration and assimilation, saying:

> My opinion, with respect to emigration [immigration], is, that except of useful Mechanics and some particular descriptions of men or professions, there is no need of encouragement: while the policy or advantage of its taking place in a body (I mean the settling of them in a body) may be much questioned; for, by so doing, they retain the Language, habits and principles (good or bad) which they bring with them. Whereas by an intermixture with our people, they, or their descendants, get assimilated to our customs, measures and laws: in a word, soon become one people.[49]

In a 1790 speech to Congress on the naturalization of immigrants, James Madison stated that America should welcome immigrants who could assimilate, but "exclude those" who would not "incorporate themselves" into our society. Both Thomas Jefferson and Alexander Hamilton saw advantages to immigration, but worried about the assimilation of newcomers, and insisted that their patriotic integration was necessary for the preservation of the

American constitutional republic. In *Notes on the State of Virginia,* Jefferson worried that a "greater number of emigrants" came from countries with "absolute monarchies," and he feared:

> They will bring with them the principles of the governments they leave, imbibed in their early youth; or, if able to throw them off, it will be in exchange for an unbounded licentiousness, passing, as is usual, from one extreme to another. It would be a miracle were they to stop precisely at the point of temperate liberty. These principles, with their language, they will transmit to their children.[50]

Jefferson's chief political rival among the Founders, Alexander Hamilton, expressed similar concerns about the need for assimilation: "The safety of a republic depends essentially on the energy of a common national sentiment; on a uniformity of principles and habits; on the exemption of citizens from foreign bias and prejudice; and on the love of country which will almost invariably be found to be closely connected with birth, education, and family." In the end, Hamilton believed, the maintenance of America's democratic republican regime depended on "the preservation of a national spirit and a national character" among both immigrants and the native-born.[51]

Hamilton opposed granting citizenship immediately to new immigrants: "To admit foreigners indiscriminately to the rights of citizens, the moment they put foot in our country ... would be nothing less than to admit the Grecian horse into the citadel of our liberty and sovereignty." Instead, he recommended drawing newcomers gradually into American life, "to enable aliens to get rid of foreign and acquire American attachments; to learn the principles and imbibe the spirit of our government; and to admit of a probability, at least, of their feeling a real interest in our affairs."[52]

During the Washington administration, Congress passed the Naturalization Act of 1795, requiring new citizens to take an oath not only swearing allegiance to the U.S. Constitution, but also renouncing all former allegiances as well. Moreover, the new citizens had to satisfy a court of admission that they were of "good moral character" and "attached to the principles of the Constitution" and the "good order and happiness of the United States."

The renunciation oath made sense to the Founders, because their concept of assimilation meant that the newcomer was leaving an old political community and joining a new one—the American liberal democratic nation-state. The immigrant was leaving a previous "people" and joining the American people, becoming one of "the People of the United States." The idea of renouncing old allegiances and embracing a new American national identity is consistent with the Founders' concept of civic nationalism rather than ethnic, racial, or religious nationalism. Abraham Lincoln remarked that although immigrants were not directly descended from the founding generation, by accepting the American creed as expressed in the Declaration of Independence they became "as though they were blood of the blood, and flesh of the flesh of the men who wrote that Declaration, and so they are."[53]

American political leaders during the great immigration wave of the early twentieth century, particularly Theodore Roosevelt and Woodrow Wilson, echoed the Founders' concept of immigration and civic nationalism: the transfer of allegiance and national identity from a previous people to the American people. The *Federal Textbook on Citizenship Training* for immigrants included a statement by Roosevelt explaining that equality for immigrants depended on undivided loyalty:

> In the first place we should insist that if the immigrant who comes here in good faith becomes an American and assimilates himself to us, he shall be treated on an exact equality with everyone else, for it is an outrage to discriminate against any such man because of creed [religion], or birthplace, or origin. But this is predicated upon the man's becoming in very fact an American, and nothing but an American. . . . There can be no divided

allegiance here. Any man who says he is an American but something else also, isn't an American at all.[54]

In a major article titled "True Americanism," Roosevelt praised a German-born congressman from Wisconsin, Richard Guenther, as an exemplar of immigrant loyalty during the American-German war scare over the Samoan Islands in 1888–89. Representative Guenther had told his fellow congressmen:

> We will work for our country.... When I say our country, I mean of course, our adopted country. I mean the United States of America. After passing through the crucible of naturalization, we are no longer Germans; we are Americans.... We will fight for America whenever necessary. America, first, last, and all the time. America against Germany.... We are Americans.[55]

Woodrow Wilson was a major political rival of Theodore Roosevelt, but sounded a similar note on patriotically integrating immigrants. At an "Americanization Day" event in Philadelphia on May 10, 1915, Wilson spoke directly to the new citizens and attacked what would later be called multiculturalism:

> You cannot dedicate yourself to America unless you become in every respect and with every purpose of your will thoroughly Americans. You cannot become thorough Americans if you think of yourselves in groups. America does not consist of groups. A man who thinks of himself as belonging to a particular national group in America has not yet become an American.[56]

On July 5, 1915, one of President Wilson's chief allies, Louis Brandeis, a leading progressive who was foreign-born, addressed another group of new citizens at Faneuil Hall in Boston on the topic of "What is Americanization?" Sounding very much like Alexander Hamilton, Brandeis stressed the need for immigrants to internalize America's ideals:

However great his outward conformity, the immigrant is not Americanized unless his interests and affections have become deeply rooted here. And we properly demand of the immigrant even more than this—He must be brought into complete harmony with our ideals and aspirations and cooperate with us for their attainment. Only when this has been done, will he possess the national consciousness of an American.[57]

From Washington and Hamilton to Theodore Roosevelt and Louis Brandeis, American leaders wanted to assimilate immigrants and strengthen national identity for the purpose of improving and sustaining American liberal democracy. Washington's call for "one people," Hamilton's emphasis on a "national character" and "national spirit," Roosevelt's advocacy of "Americanization," and Brandeis's reference to the "national consciousness of an American" are all of one piece. Since the beginnings of the republic, American leaders realized that our constitutional democracy required a robust national identity embraced by immigrants and native-born alike.

CHAPTER FOUR

Liberalism
under Assault

For two hundred years, from the eighteenth to near the end of the twentieth century, liberal democracy met and defeated its major ideological opponents: premodern autocracy, fascism or national socialism, and communism. In 1776, the Western world was dominated by the autocratic "old regime" of Throne and Altar, which we could call the "party of tradition." Throughout the nineteenth century, the aristocratic party of tradition—fortified by the skillful diplomacy of the Austrian foreign minister Metternich, the philosophy of reactionary thinkers like Joseph de Maistre, and the military forces of the Russian czar—resisted the rise of liberalism and democracy in Europe.

By the end of the First World War, with the collapse of the Hapsburg (Austro-Hungarian), Hohenzollern (German), and Romanov (Russian) empires, the party of tradition was pretty much defeated. In *The Closing of the American Mind,* Allan Bloom suggested that the death of Francisco Franco in the 1970s was the last gasp of a premodern traditionalism that resisted the Enlightenment. But in fact, the anti-Enlightenment banner was carried into the 1980s by the Argentine junta—whose ideologists were followers of the premodern European right and whose security forces were students of the counterrevolutionary theorists of the French Secret Army

Organization—until they were militarily routed by Margaret Thatcher's men in the Falklands.[1]

During a good part of the twentieth century, liberal democracy confronted a challenge from the twin totalitarianisms of Nazism/fascism and communism. Nazi Germany was utterly crushed in 1945 and the Soviet Union collapsed in 1991. The liberal democratic nation-state had triumphed over the fascist and communist states. In a famous article and later a book, Francis Fukuyama declared "the end of history," by which he meant that liberal democracy was the endpoint of humankind's ideological evolution. While Fukuyama acknowledged that the ideas of liberal democracy would continue to be challenged, he insisted that no "serious" rivals would appear in the future because any competitor to liberal democracy would not possess universal appeal. For example, he argued that radical Islam would not have widespread appeal throughout the West, like communism and fascism had in the past.[2]

A major premise of this book is that Fukuyama was wrong and that a rival ideology, which I am calling "transnational progressivism," will be a major ideological competitor to liberal democracy and therefore a threat to the liberal democratic nation-state.

Progressive Liberalism

The American liberalism of the mid-twentieth century, which defeated Nazism/fascism and then confronted Soviet communism, differs from traditional liberalism. For over a hundred years, the natural rights theory of the Founders and Abraham Lincoln had served as the philosophical foundation of the American regime, combining traditional liberalism with civic republicanism. This foundation was challenged by the progressive movement of the late nineteenth and early twentieth centuries. According to John Dewey, a leading progressive thinker, "Natural rights and natural liberties exist only in the kingdom of mythological social zoology."[3] Another major progressive, Charles Merriam, said, "The individualistic ideas of the 'natural right' school of political theory, endorsed in the Revolution, are discredited and repudiated."[4]

The Founders and Lincoln believed that a permanent standard of right is founded in "nature and nature's God," that humans are "endowed by their Creator" with "unalienable rights," and that there is an immutable human nature. The progressives, by contrast, believed that the standard of right is historical (Dewey spoke of "historical relativity"), that moral standards evolve over time, that rights cannot be gleaned from nature, and that human nature itself is malleable. Progressive intellectuals emphasized "historical development," the "historical process," or the "march of history" as leading to moral, social, psychological, and political progress. This progress was to be based on human will, and informed by science and experimentation.

In politics, the progressives endorsed two broad themes that were sometimes contradictory: democratic reforms and apolitical managerial expertise. On the one hand, progressives supported an array of measures designed to promote more direct democratic input from the people, including direct election of U.S. senators, direct primaries, state ballot initiatives on specific legislation, and referenda on the recall of state officials. At the same time, progressives supported the "scientific management" of government, which often put political decision making in the hands of ostensibly apolitical bureaucracies, "nonpartisan" commissions, and regulatory agencies remote from democratic accountability and popular participation.

The progressives opposed monopolies and trusts, and favored regulating railroads, utilities, and large business combines. They favored social welfare legislation concerning child labor, workplace safety, increased pensions, and the like. All of this led to the formation of the modern administrative state. Progressive historians like Vernon Parrington, Frederick Jackson Turner, and Charles Beard created a "usable history," a narrative in which "reform-minded" and "democratic" forces (usually embodied by Thomas Jefferson and Andrew Jackson, and later Theodore Roosevelt and Woodrow Wilson) fought corporate interests and their wealthy big-business supporters. The latter group is usually represented by Alexander Hamilton, the old Federalist Party, the Whigs, and the post–Civil War Republican Party—thus deliberately excluding Lincoln but including McKinley, Taft, and Democrats like Grover Cleveland who favored the gold standard and limited government.

The progressive movement prefigured the liberalism of the New Deal, but there were some important differences. Whereas the progressives of the early twentieth century had substantial support in both major political parties, the liberalism of the midcentury was essentially a Democratic Party affair. The New Dealers, as Richard Hofstadter explained, were less moralistic and more attuned to partisan politics than the progressives had been.[5] They put more emphasis on the working class and labor unions, and less on the middle class. In *Camelot and the Cultural Revolution*, James Piereson argues that the New Deal liberals, unlike the progressives, "accepted the reality of modern industrial organization and sought to respond to it, not by restoring the influence of the individual farmer, worker, and businessman, but by building a parallel capacity in the national government to regulate and direct it."[6]

Modern American liberalism, or progressive liberalism, combined the traditional liberalism of the Founders and Lincoln with the liberalism of Franklin D. Roosevelt. The older liberalism consisted of negative rights that individuals possessed against governmental power: freedom of speech, freedom of the press, freedom of association, habeas corpus, freedom from arbitrary arrest and imprisonment, freedom of religion, property rights, trial by a jury of one's peers, and the like. Progressive liberalism emphasized positive rights to specific social benefits, such as a pension and unemployment insurance.

Nowhere was this new liberalism expressed more forcefully than in FDR's State of the Union message of January 11, 1944, in which he endorsed a concept of positive rights and called for a "second bill of rights," including "economic security":

> The Republic had its beginnings, and grew to its present strength, under the protection of certain inalienable political rights—among them the right to free speech, free press, free worship, trial by jury, freedom from unreasonable searches and seizures. They were our rights to life and liberty. As our nation has grown in size and stature, however—as our industrial economy expanded—these political rights proved inadequate to assure us equality in the pursuit of happiness.... [T]rue individual freedom cannot exist without economic security and independence.... We have accepted, so to speak, a second Bill of Rights....
> Among these are:
> The right to a useful and remunerative job ...;
> The right to earn enough to provide adequate food and clothing and recreation;
> The right of every farmer to raise and sell his products at a return which will give him and his family a decent living; ...
> The right of every family to a decent home;
> The right to adequate medical care and the opportunity to achieve and enjoy good health;
> The right to adequate protection from the economic fears of old age, sickness, accident, and unemployment;
> The right to a good education.

From the New Deal to the mid-1960s, modern liberals dominated American political thought and practice. The quintessential liberal diplomat Chester Bowles wrote in the *New York Times Magazine* on April 19, 1959, "To paraphrase a Victorian Tory statesman, we are all liberals now."[7] Even when there was a Republican Congress (1946–48, 1952–54) and a Republican president (1952–60), the public debate stayed within the boundaries set by modern liberalism. For the most part, the basic premises and major legislation of the New Deal were accepted by both parties. The issue that remained was who could best manage the administrative, regulatory, and welfare state.

Some earlier progressive historians had taken a "debunking" approach to American history. The leading progressive educator, John Dewey—disagreeing with Jefferson, the Founders, and Lincoln—worried that teaching patriotism might require an "avoidance of the spirit of criticism in dealing with history, politics, and economics."[8] After World War I, the progressive historian Charles Beard famously wrote that the U.S. Constitution was essentially created to protect the propertied classes and hardly a document to be revered.[9] Another progressive historian, Carl Becker, "deconstructed" the Declaration of Independence and argued that its philosophical core was not credible.[10]

In the face of the Second World War and the onslaught of totalitarianism, Beard and Becker embraced a more positive view of America's past and a patriotic faith in American political institutions.[11] They joined other historians in 1941 to endorse a public statement by the American Historical Association, written by Arthur Schlesinger Sr. (father of the now more famous Arthur Schlesinger Jr.), declaring that "genuine patriotism" called for "sound scholarship" and "a truthful picture of the past":

> The history of the American people has been hammered out on the anvil of experience. It is a story of achievement, often against heavy odds. Some of the most glorious passages have consisted in the struggle to overcome social and economic injustices. Failures as well as successes carry lessons of which posterity can ill afford to be ignorant. In discussing controversial issues the textbook writer has an obligation to give both sides. By so doing he not only upholds the ideal of presenting a truthful picture, but also of encouraging in young people that spirit of inquiry, open-mindedness and fair play which lies at the root of our democratic institutions.[12]

On the evening of June 6, 1944, as American troops were fighting on the coast of Normandy, President Roosevelt read over the radio a prayer he had composed:

> Almighty God: Our sons, pride of our nation, this day have set upon a mighty endeavor, a struggle to preserve our Republic, our religion, our civilization, and to set free a suffering humanity.... Their road will be long and hard. For the enemy is strong.... Success may not come with rushing speed, but we shall return again and again; and we know that by Thy grace, and by the righteousness of our cause, our sons will triumph.[13]

This was civic nationalism par excellence, an unembarrassed patriotism that echoed the historic addresses of Washington and Lincoln in times of national peril.

Leading progressive liberals spoke in boldly optimistic and patriotic language, exhibiting a positive sense of American national identity. Liberal historians, social scientists, and media figures—including Arthur Schlesinger Jr., Richard Hofstadter, Seymour Martin Lipset, Louis Hartz, Henry Steele Commager, David Riesman, Archibald McLeish, John Kenneth Galbraith, and Edward R. Murrow—interpreted America's past, analyzed its present, and outlined its future. In effect, they "owned" the national narrative.

While concerned about the work yet to be accomplished, particularly in civil rights, modern liberals for the most part were proud of what Roosevelt and Truman had accomplished and proud to be Americans. After all, the American democratic nation-state under liberal leadership emerged in the mid-twentieth century as the greatest military, economic, intellectual, and moral power in the world. Liberal-led America had defeated the totalitarian powers of Nazi Germany and imperial Japan, and with the Truman Doctrine it prepared for the "long twilight struggle" against the new totalitarian foe, Soviet communism.

During the 1940s, however, a fierce internal struggle was fought out on the American left between anticommunist liberals and those who favored a "Popular Front" or a broad coalition of the left including communists. The anticommunists were led by Hubert Humphrey, union leaders Walter Reuther and David Dubinsky, theologian Reinhold Niebuhr, and historian-activist Arthur Schlesinger Jr., who sought to purge liberal organizations of communists and confront the Soviets in foreign affairs. On the other side were the progressives, supporters of the Popular Front led by former vice president Henry Wallace; CIO-PAC, the political action committee of the CIO; the National Farmers Union; the *New Republic* and *Nation* magazines; and the "eleven CIO unions that had substantial communist leadership." They argued for peace with the Soviet Union abroad and "no enemies on the left" at home. Both sides favored an expansion of New Deal programs, but they differed on the threat of the Soviet Union and the role of communists in political organizations and labor unions.

The two factions fought it out in union halls, newspaper offices, editorial meetings at small periodicals, Democratic Party primaries and conventions, at meetings of women's, veterans', civil rights, and ethnic organizations. The anticommunists created first the Union for Democratic Action (UDA) and then Americans for Democratic Action (ADA), which battled Henry Wallace's Progressive Citizens of America.

Some liberals believed the anticommunists were too strident. For example, Chester Bowles refused ADA membership for a time, saying, "I thought that the ADA was concentrating too much of its time on opposing communism and not enough on opposing the Republican Party, which is the major threat in this country."[14] Steven Gillon, a Yale historian and major chronicler of the ADA, writes that the grande dame of American liberalism, Eleanor Roosevelt, after a period of hesitation "found herself moving, albeit reluctantly, toward the anti-communist position of the UDA," and she became a founding member of the ADA.[15]

In 1948, President Harry Truman defeated the Republican Thomas Dewey, the Dixiecrat Strom Thurmond, and Henry Wallace running under the banner of the newly formed "Progressive Party." Truman's victory strengthened the forces of anticommunist liberalism against the weakened supporters of the Popular Front. As the Cold War intensified, the anticommunists finally routed their Henry Wallace–style rivals on the American left.

During this period, Arthur Schlesinger Jr. emerged as a leading ideological spokesman for the postwar anticommunist left. In 1949 he wrote *The Vital Center,* which became a manifesto of modern American liberalism, advocating strict regulation of business, expanded social welfare programs, and strengthened civil rights, along with anticommunism.[16] Drawing heavily on the Christian realist philosophy of Reinhold Niebuhr, Schlesinger attacked the utopianism of the Marxist left, which leads to tyranny, and that of the Wallace progressives, which leads to national weakness. He praised the realism of the Founding Fathers, and unlike some fellow liberal historians such as Richard Hofstadter, he accepted the Founders' concept of a more or less unchanging human nature with both positive and negative characteristics.

Civil Rights

Liberalism both traditional and modern emphasized equal rights and opportunities for individuals. Liberals rejected the premodern aristocratic value of "ascribed status," derived from social class, race, ethnicity, or national origin; they argued that people should be judged as individuals, not as members of a group that they were born into.

In 1964, the U.S. Congress passed the Civil Rights Act, which its chief sponsors described as exemplifying the liberal principle of equality of individual opportunity. The legislation outlawed discrimination on the grounds of race, color, religion, sex, or national origin in employment, voting, public accommodations, and federal programs. The Senate leaders of the broad civil rights coalition were Hubert Humphrey of Minnesota, a liberal Democrat, and Everett M. Dirksen of Illinois, a conservative Republican.

Opponents of the Civil Rights Act asked if it would require companies to hire blacks, ethnics, and women in proportion to their availability in the labor force, thus achieving equality of result for groups instead of equality of opportunity for individuals. Would the legislation lead to numerical quotas and coercion? Supporters of the bill answered absolutely not, and just to make sure, they added Section 703(j) to Title VII (employment), stating:

> Nothing contained in this title shall be interpreted to require any employer ... to grant preferential treatment ... to any group because of their race, color, religion, sex, or national origin ... on account of an imbalance which may exist with respect to total number or percentage of persons of any race, color, religion, sex, or national origin employed by the employer ... in comparison with the total number or percentage [of such groups] in any community, State, or other area....[17]

According to Senator Dirksen, the substitute bill "expressly provides that an employer does not have to maintain any employment ratio, regardless of the racial ratio in the community."[18] Senator Humphrey, in a debate with an opponent of the bill (Senator Robertson, D-VA), declared, "if the Senator can find in Title VII ... any language which provides that an employer will have to hire on the basis of a percentage or quota related to color, race, religion, or national origin, I will start eating the pages one after another, because it is not in there."[19]

In the end, the Civil Rights Act passed overwhelmingly and enshrined the principle of equality of individual opportunity. But the passage of civil rights legislation in the mid-1960s (including the Voting Rights Act in 1965) turned out to be, in retrospect, perhaps the high-water mark of the robust modern American liberalism of the twentieth century.

At midcentury, modern American liberalism supported a positive view of the nation and a vigorous civic nationalism, an emphasis on what Americans held in common, antitotalitarianism and anti-communism, individual rights over group rights, equality of opportunity for individuals, realism over utopianism, free speech and a free press. In the decades that followed, all of these established liberal positions came under assault. The attacks went under various names and were often tied to major political issues of the day, such as the Vietnam War or the changing definition of racial, ethnic, and sexual equality. Some actions were overdue positive reforms to end old prejudices; others were destructive, undermining the foundational principles of the liberal democratic nation-state.

Multiculturalism

The concept of "multiculturalism" was highly influential in educational and media circles during the last few decades of the twentieth century, and it remains so today. Of course, multiculturalism can mean different things. A "soft" multiculturalism might include the celebration of ethnic festivals, for example, to which few would object. The "hard" multiculturalism of some academic theorists, on the other hand, challenges the liberal principle of equal citizenship for individuals, instead favoring a group-oriented concept of citizenship. The political argument of multicultural advocates runs as follows:

"The idea of a dominant mainstream culture to which all should adhere is anathema. The United States should be thought of as a multicultural society in which different 'cultures' (including African Americans, Hispanic Americans, Asian Americans, Native Americans, and also women) have their own perspectives, values, histories, and identities separate from (and sometimes in opposition to) the 'dominant Anglo white male' culture. These different 'cultures' should be considered of equal value to the predominant Western culture. Further, the 'melting pot' concept of immigration should be replaced by a 'mosaic' or 'salad bowl' in which newcomers retain their old languages, identities, and cultures."

The core premise of multiculturalism turns Woodrow Wilson's Americanization Day speech of May 10, 1915 (discussed in the previous chapter) on its head. President Wilson said, "You cannot become thoroughly Americans if you think of yourselves in groups.... A man who thinks of himself as belonging to a particular national group in America has not yet become an American." Multiculturalists argue, on the contrary, that one should think of oneself first as a member of a particular group in America, not primarily as an American citizen. In practice, multiculturalism attacks three pillars of the liberal democratic nation-state: (1) liberalism, by putting ascribed group rights over individual rights; (2) a strong and positive national identity, by emphasizing subnational group consciousness over national patriotism; and (3) majority-rule democracy.

Prominent educators gave their support to multiculturalism in the 1990s. For example, Amy Gutmann, then a professor at Princeton (now president of the University of Pennsylvania), edited a collection of essays promoting multicultural education and a "politics of recognition," published in 1992. In her introductory essay, Gutmann wrote of the need for "public recognition and preservation" of "discrete ethnic, linguistic, and other cultural groups," as well as recognition of our more universal identity as persons. Missing in her essay is any reference to national identity or national citizenship.[20]

Two years later, Gutmann described the idea that American students should "learn that they are above all citizens of the United States" as a "repugnant position." American schools, she wrote, "must move beyond the morally misguided and politically dangerous idea of asking us to choose between being, above all, citizens of our own society or, above all, citizens of the world. We are, above all, none of the above." In Gutmann's view, "Our primary moral allegiance is to no community," such as the United States, but rather to "justice," and more specifically to "furthering social justice for all individuals." Basing education on "shared national values" is something "abhorrent" to Gutmann, who says it "would clearly be incompatible with a commitment to the teaching of democratic humanist values."[21]

During deliberations over the New York State social studies curriculum, a leading textbook author of the 1990s, Professor Jorge Klor de Alva of Stanford, argued that Latino subgroup loyalty should trump American national loyalty.[22]

Besides challenging liberalism and national identity, advocates of multiculturalism even questioned the traditional democratic principle of majority rule. In 1992, Will Kymlicka, an influential Canadian theorist of multiculturalism, stated that "liberal principles of justice are consistent with, and indeed require, certain forms of special status for minority cultures."[23] Kymlicka noted that this view of liberalism, "defended by [John] Rawls and [Ronald] Dworkin," posits that "justice requires removing or compensating for undeserved 'morally arbitrary' disadvantages." He maintained that "some minority cultures may need protection from the economic or political decisions of the majority culture" and, thus, "they may need veto power over certain decisions regarding language and culture."[24] Ironically, this idea resurrects John C. Calhoun's "concurrent majority" argument of pre–Civil War America, by which a minority bloc (the South) should be given veto power over national law.

In the United States as well, leading multicultural educators have redefined democracy, from a system of majority rule limited by individual rights, to one of power sharing among the different cultural groups or "peoples" that compose the nation. According to Professor James Banks, a major textbook author who was a key figure in the development of the National Council for the Social Studies guidelines on multicultural education, "To create an authentic democratic *unum* with moral authority and perceived legitimacy, the *pluribus* (diverse peoples) must negotiate and share power." This statement in the 1990s by a leader of the largest civic education organization in the United States implies that the American democracy consists of "diverse peoples" rather than individual citizens, that an "authentic democratic *unum*" is yet to be created, and that therefore the current U.S. political system is not fully legitimate.[25]

A series of major educational documents in the early 1990s began to refer to the American "peoples" rather than the American "people." As the old Marxists of the 1930s would have said, this was no accident. The concept of the American "peoples" implies that the United States is a multinational state, in which different "peoples" have the attributes of separate nations with distinct histories and cultures.

To speak of the American "peoples" inverts the language of American unity as expressed in the Declaration of Independence ("one people") and in the Constitution ("We the People of the United States"). The notion of the "peoples" of the United States is a counterpatriotic ideological weapon to subordinate the *unum* to the *pluribus*. This is what postmodernists call "rhetorical subversion."

During the 1990s, the American "peoples" found their way into academic standards and curricula. In July 1991, New York State released a social studies curriculum titled "One Nation, Many Peoples: A Declaration of Cultural Interdependence." Despite strenuous criticism from historians like Arthur Schlesinger Jr., a revised version of the curriculum released in 1995 still referred to the American "peoples." Also in 1995, the Colorado State Board of Education adopted history standards recommending that students describe the "interaction" of the "various peoples" living in the United States, identified as "African, Asian, European, Latino, and Native American," as if these often bureaucratic categories constituted separate nations. In 1996, the Maryland State Board of Education adopted social studies standards that referred to the "peoples of the United States." What is particularly interesting about this curricular decision is that the president of the state board, Christopher T. Cross (also president of the Council for Basic Education), had been a Republican assistant secretary of education and a director of the Business Roundtable's Education Initiative.

One of the major events of the so-called "culture wars" was the battle over the National History Standards. During the late 1980s, in an attempt to improve academic achievement, the federal government under George H. W. Bush's administration funded academics and educators in various disciplines to develop a series of voluntary national standards to provide guidelines for the states and localities. In 1994, the National History Standards were published to a storm of criticism and controversy. Lynne V. Cheney, who as chairman of the National Endowment for the Humanities had helped launch the project, attacked the final product as biased. So did others who had supported the original concept of national standards, including Chester Finn and Diane Ravitch, both former assistant secretaries of education, and Albert Shanker, president of the American Federation of Teachers.

In January 1996, the U.S. Senate agreed with the critics, condemning the National History Standards by a vote of 99 to 1. Other historians and educators joined in the criticism.* In my view, the standards were indeed biased: a document that was supposed to examine what is most important for American students to know did not mention Daniel Webster, Robert E. Lee, Thomas Edison, or Albert Einstein, but did include Speckled Snake, Wovoka, Ellen Levine, and Madonna. A content analysis of the standards by Robert Lerner and Althea Nagai found that issues of race, ethnicity, and gender were emphasized nearly three times as much as political liberty and democracy.

---

*They included Walter McDougall, John Patrick Diggins, Forrest McDonald, Herman Belz, Burton W. Folsom Jr., Wilcomb Washburn, Gertrude Himmelfarb, Elizabeth Fox-Genovese, Donald Kagan, Paul Gagnon, Stephan Thernstrom, Arthur Schlesinger Jr., Albert Shanker, and Gilbert T. Sewall.

References to the American "peoples" abound in the history standards. For example, one "core standard" instructs that students should understand how "big business, heavy industry, and mechanized farming transformed the American peoples" in the late nineteenth century. The standards describe the formation of the United States not as a product of Western civilization, with political institutions and early settlers mainly from the British Isles, but instead as a "convergence" of three civilizations: European, West African Islamic, and Amerindian ("three worlds meet").

In an effort to rescue the history standards, the Council for Basic Education under Christopher Cross's leadership convened a group of academics to revise the document. The new product eliminated the most egregious examples of bias, but maintained the multicultural framework. The standards still emphasized fostering "mutual respect" among the "many peoples" of the United States, and still described the United States as a product of the "convergence" of three civilizations. A new content analysis by Lerner and Nagai still found a roughly three-to-one ratio of race, ethnicity, and gender over political democracy.

The "multicultural conventions" embodied in the history standards were reflected in the new textbooks published after the debate, as noted by Gilbert T. Sewall, president of the American Textbook Council. Sewall warned that history content is "increasingly deformed by identity politics and pressure groups."[26] The *Education for Democracy* statement published by the Albert Shanker Institute in 2003 quotes Diane Ravitch's criticism of how the standards affected textbook content:

> The new textbooks have adopted the "three worlds meet" paradigm that the UCLA history center advocated as part of its [1994] proposed national standards for U.S. history.... [T]he texts downplay the relative importance of the European ideas that gave rise to democratic institutions and devote more attention to pre-Columbian civilizations and African Kingdoms....

The textbooks ... have nearly buried the narrative about the ideas and institutions that made our national government possible.[27]

The multicultural project in general and the National History Standards in particular were a major ideological assault on modern liberalism. Besides an emphasis on group consciousness over individual citizenship, and on ethnic subcultures over national identity, the standards described the Cold War in terms of moral equivalence (the "sword play of the US and the USSR") and flirted with a utopian outlook ("Americans believed in the perfectibility of man"). Thus, the multiculturalists rejected the major tenets of modern liberalism: emphasis on equality of individual citizenship, strong American identity, anticommunism and realism. They were closer to the progressive utopianism of Henry Wallace than the anticommunist realism of Harry Truman. It is no wonder that Arthur Schlesinger Jr. launched a vigorous attack on the multicultural project in his book *The Disuniting of America: Reflections on a Multicultural Society.*

The Diversity Agenda

There is a difference between the traditional definition of diversity and the contemporary ideological use of the concept, which I will call the "diversity agenda" or the "diversity project." We should make some distinctions.

Diversity as a natural result of a free society. There is a diversity that follows from the free choices of individual citizens and the robust interplay of the voluntary institutions of civil society within the liberal democratic nation-state. A vibrant civil society includes diverse individuals, viewpoints, and institutions: neighborhood associations, civic groups, charitable organizations, churches, clubs, ethnic associations, religious associations, veterans' groups, women's groups, fraternal organizations, sports and leisure groups, health

clubs. These have been acknowledged as part of the healthy pluralism of American civic life since Tocqueville's visit to the United
States in the early 1830s.

Diversity as the goal of society. The "diversity agenda" promotes
"diversity" as an end in itself, an outcome that political, civic, and
social forces should consciously seek to achieve. In the different
sectors of society—government, education, employment, law, culture,
media—diversity is defined in group terms, and the groups concerned
are almost always racial, ethnic, and gender groups. Religious groups
have rarely been considered as part of the diversity agenda, although
recently the Muslim minority in America has come to be seen as sufficiently different from the mainstream to qualify as an identifiable
"other," and thus to receive the attention of the diversity project.

In boardrooms, courtrooms, schools and universities, law firms,
television studies, and government bureaucracies, the question is
always asked: How can we measure our progress in achieving diversity? The answer is pretty much the same everywhere: Let's look
at the numbers. How many women, African Americans, Latino
Americans, Asian Americans have we hired, employed, retained,
admitted, graduated? What should our numbers be in relation to
the percentage of these groups in the local population?

The standard measurement for achieving "diversity" is group
proportionalism, or statistical equality for groups. For example, in
employment a major assumption is that the various racial, ethnic,
and gender groups should fill all job categories in proportion to
their percentages in the local work force. If 10 percent of all potential
workers in a given labor market are Asian Americans and 50 percent
are women, then all job categories (accountants, park rangers, attorneys, electricians, clerical employees, etc.) should be filled propor-
tionately: 10 percent by Asian Americans and 50 percent by women.
If this does not happen—and in a free society it never does—there
is a problem of "underrepresentation" that must be solved.

Soon after the civil rights legislation of the mid-1960s was passed,
the original intent of equal opportunity for individuals—regardless

of race, ethnicity, or sex—began to morph into statistical equality of results for racial, ethnic, and gender groups. The first indication of change was the use of the "disparate impact" concept by the Equal Employment Opportunity Commission in 1966. If business practices (tests, requirements, etc.) resulted in a "disparate impact" on "protected classes," so that minorities or women were statistically "underrepresented," the assumption was that there was probably something discriminatory about the practice. In 1971, the U.S. Supreme Court in *Griggs v. Duke Power Company* adopted the "disparate impact" rationale, requiring employers to prove that practices resulting in the "underrepresentation" of women and minorities were justified by business necessity. Supreme Court decisions after *Griggs* in the 1970s and 1980s reinforced the concept of group proportionalism.

In the landmark *Regents of the University of California v. Bakke* (1978), the Supreme Court approved using race as a factor in school admissions. But more importantly in the long run, Justice Lewis Powell, writing the majority decision, declared that "the goal of achieving a diverse student body" was compelling. More than any single action, Powell's phrase launched the diversity agenda as a major force in American public life.

In the 1980s, the Reagan administration challenged the central premises of group preferences. The assistant attorney general for the Civil Rights Division of the Justice Department, William Bradford Reynolds, told Congress in 1981, "We no longer will insist upon or in any respect support the use of quotas or any other numerical or statistical formula designed to provide non victims of discrimination preferential treatment based on race, sex, national origin or religion."[28] Although not supported by all elements of the Reagan administration, the Justice Department, first under William French Smith and later under Edwin Meese, fought gamely against group proportionalism, with mixed success. During the late 1980s and early 1990s, Supreme Court decisions seesawed back and forth on the issue of group preferences for "protected classes."

During this period, however, the forces favoring group preferences, slowly at first but with growing intensity, seized upon Justice
Powell's "diversity" comments and changed the entire public debate.
For decades, the argument had been that remedies (usually affirmative action) were needed to make up for previous discrimination.
By the early 1990s, the argument of "past discrimination" was passé.
The new rationale was that "diversity," meaning essentially group
proportionalism, was a good in itself and should be a major goal of
educational, business, and governmental institutions at all levels.

In the Supreme Court case *Grutter v. Bollinger* (2003), the diversity agenda achieved a major breakthrough. In a 5-4 decision, the
majority opinion written by Justice Sandra Day O'Connor ruled
that the University of Michigan Law School could use race as a
factor in admitting students in order to further a "compelling state
interest" in the "educational benefits" of a "diverse student body."
O'Connor declared that the law school had an interest in attaining
a "critical mass" of minority students for the sake of diversity.

Justice O'Connor was particularly impressed by the support of
American business leaders for the law school's diversity program.
A friend-of-the-court brief supporting the school's race-based
admission policies was filed by sixty-five leading American corporations, including Coca-Cola, Boeing, Chevron, Dow Chemical,
Intel, Microsoft, Nike, GE, Pricewaterhouse, Procter & Gamble,
and Xerox. At the heart of the amicus brief was the "postliberal"
notion that admission of a "critical mass" of people from specific
racial, ethnic, and gender groups to the institutions of higher education trumped individual merit and opportunity. The brief essentially repeated the standard multicultural arguments of the past
thirty or forty years. The brief even parroted the slogans of the pro-
multicultural historians by referring to the United States as "this
nation of many peoples."

Indeed, American business has been a major supporter of the
diversity project, multiculturalism, affirmative action, and almost
all efforts that place ethnic, racial, and gender group rights and

consciousness over individual rights. In *The Diversity Machine*, Fred Lynch describes in detail how American corporate interests have promoted public policies that challenge the core principles of the American regime. Speaking of the diversity agenda, he writes:

> Both the ends and the means of this policy movement pose a substantial threat to the values of the generic liberalism enshrined in modern American law and culture: free speech; individualism; nondiscrimination on the basis of ethnicity, gender, or religion; equality of opportunity; equal treatment under universalistic laws, standards, and procedures; democratic process; and, above all, a sense of national unity and cohesion embodied in the spirit of *E Pluribus Unum*.[29]

Ward Connerly, an African American businessman and former regent of the University of California, led a series of successful statewide referenda against group preferences in employment and education in California, Washington, and Michigan (he was defeated in Nebraska). In his autobiography, *Creating Equal*, Connerly recalls the vigorous opposition that his efforts faced from corporate interests that backed racial, ethnic, and gender preferences. Recounting his successful initiative against group preferences in the state of Washington (I-200), Connerly wrote that

> the most significant obstacle we faced in the Washington campaign was not the media or even the political personalities who attacked us, but the corporate world.... Boeing, Weyerhaeuser, Starbucks, Costco, Microsoft, and Eddie Bauer all made huge donations to the No on I-200 campaign.... The fundraising was spearheaded by Bill Gates' father, Bill Gates, Sr., a regent of the University of Washington whose famous name seemed to suggest that the whole of the high-tech world was solemnly shaking its head at us.[30]

As Connerly understands, racial, ethnic, and gender "underrepresentation" in job categories or school admissions is not prima facie evidence of discrimination. To regard it as such is to ignore how people actually behave in free societies, or, indeed, in any society that has ever existed in the history of the world.

Professors Donald Horowitz (Duke University), Myron Weiner (Massachusetts Institute of Technology), Cynthia Enloe (Clark University), and Thomas Sowell (Hoover Institution) have spent years studying the distribution of racial, ethnic, and gender groups in numerous occupations all across the planet.[31] They have found no evidence to support the assumption that without discrimination and prejudice different ethnic groups would be proportionally distributed across occupations. Everywhere in the world, in every occupation, some ethnic groups are "underrepresented" and some are "overrepresented." In studying armed forces, police, and government civil services, Professor Enloe found that none of these institutions anywhere in the world "mirror" the ethnic composition of their countries. She believes this is true because different ethnic groups use different "mobility ladders" to advance economically.

Throughout the world, different ethnic groups have been "overrepresented" in various occupations, including: Ibos in banks and railways in northern Nigeria; Chinese in the air force and within the detective ranks in the police service in Malaysia; East Indians as dentists and veterinarians in Malaysia; Germans in optics, piano manufacturing, and beer brewing in western Europe, Russia, and North and South America; Italians in the wine industry in Brazil and California; Jews in the clothing industry in the United States, South America, and Australia—to name a few examples. In one particular case of "overrepresentation," the *Wall Street Journal* reported in 1995 that more than four-fifths of all doughnut shops in California were owned by people of Cambodian origin. Ownership of these small businesses is what Professor Enloe called a "mobility ladder" for many Cambodian Americans. And since Cambodian Americans are a relatively small percentage of the population, their dominance of one occupation would mean they are "underrepresented" in many other occupations.

One could ask why these statistical disparities are a problem for people living in a free society. Why should we imagine that racial, ethnic, and gender proportionalism that has never existed anywhere in the world should be the norm? How could a policy of proportional representation be consistent with a free society? Professor Donald Horowitz, after finding no multiethnic society in the entire world where ethnic groups were proportionally represented throughout the workforce, stated that "it remains problematic whether any but the most heavy-handed preferential policies, operating in a command economy, can actually move a society to such a state."[32]

Critical Theory

Anyone who has attended classes at an American (or any Western) university during the past thirty years or so has heard a familiar set of theories that go something like this:

"Throughout history, all societies are divided between two basic groups: the privileged and the marginalized, the dominant and the subordinate, the oppressor and the oppressed. The marginalized groups of history have included women, the poor, religious, racial and ethnic minorities. Power is exercised by the privileged groups in two ways: through coercion, or more importantly through 'ideological hegemony,' which means the supremacy of the worldview or value system that supports the collective interests of the predominant groups. Subordinate groups are influenced to internalize the value system and worldview of the privileged groups.

"For example, the dominant values of a patriarchal system serve the interests of males as a group and oppress the interests of females. A racist system means that whites are privileged as a group (having 'white skin privilege'), and nonwhites are oppressed. The dominant groups establish their hegemony throughout every part of society, so that the systems and institutions of society are themselves oppressive. Women and nonwhites who regard these systems as

legitimate—with their institutional sexism and systemic racism—
are consenting to their own marginalization.

"To empower the marginalized groups, it is necessary to create
a 'counter-hegemony,' a new value system to replace that of the
dominant group. First, the members of subordinate groups must
understand how the system is oppressive and how it marginalizes
them. Unfortunately, many of them possess 'false consciousness';
they accept the conventional assumptions and values of the dominant groups as legitimate, natural, or just. Hence, 'raising consciousness' is crucial to transforming the system. Because the
hegemonic values permeate all aspects of life—family, marriage,
church, work, leisure, media, art and literature—these are all bat-
tlegrounds in which to seek this transformation by throwing the
dominant groups out of power.

"Morality is not universal but group-based. What is moral is
what serves the interests of the 'oppressed' or 'marginalized' ethnic,
racial, or gender groups."

Critical theory says that "the system" is not capable of reform,
but needs to be transformed in a revolutionary fashion. It holds
that the core principles of liberalism (both traditional and modern)—equality of opportunity for individuals, free speech, a positive
national identity, and a faith in American constitutional democracy
as it is actually practiced—are all fraudulent, merely instruments
of domination employed by the privileged groups to keep the subordinate groups in an inferior status.

The origins of critical theory can be found in the writings of
Hegelian or "cultural Marxist" intellectuals. Particularly influential
was the work of Theodore Adorno, Max Horkheimer, Herbert Marcuse, and others associated with the "Frankfurt School," or the
Institute for Social Research in Frankfurt, Germany, in the 1920s,
which sought to combine the insights of Marx and Freud. In addition, the critical theorists were greatly influenced by Antonio Gramsci, a leading Marxist intellectual and a founder of the Italian
Communist Party.

Whereas the classical Marxists emphasized economic conditions as a prelude to revolution, the cultural Marxists emphasized ideology. They argued that the decisive struggle to overthrow the bourgeois regime (middle-class liberal democracy) would first be fought out at the level of "consciousness." That is, the current system had to be rejected by its citizens intellectually and morally before power could be transferred from dominant to subordinate groups. During the past few decades, concepts like "false consciousness," "systemic oppression," "dominant" and "marginalized" groups, and "ideological hegemony" have influenced various oppositional forces including ethnic militants, environmental activists, animal rights advocates, radical feminists, the New Left, and student radicals.[33]

One example is the prominent feminist Catharine MacKinnon, a law professor at the University of Michigan. In *Towards a Feminist Theory of the State*, MacKinnon wrote, "The rule of law and the rule of men are one thing, indivisible," because "State power, embodied in law, exists through society as male power." Therefore, "Male power is systemic. Coercive, legitimized, and epistemic, it is the regime." MacKinnon argues that "a rape is not an isolated event or a moral transgression or individual interchange gone wrong but an act of terrorism and torture within a systemic context of group subjection, like lynching."[34] In the same vein, Professor MacKinnon claims that sexual harassment is not an individual issue, but a matter of power exercised by the dominant group over the subordinate group.

MacKinnon's contempt for the American regime is clear, and her legal theories are obviously in direct conflict with almost any understanding of constitutional precedent or liberal democratic jurisprudence, since she portrays the entire liberal democratic system as "oppressive." Nevertheless, MacKinnon's writings have proved to be influential. The United States Supreme Court adopted her theories as the basis for interpreting sexual harassment law in the landmark *Meritor Savings Bank v. Vinson* case in 1986.

Another leading feminist critical theorist who was influential during this period was Carol Gilligan, an education professor at

Harvard and the author of *In a Different Voice: Psychological Theory and Women's Development*.[35] Her main argument is that the "patriarchal social order," "androcentric and patriarchal norms," and "Western thinking" are the major obstacles to educational opportunities for American girls. In other words, the American liberal democratic "system" is the problem.

Professor Gilligan's educational theories were promoted by the American Association of University Women and influenced Congress to pass the Gender Equity in Education Act. In supporting the act, Senator Olympia Snowe of Maine, a Republican, employed a classic argument of critical theory and cultural Marxism, saying that the problem of discrimination against girls in American education was "systematic."[36] Patsy Mink, a Democrat from Hawaii, decried the "pervasive nature" of the antifemale bias in American education.[37]

In 1994, Congress passed the Violence Against Women Act. Channeling Catharine MacKinnon, the bill's supporters filled the Congressional Record with the critical theorist group-based concept that women were being attacked because they were members of a subordinate group; that the attacks were not simply individual crimes but "motivated by gender"; and that they "reinforce and maintain the disadvantaged status of women as a group."[38] Senator Joe Biden of Delaware stated that "the whole purpose" of the bill was "to raise the consciousness of the American public."[39]

This is not to suggest that politicians like Snowe, Mink, or Biden actively or consciously support critical theory or that they are cultural Marxists. It is to suggest, however, that the arguments of cultural Marxism and critical theory are "in the air" and influence public policy. The public debate has moved beyond liberalism, both traditional and modern. Postliberal or even antiliberal ideas have gained a foothold.

A major premise of this book is that the triumphalist Fukuyama-inspired "end of history" argument—that the principles of liberalism, individual rights, and traditional representative democracy have defeated all ideological competitors—is wrong. On the contrary, postliberal ideas of group consciousness and other challenges to traditional liberal democracy are on the rise in the developed world. There is no united liberal West that "shares values." There is instead an ideological civil war between the liberal West (meaning "liberal" in the broad traditional sense that includes political conservatives) and the postliberal West.

Vladimir Lenin always posed the question "Who pays?" Who is funding some specific political action or propaganda operation? If the question were asked who is funding multiculturalism, the diversity agenda, and critical theory, the answer would be in part the federal government, along with some state and local governments, but to a large extent American philanthropy. Major foundations—particularly Ford, Rockefeller, Carnegie, MacArthur, and Charles Stewart Mott—have for decades poured millions of dollars into multicultural, diversity, and "critical theory" projects. For example, Heather Mac Donald writes that between 1972 and 1992, Ford, Rockefeller, Mellon, and other large foundations spent around $36 million on radical feminist projects.

The purpose of this spending by major foundations is described by Alan Kors, a history professor at the University of Pennsylvania. "At almost all of our campuses, some form of moral and political re-education has been built into freshman orientation," writes Kors, explaining that "a central goal of these programs is to uproot 'internalized oppression,' a crucial concept in the diversity education planning documents of most universities." The concept of "internalized oppression" is the same as the cultural Marxist notion of "false consciousness," in which members of subordinate groups "internalize" or accept as legitimate the values and worldviews of the "oppressors" in the privileged groups. Thus, nonwhites who accept "white values" or college females who accept "male values" have "internalized" their own "oppression."[40]

Professor Kors describes one academic conference sponsored by the University of Nebraska in which attendees expressed the viewpoint that "White students desperately need formal 'training' in racial and cultural awareness. The moral goal of such training should override white notions of privacy and individualism." Hugh Vasquez of the Todos Institute produced a film titled *Skin Deep,* funded by the Ford Foundation, to "train" students in recognizing "internalized oppression" and "white privilege." The film asserts that a member of a dominant group who rejects his or her "unmerited privilege" and becomes an advocate for the subordinate group turns into an "ally."[41]

Herbert Marcuse of the Frankfurt School was perhaps the leading intellectual advocate of the 1960s New Left and counterculture. He was immensely popular with student radicals and avant garde intellectuals in both the United States and West Germany in the 1960s and early 1970s. Marcuse detested the liberal "system" built by FDR, Truman, JFK, and LBJ, with its "tyranny of the majority," its anticommunism, its "neocolonialism," its stifling bureaucracy, its suffocating affluence and consumerism, its lowest-common-denominator media propaganda machine, its careerist education, its "sexual Puritanism," its violent police, and its "repressive tolerance," giving only the illusion of a genuine democracy. In a sense, Marcuse was the anti-Schlesinger.

In an essay titled "Repressive Tolerance" (1965), Marcuse argued that the liberal version of free speech—extending to all parties and individuals, left, right, and center, fascist and communist, "crusaders for armament and disarmament," "intelligent" opinion and "stupid" opinion, "false" opinion and factual opinion—was fundamentally "repressive." He claimed that in the contemporary liberal system with its materialistic, affluent majority, the "regressive" forces were permitted free speech that actively harmed vulnerable minorities and the underprivileged. Cultivating a true democracy with a different type of majority "may require apparently undemocratic means," he said.

They would include the withdrawal of toleration of speech and assembly from groups and movements which promote aggressive policies, armament, chauvinism, discrimination on the grounds of race and religion, or which oppose the extension of public services, social security, medical care, etc. Moreover, the restoration of freedom of thought may necessitate new and rigid restrictions on teachings and practices in the educational institutions which, by their very methods and concepts, serve to enclose the mind within the established universe of discourse and behavior—thereby precluding a priori a rational evaluation of the alternatives.[42]

Marcuse assumed that freedom of thought did not truly exist in the consumerist America of 1965, hence the need for "restoration." Creating true tolerance and real democracy would depend on "the systemic withdrawal of tolerance from regressive opinions and movements."

Although Marcuse's influence had waned by the late 1970s, the idea of restricting the speech of "regressive" forces, of racists and haters, and indeed any speech considered offensive to minorities and "protected" groups, has gained more and more currency since then. One has only to examine the situation on American campuses. The Foundation for Individual Rights in Education surveyed 364 institutions of higher education in 2009 and reported that 270 of them, or 74 percent, maintained policies that clearly restricted speech that would otherwise be protected by the First Amendment. In 2008, university administrators investigated more than 500 cases of "harmful" and "inappropriate" speech, almost invariably directed at some "protected" group.

Marcuse's notion of restricting "regressive" speech is spreading beyond academia as well. On February 1, 2008, the *New York Times* reported that Janet Murguia, the president of the National Council of La Raza, "argued that hate speech should not be tolerated, even if such censorship were a violation of First Amendment rights." Speaking at the National Press Club, Murguia said that La Raza had contacted network executives at the leading cable networks—

CNN, MSNBC, and FOX News—and asked them to stop providing a platform for pundits who "consistently disparage the documented and undocumented Hispanic immigrant population." Murguia specifically named Glenn Beck, Lou Dobbs, Sean Hannity and Alan Colmes, along with "most of their guests," as "major vigilantes" who needed to be "kept in check."[43]

For the past forty years or more, the "liberal" aspect of the liberal democratic nation-state has been undermined by multiculturalism, the diversity project, and critical theory or cultural Marxism. By promoting racial, ethnic, and gender group consciousness, these forces have weakened the sense of national identity that a healthy liberal democracy requires—at the same time as the liberal democratic nation-state faces an even greater challenge from transnationalism.

CHAPTER FIVE

The Rise
of Transnationalism

With the fall of the Berlin Wall and the Soviet Union, the age-old arguments for some form of global political authority have gained a new currency. Transnationalism, globalization, interdependence, universal jurisdiction, global rules and "evolving norms of international law" are now in vogue. These trends are the latest historical incarnation of what we are calling the perennial party of global governance. Once again, as in the days of Alexander the Great, it is argued that global problems require global solutions that are beyond the capacity of independent sovereign governments.

Unlike the post–World War II era, there is now little talk of "world government" or "world federalism" among global elites. Instead, the preferred concepts are "global governance" and "transnationalism." Serious analysts do not talk about the disappearance of the nation-state, but envision its subordination to new (as yet undetermined) political forms at the global or transnational level. T. Alexander Aleinikoff, dean of the Georgetown Law Center, explained the concept in the *Opinio Juris* blog:

> But while it is perhaps true that the nation-state form is evolving (even declining), what is ascendant is not a set of other

non-political associations; we are not witnessing the rise of world anarchy or the end of history. Rather, we are likely to see the development and strengthening of other political institutions—regional, transnational, some global. These political organizations, institutions, associations—exercising what will be perceived as legitimate legal and coercive authority—will have (and need) members. That is, a decline in citizenship in the nation-state is likely to be accompanied by new kinds of citizenships associated with "polities" that tax and spend, organize armies and police, establish courts, and promulgate what are perceived to be binding norms. There is no reason that standard accounts of citizenship that link governance and a people cannot be stated at the appropriate level of abstraction to apply to new forms of political association.[1]

Transnationalism (or globalism) is not the same as internationalism. As noted in the Introduction, Harvard's John Ruggie, a former deputy secretary general of the United Nations, stated that "postwar institutions, including the United Nations, were built for an *international* world, but we have entered a *global* world," one in which "our challenge today is to devise more *inclusive* forms of global governance."[2] In other words, unlike the traditional international system of sovereign nation-states, the new global system would establish transnational and supranational laws, regulations, and institutions that reach into (transnational) and above (supranational) nation-states, including democracies. Nation-states continue to exist, but they are subordinate to transnational authority.

The U.S. Constitution would become a part of the global legal system, and therefore, by definition, subordinate to it. The relationship of the U.S. Constitution to international law, as many observers describe it, would be analogous to the relationship between American state constitutions and the U.S. Constitution. In the global governance arrangement, authority would be exercised by "evolving norms" of international (really transnational) law; by myriad UN conventions that establish new global norms, particularly in the area of human rights; by supranational institutions like the European Union; and by supranational courts like the International Criminal Court.

Crucial to the success of global governance are national courts, acting as enforcers of "evolving global norms" and transnational law as binding domestic (constitutional) law. Harold Koh, former dean of Yale Law School and current legal advisor to the U.S. Department of State, asserts that "domestic courts must play a key role in coordinating U.S. domestic constitutional rules with rules of foreign and international law."[3] This is essentially what has happened within the European Union: national courts have enforced the decisions of pan-European courts as national law.

Transnational or global governance is clearly a new form of political regime. If its proponents are successful, it will become the political superior of liberal democratic nation-states. The proposed global regime would not be democratic in the way democracy has traditionally been understood; it could be regarded as a "postdemocratic" regime. For the past two decades, the transnationalist–global governance project has advanced in major sectors of education and the culture generally, as well as in the American legal system. This transnationalist offensive challenges traditional concepts of American citizenship, national identity, and international law.

From Multicultural Citizens to Transnational Citizens

By the late 1990s, transnationalism was being promoted in universities, foundations, and legal circles by roughly the same intellectual-ideological forces that had previously developed the concepts of multiculturalism, the diversity agenda, and critical theory. Just a few years earlier, multiculturalism had been ascendant. In the early 1990s, Joyce Appleby, a prominent historian involved in creating the National History Standards (and later president of the American Historical Association), had promoted a "multicultural" vision for America, saying:

> The demographic reconfiguration of the American population and the enduring vitality of ethnic differences make it increasingly clear that the exclusive dominance of European cultural forms in the United States is now consignable to a specific time period, let us say 1676 to 1992 (a terminal date fittingly coincident with the Columbian quincentenary). It is no longer a question of whether Americans must work on a multicultural understanding of their past, but how. The very inevitability of this development raises the stakes in current discussions of national history.[4]

Within a short period of time, however, this need for a "multicultural understanding" gave way to a need for a "transnational understanding." Whereas historians and other educators in the early 1990s talked about the benefits of "multicultural citizenship," by the end of the decade they were speaking in terms of "transnational" and "postnational" citizenship. In either case, American citizenship and American national identity would be de-emphasized and diminished.

For example, in a version of her presidential address to the Organization of American Historians published in *Dissent,* Professor Linda Kerber (later president of the American Historical Association) asks: "Do we need citizenship? We are embedded in postnational and transnational relationships that may be changing the meaning of citizenship beyond recognition." Professor Kerber answers her rhetorical question by stating that we need new types of "transnational" and "postnational" citizenship. After asking, "What elements of citizenship are needed in this postnational world?" she suggests, rather vaguely, that this new world "needs" individuals with "multiple memberships" that are "reciprocal." Kerber does not explicitly say how a postnational world would (and should) affect American identity and citizenship, but the inference is clear: American national identity and citizenship are (and should be) diminished.[5]

On April 7, 2006, the *Chronicle of Higher Education* published "No Borders: Beyond the Nation-State" by Thomas Bender, a professor of history at New York University. The article begins:

> I want to propose the end of American history as we have known it. "End" can mean both "purpose" and "termination," and I have in mind both those meanings. I want to draw attention to the end to which national histories, including American history, have been put. They are taught in schools and brought into public discourse to forge and sustain national identities, presenting the self-contained nation as the natural carrier of history. That way of writing and teaching history has exhausted itself. In its place, I want to elaborate a new framing for U.S. history, one that rejects the territorial space of the nation as a sufficient context and argues for the transnational nature of national histories.[6]

Professor Bender says he wants to "argue against American exceptionalism." After all, the American "founding" (a word that is revealingly put in quotation marks) "depended upon the 'plantation complex,'" in his view. "Emergent capitalism and slavery (and the connection between them), not a band of Pilgrims, mark the American beginnings." The purpose of changing "the core American narrative" through "the use of a wider context," Bender says, is to replace "a narrow exclusive notion of citizenship" with "the kind of cosmopolitanism that makes us better citizens of both the nation and world."[7]

Likewise, the Organization of American Historians and New York University recommended rewriting the narrative of American history in the *La Pietra Report: Project on Internationalizing the Study of American History,* published in 2000.[8] The American Historical Association conducted an NEH-funded summer institute called "Rethinking America in a Global Perspective." American history survey courses are criticized for their "insularity." Teachers and students, we are told, should look at American history globally and rid themselves of an "exceptionalist orientation."

There is, of course, nothing wrong with having an international perspective in the study of history or any other discipline. However, the rhetoric used to criticize the traditional American narrative— with terms such as "narrow," "insular," "provincial," "nationalist," "outdated"—suggests that there is something else at work, an ideological agenda to diminish American identity.

This transnational ideological agenda is usually presented in descriptive (and determinist) rather than normative terms. The professors do not say, "*My ideological preference* is to transnationalize American history and de-emphasize American exceptionalism and national identity." Instead they say, "Today's postnational and interdependent world *requires* schools to transnationalize American history. We have to keep up with the times."

I suggest that this is not an "academic issue," or an argument about "new" versus "old" scholarship, or a "liberal" versus "conservative" argument. Instead, it is what Professor James W. Ceaser calls a "regime issue."[9] The purpose of "transnationalizing" the curriculum is to diminish the emotional attachment of American students to an American national identity and an American way of life. The goal is to transform the American regime. As Professor Ceaser writes, "Strategies, sometimes delicate, can be devised to alter the actual character of the regime, usually in its civil aspect, before directly redefining the public principle of rule—or, in rare cases, without ever directly confronting it."[10] Indeed, the aim (generally implicit but occasionally explicit) of much "new scholarship" is to change the culture and mores of the American nation.

If historians like Linda Kerber and Thomas Bender employ indirect language in predicting and promoting a transnational age, others are more direct. Arjun Appardurai, an anthropologist with the University of Chicago's prestigious Committee on Social Thought, predicts that large-scale immigration (without assimilation) will be a key factor in transforming America's regime. The United

States, he writes, is in transition from being "a land of immigrants" to being "one node in a postnational network of diasporas."[11] According to Benjamin Barber, a prominent political theorist,

> The Declaration of Independence ... has achieved its task of nation-building. To build the new world that is now required calls for a new Declaration of Interdependence, a declaration recognizing the interdependence of a human race that can no longer survive in fragments—whether the pieces are called nations or tribes, peoples or markets.[12]

Professor Linda S. Bosniak of the Rutgers School of Law, in "Citizenship Denationalized," explains the emergence of "transnational citizenship" as a direct challenge to national citizenship, national identity, and the nation-state itself:

> In the past few years, a handful of scholars and activists have announced the growing inadequacy of exclusively nation-centered conceptions of citizenship. Citizenship is becoming increasingly denationalized, they have argued, and new forms of citizenship that exceed the nation are developing to replace the old. They have coined phrases for these alternatives: "global citizenship," "transnational citizenship," "post-national citizenship."[13]

Bosniak sees the possibility (and desirability) of transnational political forms beyond the democratic nation-state, with new types of multiple, overlapping, and plural citizenships.

Professor Bosniak asserts—correctly, in my view—that "there is a great deal at stake" in redefining citizenship, because "notions of transnational or postnational or global citizenship challenge the conventional presumptions that the nation-state is the sole actual and legitimate site of citizenship."[14] The transnationalists are not seeking to eliminate national citizenship and the nation-state altogether, but to subordinate them to a higher global authority. The transnational goal is "decentering or 'demoting' the nation from its privileged status in political thought," and this, as Bosniak notes, is "a fundamental challenge" to the sovereign nation-state.[15]

Professor Bosniak cites a prominent Harvard political theorist, Michael Sandel, who "advances a vision of a 'multiplicity of communities and political bodies—some more, some less extensive than nations—among which sovereignty is diffused' and 'citizenship' [is] formed across multiple sites of civic engagement."[16] Indeed, as early as 1992, Professor Sandel wrote that "the moral and political institutional scheme of liberal democracy no longer fits the moral and political aspirations of its citizens." Arguing that the liberal democratic nation-state as the "primary unit of sovereign self-rule" is becoming obsolete, Sandel endorses a new form of regime, combining transnational and multicultural governance. This regime would increase the autonomy of "particular communities, be they ethnic, linguistic, or religious," at the subnational level, and simultaneously ensure the "universalization of rights" at the "supranational level," beyond the nation-state.[17]

The concept of "multiple and plural" citizenships is promoted at the highest level of American elite opinion. Thus the Carnegie Endowment for International Peace, under the leadership of Jessica T. Mathews, published two books that focus on "challenging traditional understandings" and "rethinking the meaning of citizenship." Scholars from the United States, Canada, the United Kingdom, Germany, and France contributed to the books, *From Migrants to Citizens: Membership in a Changing World* (2000), and *Citizenship Today: Global Perspectives and Practices* (2001).[18] Although written in the neutral language of social science, the essays for the most part are critical of a strong, exclusive national commitment, favoring multiple, dual, and transnational citizenships.

All this talk of transnationalizing American history, diminishing American national identity, and promoting multiple citizenships is a clear repudiation of the civic nationalism that has traditionally buttressed American liberal democracy. It is also an ideological attempt to replace traditional American civic nationalism with a new ideology, an untried and often vague vision of transnationalism.

If one speaks today at a public gathering in the language of the Founders, or Lincoln, or Franklin D. Roosevelt ("to preserve our Republic," "our civilization," "our religion," "our sons, pride of our nation"), many academics, journalists, and others among American elites will raise their eyebrows at this supposed lack of sophistication. Yet these same people—in direct contrast to, say, the authors of *The Federalist Papers*— will advance speculative and utopian notions of "new forms of global governance," a "new global world," a "Declaration of Interdependence," and the like.

From International Law to Transnational Law

International law as developed by Grotius, Pufendorf, and Vattel addresses relations between sovereign nation-states, not relations between states and their citizens or between states and the citizens of other countries. This is the traditional "law of nations" that the American Founders understood as international law. Since the end of the Cold War, a "new" international law has emerged.

David Rivkin Jr., an international lawyer who has practiced before the International Court of Justice and the International Criminal Tribunal for the Former Yugoslavia, is a leading critic of this "new" international law. Along with his law partner Lee A. Casey, Rivkin explained what this kind of law would do in the *National Interest* in 2000:

> Since the Cold War's end, a number of international organizations, human rights activists and states have worked to transform the traditional law of nations governing the relationship between states into something akin to an international regulatory code. This "new" international law purports to govern the relationship of citizens to their governments, affecting such domestic issues

as environmental protection and the rights of children. Among other things, it would: nearly eliminate the unilateral use of military force; create the unattainable requirement of avoiding all civilian casualties in combat; promote the criminal prosecution of individual state officials by the courts of other states and international tribunals; and permit—or even require—international "humanitarian" intervention in a state's internal affairs.[19]

Rivkin and Casey argue that "new" international law is "a frontal assault on sovereignty as the organizing principle of the international system." This is significant, they maintain, because "as a philosophical matter, any attack upon the principle of sovereignty threatens the very foundation of American democracy. Sovereignty is the necessary predicate of self-government." They continue by asserting that "for all of its humanitarian and democracy-building rhetoric, the new international law is profoundly undemocratic at its core. Indeed, with its lack of accountability and disdain for democratic practice (as opposed to rhetoric), it arguably poses the greatest challenge to Francis Fukuyama's anticipated global triumph of liberal democracy."[20]

The "new" international law that Rivkin and Casey criticize is distinct from traditional international law, or the law of nations. In fact, it is more transnational than international. It began to emerge, both in treaty law and in customary international law, after World War II, particularly after the end of the Cold War. The trial of Nazi leaders at Nuremberg, the establishment of the United Nations, and the passage of the UN Declaration of Human Rights led to some rethinking of international law, extending it to individuals as well as states. A number of multilateral human rights treaties have been passed, in which nations promise not to violate the rights of their citizens relating to genocide, racial discrimination, economic and cultural rights, civil and political rights, women's and children's rights. Massive crimes such as genocide are now considered violations of customary international law.

Many UN leaders, international lawyers, international jurists, academics, human rights activists, and officials of international organizations feel that the time is right to expand the reach of international law and transform its meaning. Two major concepts of international law have emerged: the "new" customary international law and the theory of universal jurisdiction.

Customary International Law: Traditional and New

The original concept of "customary international law," which nations have recognized and mostly followed for centuries, was based on these premises: (1) Practically all nation-states in their relations with each other repeat certain behaviors year after year. (2) This state behavior becomes habitual and customary over a long period of time. (3) States consent or agree that these behaviors are part of the law of nations. (4) The practice then becomes part of international law. These longstanding state practices include not harming diplomats from other countries or firing on soldiers carrying a flag of truce.

Customary international law, by definition, developed slowly because it grew out of habitual behavior, from "a general and consistent practice of states followed by them from a sense of legal obligation."* In the traditional understanding, it was "grounded in state consent," as the law professors Curtis Bradley and Jack Goldsmith observe. They cite the famous *Lotus* decision of 1927, where the Permanent Court of International Justice in The Hague declared: "International law governs relations between independent States. The rules of law binding upon States therefore emanate from their own free will." To ensure that states had in fact consented, Bradley and Goldsmith explain, "the passage of a substantial period of time was generally required before a practice could become legally binding."[21]

---

*This definition comes from §102 (2) of *The Restatement (Third) of the Foreign Relations Law of the United States,* published by the American Law Institute, 1987.

Traditional customary international law, then, rested on the relationship of nation-states to each other; on what nations have actually done in practice; on rules that developed slowly through repeated practice; and on agreement by the nation-states themselves. The "new" customary international law rejects all these premises. It is no longer based on the actual practice of states or even the consent of states. Instead, the American and foreign courts that interpret customary international law now look to UN "General Assembly resolutions, multilateral treaties, and other international pronouncements."[22]

Indeed, the very meaning of "state practice" has been changed. Paul B. Stephan, a law professor at the University of Virginia, notes that under the "new" customary international law, "state practice entails not the observable behavior of states, which is messy and often lawless, but rather what states assert as norms."[23] Thus, state "practice" becomes what states promise they will do. Many undemocratic and tyrannical regimes vote in the UN General Assembly and ratify multilateral treaties that endorse a whole range of "human rights" that become the rules of customary international law, although they have no intention of following those rules.

The consent of states is no longer required either. Professors Bradley and Goldsmith note that the new customary international law includes "peremptory norms," which are "said by courts and commentators to be binding on states regardless of consent." These "peremptory norms" are created by decisions of international (or transnational) courts such as the International Court of Justice, in multinational treaties, whether the democratic states have agreed to those treaties or not.[24] In other words, global "laws" are made by transnational courts and their academic interpreters, outside of any recognizably democratic arena.

The "new international law," as Professor Stephan puts it, "embraces a system of formulating and imposing norms on state and individual behavior that operates outside of any publicly accountable institution."[25] He describes the process of deciding what constitutes an international consensus on the new customary international law with the following syllogism:

> (1) specialists in international law, and academics in particular ... determine whether a consensus has formed within the international community as to the existence of a particular right; (2) those rights that exist constitute customary international law, and thus apply within the United States as federal law; therefore (3) those rights that academics perceive to rest on international consensus bind the United States and are enforceable by US courts.

This, Stephan exclaims, is "the antithesis of democracy."[26]

When the concept of "peremptory" or binding global norms first appeared in the new customary international law, these rules were limited to the outlawing of a few major human rights violations, such as slavery and genocide. Since then, however, the list of peremptory norms has grown to include (as many academic commentators believe) prohibitions on "systemic racism" and apartheid. As discussed in Chapter One, many human rights lawyers and activists regard the American political system itself as one built on "systemic racism." Later, we will examine how some in the human rights community consider Israel to be an "apartheid state."

Some human rights activists would like to add a prohibition on capital punishment as a binding global norm. Indeed, what constitutes the "peremptory norms" is a matter of dispute. Global norms are often ambiguous, hard to define, and open to many different interpretations. The crucial issue is, as always, who decides? Who possesses law-making authority, and by what right? Who interprets what the global norms mean? Since there is no democratic answer to any of these questions, we can conclude that the Rivkin-Casey critique is essentially right—that the "new" international law is "profoundly undemocratic at its core."

Universal Jurisdiction

The traditional law of nations identified piracy as a crime committed outside the territory of any particular nation and an act against all nations. Consequently, under traditional customary international law, states could arrest and try pirates of any nationality. The nationality of the victims did not matter; any state could apprehend pirates who were regarded under traditional international law as "enemies of the human race." Slave traders were later added to this international outlaw category.

In the later half of the twentieth century, a new concept emerged in international law, called "universal jurisdiction." Henry Kissinger noted that "universal jurisdiction" was so new that the term was not even listed in the sixth edition of *Black's Law Dictionary,* published in 1990. Universal jurisdiction means that a state can try a defendant of any nation for certain human rights crimes committed anywhere in the world. These crimes are regarded as particularly heinous and, therefore, as crimes against all humanity. In addition to piracy and slavery, many believe, they currently include war crimes, crimes against peace, crimes against humanity, genocide, and torture. International lawyers insist that many more will be added.

Amnesty International USA notes that "over 125 countries" have enacted universal jurisdiction laws. And further, "since the end of the Second World War more than a dozen states have conducted investigations, commenced prosecutions and completed trials based on universal jurisdiction." These nations include: "Australia, Austria, Belgium, Canada, Denmark, France, Germany, Israel, Mexico, Netherlands, Senegal, Spain, Switzerland, the United Kingdom, the United States."[27]

The increasing acceptance of "universal jurisdiction" serves to strengthen transnational law. But Henry Kissinger attacked the concept in *Foreign Affairs,* saying it risks "substituting the tyranny of judges for that of governments; [because] historically, the dictatorship of the virtuous has often led to inquisitions and even witch-hunts."[28]

Alien Tort Statute in the United States

In 1789, the United States Congress passed the Alien Tort Statute as part of the original Judiciary Act. The statute declared: "The district courts shall have original jurisdiction of any civil action by an alien for tort only, committed in violation of the law of nations or a treaty of the United States." At the time, this probably meant (we don't know for sure because there is little legislative history) that the young American republic would follow the traditional law of nations: protecting the rights of foreign diplomats on mission and ensuring fair business practices such as the enforcement of contracts involving aliens.

The Alien Tort Statute, sometimes called the Alien Tort Claims Act, was rarely used for two hundred years, and only once prior to the 1960s. All of this changed in 1980 with a landmark decision of the U.S. Court of Appeals for the Second Circuit in *Filartiga v. Pena-Irala*. Two Paraguayans living in the United States had sued a former Paraguayan police official, also living in the United States, for financial damages resulting from crimes committed in Paraguay. The plaintiffs charged that the official had kidnapped, tortured and murdered a relative of theirs as part of the Paraguayan state's violent crackdown on political opponents. Invoking the Alien Tort Statute, the plaintiffs asserted—with vigorous help from U.S. law professors—that these actions violated customary international law as currently understood by a consensus of expert international opinion. The appeals court agreed and awarded damages to the plaintiff, but the former police official had already fled the United States.

Human rights lawyers and activists (who were deeply involved in the case) heralded *Filartiga* as a major breakthrough decision. Harold Koh, the dean of Yale Law School at the time, remarked that with this case, "transnational public law litigants finally found their *Brown v. Board of Education*."[29] Transnational law had arrived in America. It was now possible in a U.S. federal court for foreigners to sue foreigners for alleged crimes committed in a foreign country. Other cases followed in the wake of *Filartiga*, which had transformed the almost dormant Alien Tort Statute of 1789 into an American facsimile of universal jurisdiction.

Foreign Law at the United States Supreme Court

In his book *Coercing Virtue: The Worldwide Rule of Judges*, Robert H. Bork recalls the American Bar Association's annual meeting of 2000, which took place in London. With four American Supreme Court justices in attendance "a prominent London barrister rose to accuse the United States Supreme Court of 'turning its back on the Continent,'" complaining that the justices "rarely cite the decisions of European courts."[30] While many of the American lawyers and politicians at the meeting responded apologetically, Bork notes, Justice Anthony Kennedy "did not succumb to this combination of insolent foreign browbeating and pusillanimous American response." Instead, Justice Kennedy forthrightly told the assembled European and American lawyers that if U.S. courts cede authority to remote foreign courts "there is a risk of losing the allegiance of the people."[31]

Even so, Kennedy is one of the justices on the Supreme Court who cite foreign law in making decisions. Writing for the majority (5-4) in *Roper v. Simmons* (2005), a case outlawing the death penalty for criminals less than eighteen years of age, Justice Kennedy commented favorably that the United Nations Convention on the Rights of the Child and the International Covenant on Civil and Political Rights prohibit capital punishment for juveniles under eighteen. He also cited a friend-of-the-court brief by the European Union. Kennedy argued that while foreign practice and opinion are not "controlling," the Court "has referred to the laws of other countries and to international authorities as instructive for its interpretation of the Eighth Amendment's prohibition of 'cruel and unusual punishments.' "[32]

Justice Antonin Scalia, joined by Justices Rehnquist and Thomas, issued a blistering dissent to Kennedy's argument in *Roper*, saying, "I do not believe that approval by 'other nations and peoples' should buttress our commitment to American principles any more than (what should logically follow) disapproval by 'other nations and peoples' should weaken that commitment. More importantly," foreign sources were being cited "*not* to underscore our 'fidelity' to the Constitution" or to the American heritage, but rather "*to set aside* the centuries-old American practice—a practice still engaged in by a large majority of the relevant States—of letting a jury of 12 citizens decide whether, in a particular case, youth should be the basis of withholding the death penalty."[33]

Scalia further argues that invoking the UN Convention on the Rights of the Child was not convincing because the United States had refused to ratify the agreement. Likewise, while the United States did ratify the International Convention on Civil and Political Rights, Scalia remarks that the U.S. explicitly added reservations to the convention declaring that it "reserves the right" to "impose capital punishment" subject to its own Constitution and laws. Thus, Scalia mockingly says, "Unless the Court has added to its arsenal the power to join and ratify treaties . . . I cannot see how this evidence favors, rather than refutes, its position."[34]

Scalia points out that the Supreme Court justices who cite international opinion do so only when that opinion conforms to their own (mostly liberal) preferences. He notes that the exclusionary rule (forbidding use of illegally obtained evidence in prosecutions) is "exclusively American"; that U.S. abortion laws are among the most liberal in the world; and that American law is more restrictive than the laws of any European nation on providing government support for churches and the teaching of religion in public schools. In those instances when American legal practice is more "liberal" than foreign law, these same justices do not cite or praise international legal opinion, Scalia remarks. "To invoke alien law when it agrees with one's own thinking, and ignore it otherwise, is not reasoned decision-making, but sophistry."[35]

Besides Justice Kennedy, during the past few years Justices Stephen Breyer, Ruth Bader Ginsburg, Sandra Day O'Connor, and John Paul Stevens have invoked foreign law in making decisions and filing dissents. Justices Breyer, Ginsburg, and O'Connor even met with the French president Jacques Chirac in July 2003 to discuss French views on the death penalty—at the same time that France as a leading member of the Council of Europe announced that "abolishing capital punishment in the United States was one of its priorities," as Ken Kersch noted.[36]

In *Grutter v. Bollinger* (2003), a case about affirmative action admissions at the University of Michigan Law School, Justice Ginsburg (joined by Breyer) cited the UN Convention on the Elimination of All Forms of Discrimination against Women (CEDAW) and the Supreme Court of India as evidence of an "international understanding" supporting "temporary special measures" to accelerate the achievement of "de facto equality."[37] Critics of Ginsburg's position observed that the U.S. Senate had not ratified CEDAW specifically because of controversies over proposed "temporary special measures" or gender preferences and other issues (e.g. abortion) that are contested within American democratic politics and therefore cannot be settled judicially by reference to UN treaties.

Ginsburg argued that "conclusions reached by other countries" and international authorities should sometimes constitute "persuasive authority" in decisions made by U.S. courts.[38] According to Jeffrey Rosen, a legal writer for the *New Republic*, Justice O'Connor's 5-4 majority decision in *Grutter*, in favor of permitting racial preferences in admissions, was influenced by her meeting with justices of the Indian Supreme Court.[39]

In *Lawrence v. Texas* (2003), which overturned state law on homosexual sodomy, Justice Kennedy's majority opinion (5-4) cited the European Court of Human Rights and a friend-of-the-court brief on foreign law and foreign decisions filed by the UN human rights commissioner, Mary Robinson.[40]

Justice Breyer is usually regarded as the intellectual leader of the transnationalist wing on the U.S. Supreme Court. In *Printz v. United States* (1997), Breyer dissented from the majority by touting European Union concepts of federalism, while the majority decision reinforced American federalism by restricting federal authority over American states on the matter of gun control.[41] In *Knight v. Florida* (1999), concerning delays in capital punishment, Breyer said he found decisions of the Supreme Court of India, the Privy Council of Jamaica, and even the Supreme Court of Zimbabwe to be "useful."[42]

Scalia vs. Breyer at American University

On January 13, 2005, Antonin Scalia and Stephen Breyer squared off at American University in Washington, D.C., to debate the relationship between the U.S. Constitution and foreign law. The dean of the university's Washington College of Law, Claudio Grossman, opened the exchange on the "Constitutional Relevance of Foreign Court Decisions" by saying that the issues to be discussed "are crucial in today's age of globalization for they relate to sovereignty, the relationship between domestic and international concerns, and ultimately our theories and concepts underlying sovereign international law and democratic government."[43]

Scalia led off by saying, "I do not use foreign law in the interpretation of the United States Constitution." In explaining why, he noted, "[W]e don't have the same moral and legal framework as the rest of the world, and never have. If you told the framers of the Constitution that [what] we're after is to ... do something that will be just like Europe, they would have been appalled. And if you read the Federalist Papers, it's full of, you know, statements that make very clear they didn't have a whole lot of respect for many of the rules in European countries. Madison, for example ... speaks contemptuously of the countries on continental Europe, quote, 'who are afraid to let their people bear arms,' closed quote."[44]

Scalia then repeated his arguments in *Roper* that the justices who cite foreign law do so very selectively, only when it agrees with them. When American law is more liberal than foreign law, as in the case of abortion and the exclusionary rule, these same justices do not cite European judges. "We said not a whisper about foreign law in the series of abortion cases," Scalia remarked.[45]

Breyer commented that law emerges out of a "conversation among judges, among professors, among law students, among members of the bar." He pointed out that judges in other societies similar to ours are dealing with similar problems, and said that understanding how they grapple with these issues should help American judges in interpreting American law. "This world that we live in is a world where I think it's out of date for people to teach about foreign law in a course called 'foreign law,'" Breyer said. He noted that "business is international; of course law is more and more international; and of course, human rights, too, are more and more international." Therefore, in dealing with issues concerning the environment, trade, and human rights, "we are going to have to know" foreign law.[46]

When asked why he cited judicial decisions from India, Jamaica, and Zimbabwe, Justice Breyer answered, "Do you think things outside the United States cannot be relevant to an understanding of how to apply the American Constitution? That's what's at issue. What is at issue is the extent to which you might learn from other places facts that would help you apply the Constitution of the United States. And in today's world, as I've said, where experiences are becoming more and more similar, I think that there is often—not a lot, not always—but in a finite number of instances there is something to learn about how to interpret this document [the Constitution]."[47] Breyer concluded his answer with a reference to the Founders: "I've been reading about the Founding Fathers, and I think Franklin and Hamilton and Jefferson and Madison and maybe even George Washington all would have thought that we, on occasion at least, can learn something about our country and our law and our document from what happens elsewhere."

Scalia pointed out that Hamilton and the Founders searched out foreign material because they were creating a new constitution, not interpreting an established one. He suggested that legislators could find foreign practices useful because they are making laws, while federal judges are interpreting laws that have already been made.[48]

Scalia was asked by the moderator, Professor Norman Dorsen (a former president of the ACLU): "If our courts look at another country's courts and they're able to find opinions that are persuasive on the merits, why couldn't that be a way of informing our judges in a positive way?" Scalia retorted, "your question assumes that it is up to the judge to find THE correct answer. And I deny that. I think it is up to the judge to say what the Constitution provided, even if what it provided is not the best answer, even if you think it should be amended."

Throughout the discussion, Scalia returned again and again to his key point that moral and policy solutions should be determined by the democratically elected legislative branch. The role of the judiciary is to interpret the U.S. Constitution, not to make the "best" or "most just" possible decision in any particular case; and therefore, foreign law is simply irrelevant. Breyer, on the other hand, emphasized that although foreign law is not authoritative, in today's globalizing world it makes sense to cite foreign sources and see if they can be of use in informing American constitutional jurisprudence.[49]

The Future Direction of American Courts

Some past and present justices of the Supreme Court, including Sandra Day O'Connor and Stephen Breyer, clearly believe that increasing transnationalism is the wave of the future. In 2003, Justice O'Connor told the Southern Center for International Studies in

Atlanta that U.S. courts should pay more attention to international court decisions because to do so "may not only enrich our own country's decisions, I think it may create that all important good impression." As for the future, O'Connor said, "I suspect that over time we will rely increasingly, or take notice at least increasingly, on international and foreign courts in examining domestic issues." Likewise, referring to new global legal issues in commerce and human rights, Justice Breyer told the gathering at American University, "these things have to be taught, we have to adjust to them, they have to come into our law."

In 2006, Harold Koh argued that "transnational law is becoming increasingly important because it increasingly governs and influences our lives."[50] Koh divided the U.S. Supreme Court into the "transnationalist faction" (Breyer, Souter, Stevens, Ginsburg, and sometimes Kennedy) and the "nationalist" bloc (Scalia, Thomas, Roberts, and Alito), and summed up their differences on issues of international law:

> The transnationalists view domestic courts as having a critical role to play in domesticating international law into U.S. law, while nationalists argue instead that only the political branches can internalize international law. The transnationalists believe that U.S. courts can and should use their interpretive powers to promote the development of a global legal system, while the nationalists tend to claim that U.S. courts should limit their attention to the development of a national system.[51]

Besides favoring the transnational approach as a matter of preference, Koh sees the incorporation of global law into the Constitution as likely, and therefore "legal education and American law schools should act to keep pace with the ascendancy of transnational law." Yale Law School, he noted, was now recommending that upper-level students take a course in transnational law "to shift the students' minds from the largely domestic first-year curriculum into a transnational mindset."[52]

Harold Koh has written extensively—sometimes clearly, sometimes obtusely—on transnational law and the "transnational legal process." In a rather clear paragraph in the *American Prospect*, Koh explains how the system works:

> Transnational legal process encompasses the interactions of public and private actors—nation states, corporations, international organizations, and non-governmental organizations—in a variety of forums to make, interpret, enforce, and ultimately internalize rules of international law. In my view, it is the key to understanding why nations obey international law. Under this view, those seeking to create and embed certain human-rights principles into international and domestic law should trigger transnational interactions, which generate legal interpretations, which can in turn be internalized into the domestic law of even resistant nation-states.[53]

The crucial mechanism for incorporating global norms that are "created" and "interpreted" in transnational forums into American constitutional law is the American judiciary. As noted earlier, Koh insists that domestic courts should coordinate "constitutional rules with rules of foreign and international law." The purpose is "not simply to promote American aims, but to advance the broader development of a well-functioning international judicial system."[54]

The "transnational legal process" described by Harold Koh is not democratic. To "make, interpret, enforce" international law that can then "be internalized into the domestic law of even resistant nation-states" is to exercise governance. But it is not government by the consent of the governed, for two basic reasons. First, the elected representatives of the people have no direct input either in writing the global laws or in consenting to their domestic internalization, as would be the case when the Senate ratifies a treaty or the Congress passes enabling legislation for a non-self-executing treaty.

Second, there is no democratic mechanism to repeal or change international rules that are incorporated into U.S. law. What if the

American people decide that they object to the global norms and transnational laws that were imposed upon them without their consent—for example, concerning the death penalty, internal security, immigration, or family law? What if the American people first approved but later changed their minds on some of these issues: how could the global norms, now part of international law and U.S. constitutional law, be repealed? Legislation to repeal the global norms could be deemed "unconstitutional." In short, there are no democratic answers to these questions consistent with the transnational legal process, because it is not a democratic process.

The "Disaggregated" American Nation

Anne-Marie Slaughter, a former director of policy planning at the U.S. State Department, also sees a steady advance of transnational law. In 1997, while she was a professor at Harvard Law School, she wrote in *Foreign Affairs* about an emerging "new world order" in which the nation-state is "not disappearing" but rather "disaggregating."[55] Distinct units or parts of the United States and other nation-states (judges, soldiers, diplomats, environmental officials, etc.) are pursuing their own particular interests, which may differ from the interests of other parts of the same government. These disaggregated units—including "courts, regulatory agencies, executives, and even legislators—are networking with their counterparts abroad, creating a dense web of relations that constitute a new, transgovernmental order."[56]

Across nation-states, Slaughter observes, "Judges are building a global community of law. They share values and interests based on their belief in the law as distinct, but not divorced from politics and their view of themselves as professionals who must be insulated from direct political influence." Slaughter is an advocate of this trend toward "transjudicialism," through the networking of American and foreign judges, and the resulting creation of "a genuine global rule of law."[57]

As Slaughter argues, "The disaggregation of the state creates opportunities for domestic institutions, particularly courts, to make common cause with their supranational counterparts against their fellow branches of government."[58] In the case of the American nation-state (although she does not explicitly spell out this conclusion), transjudicialism logically means that U.S. judges would, and apparently should, make common cause with European judges against American legislators and the president, who are elected by the American people. Clearly this kind of collaboration would weaken American self-government and democratic accountability.

Peter Spiro, an influential law professor and leading transnational law theorist, is even blunter than Koh and Slaughter in predicting the subordination of U.S. constitutional law to transnational law. Spiro portrays not only the state but society itself as "disaggregated," and he sees the "interests" of disaggregated elements within the American nation-state working together with transnational forces to limit American sovereignty.

In a paper titled "Disaggregating U.S. Interests in International Law," published in 2004, Spiro notes that American judges are becoming more inclined to regard themselves as part of a "global community of courts," in part because of networking and interaction with judges who sit on foreign and international tribunals. Judges value the respect of their international "peers," and American judges "will naturally want to garner respect rather than opprobrium when they find themselves, on a repeat basis, interacting with non-U.S. judges."[59] Consequently, Spiro predicts,

> the Constitution is likely to be increasingly entangled in the tentacles of international norms. As a formal matter, of course, the Constitution will remain supreme. . . . But the formal subordination of international sources may mask their growing constitutional consequence. Even though many cases will involve choices between domestically and internationally established norms, few cases will present an inescapable conflict between

them. International norms can thus be adopted under the cover of constitutional supremacy.[60]

Spiro expects that "when constitutional norms are changed to conform with international ones," American courts will claim that they are interpreting U.S. domestic law and that the Constitution is still "authoritative" or "controlling." This window dressing will "obscure the infiltration of international law," writes Spiro. "Below the surface, however, U.S. constitutional decisionmaking may nonetheless be increasingly constrained by internationally determined standards."[61]

As Professor Spiro explains, "To tether constitutional law to some other source of law is to demote it so that it is no longer supreme." Indeed, he boldly asserts, "There will likely come a point at which domestic constitutional law is effectively, if not formally, subordinated to international law."[62] Thus, the expansion of transnational law and transnational politics will have far-reaching implications:

> Judges and other constitutional actors will face incentives to incorporate international norms in their constitutional decision-making. To the extent that the Constitution becomes transnationally determined, self-determination will be limited, not only in law making but also, in the American case, in sustaining a distinctive national identity. This by itself is something to be neither lamented nor valorized. But the prospect should draw greater attention to the global institutions in which increasingly consequential norms are being contested and generated.[63]

From Internationalism to Transnationalism

Whether there will come a time when constitutional law is "subordinated" to international law is an open question. It will be decided in a great political struggle that is just beginning and will last for decades to come. The stakes are enormous. Will Americans retain self-government, or will they eventually be subordinated to some global politico-judicial authority—just as Britons, Germans, Italians, and Frenchmen today are subject to transnational European authority in vast areas of their lives? One thing is clear: transnationalism is on the rise. The "transnational mindset" that Harold Koh hopes to instill in his law students at Yale is being cultivated in a broad swath of American educational, legal, and cultural institutions. The multicultural outlook of the 1970s through the 1990s has been smoothly absorbed into a broader transnational perspective.

This transnationalism is not merely a new version of twentieth-century internationalism. The liberal internationalism of Franklin Roosevelt and the postwar initiatives of the Truman administration, such as the Marshall Plan, were built upon a robust American national identity, which was not diminished by the assumption of global leadership and generous assistance to others. Traditional liberal internationalists would see national pride and the concept of American exceptionalism as underpinnings of America's role in strengthening global security and international cooperation.

For today's transnationalists, American national pride and American exceptionalism are problematic. This mindset is illustrated by an advertisement from New York University's Center for Global Affairs that appeared in the March/April 2008 issue of the venerable *Foreign Affairs* magazine. The ad pictures two students in front of the United Nations building in New York, with a caption asking, "As a global citizen, to whom do I pledge allegiance?"[64] The words obviously evoke the Pledge of Allegiance—an affirmation of American national identity and a central ritual of America's "civil religion." But the question mark at the end is just as obviously meant to challenge—or "problematize," as the academics might put it—the very concept of national loyalty. In fact, while the "global citizen" is affirmed, the "American citizen" disappears.

If challenged, the NYU officials might say, "Well, we have many foreign students; we are not strictly an American institution." This is partly true, but of course the majority of their students and graduates *are* American citizens, and the university receives funds from the U.S. Congress specifically authorized for the purpose of strengthening American defense and foreign policy interests. If NYU's Center for Global Affairs were run by liberal internationalists rather than transnationalists, the curriculum and any advertisement would emphasize America's role in international relations, its leadership, security interests, challenges, opportunities, and global responsibilities. A confident internationalist NYU administration would tell foreign students, "You are certainly welcome and we are glad to have you. At the same time, you should not be surprised to realize that we are an American university, whose international relations program is presented mainly from the perspective of America's role in world affairs."

CHAPTER SIX

The European Union:
A Model of Global Governance

Although the idea of European unity has existed for centuries, if not millennia, the "official" history of the European Union begins in the aftermath of World War II, when many European leaders believed that peace on the continent could be achieved by the creation of a supranational "United States of Europe." And so they launched the project for European integration.

From the 1950s through the first decade of the twenty-first century, European integration proceeded by what has been called the "Monnet method." Named after Jean Monnet, a founding father of the European Union, this process first emphasized economic integration, which would then "spill over" into the judicial and political arenas. The Monnet method has also been called "integration by stealth," even by supporters of the European Union.

In 1951, France, Germany, Italy, the Netherlands, Belgium, and Luxembourg accepted the "Schuman Plan," proposed by the French foreign minister Robert Schuman, to create the European Coal and Steel Community. The ECSC was run by a supranational High Authority, headed by Jean Monnet, which oversaw the coal and steel industries of the six countries. In 1957, the same European nations signed the Treaty of Rome, which created the Common

Market and a customs union. The Treaty of Rome is considered the founding document of the European Economic Community (EEC), soon simply called the European Community (EC), and after 1992, the European Union (EU).

The Treaty of Rome was originally considered, for the most part, an international treaty among sovereign nation-states, although it had supranational aspects. Scholars of European integration have noted the longstanding conflict between two forces, representing two different visions of Europe. The intergovernmentalists see the EC/EU as an international organization serving the interests of the member states, while the federalists or supranationalists favor a politically integrated Europe in which the member states are sometimes subordinate to the European institutions.

We will describe this conflict as one between democratic sovereigntists and transnationalists. From the 1950s through the 1990s, two very different statesmen emerged as champions of democratic sovereignty: Charles de Gaulle and Margaret Thatcher. De Gaulle was a protectionist; Thatcher leaned toward free trade. De Gaulle kept the British out of the European Community; Thatcher distrusted French maneuvering in European institutions. Nevertheless, both opposed supranationalism and vigorously supported democratic sovereignty. With similar rhetoric, de Gaulle called for a *"Europe des États"* (Europe of states), and Thatcher for a European "family of nations."[1]

During his years as president of France, de Gaulle fought against attempts to move the European Community in a supranational direction. After he fell from power, Britain joined the EC in 1973, along with Ireland and Denmark. Greece, Spain, and Portugal entered in the 1980s. In 1986, the Single European Act eliminated the barriers that still existed to the free movement of goods, services, capital, and people within the EC. During the late 1980s, Prime Minister Thatcher clashed with Jacques Delors, president of the European Commission (a major administrative-legislative organ of the EC), over issues of democratic sovereignty—just as de Gaulle had clashed with Walter Hallstein, the head of the European Commission twenty years earlier.

On November 1, 1993, the European Community became the European Union with the Maastricht Treaty, which expanded the powers of EU institutions and led to the creation of a single currency, the euro, for most member states (the British and the Danes opted out). During the 1990s, Austria, Sweden, and Finland joined the EU. In 2004, eight nations from central and eastern Europe (the Czech Republic, Estonia, Hungary, Latvia, Lithuania, Poland, Slovakia, and Slovenia) along with Cyprus and Malta joined the EU. They were followed by Bulgaria and Romania in 2007.

Germany's foreign minister, Joschka Fischer, in a major speech at Humboldt University in May 2000, challenged the democratic credentials of the European project and argued that reforms must be made.[2] Partly in response to Fischer's comments, European leaders issued the Laeken Declaration on the Future of the European Union in December 2001, calling for a convention and the development of a "constitutional text" for the EU. Under the leadership of the former French president Valéry Giscard d'Estaing, the convention developed a constitution that was sent to the member states for ratification. In 2005, however, the Dutch and French publics defeated the proposed EU constitution, worrying about a further loss of sovereignty.

The leaders of the EU then revised and repackaged the constitution as a "Reform Treaty" (later called the Lisbon Treaty), keeping much of the substance of the original text. This time, the EU elites did not submit the de facto constitution to the voters of the European publics, except in Ireland, where a referendum was required by Irish law. In June 2008, the Irish voted against the Lisbon Treaty, temporarily stalling further integration. But the treaty was resubmitted to the Irish in October 2009 and this time it received a "yes" vote. After it was ratified by all twenty-seven member nations of the EU, the Lisbon Treaty went into effect on December 1, 2009.

A New Type of Governing Institution

Political theorists from Aristotle through Madison to Marx have noted that new types of political regimes will emerge under new circumstances. The European Union is one example. It is not a government, nor is it a state. In theory, it is a transnational institution empowered by nation-states in a treaty. In practice, judicial and administrative organs of the European Union make laws and regulations that exercise authority over these democratic nation-states. While the EU is not a supranational European government, it does, in many policy areas, exercise "supranational governance" with legal and administrative authority over nation-states. The main institutions of the European Union (or the European Community prior to 1993) include: the Council of Ministers, the European Commission, the European Parliament, the European Council, the European Court of Justice, and the European Central Bank.

Council of Ministers. Called the *Council of the European Union* since 1993, it is composed of national ministers of the member states, permanent representatives of the member states, and a secretariat (bureaucracy) based in Brussels. Although the Council cannot initiate legislation, it is described as a "legislative body" because, under the Lisbon Treaty, it shares authority with the European Parliament to accept or reject laws proposed by the European Commission on most issues. In the past, decisions of the Council on most issues were required to be unanimous; since the Lisbon Treaty was enacted there has been a movement toward qualified majority voting for more issues. This means that some member states can find themselves outvoted and their national concerns overridden.

The Council has been described as "a vast and complex hierarchy of separate bodies. . . . It meets in more than twenty different formations according to subject matter. Every working week one or more councils meet for upward of three days. Preparations account for three more days. The Council's reproduction service issues more than 100,000 documents annually."[3]

European Commission. The Commission has both legislative and executive functions and is the principal bureaucracy of the EU. It proposes legislation that is then accepted or rejected by the Council and the European Parliament. The Commission is also the main administrative institution of the EU. It executes policy and each year issues some five thousand directives, regulations, and decisions that implement EU policy in a range of areas including labor market, social welfare, environmental, and economic policies. The Commission is also considered the "guardian of the treaties" that provide the overall legal authority of the EU. In this capacity, the Commission may bring member states before the European Court of Justice for failure to adhere to their EU obligations.

The Commission consists of a College of Commissioners, headed by a president. Since the Lisbon Treaty, the Commission president must reflect the political makeup of the European Parliament (e.g., if there is a center-left majority, the president should be center-left). The commissioners serve five-year terms and can be reappointed; they are nominated by the member states (in consultation with the president of the Commission), appointed by the Council, and approved by the European Parliament, which must either accept or reject all the commissioners as a group. The Parliament has the power to remove all the commissioners by a two-thirds vote. (This is an unlikely scenario and has never happened.)

The commissioners are assisted by a staff (*cabinets* in the French administrative style), usually of seven members, including political appointees from their home countries and career civil servants. There are approximately seventeen thousand European civil servants (sometimes called the Eurocracy) working for the Commission. The European Commission emphasizes its supranational rather than intergovernmental orientation, and the commissioners are supposed to promote common European interests. Moreover, they take an oath renouncing any defense of the national interests of their home countries. The Commission has traditionally been "at the heart of the Union," and historically it has been the engine of European integration.

European Parliament. Unlike the national parliaments of democratic nation-states, the European Parliament (EP) cannot initiate legislation and it does not consist of government and opposition political parties. Further, although the European Parliament can force the European Commission to resign via a motion of censure approved by a two-thirds majority of votes cast, it cannot bring down an elected government via a "no confidence" vote as a national parliament can. The Parliament does have the power of "co-decision" with the Council (on most issues) to accept or reject legislation proposed by the Commission.

The Lisbon Treaty attempted to strengthen the Parliament by giving it enhanced "co-decision" authority in new policy areas with the Council and new budget powers. The Commission must submit the budget of the EU directly to the Parliament for approval. In addition, the Parliament has a voice in EU enlargement and in international agreements that the EU makes.

The European Parliament under the Lisbon Treaty will consist of 751 members including a president elected for five-year terms. Member states are afforded a certain number of seats based mostly on population, but the system has been weighted in favor of small nations. In the past, it has met in plenary sessions an average of four days a month in Strasbourg, France. The committees of the Parliament meet in Brussels (along with some plenary sessions), while two-thirds of the staff are housed in Luxembourg and the rest in Brussels. With the Lisbon Treaty, the European Parliament has gained more authority, but it remains far short of holding the powers of a traditional democratic parliament.

European Council. The heads of government or heads of state of the European Union nations, as well as the president of the European Council and the president of the European Commission, constitute the European Council. It was not part of the original Treaty of Rome, but it became important because it was essentially a summit of the EU political leaders. The semiannual summit meetings started in 1974 at the instigation of Giscard d'Estaing and have established the general political guidelines for the direction of European integration. The inclusion of the European Commission president increased the Commission's importance in inter-EU politics.

The European Council summit meeting in Milan in 1985 resulted in the Single European Act (free flow of goods, services, and people) in 1986. The summit in Dublin in 1990 led to the Treaty on European Union (Maastricht Treaty) in 1992, creating the European Union and a single currency. The summit in Berlin in 2007 led to the drafting of the Lisbon Treaty after the proposed constitution was rejected by the Dutch and French voters. The Lisbon Treaty established the office of president of the European Council (chosen by the Council itself), who serves a term of two and a half years and can be re-elected. The treaty gives the European Council and other EU bodies greater authority over the nation-states in the areas of justice, police, foreign policy, and constitutional issues. The European Council should not be confused with the Council of the European Union (discussed above) or with the Council of Europe, which is not a part of the EU.

Court of Justice of the European Union. The judicial arm of the European Union is located in Luxembourg. It consists of three bodies: the European Court of Justice, which is the direct descendant of the original European Community court dating back to the 1950s, and two lower courts established later to help ease the case load, the General Court and the Civil Service Tribunal. Today, the Court of Justice (more commonly called the European Court of Justice, or ECJ)★ is composed of judges from each of the member states.

Originally, under the Treaty of Rome, the European Court of Justice had little authority; but with two important decisions in the 1960s it established supranational authority over the constitutional law of the democratic states within the European Community. In *Van Gend & Loos* (1963), the ECJ created the doctrine of "direct

---

★In this chapter, we will employ the original and most commonly used name, the European Court of Justice, or ECJ.

effect" by ruling in favor of an individual litigant against its own national government. The Court authorized the Dutch national court to apply the ECJ judgment against the Dutch government, which it did. In *Costa v. ENEL* (1964), ruling against the Italian government, the ECJ claimed the supremacy of European Community law over Italian constitutional law in this case, and over national law in general throughout the EC. In both of these precedent-setting cases, the European Commission and national judges in the affected nation-states worked with the European Court against the nation-state.

During the 1970s and 1980s, the European Court of Justice acquired more authority. In *Francovich v. Italy* in 1991, the ECJ declared that national governments could be required to pay compensation to individuals hurt by the national government's failure to implement EEC Council directives in a timely manner. Today the ECJ acts as the supreme constitutional authority of the European Union. It reviews the validity of EU laws, hears disputes between the EU and national governments and between different institutions of the EU, and ensures nation-state compliance with European law.

European Central Bank. Established in 1998, the European Central Bank (ECB) is located in Frankfurt, Germany. It is a supranational organization that has responsibilities within the single-currency eurozone and administers the European Monetary Union. The ECB oversees the monetary policies of the member states that use the euro, including issues pertaining to interest rates, budget deficits, and inflation rates. It is run by a six-member executive board appointed by the European Council for eight-year nonrenewable terms. Along with the governors of the national central banks, the executive board constitutes the governing council of the ECB. With the Lisbon Treaty, the European Central Bank became an official EU institution.

In general, the Lisbon Treaty strengthened EU institutions *vis-à-vis* member states in the areas of crime and justice, homeland security, and foreign affairs. The treaty established an EU "high representative for foreign affairs and security policy" and an External Action Service (a diplomatic corps). The treaty states that the Council, with the approval of the Parliament, may establish a European Public Prosecutor's Office to combat transnational crime. The EU is given a legal personality, permitting it to enter into international treaties in its own right. Although technically not considered part of the treaty itself, the Charter of Fundamental Freedoms (a type of "bill of rights") is mentioned in the treaty as legally binding throughout the EU.★ In addition to civil and political rights, the Charter outlaws the death penalty and includes a range of social, economic, and cultural rights, including an annual paid vacation, parental leave, housing assistance for the needy, preventive health care, and free access to placement services.

Robert Cooper (a former British and current European Union senior diplomat) calls it a "conscious and successful attempt to go beyond the nation state."[4] The EU does not "emphasize sovereignty or the separation of domestic and foreign affairs," he says. On the contrary, it is "a highly developed system for mutual interference in each other's domestic affairs, right down to beer and sausages."[5] For Cooper, the creation of the European Union represents the beginning of a new era in world politics with an emergent "postmodern" transnational system, distinct from the modern international system that prevailed from the Treaty of Westphalia in 1648 through the end of the Cold War. Postmodern global ideology rejects nation-state rivalry, balance-of-power politics, an exclusive national sovereignty, the separation of foreign and domestic policy. Instead, it embraces the authority of transnational law over national law, the interdependence of nation-states, reduced sovereignty, and the United Nations as the final arbiter of war and peace.

★It is possible to "opt out" of all, or part, of the Charter of Fundamental Freedoms. Britain, Poland, and the Czech Republic have used this opt-out provision.

The postmodern order is built upon a new type of nation-state that Robert Cooper calls the "postmodern state," which "pools" its sovereignty with other states and accepts transnational and supra-national legal authority above its own national law.[6] The postmodern European states "share" sovereignty and adhere to a "European rule of law" that stands above the constitutional law of the demo-cratic nation-states. In contrast, Cooper notes that countries such as the United States, India, and China are modern states interested in exercising their exclusive sovereignty in legal, political, and inter-national relations. The postmodern European order described by Cooper has established a new type of postnational political com-munity, in which national sovereignty and democratic accountability have been diminished. We will look closely at one crucial aspect of "Eurogovernance": the transnational or supranational legal order that trumps the political authority of democratic national parliaments.

The "Constitutionalization" of the European Union

Leading scholars of European integration, including political sci-entists and law professors on both sides of the Atlantic, have devel-oped a large body of research examining the "constitutionalization" of the European Community and the European Union.* By this they mean the process by which the original Treaty of Rome,

---

*In an important scholarly book, *Power and Legitimacy: Reconciling Europe and the Nation-State* (Oxford University Press, 2010), Peter Lindseth argues against the "constitutionalization" theory of the European Union. He maintains that European governance is administrative rather than constitutional. Lindseth explains that the supranational regulatory and legal authority of the European Union is dele-gated to it by the democratic institutions of the nation-states. Thus, the EU insti-tutions do not possess autonomous legitimacy; instead, the legitimacy of European governance resides in the democratic elements of the nation-states and in the

designed by the democratic nation-states of Europe to serve their interests, developed over time into a de facto constitution exercising legal authority over the nation-states that had created the European system in the first place. As Alec Stone Sweet and Thomas Brunell explained in 1991,

> The constitutionalization of the treaty system refers to the process by which the EC treaties have evolved from a set of legal arrangements binding upon sovereign states [i.e., from an international treaty] into a vertically integrated legal regime [i.e., a supranational authority] conferring judicially enforceable rights and obligations on all legal persons and entities [nation-states], public and private, within EC territory. The phrase ["constitutionalization of the treaty system"] thus captures the transformation of an intergovernmental organization governed by international law into a multi-tiered system of governance founded on higher-law [supranational] constitutionalism. Today legal scholars and judges conceptualize the EC as a constitutional polity, and this is the orthodox position.[7]

The European Court of Justice is the "constitutional court" of the European legal system and its supreme interpreter, says Joseph Weiler, a prominent legal scholar.[8] In fact, the ECJ explicitly refers to the EC/EU treaties as a form of "constitutional charter." The function of the Court is "to enforce compliance with EC law."[9] And as Stone Sweet and Brunell remark, "it cannot be stressed

---

process of "reconciling" the role of EU institutions with member states. Lindseth says that national mechanisms provide for collective oversight of the supranational legal and regulatory authority of EU institutions, which are thus ultimately dependent on the nation-states. I will argue that while national oversight processes technically exist, they are weak and rarely exercised. Most importantly, the "democratic deficit" remains at the heart of European governance. Whether it is administrative or constitutional, delegated or legally controlling, this European governance is not democratically accountable, in any serious sense, to a body politic, or a people (*demos*) constituted as a political community.

enough that the EC legal system was constructed without the explicit consent of the member states."[10] Walter Mattli and Anne-Marie Slaughter likewise argue that the European supranational legal system was built "against the wishes, or at least behind the backs, of Member State Governments."[11]

How did it happen that a supranational European legal system, a de facto constitution, evolved despite the opposition of the elected representatives of Europe's democratic nation-states? In case after case, individual litigants (mostly corporations in the early years, and later also social activists) sued in national courts to overturn national laws in favor of European rules and regulations that they deemed more favorable. The national courts referred these cases to the European Court of Justice, which then authorized the national courts to enforce European Community law. The national courts usually did so, over the protests of their own democratic governments. To get a snapshot of the European judicial conflict between the democratic nation-states and a coalition of transnational forces including EC/EU officials and some elements within the nation-states themselves (judges, corporations, interest groups), we will look again at the landmark *Van Gend & Loos* and *Costa v. ENEL* cases.

Van Gend & Loos

The first major case that integrated the European legal system or the "direct effect" of European Community law was *Van Gend & Loos*. In 1963, a Dutch transport company that imported chemicals from Germany sued the Dutch government over an increase in the tariff, arguing that it violated the European Community Treaty. A Dutch court asked the European Court of Justice for an opinion on whether individual litigants, such as the Van Gend & Loos company, could directly invoke EC Treaty law instead of national law.

Testifying before the European Court of Justice, the elected democratic governments of the Netherlands, Belgium, and West Germany declared that the Court did not have jurisdiction in this case. Arguing on the grounds of traditional international law with respect to treaties, the democratic nation-states asserted that only the member states of the European Community (and the European Commission), as the treaty signatories, could charge a member state with a treaty violation. They argued that this question "must be determined exclusively by Dutch constitutional law."[12] The European Court of Justice, supported by the European Commission, ruled otherwise: that individual litigants could appeal directly to European Community law, and that national courts were required to enforce this law. In their decision, the ECJ declared that the European Community

> constitutes a new legal order of international law for the benefit of which the states have limited their sovereign rights, albeit within limited fields, and the subjects of which comprise not only Member States but also their nationals. Independently of the legislation of Member States, [European] Community law therefore not only imposes obligations on individuals but is also intended to confer upon them rights which become part of their legal heritage.[13]

Costa v. ENEL

In 1964, an Italian citizen challenged an Italian law that nationalized the electric power industry, charging that this act of the Italian parliament violated both the Italian Constitution and the European Community Treaty. A justice of the peace in Milan referred the case to both the Constitutional Court of Italy and the European Court of Justice. The Italian court ruled that because the Italian parliament adopted the law after acceding to the European Community Treaty, the parliamentary law would prevail and there was no reason to appeal to the European Court of Justice (ECJ).[14]

In proceedings before the ECJ, the democratic Italian government declared that referring the case to the European Court was "absolutely inadmissible" based on the ruling of the Italian Constitutional Court.[15] The Italian government repeated the arguments of the Dutch and Belgian governments in *Van Gend & Loos* that only a member state (or the European Commission), not an individual litigant, could challenge the actions of another member state on the basis of the Treaty of Rome. However, the European Court of Justice (supported by the European Commission) ruled that in the case of a conflict between European Community law and national law, the former is supreme. Further, the ECJ ruled that laws passed by a national parliament either before or after a European nation has joined the European Community Treaty are automatically invalid if they conflict with European Community law.

In *Costa*, the ECJ for the first time declared explicitly that European Community law was superior to national law, even though the democratic nation-states that drafted the Treaty of Rome had rejected a proposal recommending exactly that. The ECJ ruling said:

> By creating a Community of unlimited duration, having its own institutions, its own personality, its own legal capacity ... and, more particularly, real powers stemming from a limitation of sovereignty or a transfer of powers from the States to the Community, the Member States have limited their sovereign rights ... and have thus created a body of law which binds both their nationals and themselves....
>
> The transfer by the States from their domestic legal system to the Community legal system of the rights and obligations arising under the Treaty carries with it a permanent limitation of their sovereign rights, against which a subsequent unilateral act incompatible with the concept of the Community cannot prevail.[16]

The ECJ ruling in *Costa* was not unanimous—although the Court does not permit the publication of dissenting opinions. Years later, in 2002, a Danish member of the European Parliament called the decision a "coup d'état."[17]

Expansion of the ECJ'S Supranational Legal Authority

From the mid-1960s through the early 1980s, the European Court of Justice gradually enlarged its authority over the democratic nation-states. Professor Eric Stein examined ten cases beginning with *Van Gend & Loos* that pitted democratic governments (including Belgium, the Netherlands, Germany, Italy, Ireland, and Great Britain) against transnationalists (the European Commission, corporations, social activists). In every case, the democratic sovereigntists lost and the transnationalists won. The European Court of Justice ruled in favor of the transnational position, and the ruling was upheld by a national court against its own democratic government.

The flavor of this twentieth-century European judicial conflict is exemplified by the *Vabre* controversy in France. In 1975, both the Paris Court of Appeal and the Court of Cassation (France's highest civil and criminal court) refused to enforce a French law on custom duties that had been enacted in 1966. The high court ruled in favor of the litigant, the French company Société des cafés Jacques Vabre, and against the French government on the grounds that the Treaty of Rome had created a separate legal order that was binding on the national courts. The French court, in effect, endorsed the supremacy of EC Treaty law over national law.

Democratic sovereigntists struck back. In 1981, a Gaullist deputy, Michel Aurillac, introduced legislation to prevent French courts from exercising legislative powers by refusing to enforce laws passed by the French parliament. As Professor Karen Alter writes, "The Parliamentary debate surrounding the Aurillac amendment made it clear it was politically unacceptable for a court not to follow the will of Parliament, and that the *Vabre* jurisprudence should be reversed."[18] The democratic French government weighed in to support the Aurillac amendment. During the debate in the National Assembly, the minister of justice declared that if the judge takes upon himself the authority to refuse to apply a [French national] law under the pretext that he estimated that [the law] was contrary to an international accord, in the case where that law was subsequent to the accord in question, that would imply that the judge is assuming the right to disregard a law, thus scorning the will of the parliament.... This could clearly not be accepted.

The Aurillac amendment passed the National Assembly over-whelmingly, 343 to 4, but it died in the French Senate because, Professor Alter speculates, "the likelihood that a Senate decision in favour of the Aurillac amendment would be appealed [to a higher court] effectively killed the legislative attempts to reverse" the *Vabre* jurisprudence. Alter concludes that "the failed Aurillac amendment revealed that politicians' threats against the national judiciary were empty and their formidable tools of judicial influence of little consequence."[19] Thus, *Vabre* and its aftermath constituted a defeat for democratic sovereignty and a victory for transnationalism.

Why Did European Elites Accept a Transnational Legal Regime?

We have discussed *how* the European Community was transformed from an international organization—created by democratic nation-states and based on a treaty, ostensibly conforming to traditional international law—to an integrated transnational and in some cases supranational legal regime that exercises authority over the democratic states. The next question is *why* did this happen? More specifically, why did European judges, politicians, corporate leaders, and social activists accept this change from national democratic sovereignty to transnational governance?

One answer is ideological. That is the "official" reason, repeated endlessly in European Union publications, proclamations, and conferences: the belief in the European ideal of peace, harmony, and universal law; the rejection of nationalism in all its forms; the conviction that only a united Europe could prevent another outbreak of war on the continent; the fulfillment of the dream of Kant and Monnet in transnational governance. Other explanations could be found in a body of social science research that suggests more material and interest-based motivations.

Scholars of the EU argue that the self-interest of national judges, European court judges, bureaucrats, private litigants (including corporations and social activists), and legal scholars played an important part in advancing European legal integration. In this vein, Karen Alter writes that the incentive structure of the European court system offered to advance the "financial, prestige or political power of national legal actors,"[20] giving them a direct stake in promoting legal integration:

> [L]awyers specializing in EC law got more business through the growth and expansion of EC law; legal scholars supported legal integration through favourable doctrinal writings which parenthetically increased the demand for university professors to teach EC law and enhanced individual career prospects ... national judges [gained] more power *vis-à-vis* politicians ... and the ECJ enhanced its own prestige and authority through its far-reaching decisions.[21]

Alter argues that viewing courts as "bureaucracies and sub-bureaucracies with their own interests and bases of institutional support can offer insight into why some courts readily accepted EC law supremacy." Thus, "bureaucratic politics" was one important "motor of legal integration" in Europe.[22]

In 1993, Anne-Marie Burley (Slaughter) and Walter Mattli wrote that the European Court of Justice created "opportunities, providing personal incentives for individual litigants, their lawyers, and lower national courts to participate in the construction of the [European] community legal system. In the process, it enhanced its own power and the professional interests of all parties participating directly or indirectly in its business."[23] Karen Alter later noted that "national courts use EC law in bureaucratic struggles between levels of the judiciary and between the judiciary and political bodies, thereby inadvertently facilitating the process of legal integration."[24]

Examining the relationship between national judges and the European Court in 1998, Walter Mattli and Anne-Marie Slaughter asserted that the "quest for power" by national judges "has both personal and professional aspects." This includes a desire for prestige and personal recognition, for advancing one's career and institutional interests, and for promoting one's own ideals packaged as the "rule of law." Mattli and Slaughter outline three areas where national judges have sought to increase their power through the European legal system. The first is in relation to their own national legislatures. The second is in relation to other judicial bodies in the same national judicial system. Third, judges have "the power to promote certain substantive policies through law. In other words, where European law and national law promote different policies . . . a national judge may have the opportunity to achieve the result that she favours through the application of European law."[25]

One example of national courts preferring to use European law rather than national law in order to obtain the results that the judges favored is cited in a study of the relationship between German courts and European courts. The researcher, Juliane Kokott, found that German labor courts would often refer cases to the European Court of Justice on the assumption that European law was more "employee-friendly" than German national law, which the labor court judges considered too employer-friendly.[26]

Complementary and sometimes coordinating transnational forces (judges, EU officials, international lawyers, law professors, etc.) have developed a network in European legal circles over the past few decades with material-personal and philosophical-ideological interests in promoting supranational law at the expense of national law. As Mattli and Slaughter explain, "EU lawyers themselves are increasingly willing to acknowledge the existence of a closely constructed network of sub- and supranational actors acting within an insulated and self-consciously constructed 'community of law.' "[27]

Moreover, the European Court of Justice has sought allies among national judges and lawyers. Mattli and Slaughter note that the ECJ worked "to make European law attractive to individual litigants and their lawyers through its case law and its efforts to educate and appeal to national judges through tactics ranging from weekends in Luxembourg to tacit offers of a judicial partnership."[28] The European Court of Justice's far-reaching actions in *Van Gend & Loos* encouraged Dutch courts to exercise their power against the elected Dutch legislature. Likewise, the ECJ's jurisprudence in the *Factortame* case (which will be discussed shortly) encouraged British judges to assert power against the House of Commons.

The last chapter introduced the theory of the "disaggregated" nation-state or "disaggregated" sovereignty. This means that various units or parts of a nation-state have their own particular material and institutional interests, distinct from those of other parts of the same nation-state, and therefore they sometimes work with like-minded foreign and transnational forces against their fellow citizens in other units of government or sections of the same nation that have different interests. As Anne-Marie Slaughter points out, courts in particular can "make common cause with their supranational counterparts against their fellow branches of government."[29] The theory of the "disaggregated" nation appears to be directly applicable to those national judges in European states who have worked with European Community judges and officials against their own democratically elected officials. Mattli and Slaughter summarize how disaggregation has served to advance European integration more broadly:

> Yet closer examination of the actual process of integration, with starts and stops, as well as national variation, reveals courts, legislatures, executives, and administrative bureaucracies as

quasi-autonomous actors. Each of these institutions has specific interests shaped by the structure of a particular political system.... [T]he picture that emerges is one of "disaggregated sovereignty," an image of different governmental institutions interacting with one another, with individuals and groups in domestic and transnational society and with supra-national institutions.[30]

Why Did Democratic Governments Accept a Loss of Sovereignty?

In country after country across Europe, elected democratic governments and national parliaments opposed the transfer of democratic sovereignty from their own political and judicial institutions to the supranational European judiciary. In the end, they lost. Karen Alter writes that some scholars explain this acquiescence "through the incremental nature of the legal integration," which made "little steps in integration seem tolerable." At the same time, the democratic politicians feared that they might be considered unreasonable if they did not accept these small legal measures.[31] Alter cites Anne-Marie Burley and Walter Mattli's argument that "the technical nature of law provides a 'mask' and a 'shield' which limits the ability of politicians to influence legal integration."[32]

At the national level, one could argue that it is generally difficult for democratic politicians to reverse judicial rulings that they oppose because of the cumbersome legislature process, as well as the prestige usually granted to judicial institutions in liberal democratic societies. President Franklin Roosevelt's battle with the Supreme Court in the 1930s reminds us that even a popular democratic leader often has difficulties reversing the decisions of judges. At the transnational level, where the number of actors and roadblocks are more numerous, it is perhaps even more difficult for democratic politicians to defeat judges.

The *Factortame* case in the United Kingdom illustrates this difficulty.[33] Factortame was a Spanish fishing company that was involved in commercial activity in the West Country ports of the UK. In 1988, Parliament passed the Merchant Shipping Act to prevent companies using foreign ships registered as British vessels from fishing in UK waters. The Spanish company appealed the restrictions in a British court on the grounds that the laws of the European Economic Community permitted it to fish in the UK.

First, the British High Court sided with Factortame and obtained an injunction from the European Court of Justice that suspended enforcement of the section of the Merchant Shipping Act that went against European Community law. However, a court of appeals overturned the suspension in March 1989. This result was confirmed by the House of Lords, the highest court in Britain, which said it did not have the authority to suspend an act of Parliament. The Lords then referred the matter to the European Court of Justice, as was legally required under the European Communities Act of 1972.

In June 1990, the ECJ ruled that national courts could strike down national laws that violated European Community laws. On this basis, the House of Lords ruled in favor of Factortame, in effect nullifying an act of Parliament. The Lords reasoned that by joining the EC in the European Communities Act in 1972, Parliament had implicitly agreed that EC law was in some areas superior to national law.[34]

In the end, why did Margaret Thatcher's government submit to European legal supremacy? After all, Thatcher, the victor of the Falklands, was a quintessential democratic nationalist. There is no doubt that she believed in democratic sovereignty and the supremacy of the House of Commons. Her government strongly opposed the European Court of Justice's decision in *Factortame*. Technically, democratic Britain through the Tory majority in the Commons had the authority to block the ECJ decision. It could have repealed the European Communities Act of 1972, or legally withdrawn from the European Community itself. But these actions would have incurred tremendous political and economic costs, provoked a major showdown with the rest of Europe, and perhaps split the Conservative Party and brought down the government.

A few years earlier, in 1986, Thatcher under great pressure had reluctantly agreed to the Single European Act, ceding considerable sovereign rights in the economic sphere to the EC. After this, it was much harder for the Thatcher government to make the case against *Factortame*. Some former Thatcher advisors believe that there was a realistic alternative to either withdrawal from the EC or repeal of the European Communities Act: the Thatcher government could (and should) have "amended" the European Communities Act and reasserted the principle that an act of Parliament is supreme in the United Kingdom.[35] But this action also would probably have led to a major crisis with the EC and consequences that the government was unwilling to face.

This was a watershed moment in the history of British democracy. For approximately three hundred years, since the Glorious Revolution of 1688–89, the British political system was based on the principle of parliamentary sovereignty. Since the early twentieth century, ultimate authority resided in the elected members of the House of Commons. But *Factortame* demonstrated that the legal supremacy of the European Community had supplanted the political supremacy of the House of Commons, profoundly altering British parliamentary democracy.

A Postdemocratic Regime

Since the Treaty of Rome in 1957, more and more issues of public policy have been transferred from the democratic legislatures of Europe to transnational bureaucracies. The Maastricht Treaty of 1992 ceded wide policy areas to the European Union, including aspects of economic policy, social policy (labor, employment, discrimination issues), public health, consumer protection, telecommunications, energy, education, vocational training, transportation, environmental law, even town and country planning.

In EU terminology (from the Maastricht Treaty), these policy areas are called "competences." The authority over the different "competences," either European Union or member state, is listed in the various EC/EU treaties. Because the language is often ambiguous, however, decision-making authority is sometimes unclear. There are generally three types of competences: "exclusive competences" (all EU), "shared competences," and "supporting, coordinating, and complementary competences." If there is a dispute between the EU and a member state over a particular competence, the European Court of Justice usually decides in favor of the EU.

Trade has been an "exclusive competence" of the European Union, which prevents nations such as Britain from lowering or abolishing their trade barriers and thus fostering economic growth with trade partners from the developing world. With the Lisbon Treaty, the European Union has "exclusive competence" over the nation-states in these areas: customs union; establishing the rules of competition for the functioning of the internal market; monetary policy for member states whose currency is the euro; and conservation of marine biological resources under a common fisheries policy.*

Both the Maastricht Treaty and the Lisbon Treaty promised that the EU would adhere to the principle of "subsidiarity," which means that decision-making authority should be exercised at the most appropriate and lowest possible level of governance. Not surprisingly, there is wide disagreement over the extent to which subsidiarity has been respected.[36] The postmodern European system means centralization of authority and EU interference in the domestic affairs of the democratic nation-states. On issues ranging from

---

*Fisheries policy in general is a shared competence among the EU and the member states.

standards for French cheese, German beer, and Scottish haggis, to regulations for electronic devices for dredging work, to requirements that small business owners build showers for visiting truck drivers, it is EU officials rather than local producers and manufacturers or even national or provincial agents who exercise the final authority.[37]

There are no agreed-upon statistics for the ratio of laws still made by the nation-states in proportion to laws initiated by the European bureaucracy in Brussels. According to a story published in 2003 by the *Economist,* "In most EU countries more than half of new laws are already drafted in Brussels and then simply translated into national law." The magazine asked EU institutions and embassies in Brussels for their estimates, and reported that the Austrians believed that 60 to 70 percent of their laws were made in Brussels. A British member of the European Parliament put the figure for the UK at about 50 percent. France's Council of State estimated in the early 1990s that 55 percent of French laws came down from Brussels.[38] In October 2010, I spoke with the deputy head of the EU delegation to the United States, who estimated that over 60 percent of member-state laws were initiated by EU institutions.[39]

From the beginnings of the European project, prominent politicians of both the left and the right have feared the loss of democratic sovereignty. The Labour prime minister Clement Attlee rejected the European Coal and Steel Community (ECSC). In 1950, Attlee declared that Britain would not accept that "the most vital economic forces of this country should be handed over to an authority that is utterly undemocratic and is responsible to nobody."[40] In France, the Gaullist deputy Jacques Soustelle likewise opposed the ECSC, saying, "Instead of delegating our powers to a democratic Assembly, we are asked to abandon an important sector of our economy to a stateless and uncontrolled autocracy of experts."[41] The left-of-center premier Pierre Mendès-France, quintessential French secular republican of the Fourth Republic, voted against the Treaty of Rome in 1957. Inadvertently updating and paraphrasing John

Locke, he announced: "A democrat may abdicate by giving in to an internal dictatorship, but also by delegating his powers to an external authority."[42]

Margaret Thatcher, in her famous Bruges speech in 1988, said, "We have not successfully rolled back the frontiers of the state in Britain, only to see them re-imposed at a European level with a European super-state exercising a new dominance from Brussels."[43] Objecting to the subordination of Britain to European transnational authority, she asked rhetorically in her memoirs: "Were British democracy, parliamentary sovereignty, the common law, our traditional sense of fairness, our ability to run our own affairs our way to be subordinated to the demands of a remote European bureaucracy, resting on very different traditions?"[44]

The Lisbon Treaty and the "Democratic Deficit"

By the end of the twentieth century, many EU leaders and scholars of the European project were acknowledging and discussing a "democratic deficit" in the European Union. The German foreign minister Joschka Fischer explicitly addressed the problem in his famous Humboldt University speech in 2000.[45] The imperative to overcome the democratic deficit was put front and center in 2001 by European political leaders in the Laeken Declaration, which said that the European Union "needs to become more democratic, more transparent and more efficient."[46]

The EU leaders attempted to achieve this goal first with the proposed constitution, and later, when the constitution failed, through the Lisbon Treaty. The official EU website heralds the treaty as creating "a more democratic and transparent Europe with a strengthened role for the European Parliament and national parliaments, more opportunities for citizens to have their voices heard and a clearer sense of who does what at European and national level." The website poses the question "Does the Treaty of Lisbon make the decision-making process more democratic?" It answers "yes," saying that the treaty "increases the number of policy areas where the directly elected European Parliament has to approve EU legislation together with the Council," and that "National parliaments are for the first time fully recognised as part of the democratic fabric of the European Union."[47]

These statements are technically true, but substantively insignificant. To be sure, under the Lisbon Treaty, the European Parliament "co-decides" proposed laws in more policy areas than previously. But EU legislation is still initiated by the unelected bureaucracy, the European Commission, while the Parliament and the Council for the most part only approve or disapprove the Commission's legislative proposals. The European Parliament does not have the authority or accountability of a typical parliamentary democracy (such as the British House of Commons or the German Bundestag), with a responsible governing majority, votes of confidence, legislative supremacy, and the like.

Under the Lisbon Treaty, the Commission's legislative proposals are sent to the national parliaments at the same time that they are sent to the European Parliament and the Council.* If the national parliaments believe that the proposed EU legislation violates the principle of subsidiarity, they have eight weeks to send a "reasoned opinion" to the EU Commission.[48] The Commission is required to "take account of the reasoned opinion" and to "review" the draft of the proposed legislation. At that point, "the Commission . . . may decide to maintain, amend or withdraw the draft. Reasons must be given for this decision . . . to justify why it [the Commission] considers that the proposal complies with the principle of subsidiarity." The

---

*The national parliaments are also sent proposed initiatives from the European Parliament and member states, requests from the Court of Justice and the European Investment Bank, and recommendations from the European Central Bank, to examine for compliance with the principle of subsidiarity. The EU institutions are required to respond to the national parliaments in the same way as the Commission. But the final decision on what constitutes subsidiarity rests with the EU institution.

proposal is then submitted to the Council and the European Parliament. If a majority opposes the proposal, it is dead; otherwise it passes.[49] In other words, the final decision on what constitutes "subsidiarity" is made by EU institutions, not the nation-states through their democratically responsible national parliaments.* In short, the Lisbon Treaty does not solve the democratic deficit.

It would not be inaccurate to describe this form of Euro-governance as "postdemocratic." True, there are democratic governments within the European Union, but they have ceded extensive authority to supranational governance in critical areas: judicial, administrative, and legislative. This supranational governance is not democratically accountable by any standard definition of the term. Moreover, it will be difficult for European nation-states to recapture the robust democratic authority they once exercised, as the reaction of the Thatcher government to the *Factortame* case indicates.

European Public Opinion and the EU

The peoples of Europe have shown, time and again, before and after the Lisbon Treaty, their lack of confidence in the European Union, its institutions, and its claim to represent them. When given the opportunity to vote directly in referenda on strengthening the EU and furthering European integration, the people usually vote no. The only European peoples who were permitted to vote directly on the EU constitution, the French and the Dutch, voted no. The only European people who were permitted to vote directly on the Lisbon Treaty, the Irish, at first voted no, before agreeing to accept the treaty in a second vote a year later. There is little doubt that the British people would have voted against the Lisbon Treaty if they

---

*The official EU website also touts a new Citizens' Initiative as promoting more democratic governance. Under this measure, one million citizens from different EU nations could propose legislation that the Commission must consider, but final authority rests with the Commission.

had been given the opportunity, but the pro-EU forces in the UK worked relentlessly and successfully to prevent a referendum.

Before the Lisbon Treaty, public opinion polls confirmed widespread skepticism over the EU project. In 2002, Professor Robert Rohrschneider found that a majority of citizens in Great Britain, France, Germany, Spain, Italy, Netherlands, Denmark, Portugal, and Greece did not believe that the EU "represented them" in the sense of representative democracy. Only in Luxembourg, Belgium, and Ireland did citizens believe that they were represented by the EU. From these responses, Professor Rohrschneider concluded that the EU's democratic deficit was "a serious liability to Europe's political integration."[50]

Professor Lauren McLaren reviewed the polling literature in 2005 and listed three main reasons for the broad "Euroskepticism among the mass publics of the EU." First was "concern about the loss of national identity and culture due to European integration." Second was "distrust of EU institutions." Third was the "personal utilitarian dimension," the notion that the citizen had not personally benefited from being in the EU.[51] Geoffrey Van Orden, a British member of the European Parliament, wrote in 2007 about an Open Europe poll revealing that 75 percent of EU citizens wanted to vote in a referendum on whether to accept or reject the Lisbon Treaty. The number rose to 80 percent for the British, French, Irish, and Czechs.[52]

Reviewing the key polling research in 2008, the American communitarian scholar Amitai Etzioni said "it is widely agreed that there is a considerable level of disaffection from the EU project and EU authorities."[53] Etzioni cited a study from 2002 showing that a "majority of West Europeans does not believe that the EU represents them." In 2008, he noted, "26 out of 27 national governments—including 11 governments that had previously committed to doing so—did not allow their citizens to vote on the Lisbon Treaty, presumably fearing its rejection."[54]

After the implementation of the Lisbon Treaty, the EU's own polling, the Eurobarometer, found that "trust" in the EU declined

from 48 percent in the autumn of 2009 (before Lisbon) to 42 percent in spring of 2010 (after Lisbon). In May 2010, the Eurobarometer reported that 47 percent of EU citizens "tend not to trust" the
EU, while only 42 percent "tend to trust the EU." A majority of citizens in the UK, Germany, France, Austria, Sweden, Greece, Latvia,
and Cyprus "tend not to trust" the European Union.[55]

Postliberalism in Europe

In addition to having a "democratic deficit," European society today
has what could be called a "liberal deficit." Chapter Four examined
the assault on traditional liberal values such as individual rights and
free speech in the United States, in the name of multiculturalism,
the diversity agenda, and critical theory. These forces have appeared
in Europe also, in slightly different forms and circumstances. The
liberal deficit exists not only in the institutions of the European
Union, but also in the actions of the nation-states and in the projects
of civil society. Two traditional liberal values in particular are under
assault: equality of citizenship and freedom of speech. There is little
doubt that the curtailment of these two liberal principles is the result
of European elites' response to large-scale Muslim immigration.*

Historically, the concept of equal citizenship in liberal societies
meant that citizenship was based on equality of the individual. All
citizens would be subject to the same laws, regardless of the ascribed
group (religious, racial, ethnic) they were born into.[56] Today in
Europe, this notion of equality has to a great extent been abandoned.
Leading European elites have dealt with "the Muslim community"

---

*In 2011, Angela Merkel in Germany, David Cameron in Great Britain, and Nico-
las Sarkozy in France all stated that multiculturalism was a failure in integrating
immigrants into their respective societies. It is too early to tell whether this rhetorical shift by major European leaders signifies any serious changes in policy.

as a de facto autonomous community within nations, endowed with special privileges as a group.

The archbishop of Canterbury, Rowan Williams, ignited controversy when he famously declared that adoption of Islamic law (Sharia) in some form in Britain "seems unavoidable."[57] The archbishop told BBC Radio that the United Kingdom has to "face up to the fact that some of its citizens" do not relate to the British legal system and that adopting parts of Islamic law would strengthen social cohesion. "An approach to law which simply said—there's one law for everybody—I think that's a bit of a danger," he opined. Williams' comments drew heavy criticism. A particularly forceful refutation came from the Pakistani-born Anglican bishop of Rochester, Michael Nazir-Ali, who argued that Sharia "would be in tension with the English legal tradition on questions like monogamy, provisions for divorce, the rights of women, custody of children, laws of inheritance and of evidence."[58]

Despite such protests, Archbishop Williams' views on ending the "legal monopoly" of British common law had already been accepted and implemented in the United Kingdom. About the same time that Williams spoke favorably about using parts of Islamic law, the British government announced that it recognized foreign polygamous marriages of resident Muslims as legitimate in the UK, and thus would provide welfare, housing, and tax benefits for their multiple wives. Two years earlier, in November 2006, the *Daily Telegraph* reported that even in criminal cases, "Sharia courts now operate in most larger cities, with different sectarian and ethnic groups operating their own courts that cater to their specific needs according to their traditions."[59]

Five months after Archbishop Williams' lecture on Sharia, the *Daily Mail* reported that Britain's most senior judge, Lord Phillips, "gave his blessing to the use of Sharia law to resolve disputes among Muslims." Backing Archbishop Williams, the Lord Chief Justice said it was "not very radical to advocate embracing Sharia law in the context of family disputes." Other British lawyers disagreed, arguing that "family and marital disputes settled by Sharia could disadvantage women or the vulnerable."[60]

The Assault on Freedom of Speech

Across the European continent over the past few decades, public authorities and special-interest groups at both the European Union and nation-state level have attempted—sometimes successfully— to restrict public speech and writing that they deem racist, xenophobic, or hateful to minority ethnic and religious groups or immigrants. In practice, most of the attempts to limit speech have been directed at public figures and groups who criticize Islam in some fashion. They are said to be guilty of "Islamophobia."

In *Reflections on the Revolution in Europe,* Christopher Caldwell attributes what he calls a "criminalization of opinion" in part to fear, as European elites try to keep domestic peace among Muslim immigrants, and in part to guilt over previously excessive nationalism, and past racism and colonialism. Whatever the reasons, there is no doubt that free speech on political, cultural, and public policy issues is being curtailed in Europe. Here are some examples.

• In 2006, Tony Blair's government proposed the Racial and Religious Hatred Act, a law "against incitement to religious hatred" that would permit the prosecution of people who were "reckless as to whether religious hatred would be stirred up" by what they wrote or said. The purpose of the legislation, as the Labour politician David Blunkett admitted, was to stifle public criticism of Islamic doctrine. One member of Parliament from Birmingham, Khalid Mahmood, supported the bill because it could have been used against Salman Rushdie's *The Satanic Verses,* which portrayed the prophet Muhammad negatively.

• Geert Wilders, the leader of the Freedom Party in the Dutch parliament and a vocal critic of Islam, produced a controversial film called *Fitna,* which juxtaposes Koranic verses with images of Muslim violence. In 2008 he told the *Guardian,* "We need to stop the

Islamisation of the Netherlands. That means no more mosques, no more Islamic schools, no more imams. Not all Muslims are terrorists, but almost all terrorists are Muslims."[61] Although an elected democratic politician, Wilders was prosecuted in a Dutch court on charges of "group defamation" and "incitement to discrimination." In June 2011, he was acquitted. The Dutch court found that his speech "balances on the border of what is accepted," but ruled it permissible on the narrow grounds of "context," specifically, a politician talking about public issues. Despite this acquittal, restrictions on free speech remain in force within the European Union.[62]

• Oriana Fallaci, an Italian, was one of the best-known European journalists of the later twentieth century. A *New Yorker* profile in 2006 remarked that after 9/11, Fallaci wrote "three short angry books" advancing the argument that "the Western world is in danger of being engulfed by radical Islam."[63] In 2002, the Movement against Racism and for Friendship between Peoples (MRAP), a French NGO with close ties to French communists, tried but failed to get her book *The Rage and the Pride* banned. In 2003, Fallaci was sued in Switzerland by the Islamic Center of Geneva and SOS Racisme, who charged that *The Rage and the Pride* was racist. The Swiss judiciary, under pressure from Muslim groups, issued an arrest warrant for a criminal trial, but the Italian interior minister refused the extradition request. In 2005, Fallaci was ordered to stand trial in Italy for "vilification" of Islam in her book *The Force of Reason*. Fallaci did have friends in high places. A self-proclaimed "Catholic atheist," she had a very convivial visit with Pope Benedict XVI at Castel Gandolfo, outside of Rome, in September 2005. Fallaci's trial, scheduled for June 2006, never took place because she was ill with cancer and died later that year.

• Brigitte Bardot, the famous actress, has been found guilty of "inciting racial hatred" and fined five times for making negative comments about Muslim immigrants in France. Bardot was first convicted of "inciting racial hatred" in 1997, and fined 1,500 euros for an open letter to *Le Figaro* complaining of "foreign overpopulation" by Muslim families. Bardot was convicted again in 1998 for decrying the loss of French identity and tradition as mosques were multiplying "while our church bells fall silent for want of priests." She was fined in 2000 and 2003 for complaints about Muslims in France in two of her books. In 2008, Bardot was convicted and fined 15,000 euros for an open letter to Nicolas Sarkozy, then the interior minister, in which she objected to the ritual slaughter of sheep during the Islamic feast of Eid. France, she wrote, "is tired of being led by the nose by this population that is destroying us, destroying our country by imposing its acts."[64]

Friends and Foes of Free Speech in Denmark

While many European authorities were complicit in restricting free speech, traditional liberal forces in Denmark resisted the postliberal trend. In September 2005, the Danish newspaper *Jyllands-Posten* published twelve cartoons depicting the prophet Muhammad, some in negative ways, others positive or neutral.[65] Knowing that Islamic tradition discourages artistic portrayals of Muhammad, and highly cognizant of the growing accommodation of European elites to Muslim pressure, the editors of *Jyllands-Posten,* Carsten Juste and Flemming Rose, declared that they wanted to test whether "we still have freedom of speech in Denmark."[66]

After the cartoons were published, radical Danish imams stirred up opposition in the Islamic world. Eleven Muslim ambassadors in Copenhagen demanded to meet with the Danish prime minister, Anders Fogh Rasmussen, and called on the government "to take those responsible to task." Rasmussen refused, saying, "As prime minister I have no tool whatsoever to take actions against the media, and I don't want that kind of tool."[67] When asked to apologize, he responded, "In Denmark we do not apologize for having freedom of speech."[68]

Massive protests broke out throughout the Islamic world and within Muslim communities in Europe. Boycotts against Danish companies were launched by Muslims, including governments such as Saudi Arabia and Sudan. Syria, Kuwait, and Saudi Arabia recalled their ambassadors from Copenhagen. Libya closed its embassy. British Muslims marched in London under signs that read "Behead those who insult Islam."[69] An estimated 139 people were killed in connection with the Muhammad cartoons.

The response in the developed world and the West was equivocal. The UN high commissioner for human rights, Louise Arbour, launched investigations into "disrespect for belief" and asked for an "official explanation" from the Danish government.[70] EU officials sent mixed signals, defending free speech but with substantial qualifications. The European Commission's vice chairman, Franco Frattini, suggested that European media establish a "code of conduct" that would require "prudence" in their treatment of religion.[71] The president of the European Parliament, Josep Borrell, asserted that freedom of expression "must be within the boundaries of respect for the religious beliefs and cultural sensitivities of others" and that it "must avoid any insult."[72] The EU's chief foreign policy official, Javier Solana, when pressed by global Islamic leaders, said the EU had laws to address hate speech and declared, "We are trying to do our utmost so that things of this nature cannot be repeated."[73]

To their credit, a group of newspapers in Norway, France, Germany, Spain, the Netherlands, and Italy reprinted the cartoons in solidarity with the *Jyllands-Posten*. But the American media showed little interest in standing up for free speech in the same way.

Assessing the controversy, Paul Marshall, an expert on religious freedom, wrote that "the response to this often violent challenge to freedom of expression was distressingly equivocal: officials were not content merely to disagree with what the *Jyllands-Posten* cartoonists showed, but were even reluctant to defend their right to publish them."[74] In the end, the episode confirmed the worst fears of the *Jyllands-Posten* editors about the health of free-speech liberalism in the West today.

Even in Denmark, postliberalism is posing a serious threat to freedom of speech. Lars Hedegaard, the president of the Danish

Free Speech Society, was prosecuted on charges of racism and hate speech for telling a blogger at a Christmas party that girls in Muslim families were at risk of being raped by their male relatives. He was found guilty in May 2011 and fined 5,000 kroner for "making racially offensive comments."[75] Another Dane, Jesper Langballe, a member of the Danish parliament, was convicted of hate speech after publicly discussing the issue of Muslim fathers murdering their daughters in so-called "honor killings." Langballe was denied the opportunity to prove his allegations because the truth is no defense under Danish hate-crime law. The MP faces fines and possibly two years in jail.[76]

The EU as a Model for Global Governance

The European Union is intertwined with the global governance project in two crucial respects. First, the "governance" of the European Union provides a model for how global governance could work. Second, the European Union as an institution is an integral element of the global governance party in its worldwide conflict with the party of democratic sovereignty.

Robert Cooper argues that "the most desirable goal would be to extend the postmodern world [i.e. the European system] ever wider . . . so that domestic and foreign policies became intertwined and identities fused into a sense of a wider international community."[77] He quotes Jean Monnet's remark that the European Community "is only a stage on the way to the more organized world of tomorrow."[78] In a sense, the global governance project is the EU writ large: a postdemocratic, postliberal project.

In practical terms, the history and development of the EU as a transnational power offers a roadmap for transforming democratic nation-states (particularly the United States) into what Cooper calls "postmodern states," subservient to new forms of supranational authority. The strategic lessons of the European experience for the global governance party are clear enough and will undoubtedly be heeded. Thus, we should expect the following strategies to emerge.

Global governancers understand that business interests will be useful, at least in the beginning stages, to help break down democratic sovereignty. According to Cooper, "Strategically Monnet's greatest achievement was to involve the domestic interests of the business community," which brought "domestic lobbying power."[79] Business interests were the first litigants that the ECJ used to establish, *in principle,* the supremacy of EC law over national law. Sophisticated global governance advocates who favor the expansion of "rights" on controversial social issues realize that in promoting global law, transnational business litigants will, as a tactical matter, first have to win some lawsuits to establish the principles of global law on which the transnational social activists can then build. This is what happened in Europe with the gradual development of supranational law in the period from the 1960s to the 1980s.

In general, global governancers will find the "Monnet method" of "integration by stealth" to be useful: emphasizing economic before political integration, and promoting incremental rather than comprehensive global integration.[80] Thus, global governance, like European integration, is seen as an ongoing project that will take decades to accomplish, and perhaps a process that never quite ends.

But first and foremost, the global governance project emphasizes global legalism: establishing transnational legal authority (a "global rule of law") as superior to national constitutional law, and particularly to the U.S. Constitution. As the European experience demonstrates, in order to accomplish this "privileging" of transnational law, national judges will have to be won over and rule against their own national politicians.

Looking at the development of EU law, we have some hints about how this might proceed. In the last chapter we discussed Harold Koh's argument that American courts should coordinate "U.S. domestic constitutional rules with rules of foreign and international law" in order to "advance the broader development of a well-functioning international judicial system."[81] At his confirmation hearing in 2009 for the position of legal advisor for the U.S. State Department, suspicious senators quizzed Koh about his advocacy of transnational law. Asked specifically to choose between constitutional law and international law, he replied that of course the U.S. Constitution was always "controlling" or superior.[82] Indeed, the U.S. Supreme Court justices who quote foreign and international law in their decisions likewise insist that international law and foreign law can be used, but is not "controlling."

Examining the development of European integration, we notice that the German Federal Constitutional Court has perfected the method of rhetorically insisting upon retaining final "controlling" judicial authority and sovereignty for the nation-state while effectively ceding large sections of decision making to supranational authority. Democratic sovereigntists in Germany (including Greens on the left) objected to German ratification of both the Maastricht Treaty of 1992 and the current Lisbon Treaty on the grounds that they undermined democratic accountability by transferring critical policy areas to Brussels. The court rejected these arguments in both cases.

In 2009, the German Constitutional Court ruled that the Lisbon Treaty was compatible with German democracy and "the German people still decides essential political issues." The court emphasized the "principle of conferral," arguing that EU member states have voluntarily conferred "competences" on supranational institutions, but retain final authority. Two paragraphs later, however, the court admitted that the "parallel" competences claimed by both the EU and the member states were "not clearly assigned." On the issue of judicial supremacy, the court was ambiguous, declaring that Germany did not accept the "absolute primacy" of EU law, but also insisting that decisions of the European Court of Justice were "binding" on interpretations of the treaty and that ECJ case law was "binding on the courts of the Member States."[83]

The advance of global law will most likely come in the German constitutional manner, with national courts insisting on the "controlling" authority, even while ceding large amounts of power to transnational bodies. The last chapter quoted Peter Spiro's forecast that the United States will adhere to global law under the guise of constitutional law. "As a formal matter, of course, the [U.S.] Constitution will remain supreme," Spiro predicts, but adds that "the formal subordination of international sources may mask their growing constitutional consequence." In short, "International norms can thus be adopted under cover of constitutional supremacy."[84]

CHAPTER SEVEN

Ideas, Institutions, and Interests of the Global Governance Party

Thehe rise of modern transnationalism has reshaped world politics and given new life to the perennial dream of global governance, a dream nurtured in different forms by Alexander the Great, Dante, the Holy Roman Empire, the medieval church, Immanuel Kant, H. G. Wells, Albert Einstein, and many others. Today, the global governance agenda is entrenched among a substantial portion of the world's power brokers whose ideas and material interests converge with a political ideology of supranationalism.

The European Union provides a model for how global governance would work in practice, according to its advocates. Walter Russell Mead, a prominent scholar of international relations, coined the term "Global Union" or "GU" to describe this ideal:

> Think of the European Union blown up to a global scale; in the Global Union nations would have their own governments and their own laws, but an increasingly dense framework of commonly agreed-upon laws and norms, and an increasingly complex and effective web of global institutions would supplement and in many cases replace the authority of national governments.[1]

In other words, global governance would not mean "world government." Instead, there would be a supranational legal regime, a de facto constitutional authority standing above national constitutions but enforced mostly by national courts. Just as in the EU, there would be a set of supranational administrative and regulatory institutions with authority over certain policy areas, thus directly affecting the citizens of nation-states without being seriously accountable to them.

Transnational Progressivism and "Universal Human Rights"

A considerable part of the ideological energy and activist firepower for the global governance project comes from the progressive-left side of Western politics. To capture the essence of this movement, I have coined the term "transnational progressivism," which is meant to be neutral and descriptive, not pejorative. There are also "national progressives," who by their own account are devoted to social justice but would disagree with transnational progressives on crucial issues of democratic accountability and legitimacy.*

Activists among the transnational progressives challenge the two main elements of liberal democracy: liberalism and the democratic nation-state. Adhering to the central premises of multiculturalism, the diversity agenda, and critical theory, they generally favor group rights over individual rights, "victim groups" over "privileged groups," restrictions on speech perceived as denigrating to "victim groups," an emphasis on ethnic identity and on global solidarity over national identity, and equality of results over equality of opportunity.

The ideological heart of the global governance agenda is a belief in "universal human rights" as defined by international law and

---

*Examples of "national progressives" might include practicing politicians such as Franklin D. Roosevelt, Harry Truman, John F. Kennedy, Lyndon Johnson, Bill Clinton, Hillary Clinton, Dianne Feinstein, Charles Schumer; commentators like Chris Matthews; and political operatives like Patrick Caddell, among others.

legitimized by supranational institutions. The global governance project "seeks legitimacy not in democracy and popular sovereignty, but rather in universal principles of human rights," notes Kenneth Anderson, an American University law professor who was involved in the Human Rights Watch initiative to outlaw landmines. As Anderson points out, these so-called universal principles are "unattached" to the "will of the people," and the "legitimacy" of the global governance project "depends not on consent but on the presumed rightness of its human rights universals."[2]

Anderson observes that "international human rights, considered as an ideology, in part serves as a substitute for democracy," because it "subordinates the outcomes of elections, electoral process, popular will, and democracy to the strictures of human rights commands." The actual substance of those human rights commands is determined by transnational elites in unaccountable supranational institutions. Moreover, it is fluid and constantly "evolving."[3] Human rights are simply what transnational judges, lawyers, and activists tell us they are at any given moment. Professor Anderson calls it "serial absolutism." What is *absolute* international human rights law in 2011 was not absolute human rights law in 2001, nor will it be absolute human rights law in 2021.

Through serial absolutism, the content of universal human rights has greatly expanded. For example, the "human rights" spelled out in the UN International Covenant on Economic, Social and Cultural Rights include "periodic holidays with pay, as well as remuneration for public holidays," along with "paid leave or leave with adequate social security benefits" for working mothers before and after childbirth, and a school system in which the "material conditions of teaching staff shall be continuously improved."[4] The UN Convention on the Rights of the Child declares that a child has the right "to seek, receive and impart information and ideas of all kinds ... through any other media of the child's choice," and stipulates that "No child shall be subjected to arbitrary or unlawful interference with his or her privacy, family, home or correspondence."[5]

Millions of people in the world's democracies would not consider these to be "universal human rights" binding on all people everywhere. Surely all of the above are policy issues that should be decided by the normal give and take of democratic politics, including the option of no government action at all.

The Social Base of the Global Governance Party

Transnational progressivism is the vanguard ideology of the global governance movement, but not the only ideological force behind it. There are supporters of transnationalism on the political center and right, including some Western politicians and corporate elites, along with a few libertarians and economic theorists.* Moreover, ideology alone is not enough for a successful politico-social movement. It must have a solid institutional and social base. A great strength of the global governance project is that it appeals to material interests, not just ideals, and so its social base includes a substantial nonideological element of "transnational pragmatists."

The global governance project is an elite politico-social movement with worldwide influence. Generally speaking, its social base is embedded among: (1) American and other Western universities, (2) international lawyers, (3) NGOs, (4) global corporations, (5) American foundations, (6) international organizations (the UN among others), (7) the European Union, (8) "disaggregated" forces within the nation-state, and (9) postmodern nation-states. As Kenneth Anderson observes, there is a symbiotic relationship among the different institutional structures that support political transnationalism. There are

---

*Among Western politicians, the center-right European People's Party (EPP), the largest single bloc in the European Parliament, mostly supports political transnationalism. While some libertarians are attracted to transnationalism, there are also libertarians who vigorously defend democratic sovereignty, including Fred Smith, Myron Ebell, and Christopher Horner of the Competitive Enterprise Institute, and Roger Pilon and Ilya Shapiro of the Cato Institute, for example.

likeminded people with similar sensibilities promoting common political goals, but there are also internal disagreements over goals and tactics. There are moderate and radical elements, and there are rivalries.

Western Universities

Many American and European universities provide a comfortable institutional home for *transnational progressives* doing the intellectual spade work, and for *transnational pragmatists* doing the administrative outreach necessary to build an effective postnational intelligentsia and global governance movement. More important, however, are the academy's normative political values and the concept of citizenship that universities impart to their students.

Today, the curricula of major American universities require more courses in "multiculturalism" and "diversity" than in American history.[6] This is the opposite of what President George Washington envisioned when he proposed a "national university" in 1790 for the explicit purpose of strengthening American national identity. No doubt many universities that are physically located in the United States and run by American citizens do not think of themselves primarily as "American" universities, but as global institutions. The New York University advertisement (discussed in Chapter Five) that asked "As a global citizen, to whom do I pledge allegiance?" reveals an attitude that is perhaps not uncommon among university administrators.

International Lawyers

The practitioners of international law are largely in favor of increasing the scope and reach of global legal authority. This is particularly true for professors of international law. Deans at major law schools, including Yale and Georgetown, have been among the foremost intellectual theorists of an ever-expanding international and transnational law.

The international law section of the American Bar Association is at the forefront of promoting U.S. adherence to a wide range of international human rights conventions and other treaties. For example, the ABA issued a report suggesting guidelines for compliance with the UN Convention on the Elimination of All Forms of Discrimination against Women (CEDAW). The report discussed measures such as "training programs" to "educate judges and other legal professionals about CEDAW's precedence over national law," and indicated how the treaty could become self-executing and therefore be directly incorporated into American law without legislation from Congress.[7]

Nongovernmental Organizations

Since the end of the Cold War, NGOs have emerged as a major force in transnational politics. Leading NGOs include, among others: Amnesty International, Greenpeace, Oxfam, Human Rights Watch, the International Committee of the Red Cross, the World Wildlife Federation, Earth Charter, American Friends Service Committee, and Doctors Without Borders. UN leaders such as the former secretary general Kofi Annan have declared that NGOs represent "the peoples of the world" and "global civil society." Of course, the UN-approved NGOs are essentially pressure groups with no broad democratic accountability. They represent themselves and their funders, not "the peoples of the world."

In a sense, NGOs are the shock troops of the global governance project, providing much of the leadership, energy, ideology, and activism, particularly on issues related to human rights,* the environment, development, and population. We have discussed NGO

---

*Of course, not all human rights NGOs have a political agenda. The Human Rights Foundation (HRF) is a nonpartisan NGO that convenes the annual Oslo Freedom Forum, which is attended by a wide array of international figures from academia, media, business, and politics. Elie Wiesel, Harry Wu, Vaclav Havel, and Vladimir Bukovsky—all former prisoners of conscience—serve on HRF's International Council.

activism at the World Conference against Racism. NGOs have been effective because they network with other elements of the global governance coalition. They have formed close working relationships with medium-sized and smaller Western nations such as Canada, Germany, and Norway on certain issues (e.g., the landmines treaty and the International Criminal Court) to outflank large state interests, particularly U.S. interests. The NGOs also have a symbiotic relationship with international organizations such as the United Nations Secretariat, the World Bank, the International Monetary Fund, the World Trade Organization, and the International Criminal Court. Neither NGOs nor international organizations are democratic, but they provide each other with an aura of legitimacy. It was reported in 1999 that the World Bank president, James Wolfensohn, would not make a serious policy move before clearing it with the NGOs. As the *Economist* put it, "From environmental policy to debt relief, NGOs are at the centre of World Bank policy. Often they determine it."[8]

American Foundations

We have seen how leading American philanthropies supported the assault on liberalism by the advocates of multiculturalism, the diversity agenda, and critical theory. The same group of foundations is pouring tens of millions of dollars into the project to restrict American democratic sovereignty and promote transnationalism and supranationalism. These include the Ford Foundation, the Rockefeller Foundation, the Charles Stewart Mott Foundation, the Carnegie Endowment, the MacArthur Foundation, the Open Society Institute, and Atlantic Philanthropies (a mostly American foundation based in Bermuda, which permits it to be more explicitly political).

These foundations are the primary paymasters of the American NGOs promoting transnational progressivism. European and other Western NGOs are often funded by the EU and various European national governments. The NGO role in the World Conference against Racism at Durban was funded directly or indirectly by Ford, Rockefeller, Mott, and MacArthur. Ford in particular was heavily involved in providing money to the NGOs attacking American sovereignty and Israeli legitimacy in the name of global human rights. Clearly, large sections of mainstream American philanthropy represent "disaggregated" elements within the American nation and society.

International Organizations

The premier international organization is the United Nations. Since the period of Boutros Boutros-Ghali, the leadership of the United Nations Secretariat has made claims of transnational authority, mixed with perfunctory rhetorical respect for state sovereignty. As early as 1992, the UN leadership endorsed the recommendations of "Our Global Neighborhood," a report by the independent UN Commission on Global Governance, which declared that "Countries are having to accept" that in some areas "sovereignty has to be exercised collectively."[9] In 2005, Kofi Annan stated that the UN must "loosen the grip of large powers."[10] There is no doubt that the UN elite are part of the global governance project. They seek, as much as possible, to limit national sovereignty (particularly American and Israeli sovereignty) and promote supranational governance.

Other major international organizations include the International Court of Justice, the International Monetary Fund, the World Bank, the International Criminal Court, the World Trade Organization, the World Health Organization, and the International Labor Organization. With the exception of the International Criminal Court, these organizations began for the most part as international institutions, established to serve the interests of nation-states, not to "govern" beyond the authority of the states that created them. But since the end of the Cold War, at least, a creeping transnationalism and even supranationalism has been manifest in many of these organizations.

The World Trade Organization

In the aftermath of World War II, the major trading nations organized the General Agreement on Tariffs and Trade (GATT) after attempts to create a more formal International Trade Organization had failed. The GATT conducted multilateral trade negotiations for the purpose of reducing tariffs and trade barriers, and thereby avoiding any repetition of the damaging trade wars of the late 1920s and early 1930s. GATT negotiations proved to be very successful. From the 1940s to the 1990s they reduced average tariff levels by almost 90 percent, and promoted economic growth and prosperity.[11] The GATT was a highly effective international (not transnational or supranational) institution based on negotiations, reciprocity, compromise, and conciliation among member nation-states.

In 1995, the GATT was subsumed under a more formal legal structure, the World Trade Organization. From the beginning, the WTO's highest judicial organ, the Appellate Body, has seen its mission as not simply addressing trade disputes among nations, but incorporating trade issues within broader principles of a growing international legal regime. Thus, trade disputes that were once negotiated among nations are now settled by supranational litigation in the WTO's Appellate Body.

A German legal advisor to the WTO sees it as part of a developing "world constitution."[12] The current head of the WTO, Pascal Lamy, an ardent transnationalist,* decries the "traditional models of national democracy" as having "important limitations" in their ability to "handle global problems." He prefers the EU model as "a new paradigm of global governance," saying that "European construction is the most ambitious experiment in supranational governance ever attempted up to now."[13]

---

*An experienced Eurocrat, Lamy served for around a decade as chief of staff to Jacques Delors, president of the European Commission.

Although trade complaints to the WTO can be filed only by member governments, Professor Jeremy Rabkin of the George Mason University School of Law notes that "a more judicialized dispute-settlement process has given the WTO more direct connection with business constituencies." This has led to "a dramatic increase in complaints" as the system "has encouraged business interests to engage private legal assistance to prepare formal complaints" and lobby U.S. trade officials to sponsor their claims.[14] Like the European Court of Justice, the WTO is not simply resolving disputes among nations, but fostering supranational legal standards and building transnational constituencies of corporations, NGOs, and social activists that could benefit from its decisions.[15]

Leading scholars both right and left of center have worried about the supranationalist implications of the WTO's present course. Claude Barfield, a free-trade expert at the American Enterprise Institute, told the U.S. Congress that "the triumph of binding legalism" in the WTO is problematic. "New rules in the area of health and safety, and for the services industries—banks, insurance companies, telecommunications and the Internet, energy services and transportation, for example—meant that the multilateral trading system would be asked to deal with complex issues that go deep into the economic and social structures of its member states." Barfield quoted a former Canadian trade negotiator saying that under the WTO, "The degree of obtrusiveness into domestic sovereignty bears little resemblance to the shallow integration of the GATT." The WTO's dispute settlement system is "unsustainable," Barfield concluded, because its structure over time will "create major questions of democratic legitimacy."[16]

From across the political spectrum, Professor Jed Rubenfeld of Yale Law School, in criticizing the U.S. role in the International Monetary Fund, the World Bank, and the WTO, argues that America's "commitment to democracy" is "violated wherever U.S.-led international economic organizations cripple the possibilities of democracy under the guise of free trade principles and loan conditionality."[17] Thus, the WTO's global governance ambitions challenge both national democracy and a free and effective trading system.

Global Corporations

Many leaders of major global corporations have a symbiotic relationship with transnational NGOs and international organizations. They meet and do business at places like the World Bank, the World Trade Organization, and the International Monetary Fund. They socialize at the World Economic Forum in Davos, Switzerland. In fact, the term "Davos" has come to represent the new global power elite, corporate and otherwise, or what David Rothkopf calls the new "superclass."[18]

Some of these corporate leaders promote the global governance project, at least in some form, for pragmatic reasons. Their relationships with NGOs can be complicated. Sometimes global corporations are the targets of NGOs, but at other times they collaborate. One thing is clear: the twenty-first-century global corporation is different from the multinational corporation of the twentieth century. The American multinationals had branches in many other countries, but they were headquartered in the American nation and attached to American culture. Thus, International Telephone and Telegraph (ITT) in Chile cooperated with the CIA on issues involving American national security in the 1970s. This type of cooperation, based on instinctive patriotism, is not as likely to occur today.

Certainly, the public voice of global business today is quite different from the voice of international business yesterday. Let us listen to what some leading global business types are saying:

• Kenichi Ohmae, former McKinsey and Company partner, and author of *The End of the Nation-State,* declares that the nation-state and the global economy cannot comfortably coexist, and sees the emergence of transnational regions (Northern Italy/Rhone-Alps,

Southern California/Northern Mexico) as major forces in global economics and international politics.

• Jeff Seabright, vice president of Coca-Cola, said, "We are not 'an American company' with a presence in places like Beijing, Brunei, Bangalore, or Bucharest. Rather, we operate in Beijing, Brunei, Bangalore and Bucharest very much as members of those local communities."[19] (One wonders, if Coca-Cola is not "an American company," then what is?)

• A top executive of Colgate-Palmolive said, "The United States does not have an automatic call on our resources. There is no mindset that puts this country first."[20]

In his book on challenges to American identity, Samuel Huntington decries what he calls the "de-nationalization" of American corporate elites, and describes these "economic transnationals" as "the nucleus of an emerging global superclass."[21] Writing in the *Atlantic*, Chrystia Freeland reports a conversation with a "U.S.-based CEO of one of the world's largest hedge funds," in which he recounted comments by another senior executive of the company who said he was not concerned about a "hollowing-out of the American middle class." The CEO recalled his colleague explaining that "if the transformation of the world economy lifts four people in China and India out of poverty and into the middle class, and meanwhile means one American drops out of the middle class, that's not such a bad trade."[22]

While some business leaders who are American citizens have displayed a transnational political consciousness, this attitude is not universal in the corporate world. Some companies, such as Boeing and Lockheed Martin, have embraced the symbols of American patriotism in the post-9/11 era.

The European Union and the G20

The European Union represents a major institutional force supporting the global governance project. The elites of the EU actively promote the major tenets of the global governance agenda, including nation-state compliance with the (EU-sponsored) International Criminal Court and with the full range of UN human rights, environmental, and development conventions that the United States has been reluctant to join. The EU court system is an enthusiastic promoter of the "new" international law and the imposition of constantly evolving global norms on nation-states.

Philosophically, the EU represents a new kind of regime, a new type of political entity, above and beyond the nation-state. The international lawyers David Rivkin and Lee Casey have explained the fundamental difference between this new European supranationalism and America's liberal democracy:

> From the perspective of U.S. philosophical and constitutional traditions, the key question in determining whether any particular model of government is a democracy is whether the governed choose their governors. . . . [T]he reemergence of a pre-Enlightenment pan-European ideology that denies the ultimate authority of the nation-state, as well as the transfer of policymaking authority from the governed and their elected representatives to a professional bureaucracy, as is evident in the EU's leading institutions, suggests a dramatic divergence from the basic principle of popular sovereignty once shared by both Europe's democracies and the United States.[23]

Even some supporters of the European Union (as we saw in Chapter Six) are troubled by what is commonly called the EU's "democratic deficit," the lack of democratic accountability in its main institutions. At the same time, conversely, some EU officials suggest that this remoteness from democratic accountability is a positive attribute. According to an official European Commission white paper, "the original and essential source of the success of European Integration is that the EU's executive body, the Commission, is supranational and independent from national, sectoral or other influences."[24]

Leading figures in the EU, along with other transnational pragmatists, saw the global economic crisis of 2008–2010 as an opportunity to advance global governance and transnational regulation
in the financial sector. Peter Mandelson, a close associate of Tony
Blair who has served as EU trade commissioner (2004–2009),
posed the question of whether it was possible to "preserve the benefits" of the global economy while "respecting the choices of sovereign governments." He concluded: "The answer has to be: not
really." Chiding "free-market true believers," Mandelson said that
more "global coordination" and regulation were needed, and that
"the bill for the benefits of an open global economy . . . can only be
paid in greater global governance."[25]

After the implementation of the Lisbon Treaty, the new president
of a strengthened European Council, Herman Van Rompuy (former
prime minister of Belgium), noted in his inaugural address that he
assumed the presidency in "exceptionally difficult times," with "the
financial crisis . . . the climate crisis" and the like. Van Rompuy
trumpeted 2009 as "the first year of global governance, with the
establishment of the G20 in the middle of the financial crisis."[26]

In April 2009, the heads of state of the world's leading economic
powers, the G20,* met in London to address the global economic
crisis.[27] The summit called for the creation of a Financial Stability
Board to provide oversight of all "systemically important" financial
institutions, instruments, and markets. With a "strengthened mandate," the board was to replace the old advisory Financial Stability
Forum, which had been created for information exchange and international cooperation. The Financial Stability Board (FSB) was
envisioned as a global regulator to establish a "supervisory college
to monitor each of the largest international financial services firms."[28]

---

*The G20 was an expansion of the G8 group of leading economic nations (the
United States, Canada, the United Kingdom, Germany, France, Italy, Japan, plus
representatives of the EU). The G20 added emerging markets and developing
economies such as China, India, and Brazil.

The *New York Times* reported that "a European push for sweeping global regulation of the financial markets" with "cross-border [transnational] authority" was "blunted, to a large degree, by the United States."[29] Nevertheless, analysts have raised concerns about the potential of the Financial Stability Board to undermine democratic sovereignty in the long run. Jim Kelly, director of international affairs for the Federalist Society, wrote that the FSB "gives the international community the authority to review and regulate the financial and operational structures of private enterprises, potentially bypassing the jurisdiction of national regulatory systems." The G20 London Summit Declaration "makes it obvious that the FSB's oversight and regulatory authority will take primacy over any national regulatory agencies, thereby hampering the ability of State governments to determine their own economic policies."[30] Ted Bromund of the Heritage Foundation remarked that if the FSB "departs" from the "sensible principles" of promoting information exchange and international cooperation that guided the original Financial Stability Forum, "it will be making a serious error."[31]

The astute Gideon Rachman of the *Financial Times* portrayed the G20 itself as an instrument for the EU to promote its own "brand of supranational governance as a global model." Reporting on the Pittsburgh G20 summit of September 2009, Rachman mused:

> The realisation that the G20 is Europe's Trojan horse struck me at the G20's last summit in Pittsburgh. . . . The surroundings and atmosphere were strangely familiar. And then I understood; I was back in Brussels, and this was just a global version of a European Union Summit. It was the same drill and format. The leaders' dinner the night before the summit; a day spent negotiating an impenetrable, jargon-stuffed communiqué; the setting-up of obscure working groups; the national briefing rooms for the post-summit press conferences.

Rachman pointed out that "The Europeans did not just set the tone at the G20—they also dominate proceedings," having eight seats at the table (Britain, France, Germany, Italy, Spain, the Netherlands, the presidents of the European Commission and the European Council) and thus being "grossly over-represented." Also present were European leaders of key institutions such as the IMF (Dominique Strauss-Kahn), the WTO (Pascal Lamy), and the Financial Stability Board (Mario Draghi).[32]

"Once the EU gets its teeth into an issue, it never really lets go," Rachman noted. "Processes started at EU summits—which often seem minor bits of bureaucratic paper-shuffling—often turn out to have important political implications, years later." True, he acknowledged that there is not "much immediate prospect" that nation-states like the United States and China "will cede any serious powers" to G20 bodies, but nevertheless, "the kernel of something new has been created. To understand its potential, it is worth going back to the Schuman Declaration of 1950, which started the process of European integration. 'Europe,' it said, 'will not be made all at once, or according to a single plan. It will be built through concrete achievements, which first create a de facto solidarity.' " As Rachman concluded, "The G20 now has some achievements and a burgeoning sense of solidarity between the members of this new, most exclusive club, who knows what comes next?"[33]

Indeed, in September 2010, Javier Solana, former EU high representative for foreign and security policy, declared that "the main challenge now is to continue using the 'geometry of 20' to build instruments of world governance."[34]

In the context of the financial crisis, some on the center-right favor accepting elements of global governance. These pragmatists would support supranational regulation of financial institutions, noting (correctly) that undercapitalized banks in foreign countries could endanger domestic banks. But they would oppose supranational rules in other areas, such as health and safety, because it would lead to overregulation and hamper growth in the global economy. This argument, however, cannot be sustained in the long run. It is not based on principle, but on special-interest preferences. Advocates of more expansive global governance could argue that if supranational regulation is good for the financial sector, it is even more important in the "human" sectors of health and safety, where individuals' lives and well-being are at stake. In short, the transnational pragmatists of the center-right will lose the argument.

Disaggregated Forces within Democratic Nation-States

Transnational theorists have examined the role of "disaggregated" forces within the American nation-state in advancing the global governance agenda. In some cases, this means that particular groups in the United States—both governmental and private actors—would work with transnational forces to limit American democratic sovereignty. As we saw in the previous chapter on the European Union, one of those disaggregated elements could be national judiciaries, which in Europe showed a readiness "to make common cause" with foreign judiciaries at the expense of "their fellow branches of government."[35]

Peter Spiro argues that "discrete elements of the United States" have "institutional" and material as well as ideological interests in supporting American submission to transnational legal regimes and expanded global authority. Today, "it is more difficult to identify groups or corporations (or even individuals) as discretely 'American,'" he says. "Although corporations and the organs of civil society once functioned for the most part within the parameters of particular states, they now represent partially distinct transnational identities and enjoy autonomous power."[36]

For various NGOs and corporations, operating transnationally "changes the nature of their power and what they represent," Spiro explains. They can sometimes secure "through transnational channels what they could not secure through ordinary domestic ones." In this way, they can pursue policies detached from, and sometimes in opposition to, the American nation of which their leaders are nominal citizens. For example, "A U.S.-based group such as Human Rights Watch will work to enlist other states to influence U.S. human rights practices."[37] Spiro notes that Kenneth Roth, the executive director of Human Rights Watch, called on Canada to oppose a U.S.-supported Iraqi trial of Saddam Hussein and instead back the U.S.-opposed International Criminal Court as a venue to try Saddam.

More significantly, Human Rights Watch called on European governments to refuse the U.S. request to exempt American soldiers from prosecution by the International Criminal Court when serving in UN peacekeeping missions.[38] Thus, even though Human Rights Watch is a U.S.-based organization whose top leadership consists mostly of American citizens, as an institution it places the prerogatives of the International Criminal Court above the rights of American soldiers as guaranteed by the Bill of Rights in the Constitution of the United States. For Human Rights Watch, compliance with what the organization considers "global norms" trumps longstanding American constitutional rights, such as the right to a jury trial by one's peers.

The Postmodern, Subordinate Nation-State

The mainstream of the global governance project does not envision the *disappearance* of the nation-state, but its *demotion* in status. In this view, nation-states (democratic and undemocratic) would continue to exist and perform many important governance functions. But they would now have a "political superior," a range of supranational institutions, laws, rules, and norms that constitute a higher authority than a national constitution.

In fact, serious transnationalists desire a world composed entirely of postmodern states, or (to expand the jargon of international relations-ese) we could call them subordinate nation-states (SNS's). The goal of American transnational progressives is to turn the United States into a postmodern state whose elites agree to "pool" or "share" national sovereignty in order to establish a supranational political authority.

As discussed in Chapter Six, the EU diplomat Robert Cooper formulated the useful concept of modern versus postmodern states. Developing Cooper's thinking further, we could posit that the category of "postmodern state" is not necessarily a fixed status, but can change depending on the issues at stake or on the current national leadership. Some European states often act as postmodern states but reassert their sovereignty at other times. For example, France and Great Britain have, in postmodern fashion, acquiesced in the judicial supremacy of the European Court of Justice; yet in maintaining independent nuclear deterrence capabilities, they are acting as modern states.

Contemporary Germany has in some ways been the prototype of the postmodern state, whose elites favor limiting national sovereignty and promote global and transnational governance. These elites believe that their "interests" (they would not use so crude a term as "national interest") are better served in a world of postmodern states, in which the United States and other larger powers such as China and Russia would be constrained by supranational authority. To ensure that popular opinion did not interfere with the march toward supranationalism, German elites prevented the German people from voting on the dramatic currency change that abolished the Deutschmark and created the euro.★

German political, media, and academic elites unleashed a barrage of criticism when the country's president, Horst Köhler, made a series of perfectly reasonable observations in an interview with Deutschlandradio Kultur on May 22, 2010. Köhler said that "a country of [Germany's] size with such foreign trade orientation and foreign trade dependency also must know, when it comes down

---

★With the financial crisis in Greece and beyond, there are indications that the German middle classes are becoming more open to political challenges to their post-democratic elites.

to it, in an emergency, that military intervention is necessary to defend, for example free trade routes, or prevent whole regional instabilities which would certainly have negative effects on [the country's] trade, jobs and income." President Köhler also noted that it was "completely normal" for German soldiers in Afghanistan to say that they were involved in a "war."[39] Köhler's remarks violated the taboos of the German elites. Under a hail of elite of criticism, he resigned.

In a sense, German elites have learned the wrong lessons from World War II, which they blame on "nationalism" or the "nation-state" in general, as much as on Nazi ideology and totalitarianism. Yoram Hazony, an Israeli philosopher and political theorist, argues that Hitler was in fact not an advocate of the nation-state, but of a racial empire:

> The heart of the idea of the nation-state is the political self-determination of peoples. The nation-state is a form of government that limits its political aspirations to the rule of one nation, and to establishing national freedom for this nation. The Nazi state, on the other hand, was precisely the opposite of this: Hitler opposed the idea of the nation-state as an expression of Western effeteness. On his view, the political fate of all nations should be determined by the new German empire . . . the Third Reich. . . . The Nazis' aim was thus diametrically opposed to that of the Western nation-states. Hitler's dream was precisely to build his empire on their ruin.[40]

In Europe today, many nation-states have voluntarily given up vast areas of decision making and therefore sovereign authority to the European Union, and could thus be regarded as postmodern states. This surrender of national sovereignty has occurred, for the most part, without the explicit consent of the citizens of those nation-states.

CHAPTER EIGHT

Rethinking World Politics

S tudents of international politics traditionally are divided between realists and idealists. Realists view world politics as an arena of nation-states that seek power and influence for their rational self-interest. They act sometimes in combination and sometimes in opposition, but states working for their own material interests are the only serious players in the great game of global politics. These "cold monsters," in Nietzsche's term, must sometimes act amorally for "reasons of state." Exemplars of this realpolitik include Niccolò Machiavelli, Otto von Bismarck, and Henry Kissinger.

In the realist vision, the Cold War was primarily a strategic conflict for world hegemony between two "superpowers." The United States, a multiethnic nation-state with a capitalist free-market economy, was locked in a fierce power struggle for nearly half a century with the Soviet Union, a multinational empire with a socialist command economy. In the end, the sheer material strength of the United States—military, economic, and strategic—overwhelmed the Soviet Union, which disappeared from world history.

Idealists view world politics as an arena of competing political philosophies or ideologies, such as democracy, liberalism, constitutionalism, monarchism, authoritarianism, totalitarianism, fascism, communism, socialism, Islamism, nationalism, Third Worldism, and the like. For the idealists, it is ideas and values rather than material interests that move the world. Idealists and ideologically minded analysts often quote John Maynard Keynes to the effect that even "practical men," including the most hardnosed businessmen, "are usually the slaves of some defunct economist."[1]

In the idealist view, Marxism was influential not because of its analysis of material conditions, but because it presented an inspiring militant ideology—a cause to live for and, if necessary, to die for. Idealists viewed the Cold War as a global war of ideas between liberal democracy and communism. America and the free world eventually prevailed because the idea of freedom proved stronger than communism, to such an extent that finally even the Soviet elite no longer believed in their own system at the end. Woodrow Wilson is often portrayed as the quintessential idealist statesman.

These explanations of realism and idealism are obviously pure, theoretical types. In the actual world of international politics, realism and idealism always intersect. Statesmen (and those who study them) are well aware that there is no clear dividing line between realism and idealism, between a nation's interests and its ideals. Certainly Henry Kissinger, the arch-realist, at times used ideological and value-based arguments. Likewise, Woodrow Wilson was capable of exercising realpolitik on occasion.

Since the end of the Cold War and 9/11, both realists and idealists see a number of emerging trends. These include the increasing globalization of economics, culture, and politics; the economic rise of India and China and the ascent of Asia generally; instability in developing regions; the challenge of terrorism and radical Islam; global environmental and development issues; and potential challenges from major nondemocratic states such as China and Russia. While recognizing short-term setbacks, Western elites for the most part still view a gradual modernization and democratization throughout all regions, and the realization of a more peaceful world, as a likely long-term global trend. Hence the original Fukuyama paradigm is still widely accepted in the developed world.

How does the global governance project fit into a conceptual framework for world politics? International relations theorists of either the realist or the idealist school, or a combination thereof, have not adequately addressed this issue, which will be central to understanding global politics in the twenty-first century. Transnational theorists such as Robert Cooper, Anne-Marie Slaughter, and Peter Spiro argue (correctly in my view) that policy analysts need a new lens through which to examine world politics. This lens would reveal, for example, how some medium-sized and smaller nation-states work with international and domestic NGOs, with "disaggregated" elements of larger nation-states, and with transnational forces to restrain more powerful states.

The New Global Chessboard

Today we could identify four major competitors in the arena of world politics. Each has an ideological core and a distinct political vision, along with a solid material base and institutional resources, including nation-states and alliances with non-state actors. The competitors are (1) radical Islam, representing violent antidemocratic transnationalism; (2) China and Russia, representing authoritarian (nondemocratic) nationalism; (3) liberal democratic sovereigntists, led by the United States, representing democratic nationalism; and (4) the forces of global governance, representing postdemocratic transnationalism.

The four rivals differ on the ultimate *ends* of political society. For *radical Islam*, the goal of political society is the worldwide establishment of Sharia (Islamic law) under a caliphate governing the whole *ummah*, the global Muslim community. *Nondemocratic nationalists* of the China-Russia type are the least universalist and prefer to establish their own particular regime as a great power with full sovereignty and freedom of action. *Liberal democratic sovereigntists* believe the ends of political society are the preservation and perpetuation of self-governing liberal democratic nation-states, with no political superior. *Global governance transnationalists* aim to create some type of global or supranational political authority that is superior to that of all nation-states, including democratic ones.

The four main global protagonists differ on basic principles and values of politics and government, including the meaning of democracy, constitutionalism, the rule of law, consent, sovereignty, and self-government. They offer very different visions of world order.

An Islamist World. For radical Islamists, sovereignty does not come from the people, but from God (Allah). Legitimate political societies are those that have submitted to the will of God, which is the literal meaning of the word "Islam," and conform to Sharia. Both national (constitutional) law and international law are trumped by Islamic law. Societies that are not governed by Sharia are considered illegitimate; this includes Muslim nations such as Egypt. Islamist regimes could be established through violence (*jihad*) or through nonviolent political action or propaganda (*dawa*), but either way they are considered legitimate because they have established the rule of Sharia. Radical Islamists are ultra-transnationalists who favor the eventual establishment of an Islamist world political community superior to all nations governed by Sharia.

A Hobbesian World. In China, political legitimacy is asserted by the leadership of the Communist Party. The contemporary Russian regime claims legitimacy in the name of "sovereign democracy," which in practice means rule by the prevailing state security elite, who supposedly act in the name of the Russian people and nation. In general, Chinese and Russian nationalists see an anarchic Hobbesian world of intense state-to-state conflict and competition. They are believers in power politics in the global arena and essentially favor expanding their own power and sphere of influence as much as possible. They would follow or ignore international law depending on political expediency, and often ratify international human rights treaties that they have no intention of following.

A Lockean World. In conventional international relations thinking, the forces of liberal democratic sovereignty and global governance—of the United States and the European Union, of NATO and the NGOs—make up "the West" and a good part of the developed world. At one level of understanding this is clearly true. At a deeper level, however, there is, as Jürgen Habermas puts it, a "divided West," split between two conflicting worldviews.[2]

Western democratic sovereigntists place legitimacy in the hands of the self-governing liberal democratic nation-state. Although based on majority rule and the consent of the governed, the democracy is *liberal* because majority rule is limited by a constitution. Liberal democratic sovereigntists support traditional international law and favor an effective international system of cooperating democratic states. Most democratic sovereigntists believe in universal human rights, but unlike the globalists they reject the idea that the substance of these universal rights should be decided at the transnational level. Because democratic sovereigntists take the provisions of human rights treaties seriously, they reject treaties that are not consistent with their national constitutions or to which they could not in good conscience adhere.

A Kantian World. Western global governancers locate the highest authority not in democratic self-government (e.g., parliamentary or presidential democracy), but in global norms and universal human rights. They regard the "new" international law, embodying the latest (and most progressive) concepts of global human rights and universal norms, as superior to any national law or the constitution of any democratic nation-state. These global rights and norms are always evolving and expanding, as humans themselves progress in knowledge and empathy. International human rights treaties contain binding legal norms, but they are also aspirational, outlining the future goals of an emerging global community.

These last two global competitors, *democratic sovereignty* vs. *global governance,* represent incompatible worldviews and will be locked in ideological combat during the twenty-first century. Because the conflict is over first principles, it will be intense, whether it is acknowledged or ignored by conventional statesmen, scholars, and journalists. At the same time, it is also a zero-sum power struggle with material consequences: if one side gains more power, the other side loses power. The struggle is going on beneath the day-to-day bustle of conventional world politics, but is nonetheless real and deadly serious.

Seeing the World through Bifocal Lenses

Transnational thinkers are right to suggest that we need new lenses to bring the thickets of world politics into focus. We need bifocal lenses. While one lens focuses on conventional world politics, the other analyzes the conflict between liberal democracy and its newest rival, supranational governance, over the aims of global politics. It is also necessary to look through both lenses at the same time, because the four major forces in world politics interact like the proverbial billiard balls of traditional international relations theory. For example, transnational progressives who favor global governance react very differently to radical Islamist terror attacks than do democratic nationalists in the United States and Israel.

Radical Islam is a direct and violent threat to liberal democratic nations. Jihadists could obtain weapons of mass destruction and attack democratic nations, killing millions of people. Large-scale immigration from Muslim countries has led to pockets of support for radical Islamism throughout Europe. The United States, too, has resident radical Islamists, some of whom are immigrants and the children of immigrants, while others are native-born converts. Continuing mass immigration with weak assimilation to Western cultural norms, combined with low native birth rates, will exacerbate this problem in the years to come. Islamic law is already penetrating sections of the West, particularly western Europe.

Authoritarian China and to a lesser degree Russia present traditional geopolitical challenges to the United States. Obviously, an ascendant China is a more serious threat than a declining Russia. Both of these challenges are material rather than ideological. In an effort to undermine American and Western influence, these autocratic regimes will sometimes ally with or try to assist radical Islamists internationally, while they suppress the jihadists at home. Jockeying for greater leverage, the autocratic states will continue to cause problems for the United States and other democracies in the UN Security Council and elsewhere. If regime change eventually comes to China or Russia, it should alter their stance toward the democracies.

As Francis Fukuyama suggested in the early 1990s, neither the radical Islamists nor the Chinese and Russian autocrats present a major ideological challenge to liberal democracy in the sense of offering a compelling ideology with worldwide appeal. Unlike fascism (in its early "wave of the future" days) or communism, these contemporary rivals to liberal democracy are unlikely to attract large numbers of Westerners, or Westernized intellectuals from other parts of the world.*

On the other hand, the worldview and ideology of the global governance project has wide appeal in the West and in the broader international community. The ideology of global governance challenges the major premises of liberal democracy: individual over group rights, free speech, majority rule, democratic accountability, national identity, the primacy of the nation-state. This challenge could be considered existential, because it would transform the democratic regime into a different type of regime.

---

*Radical Islam obviously has an appeal to disaffected young men and intellectuals throughout the Islamic world, including Muslim communities in the West. But it is unlikely that Westerners will become radical Islamists in numbers comparable to the Fascist and Communist sympathizers in the 1930s and 1940s.

The conflict between liberal democracy and global governance, between democratic sovereigntists and supranationalists, will be nonviolent but juridically coercive. It will be complicated by the fact that liberal democrats will be engaged in a two-front struggle. On the one hand, there will be the ongoing violent conflict with radical jihadists—a conflict in which the forces of liberal democracy and those of global governance will often be cooperating. Manifestos will be issued about Western unity, the "norms" of the "international community," and civilizational solidarity against extremism. Much of this will be sincere, because all civilized people oppose indiscriminate terrorism.

Nevertheless, the forces in the West (and elsewhere) promoting global governance will continue their political and legal struggle to transform the modern liberal democratic nation-state into a post-modern subordinate state. This situation is reminiscent of the Cold War, when serious Western anticommunists were forced to wage a two-front ideological conflict: both against the communists and against the Western anti-anticommunists who derided the anticommunist enterprise.

Strategic Goals of the Global Governance Party

The great military strategist Carl von Clausewitz wrote that the most effective way to defeat an enemy is to strike at his "center of gravity," which is the main source of his strength, the "hub of all power and movement upon which everything depends. That is the point against which all our energies should be directed."[3] Depending on circumstances, an adversary's center of gravity could be his army or capital city, an alliance system, or popular support and citizen morale. Liberal democracy's center of gravity today is the American constitutional regime. Thus, the main obstacle to the global governance project is American sovereignty and all it entails by way of American exceptionalism in politics, culture, religion, economics, national identity, and jurisprudence. America must be brought to heel. Its political, economic, and legal system must be harmonized and integrated with myriad European and other foreign institutions, and subordinated to global norms and authority.

All transnationalists and supranationalists—progressives and pragmatists, Americans and non-Americans alike—see a sovereign, independent, unbridled United States as the major problem. America sets a "bad" example. By its very existence, a vigorous American nation-state affirms the ideal of national independence. The global governancers know that if the bridle can be put on the American nation-state, it will be much easier to harness others (including democracies like Israel, Poland, the Czech Republic, India) and limit their sovereignty.

Could America voluntarily accept the bridle and become the horse that leads the global governance cart? The more sophisticated among the transnationalists know that the global governance project will advance only under "American leadership." In this scenario, the American nation becomes a major advocate of global governance and helps establish a new global order of supranational institutions and rules. America embraces global legalism and voluntarily relinquishes a large measure of its judicial and political independence in order to "serve humanity." The American caterpillar is transformed into the global butterfly.

Today, many of the world's elites (including Americans) are committed to the project of curtailing American sovereignty. A decade ago, Jeane Kirkpatrick, former U.S. ambassador to the United Nations, noted that "foreign governments and their leaders, and more than a few activists here at home, seek to constrain and control American power by means of elaborate multilateral processes, global arrangements, and UN treaties that limit both our capacity to govern ourselves and act abroad."[4]

Kirkpatrick was stating the obvious. The American academics and professionals who seek to shrink American sovereignty use terms like "obedience," "compliance," and "submission." They describe America as part of an "axis of disobedience."[5] What is needed, say these American globalists, is "greater U.S. submission to international regimes," the "assimilation of the United States into the system of international norms," and America's "socialization" into an international human rights regime.[6]

Leading UN officials agree that American independence is the main problem confronting global governance. One of the most influential figures in the "international community" is Lord Mark Malloch Brown, a British diplomat and life peer who has served in various UN leadership positions, including deputy secretary general in 2006. In a commencement address at Pace Law School in New York in 2005, Malloch Brown described the United States as an "ungainly magnificent giant" of a nation that "cannot quite accept membership of the global neighborhood association, and the principle of all neighborhoods, that it must abide by others' rules as well as its own." He complained that "the country that most resents being subject to the constraints, rules, and ultimately laws posed by others" is the United States.[7]

Former Canadian and Mexican foreign ministers agree that American sovereignty is a problem. Lloyd Axworthy, who was Canada's foreign minister in 1996–99, has written that the "pre-eminent position" of the United States in international politics "complicat[es] the efforts to govern this global interdependence." Axworthy was upset about American "reluctance to submit to international treaties and agreements."[8] His use of the word "submit" is instructive because it highlights the agenda of the global governance party: the subordination of the American constitutional system to the "new" international (or rather, supranational) law.

Jorge Castaneda was Mexico's foreign minister during the presidency of Vicente Fox. He is usually regarded by foreign policy experts as being friendly to the United States and a supporter of the Fox-Bush *"dos amigos"* relationship. But in November 2002, he clearly expressed the viewpoint of the global governance project toward American sovereignty, saying, "I like very much the metaphor of Gulliver, of ensnarling the giant. Tying it up with nails, with thread, with 20,000 nets that bog it down: these nets being norms, principles, resolutions, agreements, and bilateral, regional, and international covenants."[9]

It is true that many Americans who aim to reduce U.S. government influence and military intervention abroad are pursuing their agenda entirely through the normal process of American democracy, without recourse to transnational political or legal authority. These citizens are acting as liberal democrats, not global governancers, because they are working within the constitutional process by which Americans regularly decide vital political questions for themselves. This is the essence of self-government.

The Anglosphere

During the past decade or so, scholars, commentators, and some practicing politicians across the English-speaking world have begun to speak about the "Anglosphere." The political, cultural, legal, historical, economic, social, and ideological affinities among the English-speaking peoples have been highlighted by the British historians Robert Conquest and Andrew Roberts, the Australian academic Keith Windschuttle, the Anglo-Canadian publisher Conrad Black, the American businessman James C. Bennett, the former Thatcher speechwriter and *National Review* editor John O'Sullivan, and Daniel Hannan, a member of the European Parliament, among others.

The Anglosphere today consists of the United States, Great Britain, Canada, Australia, New Zealand, Ireland, India, South Africa, and parts of the Caribbean, Oceania, Asia, and Africa with English-speaking societies and democratic governments based on common law. Proponents of the Anglosphere concept identify common characteristics that are "shaped by [the] values of the historical English-speaking civilization."[10] These characteristics include: a shared historical narrative (the Magna Carta, the English and the

American Bill of Rights); common law principles such as trial by jury, honoring contracts, "one's home is one's castle"; constitutional government; an independent judiciary; individual over collective identity; a strong civil society and institutions; and greater flexibility and openness to market economics, free trade, innovation, and entrepreneurship, particularly in contrast to more rigidly bureaucratic and statist attitudes in continental Europe and parts of Asia and Latin America.

Today's Anglosphere advocates see shared civic and cultural values, rather than race or ethnicity, as the basis of this "distinct branch of Western civilization."[11] It is not a "white man's club," as Daniel Hannan points out, but includes democratic Asian societies like India and Sri Lanka, and stable Caribbean nations.[12] Christopher Hitchens, a qualified sympathizer, suggests that despite some exaggerations, "properly circumscribed, the idea of an 'Anglosphere' can constitute something meaningful." Hitchens describes a visit to Oxford University in July 2005 by the Indian prime minister Manmohan Singh, who remarked that "many of India's splendors as a rising twenty-first century superpower—from railroads to democracy to a law-bound civil service—were the result of its connection with England. 'If there is one phenomenon on which the sun cannot set,' Singh observed, 'it is the world of the English-speaking peoples, in which the people of Indian origin are the single largest component.'"[13]

In terms of world politics, its adherents (mostly center-right intellectuals) see the Anglosphere as a counterweight to the EU and the forces of global governance, a bulwark against the growing threat of China, and a serious opponent of radical Islam. The Anglosphere is not viewed as supranational, but as a common cultural space with close intellectual, economic, strategic, and security connections. Supporters point to the substantial military and intelligence ties among the leading Anglosphere nations (United States, United Kingdom, Australia, Canada, and perhaps India in the future).[14]

Some of the most articulate democratic sovereigntists are self-identified supporters of the Anglosphere. At the same time, there is a sizable transnational progressive element in the Anglosphere—the BBC, the *Guardian,* universities and law schools, professionals in the British Foreign Office, and diplomats like Mark Malloch Brown, Lloyd Axworthy, Robert Cooper, and Strobe Talbott. If the conflict between democratic sovereignty and global governance is, at one level, an ideological civil war within the West, it is an even more intense intellectual-philosophical-ideological struggle within the Anglosphere.

Asian Nations

At this point, Asian democracies including India, Japan, South Korea, and Indonesia are for the most part on the sidelines in the conflict between democratic sovereignty and global governance. Their self-interest and national pride could potentially lead them to join the democratic sovereignty camp, or conversely they could believe that the forces of global governance best represent the "international community" and move in that direction. With a South Korean as UN secretary general, we might expect Korean elites to look more favorably upon the global governance project, at least in the near future. To date, under pressure from the global governancers to join the International Criminal Court, India has steadfastly refused, while Japan finally succumbed and ratified the ICC treaty. Meanwhile, Indonesia is developing closer security ties to the United States and acting like a democratic sovereigntist state.

As we will discuss in Chapter Fourteen, Asian nations in general represent a major roadblock to the ambitions of the global governancers. The dictatorships of China, Burma, Vietnam, and North Korea are obviously sovereigntist, although antithetical to democratic sovereignty. Other nations that are usually considered "partially free," such as Singapore, the Philippines, and Thailand, often line up with the United States on important sovereignty issues (such as rejection of the International Criminal Court and Additional Protocol I of the Geneva Conventions of 1977). These nations have a potential to develop into modern democratic sovereigntist states and should be courted by the United States and the forces of the liberal democratic nation-state.

The Democratic Sovereigntist Party

Besides the United States, the democratic sovereigntist bloc includes those democratic nation-states that are especially threatened by supranational forces and institutions, particularly Israel, and to some extent the relatively new democracies of central and eastern Europe—although the global governancers are gaining traction there, too. In addition, the democratic sovereigntist bloc includes "disaggregated" elements across Europe, in this case meaning those Europeans who are critical of the European Union's postdemocratic governance and want to restore democratic accountability.

In general, democratic sovereigntists aim to preserve liberal democracy in the particular nation-states of which they are citizens. Beyond this, the survival of the democratic American nation-state is connected to the perpetuation of liberal democracy throughout the world. This connection was forcefully stated by George Washington, who said that "the preservation of the sacred fire of liberty and the destiny of the republican model of government are justly considered, perhaps, as deeply, as finally, staked on the experiment entrusted to the hands of the American people."[15]

At the most idealistic level, the party of liberal democracy seeks a global order of cooperative independent democratic nation-states. From Franklin D. Roosevelt to Ronald Reagan and beyond, both liberal and conservative internationalists have articulated this vision. Liberal democrats are not Hobbesians; they believe the international system can be improved and that we are not doomed to a perpetual "war of all against all."[16] They support global institutions that are truly *inter*-national rather than *supra*-national; that are servants of democratic nation-states, not their masters.

In the liberal democratic vision, sovereignty is not "pooled" and thus subsumed by "higher" supranational authorities. Global problems, even major ones such as war and peace, do not empower supranational authority to trump independent governments that are based on the consent of the governed. In this respect, liberal democrats are Lockeans rather than Kantians. Kenneth Anderson, a professor of international law, has argued convincingly that sovereignty is the necessary precondition of democracy. While sovereignty for its own sake is not always admirable, it is sovereignty that makes democracy and political liberty possible. The sovereign nation-state, and no other modern association, provides the home in which democratic self-government and constitutional liberty are able to exist.

If the center of gravity (in the Clausewitzian sense) of liberal democracy is the sovereignty of the American nation-state, the party of global governance finds its center of gravity in the claim to global moral legitimacy. Supported by influential elements among the world's elites, global governancers often presume to speak for the planet in order to solve global problems. But a lack of democratic accountability undermines their moral claim to global leadership and weakens their center of gravity. This lack of accountability is the Achilles' heel of the transnationalists, and thus the issue that democratic sovereigntists should use against their globalist foes, or as Clausewitz would put it, "the point against which all our energies should be directed."[17]

This book was written during the Obama presidency, but the tension between liberal democracy and global governance will persist and likely increase long after Barack Obama has left the White House. In future Democratic administrations, liberal internationalists or national progressives, who see global institutions as useful to the extent they serve American national interests, will argue with transnational progressives, who support supranationalism for its own sake and hope to build real global authority. In future Republican administrations, there will likely be internal conflicts between democratic sovereigntists and transnational pragmatists, who would probably be represented by corporate interests willing to cede democratic sovereignty for short-term material benefits.

Global Governance and the Center-Right

The challenge that global governance presents to liberal democracy is beginning to be recognized and internalized by some on the American intellectual and political center-right.* On the other hand, there is a long way to go. Francis Fukuyama and Robert Kagan, both influential thinkers who have long been associated with vigorous support for liberal democracy, appear to have moved toward welcoming more supranational governance and less democratic sovereignty.

When Fukuyama turned away from his hawkish foreign policy positions, he also began to rethink the tenets of liberal democracy and constitutional sovereignty. In 2006, he wrote in *America at the Crossroads* that as a "realistic Wilsonian" he did not want "to replace national sovereignty with unaccountable international organizations." But he worried that "we do not now have an adequate set of horizontal mechanisms of accountability between the vertical stovepipes we label states."[18] Fukuyama asserts that "horizontal accountability" between nation-states is necessary because few nations "trust the United States" to be "sufficiently benevolent" without "the subjection of American power to more formal constraints."[19] In practice, horizontal accountability would have to mean transnational or supranational institutions or rules that would "subject" the United States and other democratic states to "formal constraints."

---

*For example, on March 8, 2011, Senator Jon Kyl (R-AZ) gave a speech to foreign policy experts at the Center for the National Interest (formerly the Nixon Center) in Washington, D.C., analyzing strategic challenges to American national sovereignty from forces at home and abroad. Transcript at http://www.cftni.org/kyl_speech.pdf.

In a key section of the book, Fukuyama writes: "Although international cooperation will have to be based on sovereign states in the foreseeable future, shared ideas of legitimacy and human rights *will weaken objections that the United States should not be accountable to regimes that are not themselves accountable.*" (Emphasis added.)[20] Fukuyama then addresses the question of why Americans would want to be accountable to regimes that are unaccountable. The reason, he suggests, is that Americans believe in "checks and balances," and that if "unchecked power is corrupting in a domestic context," the same holds true in foreign relations.[21]

Of course, for Americans to be accountable to an unaccountable regime—that is, to a regime outside of the American Constitution and not democratically accountable to the American people—is anathema to the American understanding of constitutional democracy and government by the consent of the governed. Nor is Fukuyama's analogy to domestic "checks and balances" persuasive.

The American system of checks and balances restrains government officials in both domestic and foreign policy within our constitutional order. But Fukuyama implies that decision making by American officials accountable to the American people, on vital questions of national security, should be subjected to a jurisdiction outside of our Constitution and democracy. It would be one thing to say that the United States, as a matter of prudence and policy, should consult and attempt to persuade allies before embarking on serious foreign policy ventures; it is quite another to recommend, as Fukuyama appears to do in *America at the Crossroads*, an extraconstitutional transnationalism that is not compatible with democratic decision making.

Robert Kagan is best known as a foreign policy hawk who encapsulated basic differences between American and European worldviews with his observation that "Americans are from Mars and Europeans are from Venus."[22] Alternatively, like Strobe Talbott, he describes the contrast in terms of a Hobbesian America and a Kantian Europe. By this he means: America is a modern sovereign state that is involved in power politics and willing to use force, while Europeans live in a postmodern world of peace and shared sovereignty, mostly eschewing "hard" military power in favor of "soft" power that comes with political and economic integration, transnational institutions, and postnational law.[23] Kagan, like Fukuyama, is not troubled by a weakening of American sovereignty. In 2008, when he was an advisor to John McCain's presidential campaign, he wrote an article in *Foreign Affairs* declaring that the United States has "little to fear" from increasing transnational and supranational authority and "should not oppose but welcome a world of pooled and diminished national sovereignty."[24]

Both Fukuyama and Kagan could be characterized as "hard" Wilsonians who conceptualize world politics in a broad bipolar fashion. On the one hand, there is the modern, democratic, and developed world; and on the other, there is the part of the world that has not yet achieved full modernity, democracy, and development. Having spent some time among European elites, Fukuyama and particularly Kagan apparently believe that the United States should concede some sovereignty issues to the Europeans, presumably in order to gain their support on other matters. The problem with this approach is that many of these sovereignty issues—for example, whether the United States should join with the Europeans and adhere to the International Criminal Court—are not simply "policy issues" of cost-benefit analysis, but "regime issues" that pertain to the core principles of liberal democracy and the American constitutional system.

Given their overall records, Fukuyama and Kagan should not be placed in the global governance camp, but neither are they democratic sovereigntists. Instead, they represent an interesting category on the cusp of the sovereignty-supranationalist divide: transnational pragmatic hawks who often combine advocacy of global law with the use of military force to uphold transnational institutions. No doubt the figure of the transnational pragmatist hawk will appear in future American presidential administrations in both political parties.★

Another major establishment figure associated with Republican administrations who has looked favorably on aspects of global governance is Richard Haass, a foreign policy realist who is president of the Council on Foreign Relations. Haass was a special assistant to President George H. W. Bush. During the administration of George W. Bush, he served as director of policy planning at the State Department and was a special advisor to Secretary of State Colin Powell. Haass asserts that it is time to "rethink" sovereignty, arguing that globalization "implies that sovereignty is not only becoming weaker in reality, but that it needs to become weaker. States would be wise to weaken sovereignty in order to protect themselves, because they cannot insulate themselves from what goes on elsewhere."[25]

Stewart Patrick, also from the Council on Foreign Relations, considers Haass to be correct in his belief that "seizing the 'opportunity' of global integration will require accepting 'a little less sovereignty.'" But he suggests that the question of "how much less" will become a matter of considerable controversy. Patrick rightly predicts that "the debate over American sovereignty will be one of the most contentious in U.S. foreign policy in the coming decades."[26]

The following chapters will examine five specific "fronts" in the epic global ideological and institutional "struggle for a new world" between the forces of global governance and the liberal democratic nation-state. These "fronts" include: initiatives by the global

---

★Analysts like Thomas P. M. Barnett (*The Pentagon's New Map; Blueprint for Action;* and *Great Powers: America and the World After Bush*) and Philip Bobbitt (*The Shield of Achilles* and *Terror and Consent*) might be placed in the transnational pragmatist hawk camp.

governance coalition to influence and alter domestic policy in the United States through the implementation of UN treaties or conventions; attempts to transform the laws of war by waging "lawfare" against the United States around the planet; the actions of the International Criminal Court in the "struggle for a new world"; the targeting of Israel by the global governance party; and finally, the advancement of multicultural and transnational allegiances at the expense of patriotic assimilation of immigrants into the democratic nation-state.

PART TWO

Struggle for a New World

CHAPTER NINE

Global Domestic Politics

T he term "global domestic politics" has been used by one of the leading political supporters of global governance, the former German foreign minister Joschka Fischer,[1] and by one of Europe's leading intellectuals, Jürgen Habermas.[2] In addition, the European Union official and global governance theorist Robert Cooper has said that in the coming global world, postmodern nation-states will actively intervene in the domestic affairs of democratic nation-states, including regulations for "beer and sausages."[3]

This chapter describes the global governance attack on domestic practices of the American democratic regime, with charges of "major human rights violations," during the Clinton administration in the 1990s. Then it examines a series of human rights and other international conventions (treaties) that the United States either has refused to ratify, or has ratified only with stringent reservations. These treaties can be—and already are being—employed to transform the arena of democratic politics and to assert global authority over the policies of liberal democratic nation-states.

The Global Governance Party Attacks
Bill Clinton's America

March 22, 1999, was the first day of the 55th session of the United Nations Commission on Human Rights. Every year, as the *New York Times* noted, Amnesty International "targets a half-dozen nations as the worst violators of human rights," and this year the organization "for the first time placed the United States on its list of human rights violators, in the company of Algeria, Cambodia and Turkey, among others." Amnesty International's secretary general, Pierre Sané, told the commission that "Human rights violations in the United States are persistent, widespread and appear to disproportionately affect people of racial or ethnic minority backgrounds."[4]

The U.S. ambassador to the commission, Nancy Rubin, objected to Amnesty's attack, but within days the offensive was joined by postmodern states when Joschka Fischer announced that the European Union "for the first time would submit an anti–death penalty resolution to the UN Human Rights Commission." American delegates were blindsided. Again, the United States was clearly targeted, as the EU resolution sought to prevent the extradition of criminals "to countries where the death penalty is in force." Then Norway, Finland, and Italy told the UN commission that capital punishment under any circumstances was an "inhuman form of punishment." Earlier in 1999, Germany had strenuously protested the execution of two German-born killers in Arizona, calling it "barbarism."[5]

The UN commission also heard from one of their own special rapporteurs, Radhika Coomaraswamy of Sri Lanka, who had returned from investigating violence against women in the United States. She reported that the United States was "criminalizing" a large segment of its population that is "overwhelmingly composed of poor persons of color and is increasingly female."[6]

The groundwork for the assault on U.S. policies by the forces of global governance was laid several years earlier. During the last year of the presidency of George H. W. Bush, in 1992, the United States joined the International Covenant on Civil and Political Rights (ICCPR). The treaty required the United States to submit a report to the UN Human Rights Commission during the first year on the status of civil and political rights in the country.

However, in 1993, before the new Clinton administration issued the report, two American NGOs—Human Rights Watch and the American Civil Liberties Union—published "Human Rights Violations in the United States: A Report on U.S. Compliance with the International Covenant on Civil and Political Rights."[7] The HRW-ACLU report was a scathing 180-page document that charged: "in the areas of racial and gender discrimination, prison conditions, immigrants rights, language discrimination, the death penalty, police brutality, freedom of expression and religious freedom ... the United States is now violating the treaty in important respects."[8] The report had two purposes: first, to assist UN investigators in identifying where the United States was, in their view, not in "compliance" with the ICCPR treaty; and second, to influence the Clinton administration, which the NGOs insisted had "an immediate legal obligation" to "remedy these human rights violations at home through the specific steps we outline." What were these human rights violations cited in the HRW-ACLU report?

Police Brutality. The report attacked American police officers in general for "persistent use of excessive force ... exacerbated by racism."[9]

Women's Rights. The report charged that "women in the US face systemic and entrenched discrimination"[10] and that "equal employment opportunities ... remain illusory for most women."[11] The report noted that 90 percent of telephone operators were women, but 99 percent of all auto mechanics and carpenters were men.[12] It complained that school curricula were "biased against women," that "textbooks include little material on women," and that "the lists of most frequently required books and authors are dominated by white males."[13]

Capital Punishment. The report strongly objected to the American reservation to the ICCPR treaty stating that capital punishment could be used in the United States "to the extent permitted under the U.S. Constitution." It called this reservation a "violation" of the treaty.[14] The HRW-ACLU report also charged that "in recent years, the United States Supreme Court has acted to limit the right to appeal ... at the federal level ... thereby eroding a fundamental safeguard in ensuring a fair trial."[15]

Immigrants and Refugees. The report criticized the U.S. Supreme Court's actions in "limiting access to federal habeas corpus" for those attempting to enter the United States illegally. It declared that "[t]he interdiction and summary repatriation of Haitian boat people is a flagrant violation of Article 12 [of the treaty] which states that '[e]veryone shall be free to leave any country, including his own.'"[16] The HRW-ACLU report also charged that human rights violations such as "beatings, rough physical treatment, and racist verbal abuse" were "common" among U.S. Border Patrol agents.[17]

Language Rights. The report objected to the U.S. "declaration" to the ICCPR treaty stating that "The United States understands distinctions based upon ... language ... to be permitted when such distinctions are, at minimum, rationally related to a legitimate government objective."[18] The ACLU and Human Rights Watch insisted on the "right" of language minorities to use foreign languages in all aspects of American life: government, voting, health, business, and education; and demanded publicly funded translators to achieve full "language rights."[19]

Racial Discrimination. The report spent about twenty pages attacking an array of U.S. Supreme Court decisions from the 1970s through the 1990s that are characterized as a "retreat" from the landmark civil rights case *Brown v. Board of Education* (1954).[20] The Court was accused of "turning its back on the commitment it made in *Brown* to ensure an equal educational opportunity to all"[21] and specifically of undermining affirmative action.[22]

Freedom of Expression. The report charged that military "restrictions on press coverage of the 1991 Gulf War . . . violated Article 19" of the ICCPR treaty.[23] The ACLU and HRW also decried an act of Congress granting power to the Justice Department to exclude from the United States any foreigners who provide financial support to terrorist organizations.[24] In addition, the report objected to deportation proceedings against "seven Palestinians and one Kenyan residing in Los Angeles." The government, it said, "alleges merely that they raised funds for a constituent group of the Palestine Liberation Organization, which the government deems a terrorist organization."[25]

Church and State. The HRW-ACLU report strenuously objected to the U.S. Supreme Court decision in *Zobrest v. Catalina Foothills School District* (1993). The Court decided that under the Educational Disabilities Act, the school district could provide a state-employed sign language interpreter to assist a hearing-impaired child at a Catholic school without violating the constitutional prohibition on the "establishment" of religion. The report stated that the Supreme Court's decision in *Zobrest* "results in the coerced taxation of citizens for the promotion of religious doctrine, a consequence anathema to any theory of religious liberty."[26]

Policy Preferences as Universal "Human Rights"

The HRW-ACLU report on "Human Rights Violations in the United States" did highlight some actual government abuses in prisons and elsewhere in America in 1993, but it was full of exaggeration and strident rhetoric. The implicit assumptions of the writers appear to have been drawn from critical theory and the diversity agenda, with their demands for statistical equality and claims that American life is riddled with "systemic inequality." Which logically means that the American democratic "system" itself is illegitimate. How else to explain the report's complaints that schoolchildren were reading more books written by men than by women, or that 99 percent of all auto mechanics were men? Do these constitute violations of human rights that an international treaty must rectify, or do they result from millions of uncoerced individual choices in a free society? Why are over twenty pages of the report devoted to Supreme Court decisions that displeased the NGOs? Did these Supreme Court decisions amount to violations of global human rights?

The section of the report on immigration argues that under the International Covenant on Civil and Political Rights, everyone is free to leave "any country, including his own." This is a principle that most Americans would agree with. However, the HRW-ACLU report implies that everyone has a right to enter any country, with or without the consent of that country's citizens. The host country is not permitted by the treaty to "interdict" or send back the unwanted migrants. Thus, the HRW-ACLU report is at odds with the democratic principle of government by the consent of the governed.

In the final analysis, what the report advocates are not universally recognized "human rights," but essentially the policy preferences of the American Civil Liberties Union and Human Rights Watch. The issues examined in the report (education, law, language, immigration) are all matters of policy that citizens in a free society can decide for themselves through the normal process of liberal democracy and their own constitutional order—rather than "human rights" issues to be decided by judges on the basis of transnational norms.

Most significantly, the ACLU and Human Rights Watch argue that the International Covenant on Civil and Political Rights should be "self-executing" and directly applied by American judges as American law. They contend that the "rights" embodied in the treaty "extend freedoms beyond the protections" of the U.S. Constitution, and that the ICCPR should trump American law in those cases where the treaty grants more "rights" than does existing American constitutional law. They also call for "repealing the restrictive reservations, declarations and understandings" that the United

States has attached to the treaty's ratification (which basically say that nothing in the treaty subordinates the U.S. Constitution or American law).[27]

We saw in Chapter Six how transnational European treaty law was "self-executing" and interpreted by national judges as superior to their own national constitutions. This strategy of expanding global legalism through treaty interpretation—and thus privileging transnational law above U.S. constitutional law—is clearly being advocated by the ACLU and Human Rights Watch in their 1993 report.

UN Special Rapporteurs Investigate the United States

The UN Commission on Human Rights (UNCHR) appoints special rapporteurs to assess allegations of human rights violations and report back to the commission with recommendations. Maurice Glélé-Ahanhanzo of Benin, the UNCHR's "special rapporteur on contemporary forms of racism, racial discrimination, xenophobia and related intolerance," was assigned to report on the racial situation in the United States. In June 1994, Glélé requested permission to visit. The Clinton administration responded "promptly and positively" and "offered to 'provide the Special Rapporteur with all the assistance he wanted.' "[28]

Glélé visited the United States from October 9 to 22, 1994.[29] He met with Clinton administration officials, but more importantly he met with NGO activists who provided him with extensive material alleging U.S. "violations" of human rights, including the HRW-ACLU report. These NGOs included, among others, the ACLU, Amnesty International, the World Council of Churches, the Arab-American Anti-Discrimination Committee, the Anti-Defamation League, the African American Human Rights Foundation, the United Methodist Church, the Center for Constitutional Rights, and the Mexican American Legal Defense and Educational Fund. Glélé also met with the Mexican ambassador to the UN and the Mexican consul general in Los Angeles.[30]

Glélé's report depicted the American political and social system as an utter failure with respect to race, saying: "The fate of the majority of Blacks is one of poverty, sickness, illiteracy, drugs and crime in response to the social cul-de-sac in which they find themselves. Even within the African American middle class, resentment is growing and doubt prevails about the possibility of a much better social status beyond a certain limit and the possibility of integration."[31] The report also alleged a "persistence" of "structural and insidious racism and racial discrimination against African Americans, Latin Americans, Asians, Indian Americans (Amerindians), Arabs and Jews in the economic and social spheres." It claimed to find "police brutality symbolized by the notorious Rodney King case," and a growing level of "incitement to racial hatred."[32] Parroting Mexican government officials and the HRW-ACLU paper, the UN report repeated claims that the U.S. Immigration and Naturalization Service and the U.S. Border Patrol "encouraged shootings." According to the UN report, "The U.S. Government has authorized a de facto 'iron fist' policy along the U.S.-Mexico border, authorizing U.S. Border Patrol agents to use deadly force by firing upon Mexican nationals who sometimes throw stones at U.S. agents."[33] Suffice to say, there is no serious evidence that the U.S. Border Patrol under the Reagan, George H. W. Bush, or Clinton administrations "encouraged shootings" or authorized an "iron fist" policy.

In addition, Glélé pontificated about American internal politics during the 1980s, stating: "The economic and social policy conducted by the Republican Administration under President Reagan and President Bush in the 1980s helped to accentuate the imbalances in the distribution of wealth, for the benefit of the rich, while a broad sector of the population, consisting in particular of persons from ethnic minorities, was impoverished and marginalized."[34] The UN special rapporteur also complained about America's single-member districts for the House of Representatives, claiming that the system "makes it difficult for people of colour to elect representatives. . . . In short, although people of colour in the United States generally have the right to vote, they do not have the equally fundamental right to representation."[35]

The report complained about the absence of "legislation to prohibit incitement to racial hatred . . . because of the sacrosanct nature of the First Amendment."[36] Glélé's recommendations for the United States included banning "racist propaganda" and prohibiting "the establishment of racist organizations," along with "revitalizing" affirmative action programs and increasing funds for public schools. The report asserted that "Everyone must be persuaded to accept the existence of the indissoluble link between civil and political rights and the economic, social and cultural rights which are their natural corollary."[37]

The UN General Assembly's Social, Humanitarian and Cultural Committee endorsed Glélé's report and expressed "full support for the work of the Special Rapporteur."[38]

The Clinton administration denounced the UN report as "an incomplete and biased analysis which does an injustice to the United States" and paints "a distorted and misleading picture." The administration responded with an issue-by-issue rebuttal of the falsehoods and errors in the report, and an attack on its statistics and methodology. The reason for the distortions, the administration suggested, was the special rapporteur's "willingness to accept every criticism" of U.S. policy "at face value."[39]

Another UN special rapporteur, Bacre Waly Ndiaye of Benin, formally asked the U.S. government in 1994 for an invitation to visit and investigate capital punishment. After his repeated requests were ignored, Ndiaye finally received permission, and visited the United States from September 21 to October 8, 1997.[40] Like Glélé, he met with American NGOs including the National Coalition to Abolish the Death Penalty, Human Rights Watch, Parents Against Police Brutality, the International Human Rights Law Group,[41] the NAACP Legal Defense Fund, American Friends Service Committee, Amnesty International, and the American Civil Liberties Union.[42]

Ndiaye's report was another savage attack on U.S. practices, cribbed for the most part from conversations with and reports from the American NGOs listed above. It vociferously objected to U.S. "reservations, understandings, and declarations" to international treaties, in which the American government spelled out the constitutional limits to their global obligations.[43] During his brief stay, Ndiaye also intervened in the death penalty case of Mumia Abu-Jamal, the Philadelphia Black Panther convicted of murdering a policeman, whose case has became an international cause célèbre.[44]

The 1990s offered a preview of the emerging struggle between the growing global governance coalition and the liberal democratic nation-state. Let us now examine how the forces of global governance are attempting to use international conventions (treaties) to expand global authority at the expensive of the liberal democratic nation-state, and specifically the American democratic regime.

Using UN Treaties to Limit Democratic Sovereignty

UN Convention on Discrimination against Women

In 1980, President Jimmy Carter signed the UN Convention on the Elimination of All Forms of Discrimination against Women (CEDAW), but it has been difficult ever since to obtain the necessary sixty-seven votes in the Senate for ratification. At a hearing of the Senate Foreign Relations Committee in 2002, Senator Joseph Biden, chairman of the committee, declared that CEDAW "can be viewed as an international bill of rights" for women, setting "basic standards." According to Biden, "Ratification of the treaty would not impose a single new requirement in our laws," because our laws already comply with the "treaty requirements."[45] Representative Lynn Woolsey (D-CA) called CEDAW "a powerful tool" to promote equal rights for women worldwide.[46]

CEDAW has been adopted by almost 170 countries, including every industrialized democracy except the United States. Representatives Carolyn Maloney (D-NY) and Connie Morella (R-MD) said that the American refusal to ratify the treaty was "embarrassing."[47] Professor Harold Koh called it a "national disgrace," arguing that "Particularly after September 11, America cannot be a world leader in guaranteeing progress for women's human rights, whether in Afghanistan, here in the United States, or around the world, unless it is also a party to the global women's treaty." By not ratifying CEDAW, said Koh, "the United States chooses to keep company with such countries as Afghanistan [under the Taliban], Iran, Sudan, and Syria."[48]

Elected officials like Biden suggested that the United States was essentially already in compliance and that the treaty would therefore "impose a minimal burden," requiring no "new laws," although Biden noted that "reservations" would be needed where the treaty was "inconsistent with our Constitution or current federal law."[49] Thus, CEDAW's effect would essentially fall on others. By contrast, the lawyers and activists supporting CEDAW emphasized that the treaty was an instrument to use domestically in the United States. Human Rights Watch pictured CEDAW as "an important tool for improving the protection of women's rights at home."[50] Professor Koh testified that U.S. ratification "would have a major impact in ensuring both the appearance and the reality that our national practices fully satisfy or exceed international standards."[51] The implication of Koh's testimony was that the "reality" of current U.S. "national practices" in women's rights did not "fully satisfy international standards."[52]

Nation-states that have joined a UN convention such as CEDAW submit periodic reports on their compliance with the treaty to a monitoring committee (or "treaty body"), which gathers information from NGOs within the country, questions the state's representatives, and then issues reports and recommendations. In 2008, the monitoring committee for CEDAW told British representatives that it was "concerned that women continue to be seriously underrepresented in political and public life, especially in leadership and decision-making positions," and noted that "women's representation currently stands at 19.3 per cent in the House of Commons." As a remedy, "The Committee calls upon the State party to take measures, with benchmarks and concrete timetables, to increase the number of women in political and public life, at all levels and in all areas .... It also recommends that the State party introduce temporary special measures [gender preferences or quotas], in accordance with article 4, paragraph 1, of the Convention."[53]

In the same report, the CEDAW Committee spelled out its "Principle of Equality":

264. The Committee welcomes the introduction [by the UK] of a Gender Equality Duty in April 2007 ... by which all public authorities are required to draw up and publish gender equality schemes (with identified objectives and steps to implement them), as well as to conduct gender impact assessments of all new policies and laws, including on employment and service delivery.... [The Committee] notes with concern, however, that varying levels of public understanding of the concept of substantive equality have resulted only in the promotion of equality of opportunity and of same treatment, as well as of gender-neutrality, in the interpretation and implementation of the Gender Equality Duty....

265. The Committee encourages the State party to develop and implement awareness-raising and education campaigns, in particular in the public sector and across all branches of Government, to broaden understanding of the provisions of the Convention, and of the content and meaning of substantive equality that goes beyond equality of opportunity and same treatment.... The Gender Equality Duty should aim to ensure the practical realization of the principle of equality between

women and men as required under article 2 of the Convention, and not solely towards the achievement of equality of opportunity. The Committee also recommends the development of appropriate mechanisms and capacity to monitor implementation, evaluate results achieved and ensure accountability.[54]

The CEDAW Committee investigating the UK also expressed "concern that although temporary special measures are provided for in some legislation, they are not systematically employed as a method of accelerating the achievement of de facto or substantive equality between women and men in all areas of the Convention."[55]

The ideological orientation of the CEDAW Committee is clear: support for equality of results on a group basis, not just equality of opportunity for individuals regardless of gender, or de jure (legal) equality. In report after report, the CEDAW Committee (and other UN monitoring committees) calls for "substantive equality," "de facto equality," or equality of condition on a gender, race, or ethnic group basis.

The CEDAW Committee admonished Denmark in 1997 because it "had yet to reach gender parity in the political sphere," although the level of women's participation in politics was at a "higher level than in other countries."[56] Belgium implemented gender quotas for electoral politics, but in 2002 the committee remained unsatisfied. "While recognizing the impressive gains achieved," the committee remarked, "the quotas have not necessarily led to the expected results."[57]

In 2007, the committee questioned Singapore's adherence to the "principle of gender-neutral meritocracy." Despite some progress since its last report, the committee noted that "the proportion of women parliamentarians is still low," and that "women continue to be underrepresented at senior levels within the public administration, including the diplomatic service, the judiciary and educational institutions, as well as the private sector, thus limiting women's equal participation in decision-making processes in all areas." The committee recommended that Singapore adopt "temporary special measures," meaning gender quotas.[58]

In 2008, the committee welcomed France's political parity act, which established quotas requiring that women constitute 50 percent of each party's candidates for local elections, but it was still concerned about an "underrepresentation of women in high-level positions in public sectors ... in academia, and in the private and business sectors."[59] The committee also called on the French to "ensure de-facto equality" in the economic sphere, "eliminat[ing] occupational segregation" and "curbing wage gaps" by instituting "financial sanctions" against companies "that do not have a plan to redress wage inequalities."[60]

As we discussed in Chapter Four, the concept of "substantive equality" for ethnic, racial, and gender groups violates a central principle of liberalism. Traditionally, the liberal believes in equality of individual opportunity in employment, education, the electoral process, and the like, based as much as possible on merit. The liberal—unlike the aristocrat, the Marxist, or the fascist—rejects the idea that people should be chosen for positions on the basis of an ascribed group that they were born into. The notion that democratic parliaments should be officially apportioned on a gender, race, and ethnic basis is antiliberal to the core. It is more akin to the aristocratic system of the Estates-General in eighteenth-century France; the "corporatist" parliaments of twentieth-century fascist regimes, divided into occupational and other fixed groups; and the legislatures of twentieth-century communist regimes, which often maintained quotas for racial, ethnic, linguistic, and gender groups.* The notion that all institutions and organizations of government, civil society, the market, and private life should show proportional equality among

---

*Suzanne Lafont complains that "The post-communist governments have replaced the quota system with democratic elections. Not surprisingly, the number of women as elected and appointed officials has decreased." See "One Step Forward, Two Steps Back: Women in the Post-Communist States," *Communist and Post-Communist Studies* 34 (2001), p. 208.

gender, racial, and ethnic groups—as repeatedly demanded by UN treaty bodies—is incompatible with the workings of a free society.

The UN Convention on the Rights of the Child

American proponents of a global human rights regime often cite the U.S. "failure" to ratify the UN Convention on the Rights of the Child (CRC) as particularly egregious. Pointing out gleefully that only the United States and Somalia have refused to join the convention, they taunt: does the U.S. want to stand alone with Somalia? But the UN committee monitoring the CRC displays the same bureaucratic intrusiveness and disregard for democratic sovereignty that characterize the committees monitoring CEDAW and other UN human rights treaties.

One might assume that Great Britain under New Labour in 2002 was pretty much in compliance with a treaty protecting the universal rights of children. Well, not exactly, if we look closely at the monitoring committee's report. To be sure, the committee said it "welcomes the abolition of corporal punishment in all schools in England, Wales and Scotland following its 1995 recommendations." Nevertheless, the committee said it "deeply regrets" that the British retain the principle of "reasonable chastisement" and have "taken no significant action towards prohibiting all corporal punishment of children in the family." They should "with urgency adopt legislation . . . to remove the 'reasonable chastisement' defence and prohibit all corporal punishment in the family."[61]

The committee poked its nose into government budget priorities and told the British to "undertake an analysis of all sectoral and total budgets" across the country "in order to show the proportion spent on children," and then create a "permanent body with an adequate mandate and sufficient resources" to implement the Children's Convention through the entire United Kingdom. The committee was particularly concerned that the "devolution of powers" to governments in Scotland, Wales, and England made it "difficult

to achieve a comprehensive and coherent child rights policy." Therefore, a new "central mechanism" was needed.[62]

With its interest in substantive equality, the monitoring committee
reprimanded Britain for "the sharp differences in educational outcomes
for children according to their socio-economic background and to
other factors such as gender, disability, ethnic origin or care status."[63]
It also was "concerned" about Britain's "wide-ranging reservation on
immigration and citizenship, which is against the object and purpose
of the Convention." The committee demanded that the UK "incorporate into domestic law" all provisions of the treaty "in order to
ensure that all legislation complies with the Convention."[64]

It is reasonable to assume that U.S. adherence to the UN Convention on the Rights of the Child would bring up many controversies concerning federalism, parental rights, juvenile justice,
privacy, and substantive equality, while expanding the scope of
transnational politics and the power of the globalists.

UN Monitoring Committees Intrude into Democracy

The intrusiveness of the UN treaty bodies into the political process
of democratic states appears to be boundless. For example, Israel
was told in 1997 to create programs for "gender sensitization of
the judiciary, police and health professionals."[65] Also in 1997, the
CEDAW Committee warned Australia's democratic representatives
about "disproportionate budget cuts" in programs affecting women.
The committee was displeased that Australia maintained reservations
to the treaty concerning women in military combat units, and failed
to guarantee paid maternity leave.[66] By 2006, the committee
applauded Australia's enactment of paid maternity leave for federal
government workers, but complained that "there is no national system of paid maternity leave" that would direct the states and territories or the private sector to follow suit.[67]

In 2004, the monitoring committee noted that the German parliament had "deliberately refrained from complying with the Committee's proposal to introduce non-transferable child-raising leave for fathers." The committee demanded to know if the German government had "undertaken a study on why fathers are so reluctant to take parental leave," and asked, "What measures, if any, is the Government envisaging to counteract such realities?"[68]

In 1999, Ireland was told to " 'genderproof' its budget" and to "allocate funds according to [the] needs" of women. The Irish were scolded because "the Irish Constitution did not include all the provisions of the Convention," and were told it was "important that Irish law include all the international human rights instruments" (CEDAW, CERD, ICCPR, and CRC).[69]

The UN committee monitoring CERD (the race convention) told the United States in 2001 to drop its reservation on First Amendment grounds and outlaw hate speech as defined by the committee.[70] The UN committee monitoring the International Covenant on Civil and Political Rights (ICCPR) complained to Australia in 2000 about its detention of illegal immigrants ("unlawful non-citizens"), and chastised the United States for an "increased level of militarization on the southwest border with Mexico." The committee said that U.S. immigration law "should be compatible with the rights guaranteed by the Covenant" and that all U.S. Border Patrol agents should be trained in these issues.[71] Also troubling to the committee was American federalism itself, where "the states of the union retain extensive jurisdiction over . . . criminal and family law," which "may lead to a somewhat unsatisfactory application of the Covenant throughout the country."[72]

And so it goes. The global governancers promote massive governmental intrusions into civil society, commercial enterprise, and private life, all in the name of "substantive equality" among ethnic, racial, and gender groups. At the same time, they insist that numerous policy issues—involving budget priorities, immigration, women in combat, police training, educational curricula, parental leave, and so on—should be removed from the democratic process and placed in the zone of "universal human rights," untouched by popular consent.

A Conversation with a Member of the CEDAW Monitoring Committee

Members of the CEDAW Committee discussed potential issues of U.S. ratification of the treaty at a small Friday-afternoon meeting of the American Society for International Law in Washington, D.C., on July 10, 2010. At the reception after the formal presentations, I spoke with a member of the committee, Pramila Patten of Mauritius.

I mentioned the committee's report on Slovenia (1997) in which the CEDAW monitors complained that only 30 percent of Slovenia's children were in day care centers.[73] Apparently, too many children were being raised at home by their parents. I asked the UN representative why this was a problem in a free society. Ms. Patten replied that she remembered the Slovenian situation well. A new government was providing benefits to stay-at-home mothers, reinforcing old stereotypes and depriving children of the educational and social opportunities of the day care centers. Further, she noted, Slovenia's policies were unfortunately influencing western European countries.

I then asked Ms. Patten: since Slovenia's government was democratically elected on a platform that included providing funds to mothers at home (as many Christian Democrats in western Europe traditionally have done), wasn't this a case of the UN committee interfering in the give and take of democratic politics? Moreover, it was certainly possible that a future Slovenian government might change these policies and institute measures closer to the committee's preferences. That's democracy, isn't it?

Ms. Patten responded that Slovenia's policy on subsidies for mothers at home was discriminatory and hurt women because it reinforced stereotypical attitudes toward motherhood. She argued that CEDAW spelled out universal norms and values that took precedence over the concept of majority consent, as exercised through a democratically elected parliament.

We also discussed the issue of "comparable worth," a concept endorsed by the CEDAW Committee, which holds that work traditionally performed by women should be paid as work of "comparable value" to work traditionally performed by men—for example, telephone operators compared to construction workers. I pointed out to Ms. Patten that "comparable worth" is a controversial political issue within the United States, having both supporters and opponents in Congress. Opponents argue that pay rates should be set mainly by market forces, with collective bargaining part of the mix.

Patten replied that equal pay for work of equal value is required for equal rights, that this is a universal norm, and that neither the private sector nor the market should be permitted to discriminate against women. Patten further emphasized to me that the goal of CEDAW is substantive or de facto equality, not simply de jure equality. At the end of our conversation, the UN representative suggested that the United States could ratify the treaty with reservations and "we could work on this [i.e., on withdrawing the reservations] later."

Does the UN's Interference in Domestic Policy Matter?

It is argued that the CEDAW Committee and the other UN treaty bodies have no enforcement power and must rely on persuasion, and thus there is little reason to be concerned that they could alter the structure of decision making within democratic states. But this reasoning ignores the dynamics of contemporary transnational politics. In fact, the UN monitoring committees, working closely with their national political and NGO allies, have influenced democratic lawmaking. For example, the American Bar Association's website notes that twenty-two countries, after ratifying CEDAW, changed their employment laws related to gender. Germany, Poland, Portugal,

Spain, the United Kingdom, the Philippines, and Guatemala altered their own government subsidies for maternity leave and child care after joining CEDAW.

In 2003, the CEDAW Committee hailed Norway as a "haven for gender equality" in many areas of politics, law, and international relations, but was concerned about "inequalities in economic decision making" in the private sector.[74] In response, the Norwegian government—against the vocal opposition of business groups—established gender quotas for corporate boards. At least 40 percent of all board members are now required to be women. Subsequently, similar quota legislation for businesses was passed in Spain, the Netherlands, and France. The *New York Times* reported that Belgium, Britain, Germany, and Sweden were considering legislation along the same lines.[75] All this suggests that "recommendations" by UN treaty monitoring committees, although unenforceable, do influence decision making within democratic states.

During the last few decades, more than a hundred countries have adopted some form of gender quotas for women candidates to elected offices.[76] Most of the leading scholars on gender quotas credit transnational advocacy networks, including the UN CEDAW process, as central to the success of implementing gender quotas in nation-states.[77] "The recommendation by the UN women's conference in Beijing about affirmative action and quota systems and the continuous international report systems in the CEDAW Convention have proved significant," wrote two Swedish theorists of gender quotas, Drude Dahlerup and Lenita Freidenvall.[78] Almost all committee reports criticize the numerical underrepresentation of women in political and economic decision making in every country that has joined CEDAW. As a remedy, the committee invariably urges nation-states to enact gender quotas in all sectors of society, public and private.

How UN Treaty Monitoring Committees Harm Democracy

First, the committees that monitor UN treaties distort the democratic self-governing process at the procedural level. Typically, the committees work closely with local NGOs and exert pressure to foster political policies that they favor. In terms of democratic political theory, the UN monitoring committees are foreign political actors, existing outside the legally constituted democratic framework where laws are made and self-government is exercised. Although they are outside the country's democratic space and unaccountable to its citizens, they nevertheless ally themselves with certain factions against other factions in the same democracy. In other words, they take sides within a democratic system of which they are not part, in a type of asymmetric political warfare that is essentially postdemocratic.

Second, the UN monitoring committees actively seek to shrink the space of democratic decision making and limit the scope of democracy itself. In addition, they claim moral authority over a wide swath of civil society and private life. They attempt to remove one policy issue after another from the give and take of democratic politics and place them all in the realm of "universal human rights," outside of democratic accountability and consent.

The goal of many American NGOs, lawyers, foundations, academics, foreign policy specialists, policy wonks, and a few politicians is the incorporation of the United States into what legal scholars call the "global human rights regime." This is also the goal of the global governance forces at the UN, in the EU, and among transnational elites worldwide. If they succeed in subordinating the U.S. Constitution to international human rights law, they will have realized the vision of "global domestic politics" as articulated by Joschka Fischer, Robert Cooper, and the intellectual prophets of the European Union such as Jürgen Habermas.

Three steps are envisioned to bend American law to global (or transnational) human rights law. First, the United States would ratify the UN human rights conventions on women (CEDAW) and on the Rights of the Child. Second, the United States would withdraw its reservations, understandings, and declarations to the major human rights conventions that it has already ratified. These include the UN race convention (CERD) and the civil and political rights convention (ICCPR). It is expected that the United States would probably ratify CEDAW and the Rights of the Child with reservations at first, but constant badgering and "shaming" by the "international community" would result in these reservations being withdrawn.

Third, the final incorporation of global human rights law would occur either by declaring the treaties to be "self-executing" (the preferred method), or through enabling legislation that would fully incorporate all aspects of the UN human rights conventions into domestic law. At that point, the UN treaties would have a "direct effect" in American courts. Scores of lawsuits could be launched to incorporate the new global rules, which over time would begin to be enforced as "American law" by national judges. This scenario would be similar to how EU law became embedded in the courts of European nation-states.

In 2002, the American Bar Association, which strongly favors U.S. ratification of CEDAW, issued a book titled *The CEDAW Assessment Tool*, detailing the measures that nation-states must implement to be in compliance with the treaty. While the ABA report examines de jure equality for women, it emphasizes substantive equality, saying that "A major focus of the diagnostic tool will be on de facto or 'real life' impediments to equality."[79] The ABA uses the official "CEDAW Commentary and Guidelines" as its authoritative source on what the treaty means. For example, on the issue of "temporary special measures," the ABA report quotes the CEDAW guidelines as declaring that gender quotas are not simply voluntary, and that CEDAW creates "an obligation to implement temporary special measures policies." The ABA report, quoting CEDAW, describes these measures as "positive action, preferential treatment or a quota system." The report also calls on nation-states "to review all negative attitudes and actions associated with these [gender quota] concepts."[80] By this line of reasoning, if the United States were a state party to the CEDAW treaty, California's Proposition 209 of 1996, which outlawed gender and racial preferences, would certainly be considered "negative action" that needed looking into.

The ABA document spells out in heavy detail what implementation of the treaty would mean in practice, listing hundreds of questions to be used to judge de facto compliance with CEDAW. The answers to the questions could also be used to provide raw material for future lawsuits. Here are a few of the ABA's questions:

Does the government coordinate with the NGO community when drafting policy recommendations to the legislature or within government agencies? If so, what is the nature and quality of the coordination? Does the national machinery or the State track national budget expenditures for programs that promote the advancement of women? What are the results of this study (e.g., percentages of funds spent on social and family support programs, awareness campaigns, temporary special measures to promote women's advancement in all fields)?[81]

The ABA also wanted to know:

Is there a national mechanism to promote de facto equality of women? If so, does it promote the use of temporary special measures when developing policies, procedures and legislation within the government institutions? Can the Ombudsperson or other legal professionals initiate suits for the lack or violation of temporary special measures? ... If so, how many cases have been filed? What were the results? ... Are there quotas, targets or specific goals regarding compliance with CEDAW? If so, what are they? Are these quotas, targets or goals being met?[82]

They were interested in what governments were doing to influence family dynamics:

What measures has the State undertaken to ensure that family education includes the concept of shared responsibility of both parents in raising children? What measures has the State undertaken to encourage shared parental responsibilities?[83]

And the ABA wanted to know what was being done to increase women's participation in politics and civil society:

Has the State allocated funds to encourage female candidates to run for office? ... Do gender quotas exist for increasing the number of women elected or appointed to government bodies? If so, how have they been implemented? ... Do voting rates differ between women in urban and rural areas? If so, has the State introduced any special temporary measures to eliminate the gap? Are female political party members involved in drafting political platforms? Are female candidates guaranteed equal access to media outlets during their political campaigns as men? Do they receive equal media attention? ... Do public education campaigns conducted by the State emphasize the importance of a balanced representation of men and women in elected bodies? ... Has the State conducted studies on the involvement of women in civil society, including NGO participation? If so, what percentage of NGO membership are women? If so, what percentage of NGO leadership is [*sic*] women? ... What percentage of judges are women? What percentage of prosecutors are women?[84]

In 2008, the American Constitution Society published and widely disseminated a paper titled "Human Rights at Home: A Domestic Policy Blueprint for a New Administration."[85] Written by Catherine Powell of the Fordham University School of Law, the paper laid out a detailed plan on how a new administration could (and should) incorporate the global human rights regime into American domestic law. On the first page, Professor Powell thanked a "Blueprint Advisory Group" that included leading American law professors, lawyers, and NGO leaders, such as Harold Koh (Yale), Christopher Edley Jr. (Berkeley), Sarah Cleveland (Columbia), Ryan Goodman (Harvard), Elisa Massimino (Human Rights First), Thomas Malinowski (Human Rights Watch), Larry Cox (Amnesty International), Wade Henderson (Leadership Council on Civil Rights), and Gay McDougall (United Nations Human Rights Council). Later, Professor Powell herself joined the Office of Policy and Planning in the Obama administration's State Department, with responsibility for human rights, international organizations, and women's issues.

Powell's blueprint for "Human Rights at Home" calls for closing the "gap" between human rights ideals and American practice. As examples of violations of human rights in America, she cites "inequalities . . . in access to housing, education, jobs, and health care"; "racial and ethnic profiling . . . used unfairly to target African Americans, Latinos, and those who appear Arab, Muslim, South Asian, or immigrant"; and a "pay gap . . . between male and female workers."[86] Echoing the critical theorists of the Frankfurt School (see Chapter Four), Powell asserts that "discrimination today is deeply structural and institutional." In other words, the problem is in the American system itself.

The U.S. Constitution's equal protection clause "has been interpreted to prohibit only intentional (or purposeful) discrimination," Professor Powell laments. Thus, "U.S. domestic law does not adequately address measures that have a discriminatory impact in the absence of a showing of discriminatory intent." By contrast, she notes approvingly, the UN's race convention prohibits discrimination that may be outwardly neutral but has a racially discriminatory "effect," and thus it "reflects a broader conception of equality" than the U.S. Constitution.[87] Powell calls for the United States to ratify all the leading human rights treaties that it has not yet joined, such as the Convention on the Rights of the Child and CEDAW, and to withdraw all the "burdensome RUDs" (reservations, understandings, and declarations) it has attached to the treaties already ratified. These treaties, she argues, should either be made self-executing in

U.S. courts, or be accompanied by detailed enabling legislation that fully obligates American law to the UN human rights regime.[88]

This chapter has examined the quiet incursion of the major EU concept of "global domestic politics" into American political life. We have seen how "disaggregated" elements within democratic nation-states work together with transnational forces to change domestic policy. We will be witnessing much more of this transnationalism in domestic policy and politics in the coming decades. Meanwhile, in the realm of foreign and security policy, the global governance coalition is attempting to dictate the rules by which America and other democracies are permitted to defend themselves, as the next chapter details.

CHAPTER TEN

Who Decides the Rules of War?

S ince the beginning of the modern international system, nation-states have acknowledged and often adhered to the "law of war" in armed conflict. These rules and customs have been codified in The Hague Convention of 1907, the Geneva Protocol of 1925, the Geneva Convention of 1929, and particularly the four Geneva Conventions of 1949. The law of war, also known as the "law of armed conflict" (LOAC) or "international humanitarian law" (IHL), is generally divided into the "Hague rules," which limit the means of war such as weapons and targets, and the "Geneva rules," prescribing humanitarian consideration for the sick and wounded, prisoners of war, and civilians. The traditional law of war has, among other measures, outlawed poison gas and authorized the International Committee of the Red Cross to monitor conditions for prisoners of war who are lawful combatants (wearing uniforms or distinctive signs, carrying weapons openly, serving in a chain of command, etc.).[1]

Protocol I Radically Revises the Law of War

At the instigation of the International Committee of the Red Cross (ICRC), a conference was convened in Geneva in 1974, under the auspices of the Swiss government, to update the law of war. The result of the Diplomatic Conference of Geneva, with four sessions from 1974 to 1977, was a radical change to the Geneva Conventions with the adoption of Additional Protocol I. One of the world's leading experts on Protocol I, W. Hays Parks, describes it as "a conscious effort by the ICRC, Switzerland and Sweden—working through the Third World—to shift the responsibility for collateral civilian casualties from the defender to the attacker."[2] The goal of the African-Arab-Asian "nonaligned nations," or "Group of 77," was to support "wars of national liberation" in general, a goal in which they were aided by the Soviet bloc. The main objective of the Red Cross, the Swiss, and the Swedes was to expand global influence over the law of war. In addition, the Swedes and the Third World wanted to limit offensive airpower.[3]

In one sense, the modern law of war became the "postmodern laws of war" with the adoption of Protocol I. Unlike the Geneva Conventions of 1949, Protocol I recognizes irregular forces and terrorists as "lawful combatants." This includes, for example, the Palestine Liberation Organization of the 1970s, which attended the Diplomatic Conference of Geneva and received strong support from the Group of 77 and the Soviet bloc. Under Protocol I, irregulars and terrorists are permitted to hide among the civilian population with concealed weapons and not reveal themselves until right before an attack.[4] This "privileges" irregulars and terrorists, while disadvantaging their conventional military adversaries—often American, Israeli, British, Indian, or other democratic militaries. It also puts the innocent civilian population at further risk by blurring the distinction between combatants and civilians—a distinction that was traditionally one of the major purposes of international humanitarian law.

During the Diplomatic Conference of Geneva, delegates from the United States and other Western nations (including Britain, Australia, and France) argued logically and vigorously against the effort by Third World nations and the Soviet bloc to rewrite the law of war. In particular, they opposed the parts of Protocol I that legitimized irregular, guerrilla, and terrorist combatants. At the end of the day, as so often happens, the Americans and their allies found themselves outvoted. Should they vote no and reject the treaty? Or stay "engaged," go along, and attempt to influence the direction of the treaty?

This kind of dilemma occurs again and again in international negotiations. The U.S. State Department usually recommends signing the proposed treaty, adding reservations if necessary, and attempting to influence its interpretation and implementation. Foggy Bottom's argument is nearly always put in pragmatic terms: "we don't want to be isolated"; "we want a seat at the table when the rules are made"; "we will lose influence if we just say no and don't participate."

The "sign on and hope to influence later" position was the original State Department stance on Protocol I. At the end of the conference, the United States and most other Western countries accepted the final document in the spirit of "consensus," although the troubling sections remained in the text.* Israel voted no. The United States signed Protocol I, and it was presumed within the U.S. government and by American allies that the United States would eventually ratify the treaty with some reservations. But first it had to be reviewed by the Joint Chiefs of Staff of the Armed Forces.

Seven years passed, during which the Carter administration gave way to the Reagan administration. In 1984, Douglas J. Feith,

---

*We could think of Protocol I as having three parts. First, the United States legally recognizes the parts of Protocol I that are consistent with the 1949 Geneva Conventions, traditional laws of war, and customary international law. Second, the United States (as a matter of policy, not law) has incorporated elements of Protocol I into its military doctrine, practice, and rules of engagement. Third, the United States objects to many sections of Protocol I and does not recognize them as part of international humanitarian law (the laws of war).

the deputy assistant secretary of defense for negotiations policy, was at a meeting when visiting German officials asked their American counterparts if Protocol I was going to be ratified by the United States. Feith met with the Army, Navy, and Air Force lawyers for the Joint Chiefs and asked them to finish their review of Protocol I without any presumptions or prejudgments that the U.S. would or would not ratify it.[5] Feith, a lawyer, believed it subverted the traditional approach of the Geneva Conventions of 1949, which had emphasized the protection of civilians, whereas the provisions of Protocol I would put civilians in greater danger. Feith led the intellectual opposition within the administration,[6] and wrote that Protocol I, by abandoning the traditional emphasis on protecting civilians, "lays waste the legal and moral achievement of ages."[7]

The Joint Chiefs of Staff finished their review in 1985 and recommended to the secretary of defense, Caspar Weinberger, that the United States reject the treaty. W. Hays Parks examined the main arguments of the Joint Chiefs and the fundamental problems with Protocol I in a book-length analysis in the *Air Force Law Review*. Parks writes that the protocol "suffers from the intentional ambiguities of its language, which places combatants carrying out lawful combat operations at an increased risk from spurious allegations of violations of the law of war if captured."[8] Further, the International Committee of the Red Cross was "unqualified to draft provisions regarding the regulation of modern war," since its "knowledge of modern war - fighting was weak," and its draft rules failed to "stay abreast of technology" and the "revolutionary" changes in modern warfare.[9]

Most significantly, Parks declares: "Notwithstanding claims to the contrary, Protocol I was not intended to protect the innocent civilian so much as it was developed as a vehicle for providing maximum psychological advantage" to the defenders "in the arena of world opinion."[10] Indeed, Parks says that the Diplomatic Conference of Geneva in 1974–77 "produced nothing that might bring some hope of amelioration of the suffering of the victims" of war.[11] Whereas American domestic law "clearly values life over property," says Parks, "Article 48 of Protocol I places the protection of civilian property on the same level as the protection of civilian lives."[12] At the same time, the provisions in Articles 48, 52, 57, and 85 "establish an intent in Protocol I to give priority to the protection of inanimate civilian objects over the lives of combatants."[13]

In terms of traditional military strategy and tactics, Parks notes that the longstanding codification (since the Hague Convention of 1907) of the principle of surprise in war has been weakened by Protocol I, Article 51, paragraph 2(c), which states: "Effective advance warning shall be given of attacks which may affect the civilian population, unless circumstances do not permit."[14] In 1986 and 1987, Australia and the United States conducted joint war games designed "specifically to evaluate Protocol I." One of the sides in the war games adhered to Protocol I and the other did not. Parks reports that the exercise revealed that "any military commander or force adhering to the requirements of Protocol I would be defeated by an opponent not following them."[15]

Reviewing the history of the Vietnam War, Parks says, "There is no doubt that under customary international law, as evidenced by the practice of nations in the wars of this century, the dams, dikes, rail lines, and roads of North Vietnam were legitimate targets."[16] However, the United States made a policy (not legal) decision not to bomb dikes and dams that were being used by the North Vietnamese for military purposes. Parks comments that this "restraint exercised by the United States—at a cost of hundreds of American lives and aircraft, if not the war"—would likely be exploited by a future adversary if the United States adhered to Protocol I as a matter of international law.[17] Policy could be changed, but international law would lock American airmen into difficult and dangerous situations.

Upon receiving the Joint Chiefs' review document, Secretary Weinberger sent a memorandum to the secretary of state, George Shultz, on July 2, 1985, declaring that he "concurred" with the recommendation against ratification:

Protocol I's key operative provisions would radically change humanitarian law in favor of terrorists and other irregulars at the expense of civilians. The unacceptable elements of Protocol I are multifarious and fundamental in nature ... the Chiefs and I have concluded that Protocol I's flaws are not remediable through reservations and understandings. We therefore recommend that the United States declare its intention not to ratify Protocol I. The Swiss Government, as depository, should be informed formally.... We are confident that a clear exposition of our case against Protocol I will win substantial support on the Hill and with the public.[18]

Secretary Shultz agreed and sent a memorandum to President Reagan with copies to the secretary of defense and the attorney general on March 21, 1986, saying: "The Joint Chiefs and the Departments of State, Defense and Justice have completed their reviews.... We have concluded that Protocol I is unacceptable." Secretary Shultz noted that Protocol I represented a "comprehensive re-working of the humanitarian law of armed conflict" and was therefore of "considerable legal and political significance."[19]

On January 29, 1987, President Reagan sent a formal letter to the U.S. Senate expressing opposition to Protocol I and declaring that it would not be submitted for ratification. Reagan's letter formally denounced Protocol I as "fundamentally and irreconcilably flawed."[20]

The editorial boards of two major newspapers that often disagreed with Reagan's foreign policy, the *Washington Post* and the *New York Times,* heartily endorsed the administration's opposition to Protocol I. A *Times* editorial on February 17, which referred to the protocol as "a shield for terrorists," said that the president had faced "probably no tougher decisions than whether to seek ratification of revisions to the 1949 Geneva Conventions.... He decided to say no, a judgment that deserves support.... Mr. Reagan made the sound choice. He notified the Senate that he would not submit the revision or protocol because it was 'fundamentally and irreconcilably flawed.' "[21] A *Post* editorial the next day, "Hijacking the Geneva Conventions," said the Reagan administration "is right to formally abandon Protocol I. It is doing so, moreover, for the right reason: 'we must not, and need not, give recognition and protection to terrorist groups as a price for progress in humanitarian law.' "[22]

Yugoslavia and International Humanitarian Law

In 1999, the Clinton administration led the NATO alliance in a sustained bombing campaign of Yugoslavia to force a Serbian withdrawal from Kosovo and halt the suppression of the Albanian population in the province. (Americans flew about 80 percent of the missions.) For years, Amnesty International and Human Rights Watch had faulted Western nations for failing to stop the human rights abuses of the Milosevic regime in Kosovo, and at first appeared, to some degree at least, to welcome NATO's action. But when the war ended, the two human rights groups, as self-described "impartial observers," issued reports on "violations" of the "laws of war," or in their preferred term, "international humanitarian law," by both sides in the conflict.

Amnesty International's report, "Collateral Damage or Unlawful Killing? Violations of the Laws of War by NATO during Operation Allied Force," charged that "NATO forces did commit serious violations of the laws of war leading in a number of cases to the unlawful killing of civilians."[23] One completely American operation, the bombing of the Serbian state radio and television building, was deemed to have "breached article 52 (1) of Protocol I and therefore constitutes a war crime."[24] Indeed, the baseline for what Amnesty International called "violations" of international humanitarian law turned out to be sections of Additional Protocol I that the United States had rejected. At the time of the war over Kosovo, France and Turkey, both NATO members, had also not accepted Protocol I.

Page after page of the Amnesty report refers to "violations" of Protocol I, with almost no mention of the Geneva Conventions of 1949. Amnesty International asserted that provisions of Protocol I cited in its report "are considered part of customary international law and are therefore binding on all states."[25]

That is not the view of the United States, nor of the other nations that have rejected Protocol I, including Israel, India, Indonesia, Turkey, Pakistan, Philippines, Thailand, Malaysia, Sri Lanka, and Singapore, among others. Furthermore, customary international law is based on two factors: first, on the longstanding actual practice of states, and second, on *opinio juris,* the belief by those states that they are adhering to those practices because they believe that they are obligated to do so under international law. If many major states that are actually involved in armed conflict neither adhere to major provisions of Protocol I in practice, nor believe that they are obligated to do so as a matter of law, then these controversial provisions of Protocol I, by definition, could not be customary international law.

Two reports by Human Rights Watch also charged NATO (and particularly American) forces with "violations" of international humanitarian law, although not "war crimes." Nine specific attacks were condemned as "illegitimate" assaults on "non-military targets," including the bombing of the radio-television station, bridges, and a heating plant.[26] The stated purpose of Human Rights Watch in producing the report was to assess the NATO nations' "compliance with their obligation" to adhere to the laws of war.[27] Like Amnesty International, Human Rights Watch used Protocol I as the standard for determining whether the laws of war had been violated, saying: "Protocol I additional to the Geneva Conventions of 1949 provides the basis for the evaluation here of NATO's bombing. This protocol has been ratified by most NATO members, and the U.S. government . . . has declared that it accepts all of the relevant standards."[28]

The claim that the United States "accepts all the relevant standards" of Protocol I is deceptive. American officials and diplomats might state in a general way that the United States fully adheres to all aspects of the laws of war, but in legal terms this means adherence to the Geneva Conventions of 1949 and only those provisions of Protocol I already accepted by the United States as part of international law. The United States follows parts of Protocol I (with its own interpretations) as a matter of policy, but this is not the same thing as accepting all the provisions of Protocol I as a matter of international law. Policy can be changed at any time.*

A Human Rights Watch report declared that NATO "did not take adequate precautions in warning civilians" of attacks.[29] Likewise, Amnesty International decried NATO's "consistent failure to give effective warning to civilians" before bombing.[30] These charges were made on the basis of Protocol I, not the original Geneva Conventions, which did not require warning civilians (and thus the enemy) before a bombing attack. Obviously, warning civilians would also alert air defenses and put American pilots at greater risk. In fact, both Human Rights Watch and Amnesty International reports explicitly complained that NATO and American military commanders were too concerned with "ensuring pilots' safety" and too "determined . . . to avoid pilot casualties."[31] Major General Charles Dunlap, USAF (ret.), called these reports "wildly inaccurate," adding that the "allegations" by Human Rights Watch and Amnesty International that American tactics were responsible for "unnecessary civilian casualties were especially infuriating to airmen," who are "convinced that they are doing everything they can to comply with LOAC" (law of armed conflict).[32]

Human Rights Watch called on NATO and the United States to "alter its targeting and bombing doctrine" to "ensure compliance with international humanitarian law" as they would define "compliance," meaning adherence to Protocol I.[33] HRW also insisted that NATO conduct an investigation of "illegitimate" bombings and "declassify" and "release comprehensive information on their

---

*See clarification of Protocol I in footnote on p. 229.

operations" in the Kosovo War.[34] Amnesty International demanded that the United States ratify Protocol I "without reservations" and change military tactics to conform to the protocol.[35]

The Kosovo reports of Human Rights Watch and Amnesty International, taken together with the other activities of these two NGOs during this same period of time, reveal a long-term strategic agenda that is in conflict with the goals of the American democratic nation-state. American goals under the Clinton administration in Kosovo were to achieve the military objectives of Serbian withdrawal from the province with minimal American casualties. Clearly, the NGOs had other goals, which are revealed by examining their public statements in the years preceding the war in Yugoslavia.

Both Amnesty International and Human Rights Watch spent a great deal of time during the Clinton years showering abuse on American institutions and characterizing America's domestic system as an "oppressive" one that routinely violates internationally recognized human rights. In 1998, a year before the war over Kosovo, Amnesty International referred to the United States as the "world leader in high tech repression."[36] Their American affiliate, Amnesty International USA, charged that the United States was guilty of a "persistent and widespread pattern of human rights violations," and that American courts were involved in "calculated killings" and "cruelty."[37] Also in 1998, Human Rights Watch labeled the United States a "laggard" in human rights. Fifty years after the Universal Declaration of Human Rights, declared the HRW executive director, Kenneth Roth, "the U.S. government stands in the way of further progress on human rights." Roth called the establishment of a global justice system "the next big step" in international human rights policy, and complained that the Clinton administration failed to support "this emerging system of international justice."[38]

Indeed, the Kosovo reports and the other initiatives of Human Rights Watch, Amnesty International USA, and a host of other NGOs through the 1990s and beyond can best be understood as part of the broader global governance project to establish "this emerging system of international justice," or in reality "transnational justice." The staffs of Human Rights Watch and Amnesty International USA are transnational progressives par excellence. They represent the ideological and activist vanguard of the global governance party, whose goal is the establishment of new forms of transnational authority, not the preservation of American democratic sovereignty. Thus their interests regarding the Kosovo War, or any other international issue, are markedly different from those of American (small *l*) liberal (small *d*) democrats. The fact that they are American citizens is not, in their view, of primary concern in the transnational politics of the twenty-first century. They are "disaggregated," in Anne-Marie Slaughter's sense.

For example, the NGO activists argued that American pilots were "obligated" (HRW's term) to fly at lower altitudes, at greater risk of being killed by anti-aircraft fire, to lessen the possibility of civilian casualties. Whereas most Americans would presumably be more interested in protecting the lives of American airmen so long as the legitimate laws of war were followed, the NGOs pursued goals that were in conflict with American interests.

For that matter, if protecting civilians is actually the primary concern of the NGOs, why do they insist that nations adhere to Protocol I when certain parts of it—for example Article 44, paragraph 3, which effectively permits terrorists to hide in crowds— would likely lead to a greater number of civilian and military deaths than the rules of the Geneva Conventions of 1949? In addition, as Hays Parks noted, Protocol I gives civilian property the same level of protection as civilian lives, and more protection than the lives of American soldiers.[39] One could well ask: what type of moral inanity is that? It appears that the NGOs are less concerned with saving civilian lives than with establishing transnational laws and subordinating nation-states (especially the American Gulliver) to those global rules that the NGOs themselves help to create.

Lawfare

The reports on Kosovo by Human Rights Watch and Amnesty International USA could be described as a form of "lawfare" against the American democratic nation-state, the purpose of which is to promote the global governance agenda. The concept of lawfare, which has entered the foreign policy and defense vocabulary in recent years, was first developed in 2001 by Major General Charles Dunlap (ret.), one of America's foremost military intellectuals.[40] The venerable Council on Foreign Relations' Roundtable on National Security discussed the idea in 2003 at a meeting titled "Lawfare, the Latest in Asymmetries."

Lawfare, as we will use the term in this book, means the use or misuse of law—litigation for harassment, propaganda, or ideological purposes—to achieve strategic, political, or military objectives.* Classic examples are the operations of Colombian Marxist guerrillas who bribe or force peasants to file false charges of war crimes against the most capable commanders in the Colombian military, forcing them into costly litigation that can effectively remove them from active service.[41] Before the controversies over the Iraq War of 2003, Dunlap worried that "the persistent criticisms of some international lawyers, NGOs, academics, and others regarding U.S. and coalition air operations in Iraq [in 1991], the Balkans, and Afghanistan have been extremely counter-productive.... In too many instances the criticisms appear alternatively uninformed or patently politicized."[42]

---

*Lawfare is also seen as a neutral concept that could be used by any type of political actor: democratic state, undemocratic state, terrorist entity, NGOs, radical Islamists, autocrats, global governancers, or democratic sovereigntists. Some analysts point to a "positive" form of lawfare that could be exercised by democracies against their opponents. One example is the U.S. lawsuit against the Libyan terrorists responsible for the Lockerbie airline massacre.

The International Criminal Tribunal
for the Former Yugoslavia

The UN Security Council established a tribunal to prosecute all war crimes committed during the Balkan conflicts of the 1990s. In 1999, the ICTY prosecutor, Carla Del Ponte, received allegations from NGOs, international lawyers, activists, and the Yugoslav government that "senior political and military figures from NATO countries committed serious violations of international humanitarian law" during the allied bombing campaign. Del Ponte established a committee to assess these charges.[43] The committee reviewed documents from Human Rights Watch, Amnesty International, the Yugoslav foreign ministry, the Russian Parliamentary Commission, NATO, and the U.S. Defense Department, among other organizations.[44]

Throughout the ICTY committee report there are references to Protocol I as the source of the criteria and guiding principles used to determine if there was enough evidence to proceed with a war crimes prosecution. For example, the committee notes that Protocol I "provides the contemporary standard which must be used when attempting to determine the lawfulness of particular attacks." The report acknowledges that "neither the USA nor France is a party of Additional Protocol I," but adds, "The definition is, however, generally accepted as part of customary [international] law."[45]

The ICTY gives special credence to the interpretation of Protocol I in the commentary by the International Committee of the Red Cross, which is clearly at odds with American understanding of the law of war.[46] The committee's report contains echoes of Hays Parks' forebodings about Protocol I. For example, in reviewing Amnesty International's allegations about the American attack on Radio Television of Serbia, the report spoke of "NATO's apparent failure to provide clear advance warning of the attack, as required by Article 57(2)," as if Protocol I were already established international law and the military principle of surprise were now forbidden by the law of war.[47]

In the end, Carla Del Ponte and the ICTY decided not to proceed with a prosecution against U.S. General Wesley Clark and
other NATO officials—not because the tribunal necessarily considered them exonerated, but because (at least officially) the war
crimes cases would have been too hard to prove. "In all cases, either
the law is not sufficiently clear or investigations are unlikely to result
in the acquisition of sufficient evidence to substantiate charges
against high level accused or against lower accused for particularly
heinous offences."[48] But perhaps there were also political reasons
for not proceeding: the time was not yet right to go after Gulliver.

Lawfare after 9/11

There is a clear continuity in the lawfare waged by the forces of
global governance against the American nation-state before and
after 9/11. The concepts and issues brought forward during the
1990s were repeated, amplified, and updated after the United States
responded to the attacks on the World Trade Center and the Pentagon. Over and over there are references to American human rights
violations at home and abroad, to the legal authority of Protocol I,
to the need for universal jurisdiction, and to the primacy of international law over national law. Thus, the broad outlines of the global
governance offensive have continued from the Clinton years through
the Bush presidency into the Obama years, and will no doubt persist
into the indefinite future.

This is so because the main obstacle to global governance is not a
particular U.S. administration or president, but the sovereign independence of our democratic nation-state and the stubborn exceptionalism of its unique culture, which is reinforced by a distinctly American
civic nationalism. American transnationalists realize this as much as
anyone, hence the strenuous efforts by some influential American
lawyers, academics, and NGO activists to subordinate both domestic
policy decisions and national security policies to global authority.

Almost as soon as American air strikes began in Afghanistan on October 7, 2001, the party of global governance started accusing the U.S. military of violating the law of war. For the human rights NGOs like Human Rights Watch and Amnesty International, the early period of the Afghan war was Kosovo 1999 revisited. Once again, there were charges that American soldiers were guilty of violating international humanitarian law and causing excessive civilian causalities. In the first month of the war, Human Rights Watch issued a backgrounder declaring that the United States "should immediately halt the use of cluster bombs in Afghanistan." HRW called for a "global moratorium" on cluster bombs, a weapon the U.S. Air Force has used effectively in the Gulf War of 1991, the Kosovo conflict of 1999, and later in Iraq in 2003.[49] The weapons are hardly unique and have been deployed by at least fourteen countries including Britain, Israel, India, Pakistan, Russia, and China, as well as the United States.[50]

From October to December 2001, the International Committee of the Red Cross and other NGOs, along with some postmodern nation-states (such as Sweden) and the European Parliament, joined Human Rights Watch and "called for an immediate stop" to the use of cluster bombs by the Americans and the British in Afghanistan.[51] Not content with opposing American actions overseas, European global governancers also objected to measures enacted by the U.S. Congress at home. In December 2001, the European Parliament condemned the USA Patriot Act as "contrary to the principles" of human rights because it allegedly "discriminated" against noncitizens.[52]

On December 11, 12, and 13, 2003, Human Rights Watch unleashed a series of press releases condemning U.S. military tactics in Afghanistan and Iraq as being responsible for "preventable" civilian deaths.[53] The December 12 report denounced U.S. "decapitation strikes" aimed at Saddam Hussein and other Baathist leaders because they had resulted in a small number of civilian deaths, although HRW admitted that they did not know how many. The executive director, Kenneth Roth, commented that "focusing on the exact number of deaths misses the point. The point is the U.S. military should not have been using these methods of warfare."[54]

The following day's press release, describing an American attack in Hutala, Afghanistan, "voiced doubt about the U.S. military's claim that it was unaware of civilians being present at the targeted locations." According to John Sifton, an HRW researcher, "Stating that the U.S. military didn't know there were civilians present at these sites is simply not an adequate response." Sifton went on to say, "The laws of war require that an attacking force take all feasible precautions to avoid civilian casualties."[55] Of course, the "all feasible precautions" standard comes directly from Protocol I, Article 57, which was ambiguous and never defined by the conference that established Protocol I, as Hays Parks pointed out, and had been the subject of serious arguments over conflicting interpretations between the NATO nations and the International Committee of the Red Cross at the conference.[56] In other words, there was no consensus on the meaning of "all feasible precautions" and it could not therefore be considered as part of customary international law and the laws of war.

In the great bulk of cases examined by Human Rights Watch, the standards for laws of war used to judge American actions were the provisions of Protocol I that the U.S. Joint Chiefs of Staff have rejected for both military and humanitarian reasons. Once again, Human Rights Watch was making assertions about what constituted customary international law that directly contradicted the practice and legal understandings of nation-states actually involved in armed conflict.

The Promotion of Universal Jurisdiction

In Chapter Five, we discussed how the ever-expanding use of "universal jurisdiction" in the late twentieth century strengthened the forces promoting new norms of "transnational" law over the traditional international law between nation-states. Historically, under the "law of nations," it was deemed proper for civilized nations to arrest and bring to justice international outlaws such as pirates and slave traders of any nationality because they were considered enemies of humanity and of all nations. Contemporary notions of "universal jurisdiction" are something quite different, however. Many nations (including the United States) have claimed the right to try foreign citizens for acts committed in foreign countries on a continuously expanding list of crimes. In recent years, "universal jurisdiction" laws have been used (and misused) particularly against the United States and Israel in a series of politically motivated charges and cases. Let us look at some examples.

Belgium. In 1993, Belgium passed a universal jurisdiction law, which was expanded in 1999. When the law came under fire from, among others, Israel (after charges were filed against Ariel Sharon), three major human rights groups issued a statement backing Belgium. In November 2000, Human Rights Watch, the International Commission of Jurists, and the International Federation for Human Rights (FIDH) declared that "Prosecutions based on universal jurisdiction are the essential part of an emerging system of international justice."[57] By the early years of the twenty-first century, a flood of war crimes cases were filed in Belgium, including a case against former president George H. W. Bush, General Colin Powell (chairman of the Joint Chiefs of Staff), and General Norman Schwarzkopf, for their alleged roles in the killing of civilians in a missile attack on Baghdad during the Gulf War in February 1991.[58]

At one point, relations between modern democratic Israel and the postmodern (and to some extent postdemocratic)* binational state of Belgium became severely strained as Binyamin Netanyahu,

---

*I use the term "postdemocratic" here because many political decisions affecting life in Belgium are made by the European Union, not the government of Belgium. There are no national political parties and very little sense of national identity in Belgium, which is essentially a binational state divided between the French-speaking Walloons and the Dutch-speaking Flemish populations.

then the Israeli foreign minister, denounced the complaint against Prime Minister Sharon and recalled Israel's ambassador.[59] At one level, the crisis exemplified the ideological conflict between the forces of global governance and the democratic nation-state. At its core, the argument between Israel and Belgium was over first principles of democratic theory, with Belgium insisting on the right to try officials of a foreign democratic state without the consent of that state, on the grounds that those officials violated international law as defined by Belgium.

The U.S. secretary of defense Donald Rumsfeld suggested, during an interview in Brussels in 2003, that if American officials were at risk of prosecution, the United States could move NATO meetings and activities out of Belgium. "It's perfectly possible to meet elsewhere," he remarked. Faced with U.S. and Israeli pushback, Belgium relented, changed the law, and considerably scaled back its jurisdiction.[60]

Amnesty International. On May 25, 2005, Amnesty International released a report accusing the United States of major human rights violations and characterizing the detention center at the U.S. Navy base at Guantanamo Bay, Cuba, as "the gulag of our times."[61] Thus, Amnesty compared an American military detention facility that held fewer than eight hundred terrorist suspects to Stalin's Siberian prison camps, where an estimated fifteen to thirty million innocent people were murdered, starved, or worked to death.[62]

William Schulz, head of Amnesty International USA, said that foreign governments should investigate American leaders responsible for alleged human rights violations if the U.S. government did not launch its own investigation. "If those [foreign] investigations support prosecution," Schulz added, "the governments should arrest any official who enters their territory and begin legal proceedings against them."[63] He listed, among others: Donald Rumsfeld, Attorney General Alberto Gonzales, former CIA director George Tenet, Lieutenant General Ricardo Sanchez (former U.S. commander in Iraq), and the Justice Department officials John Yoo, Jack Goldsmith, and

Tim Flanigan. These people, Schulz said ominously, "should think twice before planning their next vacation to places like Acapulco or the French Riviera because they may find themselves under arrest as Augusto Pinochet famously did in London in 1998."[64]

Center for Constitutional Rights. In 2004 and again in 2006, the New York–based Center for Constitutional Rights (CCR) and the German Federation of Republican Lawyers filed war crimes charges in Germany against U.S. officials (Rumsfeld, Gonzales, Sanchez, and Defense and Justice Department lawyers) under Germany's universal jurisdiction law. In 2007, working with the Paris-based International Federation for Human Rights, the CCR attempted to interest French prosecutors in bringing charges against Donald Rumsfeld under the UN Convention against Torture when he was visiting France.

The Center for Constitutional Rights was cofounded by William Kunstler, a self-described radical activist. The organization has been involved in high-profile cases such as defending the Chicago Eight after the "days of rage" following the 1968 Democratic convention, suing Israel's director of General Security Services for "war crimes," and representing Mohammed al-Qahtani, the so-called "twentieth hijacker" of 9/11. The president of the CCR, Michael Ratner, writes that we should "send a message to the world" that the former U.S. officials, "like the pirates of old, are enemies of all humankind and will be brought to justice."[65] The cases in Germany and France did not advance, but the CCR has also filed cases against Rumsfeld and the other former U.S. government officials in Sweden and Argentina.[66]

Spain. The first major "universal jurisdiction" case to achieve worldwide prominence was launched by the Spanish investigative judge Baltasar Garzón. On October 16, 1998, while the former Chilean dictator General Augusto Pinochet was visiting Great Britain, Judge Garzón issued an extradition warrant for Pinochet, who was then a senator, for alleged crimes (torture, terrorism, genocide) committed against Spanish citizens in Chile. Garzón asked the British Labour government to detain Pinochet and turn him over to the Spanish court. The British arrested Pinochet and held him until March 2000, but then declared him too ill to face trial in Spain and allowed him to return to Chile, where he eventually did face legal action.

During Pinochet's house arrest in the United Kingdom, the democratic nation-state of Chile strongly objected to the actions of Garzón and the British government. Chileans, including the center-left government, argued that Pinochet had been granted amnesty and immunity from prosecution as part of a broad national political compromise that was widely agreed upon in Chile and was crucial to strengthening the recently restored constitutional democracy. In addition, the Chileans asserted that any actions against Senator Pinochet should be taken by the Chileans themselves within the constitutional framework of their democracy, not by Europeans across the Atlantic.[67]

Nevertheless, Baltasar Garzón became a hero to the party of global governance with his warrant against Pinochet, as he did again in March 2009 when, with great fanfare, he initiated a preliminary investigation of war crimes charges against six American lawyers who had served in the U.S. Defense and Justice departments in the Bush administration. Judge Garzón acted upon a ninety-eight-page complaint filed *under Spain's universal jurisdiction law* by a Spanish legal activist group called Association for the Dignity of Prisoners, who were assisted in drafting the document by American and European lawyers.[68] The chief advocate of the Spanish group was a Madrid lawyer, Gonzalo Boyé, who represented several former Guantanamo detainees including Spanish Muslims, and who served eight years in a Spanish prison for assisting Basque terrorists in the 1988 kidnapping of a businessman named Emiliano Revilla.[69]

The forces of global governance hailed Garzón's decision to begin the transnational legal process against the Americans. Reed Brody of Human Rights Watch told the *New York Times* that the use of universal jurisdiction by judges such as Garzón in Spain is a means of "persuading or forcing" American courts to act.[70]

On April 15, 2009, the Spanish attorney general, Condido Conde-Pumpido, recommended that the case not proceed, declaring that it lacked merit. "If there is a reason to file a complaint against these people, it should be done before local courts with jurisdiction, in other words in the United States," he said.[71] Then, a Spanish high court removed Gonzalo Boyé's case from Judge Garzón's docket and reassigned it to another judge, where it appears to have stalled.[72] In June, the Spanish parliament—also under pressure from the Israeli and Chinese governments on different universal jurisdiction cases affecting their officials—decided to limit the scope of Spain's universal jurisdiction law.[73]

Despite all this, Judge Garzón initiated a new investigation of American officials. This time, Garzón was pursuing "any of those that executed and/or designed a systematic plan of torture or cruel, inhuman, and degrading treatment of the prisoners" at Guantanamo. Garzón's new focus was on "charges of conspiracy" to create "a regime of torture." The *Christian Science Monitor* reported that he was particularly interested in investigating "the conceptual legal 'framers' of then-secret memos that enabled the interrogations."[74] In other words, Garzón, as a promoter of global governance, proposed to investigate American government lawyers for their advice to an American president and perhaps see them convicted in a Spanish court. This is how the forces of global governance threaten constitutional democracy.

In April 2010, however, Garzón himself was indicted by the Spanish General Council of the Judiciary on three charges. First, that he exceeded his authority and ignored the national amnesty law in opening an investigation of crimes committed during the Spanish Civil War in 1936–39. Second, that he ordered illegal wiretaps in conversations between attorneys and clients. Third, that he dropped tax fraud charges against the president of Santander Bank in return for a bribe (the bank paid to sponsor Garzón for a sabbatical at New York University after the tax case against the bank president was dropped). In May 2010, Garzón was suspended from the bench.[75]

Transnational progressives rallied to Garzón's defense. Amnesty International denounced the charges against him as "outrageous,"[76] while Reed Brody of Human Rights Watch said that the Spanish decision to suspend Garzón marked "a sad day for the cause of human rights."[77] Carolyn Lamm, president of the American Bar Association, voiced support for Garzón,[78] as did the *New York Times*,[79] the International Criminal Court's prosecutor Luis Moreno-Ocampo,[80] and Carla Del Ponte, former prosecutor of the International Criminal Tribunal for the Former Yugoslavia.[81] In fact, as he awaited trial, Garzón was hired by Moreno-Ocampo for seven months as a consultant, with the permission of the Spanish judiciary.[82]

Judge Garzón is a prototype of the transnational prosecutors that we can expect to see in the coming years. If he is convicted, his career will be over. But in the future we will no doubt meet other global legalists who will attempt to bring war crimes charges against other democratic civilian and military leaders in disputes over the definitions of war crimes and obligations under international humanitarian law.

Lawfare against the United States in the Obama Era

The global governance challenge to American democracy is continuing in the Obama era, and it will no doubt persist for decades to come. Within three months of Barack Obama's inauguration, the UN special rapporteur on torture, Manfred Nowak of Austria, was asked by the newspaper *Der Standard,* "Has Obama violated international law?" The question referred to Obama's decision not to prosecute CIA operatives for alleged torture during the interrogation of terror suspects. Nowak replied, "Correct. It is a violation of binding international treaty law," meaning the Convention against Torture.[83] Interviewed in *Salon* magazine, Nowak said, "I do not consider this so-called 'war on terror' as an international armed conflict." Therefore, he insisted that international human rights law would apply more than the law of war (the Geneva Conventions) in the situation involving the CIA agents.[84]

Two news stories that appeared in the same week of late October 2009 illustrate the ongoing conflict between the forces of global governance and the American democratic nation-state. It was reported by the *New York Times,* the BBC, Reuters, and Agence France-Presse that the Obama administration could be "violating international law" in Afghanistan and Pakistan with its use of unmanned aircraft in missile attacks on terrorists.[85] According to the *New York Times,* the UN special rapporteur on extrajudicial executions, Philip Alston, said that the United States needed to show it was not killing people randomly on the Afghan border, and that the failure to respond to UN concerns about the use of drones was "untenable."[86] Alston maintained that "The onus is really on the United States government to reveal more about the ways in which it makes sure that arbitrary extrajudicial executions aren't, in fact, being carried out through the use of these weapons."[87]

Alston told Jane Mayer of the *New Yorker* that the United States was operating in an "accountability void," and that the drone program was "a lot like the torture issue." Mayer gave his criticisms a positive treatment, emphasizing the civilian deaths caused by the drones and dramatically stating, "There is no longer any doubt that targeted killing has become official U.S. policy."[88]

The special rapporteur also got a sympathetic hearing from Amy Goodman on the *Democracy Now* radio program, where he said that the U.S. response to the UN's concerns about the use of drone aircraft was essentially the same under the Bush and Obama administrations. The position of the U.S. government on the use of drones against terrorist targets is that the United States is complying with the law of war and that the UN Human Rights Council has neither the authority nor the competence to review American military actions in armed conflict.[89] But the global governancers are campaigning to restrict and delegitimize the use of drones as a weapon of choice by the United States in the war on terror.

Again, we are faced with a basic disagreement over political legitimacy between the competing ideologies of democratic sovereignty and global governance. The UN special rapporteur argued that the Human Rights Council has the authority to oversee, and apparently approve or disapprove, the military actions taken by liberal democratic nation-states (particularly the United States and Israel) in their own defense. This assertion is advanced despite the fact that the membership of the Human Rights Council includes undemocratic regimes such as Cuba, China, Saudi Arabia, and Russia, and in the past decade (when it was called the UN Commission on Human Rights) has included Algeria, Syria, Libya, Vietnam, and Sudan. Democratic nation-states argue that they will adhere to the laws of war and relevant treaties to which they have agreed, while ultimately determining how best to defend themselves.

The second story that illustrates the same fundamental conflict involved a UN Human Rights Council investigation into U.S. domestic affairs, specifically a lack of affordable housing in New York City. On October 23, 2009, the *New York Times* reported that "The United Nations has assigned an official, 'a special rapporteur on the right to adequate housing,' to check the city's affordable housing." The UN special rapporteur, Raquel Rolnik of Brazil, said, "I am representing the right of adequate housing as a human right." One resident of public housing told Rolnik that Mayor Bloomberg "doesn't care about the poor." The *Times* reported that "Ms. Rolnik hugged a resident herself" and insisted that the city should make affordable housing a priority.[90]

Interestingly, both of the UN special rapporteurs investigating U.S. "human rights violations" were educated in American universities. The Brazilian Raquel Rolnik was a doctoral student in urban history at New York University during the 1980s, and the Australian Philip Alston received a JSD degree from the University of California at Berkeley School of Law in 1980. Professor Alston is currently on the faculty of the New York University School of Law and codirector of the law school's Center for Human Rights and Global Justice. Rolnik and Alston appear to be typical representatives of the transnational progressive elite who provide the energy for the global government project.

CHAPTER ELEVEN

The International Criminal Court: A Supranational Judiciary

"Three times on the night of 17–18 July 1998, jubilation exploded through packed meetings of the UN Diplomatic Conference of Plenipotentiaries on the Establishment of an International Criminal Court, which was drawing to a dramatic close in Rome," reported the conference observers and NGO activists Fanny Benedetti and John L. Washburn.[1] First, the delegates overwhelmingly defeated amendments by India and the United States to restrict the power and reach of the proposed new supranational court. After the vote rejecting the U.S. proposal, according to another account, "the delegates burst into a spontaneous standing ovation which turned into a rhythmic applause that lasted close to ten minutes. Some delegates embraced one another and others had tears in their eyes."[2] On the third vote, the delegates overrode vigorous American objections and approved the final document establishing the International Criminal Court (ICC) by a vote of 120 to 7 (with 21 abstentions).[3] The cheering and applauding began again as "exhausted delegates roused themselves for another twenty minutes of exultation."[4]

Four years later, in 2002, sixty nations had ratified the Rome Statute of the International Criminal Court, a major victory for the global governance party and a direct challenge to democratic sovereignty, particularly the American liberal democratic nation-state. The Rome Statute established the ICC as a permanent treaty-based supranational court to try cases involving what are described as the most egregious violations of international humanitarian law, specifically "war crimes," "crimes against humanity," "genocide," and the "crime of aggression," to be defined at a review conference in Kampala, Uganda, in 2010. The ICC asserts jurisdiction over nation-states, even those that have not ratified the treaty.* Under the principle of "complementarity," a nation-state has the opportunity to bring its own political or military leaders to trial before the ICC would act. However, if the ICC decides that the nation-state's legal process was inadequate, the ICC could then conduct its own trial of those political or military leaders.

For example, India, the world's largest democracy, has refused to join the International Criminal Court. If Indian troops are charged with having committed war crimes while they are on a peacekeeping mission in the Democratic Republic of the Congo, which has ratified the ICC, they could be subject to the jurisdiction of the ICC without India's consent. If the soldiers are tried within the Indian judicial system and are acquitted, the ICC could, under the terms of the Rome Statute, declare India "unwilling" to conduct a serious trial and then proceed to try the Indian soldiers.

The International Criminal Court is an autonomous supranational institution that claims legal authority over the citizens of democratic nation-states against their wishes. Further, in the ratings by Freedom House, nearly 37 percent of the nation-states that belong to the ICC (42 out of 114 countries) are not completely free liberal democratic societies. On the other hand, seven totally free democratic states have refused to join the global court.[5] Put bluntly, under ICC rules, *judges from dictatorships* (Chad, Congo, Tajikistan) and illiberal, partly free

---

*That is in the cases of war crimes, crimes against humanity, and genocide, but not the "crime of aggression."

countries (Venezuela, Burkina Faso)⋆ *could sit in judgment over the citizens of fully functioning democracies* like Israel, Indonesia, and El Salvador. Hence, on universal moral grounds, the jurisprudence of the International Criminal Court is a direct affront to democracy, self-government, and the rule of law everywhere in the world.

The ICC has an independent prosecutor (a type of "global special prosecutor") and judges chosen by the nation-states that joined the treaty; but the ICC and its prosecutor are not accountable to any democratic legislature or executive. The prosecutor can proceed with a case once he or she has received the okay from two of the three judges on an ICC pretrial chamber. The ICC functions outside of any democratic space, and certainly outside the principles and limits of the Constitution of the United States. In the words of John Bolton, former ambassador to the United Nations, the ICC is simply "out there," claiming "authority to operate outside (and on a plane superior to) the U.S. Constitution."[6] As the international lawyers David Rivkin and Lee Casey explain,

> The creation of a permanent, supranational court with the independent power to judge and punish elected officials for their official actions represents a decisive break with fundamental American ideals of self-government and popular sovereignty. It would constitute the transfer of the ultimate authority to judge the acts of U.S. officials away from the American people to an unelected and unaccountable international bureaucracy.[7]

It is not surprising that some leading democracies have said no to the ICC. As of today, the world's most powerful democracy (United States), the world's most populous democracy (India), the world's most beleaguered democracy (Israel), and the world's largest Islamic democracy (Indonesia) have refused to adhere to the International Criminal Court. In fact, among the world's people who live under democratic governments, more live in countries that have rejected

---

⋆Judges are chosen from state parties that are members of the ICC treaty.

the authority of the ICC (around 1.836 billion people) than in countries that adhere to the ICC (approximately 1.299 billion people).[8]

How "Global Rules" Are Made

The process by which the International Criminal Court was established offers a case study in how global governance is advanced. Studying the lessons surrounding the birth of the ICC can help us foresee the transnational politics of the future. The coalition that built the International Criminal Court had two main elements: postmodern nation-states and NGOs.

The Like-Minded Group. First and foremost in promoting the ICC was a loose alliance of postmodern (or partially postmodern) states that were determined to subordinate modern sovereign states, particularly the United States, to global authority. This alliance, known as the Like-Minded Group (LMG), was led by Canada, the Netherlands, Germany, Norway, Finland, Sweden, Argentina, and South Africa. Western European nations were especially influential: thirteen out of fifteen EU members were part of the Like-Minded Group. The EU itself has consistently supported the idea of an independent global court for the laws of war.

NGOs. A coalition of NGOs led by human rights groups including Amnesty International, Human Rights Watch, and the Lawyers Committee for Human Rights (now Human Rights First), were firm allies of the Like-Minded Group through the entire process. The NGO bloc known as the Coalition for the International Criminal Court provided the LMG at the conference with intellectual arguments, position papers, lobbying, and even vote-counting operations. Years earlier, in fact, the NGO coalition had begun "convening working groups on key issues, arranging meetings between ... representatives of the governments involved in the ICC negotiations, and promoting awareness of ICC proposals and negotiations through newsletters, a Web page, and other media."[9]

The NGOs needed money to fund their activities, of course. Marlies Glasius, a Dutch researcher, determined that funding for the NGO coalition and its constituent organizations "initially" came from the World Federalist Movement, with additional money from the Ford and MacArthur foundations, as well as the European Union and some governments in the Like-Minded Group.[10]

Goals. The first chairman of the Rome Conference, which created the ICC, noted that the goals of the Like-Minded Group and those of the NGO coalition were "completely parallel."[11] The main goals of the coalition supporting the ICC were: (1) to create a supranational court; (2) to provide for an independent global prosecutor, free of the UN Security Council and the U.S. veto; and (3) to establish universal jurisdiction over nation-states in the areas of international humanitarian law, including war crimes, crimes against humanity, genocide, and aggression. They also wanted to define these specific crimes more expansively, in terms of Protocol 1 rather than the traditional understanding of international law including the Geneva Conventions of 1949. With some minor limitations, they were successful in achieving their goals.

Tactics for Creating the Rome Statute of the ICC

The ICC process began in 1994 with a draft document by the International Law Commission, a UN body that codifies international law and was tasked by the General Assembly to develop a first cut at a treaty. It progressed through several international meetings of the UN Preparatory Committee on the Establishment of the International Criminal Court (PrepCom), leading to the Rome Conference of June 15 to July 17, 1998. Throughout this process, the major human rights NGOs assisted the Like-Minded Group and provided substantial input into the draft documents that laid the foundation for the final Rome Statute.

The Netherlands and Canada were at the center of the Like-Minded Group, and their representatives held the crucial chairmanships in the negotiations that produced the treaty. Adriaan Bos, a legal advisor to the Dutch foreign ministry, was the influential chairman of the PrepCom meetings from 1996 to 1998. When Bos fell ill, a legal advisor to the Canadian foreign ministry, Philippe Kirsch, was elected by the delegates as chairman of the powerful Committee of the Whole for the five-week Rome Conference.

At the time of Kirsch's appointment, the Canadian foreign ministry was headed by Lloyd Axworthy, an outspoken advocate of global governance and restricting the power, influence, and sovereignty of the United States. The year before the Rome Conference, at the Ottawa Landmines Conference of 1997, Axworthy had helped organize a coalition of postmodern states and NGOs that successfully isolated the United States and rebuffed American defense concerns about the necessity of maintaining landmines on the North Korean border.

During the ICC negotiations, both Adriaan Bos and Philippe Kirsch used their role as chairmen to place representatives of the Like-Minded Group in eleven of the fifteen "coordinating" groups that developed the conceptual substance of the court. For example, three crucial issues were: establishing an independent prosecutor, unchecked by the UN Security Council; promoting the jurisdiction of the court over nation-states; and expanding the type of cases that would be admissible before the court. The subcommittees that deal with these issues were put in the reliable hands of Argentina, Finland, and Canada, all of which wanted to make the ICC as supranational as possible.[12]

As chairman of the Committee of the Whole, Philippe Kirsch, a savvy and sophisticated diplomat, coordinated strategy with the leading members of the Like-Minded Group (Germany, Argentina, Netherlands, Norway, Finland, Sweden, South Africa) and with representatives of the most powerful NGOs (Human Rights Watch, Amnesty International, Lawyers Committee for Human Rights, and the International Federation for Human Rights.

After receiving drafts of suggested ICC content from the working groups dominated by the LMG, Kirsch sent the proposed language for refinement to the drafting committee, chaired by his close ally Cherif Bassiouni, hailed as an "intellectual and entrepreneurial leader" of the coalition promoting the ICC. According to Fanny Benedetti and John L. Washburn's perceptive history of the ICC negotiations,

> Cherif Bassiouni contained in one person and in his leadership the roles of government representative (Egypt), vice-chair of the PrepCom, scholar (DePaul University Law School), and NGO activist. He was one of the few foremost authorities on international criminal law with extensive publications ... and service on innumerable committees of experts and advisory commissions and as a consultant to governments. In the Prep-Com, he drove the intellectual conceptualization and the substantive completeness of the draft treaty through his personal prestige with most of the delegations, his strong personality, and his extraordinary command of almost every aspect of the international criminal court.[13]

Bassiouni is, in many respects, the quintessential face of the new transnational politics. Born in Egypt in 1939, he immigrated to the United States and became an American citizen in 1967. Bassiouni spent most of his career as a professor of international law at DePaul University in Chicago. Despite his American citizenship—and thus his naturalization oath of loyalty to the U.S. Constitution and pledge to renounce all previous political allegiances—he represented Egypt at the Rome Conference, thus obtaining a coveted spot as chairman of the drafting committee, and worked against the democratic government of his adopted nation.

On July 5, with less than two weeks to go before the scheduled end of the Rome Conference, Chairman Kirsch called a special Sunday session of twenty-eight selected nations at the Canadian embassy, where he put forward a "package deal" paper that adhered to the main points of the Like-Minded Group. The United States attended the meeting but objected that its purpose was a "Like-Minded Group setup" and "questioned Kirsch's impartiality."[14] The next day, Kirsch issued a revised comprehensive version known as the "Bureau Discussion Paper" (informally, the "Canadian draft").

On July 8, Kirsch presented the draft paper to the Committee of the Whole. Wielding a heavy gavel, Kirsch prevented a general debate on the entire draft and instead very publicly polled the national delegations on their willingness to support the key LMG positions, including an independent prosecutor and expanded jurisdiction over nation-states. The U.S. delegation derided this "virtual voting" as a "rug sale."[15] But the NGOs, working in tandem with Kirsch, published and disseminated the "virtual votes" through their daily electronic and print newsletters and their press briefings. Kirsch's purpose was to show that there was solid majority support for a supranational court and to isolate the United States, India, and the other states who objected. In this, he succeeded.[16]

On Friday, July 10, Kirsch submitted the chairman's draft. For the next week, negotiations were intense, deals were struck, and France obtained "opt-out provisions" for itself, deserting the U.S.-India-Israel-China opposition. The British had joined the Like-Minded Group after the Labour Party victory in 1997, although the UK was not completely trusted by the LMG bloc.[17] Most significantly, the text of the treaty kept changing right up to the last minute. As noted earlier, Indian and American amendments were defeated in the final hours of the conference, and the treaty was rammed through just before the deadline as the delegates wildly cheered the American defeat.

The Clinton Administration Objects

The Clinton administration took issue with both the substance of the ICC treaty and the process of the negotiations. On the diplomatic process creating the treaty, the head of the American delegation, Ambassador David Scheffer, later wrote:

The treaty text was subjected to a mysterious, closed-door and exclusionary process of revision by a small number of delegates, mostly from the like-minded group, who cut deals to attract wavering governments into supporting a text that was produced at 2:00 A.M. on the final day of the conference, July 17. Even portions of the statute that had been adopted by the Committee of the Whole were rewritten. This "take it or leave it" text for a permanent institution of law was not subjected to the rigorous review of the Drafting Committee or the Committee of the Whole and was rushed to adoption hours later ... without debate.

Thus, on the final day of the conference, delegates were presented with issues and provisions in the treaty text that were highly objectionable to some of us. Some provisions had never once been openly considered. No one had time to undertake a rigorous line-by-line review of the final text.[18]

Even more importantly, the ambassador criticized the substance of the statute, particularly the ICC's claim to jurisdiction over American soldiers and officials even if the United States did not ratify the treaty. "A fundamental principle of international treaty law is that only states that are party to a treaty should be bound by its terms," remarked Ambassador Scheffer. "Yet Article 12 of the ICC treaty reduces the need for ratification of the treaty by national governments by providing the court with jurisdiction over the nationals of a nonparty state." Scheffer objected to the "theory that an individual U.S. soldier acting on foreign territory should be exposed to ICC jurisdiction if his alleged crime occurs on that territory, even if the United States is not party to the ICC treaty." He pronounced it "simply and logically untenable to expose the largest deployed military force in the world, stationed across the globe to help maintain international peace and security and to defend U.S. allies and friends, to the jurisdiction of a criminal court the U.S. Government has not yet joined and whose authority over U.S. citizens the United States does not yet recognize."[19]

The Clinton administration, pushing global cooperation and "assertive multilateralism," supported the general idea of an international criminal court. As Scheffer explained, "Since 1995, the question for the Clinton administration has never been whether there should be an international criminal court, but rather what kind of court it should be."[20] The International Law Commission's final draft statute for the ICC, published in 1994, "addressed many of the U.S. objectives and constituted, in our opinion, a good starting point," Scheffer said. He mentioned specifically the sections of the International Law Commission report that tilted toward Security Council approval for referring cases to the ICC and limited the prosecutor's discretion to cases submitted by state parties or the Security Council.[21]

The United States, however, was outmaneuvered at the Prep-Com meetings and at the Rome conference by the global governance coalition, which favored a strong supranational court and ignored American objections. At the same time, the Clinton administration was looking over its shoulder at the Republican Senate and the chairman of the Foreign Relations Committee, Jesse Helms (R-NC), a firm American sovereigntist. Noted for his blunt speech, Senator Helms declared during the Rome conference that any treaty suggesting that Americans could be tried by the ICC would be "dead on arrival" in his committee.[22] Addressing the UN Security Council a year and half later, Senator Helms told the delegates:

> Americans distrust concepts like the International Criminal Court and claims by the United Nations to be the sole source of legitimacy for the use of force because Americans have a profound distrust of accumulated power. . . . There is only one source of legitimacy of the American government's policies, and that is the consent of the American people.[23]

After the U.S. "no" vote in Rome, a Human Rights Watch representative, Richard Dicker, complained that "there's been no real disagreement between the [Clinton] administration and the

Congressional Republicans on the ICC."[24] Indeed, Ambassador Scheffer was "unanimously praised" by both Republican and Democratic senators on the Foreign Relations Committee "as a kind of returning hero" a few weeks after the end of the Rome conference in July 1998.[25] Nevertheless, even after the conference, the Clinton administration (unlike Helms and other conservatives) still believed that it might be possible to persuade the Like-Minded Group to accept the American proposals and make changes in the treaty that would permit the United States to join the ICC. With this hope in mind, President Clinton signed the ICC treaty on the last possible day, December 31, 2000. At the same time, however, he declared that the treaty was flawed and he would not submit it to the Senate for ratification; he also recommended that the incoming president, George W. Bush, not submit it to the Senate.

The Extraordinary Influence of the NGOs

In the process that created the International Criminal Court, NGOs such as Human Rights Watch and Amnesty International worked closely with the conference chairmen, Adriaan Bos and Philippe Kirsch, and with government representatives from the Like-Minded Group. The NGOs, said Kirsch, "provided substantial expert advice to virtually all delegations on the full range of complex legal issues contained in the statute."[26] According to Eric Leonard, a leading historian of the ICC process, "It is clear that the role of NGOs in the negotiating process was significant.... One can view the NGO presence, both prior to and during the Rome conference, as an example of the changing nature of world politics and international treaty negotiation."[27] Abram Chayes and Anne-Marie Slaughter remark that "Without the NGO community, the ICC treaty might not have been concluded."[28]

Marius Glasius, another important chronicler of the ICC negotiations, maintains that "In formulating its ICC policies, the United States was responding to NGO initiatives as much as to the policies and positions of other countries."[29] And when the United States presented arguments, the NGOs aided the LMG by quickly offering written counterarguments. Near the end of the conference, for example, a U.S. position paper calling for a limited ICC prosecutor was promptly attacked in a detailed rebuttal published by the U.S.-based Lawyers Committee for Human Rights.[30]

The academic literature on the history of the International Criminal Court singles out a number of individuals as intellectual and entrepreneurial leaders of the project. They could be characterized as "transnational norm entrepreneurs," a term coined by Harold Koh to denote those who formulate and promote new global norms through transnational interactions, negotiations, and transnational legal forums. In addition to Adriaan Bos, Philippe Kirsch, and Cherif Bassiouni, several NGO representatives are given prominence of place. William R. Pace organized and led the NGO coalition for the International Criminal Court. An American citizen, Pace has been the executive director of the World Federalist Movement (now called the Institute for Global Policy). Also cited as key players are Richard Dicker (an American citizen) of Human Rights Watch and Christopher Keith Hall (a British citizen) of Amnesty International.

Lawmaking, Global Governance Style

The process that created the International Criminal Court is a textbook case of how global governance works and how global rules are made, with a mix of transnational coalitions, negotiations, deals, and interactions among nation-states (modern and postmodern), NGOs, and international organizations (including UN bodies), along with "transnational norm entrepreneurs." This postdemocratic "lawmaking" clearly differs from actual lawmaking in the American constitutional democracy or in any other liberal democratic nation-state that exercises sovereign self-government.

In American liberal democracy, laws are made and executed by elected political leaders who are accountable to a democratic electorate in some way. If we do not like the policies enacted by these leaders, they can be reversed. Political majorities can become minorities. In any case, laws are made and administered, for good or ill, by the individuals that we, the people of the United States, have chosen and can replace. On the other hand, who are the ICC negotiators and their NGO allies accountable to? How can they be replaced? How could the ICC minority (United States, Israel, India, China) become the majority? How could the ICC process be reversed?

During the ICC negotiations, global laws that explicitly claim legal authority over Americans were made (and will be administered) not by people like Barack Obama, John Boehner, or Harry Reid, but by people like Philippe Kirsch, Adriaan Bos, Cherif Bassiouni, William R. Pace, Richard Dicker, Christopher Keith Hall, and the first ICC prosecutor, Luis Moreno-Ocampo. None of whom is remotely accountable to the American democratic electorate. It is true that America might, as the cliché puts it, have "a seat at the table" in global decision making of the ICC type, and even be ably represented by an ambassador like David Scheffer. Nevertheless, this "seat at the table" does not ensure that American self-government (or the self-government of other democratic states) will not be ignored and undermined, or prevent the enactment of transnational laws that would never have been accepted by the American people. In short, the advance of global governance presents a direct challenge to the future of liberal democracy.

As the ICC process illustrates, the transnational politics of the future will increasingly involve the phenomenon of American citizens working (particularly through NGOs) to limit American self-government and subordinate America's democratic system to global authority. Obviously there is nothing wrong with American citizens working with others to oppose the policies of a particular American administration. This has always been part of our robust democratic tradition. But what occurred at the Rome conference in the summer of 1998, and in the PrepCom meetings over the preceding two years, was something very different. Scores of Americans participating in the ICC process through NGOs were not simply opposing the policies of the Clinton administration; they were working to shift decision-making authority from American democracy to a supranational institution outside the framework of American constitutional democracy. They were seeking to subordinate the rights of fellow Americans to a supranational authority in what is clearly a zero-sum game: any power accumulated by the independent prosecutors of the ICC diminishes the guarantees of the U.S. Constitution and weakens the authority of our elected representatives.

A Counteroffensive by Democratic Sovereigntists

In his UN speech of January 20, 2000, Senator Jesse Helms, the southern populist conservative, not only attacked the ICC overreach but explicitly identified himself with an earlier American sovereigntist, previous chairman of the Senate Foreign Relations Committee, and Boston Brahmin, Henry Cabot Lodge of Massachusetts. Helms told the Security Council:

> The demands of the United States have not changed much since Henry Cabot Lodge laid out his conditions for joining the League of Nations 80 years ago: Americans want to ensure that the United States of America remains the sole judge of its own internal affairs, that the United Nations is not allowed to restrict the individual rights of U.S. citizens, and that the United States retains sole authority over the deployment of United States forces around the world.[31]

On May 9, 2001, Senator Helms, along with Senator Zell Miller (D-GA) and others, introduced the American Service-Members' Protection Act in order to "protect United States military personnel and other elected and appointed officials . . . against criminal prosecution by an international criminal court to which the United

States is not a party."³² After negotiations with the Bush administration, the bill was reintroduced in the Senate and the House in
late September 2001.

The American Service-Members' Protection Act prohibits assisting the International Criminal Court by spending taxpayer dollars
on it or sharing classified and law enforcement information. It restricts
U.S. participation in peacekeeping missions unless the UN specifically
exempts U.S. troops from prosecution by the court. It prohibits military aid to any country that is a party to the ICC unless those nations
sign an accord that they will not turn American soldiers over to the
court; there are exemptions for NATO allies and major non-NATO
allies, and the president can waive this prohibition in the national
interest. Finally, the bill authorizes the president to "take any action
necessary" to free U.S. soldiers and officials held by the court (thus
earning the nickname "The Hague Invasion Act").

On May 6, 2002, the Bush administration sent a formal letter
to the United Nations (signed by John Bolton, the under secretary
of state for arms control and international security) saying that the
United States did not intend to ratify the ICC treaty, was not bound
by the terms of the treaty, and was removing its signature of December 31, 2000. The United States essentially "unsigned" the treaty.
On July 1, 2002, after the sixtieth country ratified the Rome Statute,
the International Criminal Court formally went into effect. A month
later, on August 2, President Bush signed the American Service-
Members' Protection Act, which had passed overwhelmingly with
solid bipartisan support in both the Democratic Senate★ and the
Republican House of Representatives.

John Bolton asserted U.S. opposition to the ICC on the principled
grounds of democratic sovereignty not simply as an exercise in legal
technicalities or realpolitik. The ICC, said Bolton, "runs contrary to
fundamental American precepts and basic Constitutional principles

---

★The future vice president Joe Biden and the future secretary of state Hillary Clinton both voted for the bill.

of popular sovereignty, checks and balances, and national independence." He declared that the ICC, "with its unaccountable Prosecutor and its unchecked judicial power, is clearly inconsistent with American standards of constitutionalism. This is a macro-constitutional issue for us, not simply a narrow technical point of law."[33]

With American soldiers and officials possibly at risk of prosecution by the ICC in the future, the United States took a series of actions designed to prevent this from occurring. On June 30, 2002, the Americans vetoed a Security Council resolution to extend the mission of UN peacekeepers in Bosnia. They insisted on adding a clause to prohibit soldiers serving in the UN Bosnia mission from any country that did not belong to the ICC from being subject to the jurisdiction of the ICC without the approval of the Security Council. When the clause was adopted, the United States agreed not to veto the resolution and it passed on July 12. In June 2003, the Security Council extended the exemption for non-ICC states for another year, but in 2004 the United States lost its bid to extend the exemption again, after objections by other Security Council members.

In the summer of 2002, the United States launched a major diplomatic campaign to obtain "bilateral non-surrender agreements" with as many countries as possible. Under these agreements, the other nation would pledge "not to surrender" any U.S. military personnel or officials on their territory to the International Criminal Court. These were commonly referred to as Article 98 agreements because Article 98 of the ICC Rome Statute was worded in such a way as to suggest that under certain international agreements, persons could not be surrendered to the ICC without the cooperation of the state in which they belonged.*

---

*Article 98, "Cooperation with respect to waiver of immunity and consent to surrender," reads as follows: "1. The Court may not proceed with a request for surrender or assistance which would require the requested State to act inconsistently with its obligations under international law with respect to the State or diplomatic

The first Article 98 agreement was signed with Romania in August 2002; by June 2004, eighty-nine nations had concluded bilateral non-surrender agreements with the United States.[34] Eventually over one hundred such agreements were signed. The forces of global governance—particularly the European Union, the NGOs, and elements of the UN bureaucracy—bitterly objected to the U.S. policy of obtaining Article 98 agreements, arguing that it was undermining the ICC. In 2003, the EU formally took a "common position" in support of the ICC.[35] While the Article 98 agreements could cut off military assistance to ICC-adhering countries, in December 2004 the U.S. Congress went further and passed the Nethercutt amendment, which would cut off economic aid to nations that have ratified the ICC but not signed a non-surrender agreement with the United States. Like the American Service-Members' Protection Act, the Nethercutt amendment granted the president authority to waive the foreign aid prohibitions.

The International Criminal Court Sets Up Shop

When the International Criminal Court went into force on July 1, 2002, the top posts, not surprisingly, went to the nations of the Like-Minded Group, which had led the coalition that enacted the treaty. Philippe Kirsch was chosen as the first president of the court (2003–2009). Luis Moreno-Ocampo of Argentina, a major LMG country, was selected as the first prosecutor. Judges were chosen from the leading LMG countries, including Germany, Canada,

---

immunity of a person or property of a third State, unless the Court can first obtain the cooperation of that third State for the waiver of the immunity. 2. The Court may not proceed with a request for surrender which would require the requested State to act inconsistently with its obligations under international agreements pursuant to which the consent of a sending State is required to surrender a person of that State to the Court, unless the Court can first obtain the cooperation of the sending State for the giving of consent for the surrender."

South Africa, Finland, Brazil, Ireland, and South Korea. Bruno Cathala of France was named chief administrator of the court, as a reward to France for having shifted its support from the sovereigntist bloc to the Like-Minded Group at a crucial time in the negotiations near the end of the Rome conference.

Since 2003, Luis Moreno-Ocampo has launched a series of war crimes investigations and begun some trials. To date, the ICC has been active in Africa: in the Democratic Republic of the Congo, in the Central African Republic, in Uganda, and in Darfur, Sudan. Beginning in 2005, with the second presidential term of George W. Bush and with Condoleezza Rice as secretary of state, the United States became more accommodating to the ambitions of the global court. This trend accelerated in the early Obama years.

The first indication of change was the acceptance by the United States of an ICC role in Darfur. In 2005, under continuous pressure from the Europeans, the United States agreed to abstain and not veto a UN Security Council resolution authorizing the ICC to investigate war crimes in Darfur, thus granting a degree of legitimacy to the global court. Some democratic sovereigntists argued that an African court (like the International Criminal Tribunal for Rwanda) should have been chosen instead of the Hague-based ICC, which could be characterized as "colonialist," but in the end these views did not prevail within the U.S. government.[36]

Then, slowly but steadily, Congress removed some of the teeth from the American Service-Members' Protection Act. In 2006, Congress permitted ICC-adhering countries to receive military education and training funds, but kept the prohibition against foreign military funds for those nations that had not signed non-surrender agreements. In January 2008, all sanctions against military aid to ICC-adhering countries were removed by Congress. In 2009, the Nethercutt amendment prohibiting economic aid expired and was not renewed. The president, however, is still authorized to rescue Americans with "all means necessary" if they are held by the ICC.

The Case of Darfur/Sudan

In July 2008, the ICC chief prosecutor, Luis Moreno-Ocampo, indicted Sudan's president, Omar al-Bashir, and other officials for "war crimes" and "crimes against humanity" in their actions against the population in the Darfur region of Sudan, including large-scale killing and raping as part of a government plan. This was the first indictment of a sitting head of government. Omar al-Bashir is a ruthless killer, and many Western governments and observers have characterized the actions of his regime in Darfur as either "genocide" or very close to it. The Europeans argued that the ICC could play a constructive and practical role in Darfur through a war crimes investigation (and indictment) that would put pressure on the Bashir government and provide "leverage" for a peace settlement. The Americans eventually went along with the ICC instead of supporting a pan-African court. As John Bolton explained it, "Pressed by Europeans, the Bush Administration was essentially cornered into supporting the [ICC] investigation leading to the indictments" of the Sudanese leaders.[37]

Experts on Africa from the left and the right believed that ICC action in Sudan would make the situation worse. For example, Alex de Waal, a Harvard professor who has written two books on Darfur, and Andrew Natsios, a former U.S. special envoy for Sudan and former administrator of the United States Agency for International Development, saw both "a real potential for widespread atrocities and bloodshed," and the likely derailing of the peace process as the Sudanese government dug in.[38]

In March 2009, the ICC's Pre-Trial Chamber of judges agreed to the prosecutor's request for the issuance of an arrest warrant for Omar al-Bashir and two of his officials. The Sudanese government reacted swiftly and savagely. "Within hours," it had "expelled the biggest international aid agencies, seized their assets, and closed down Sudanese human rights organisations at gunpoint," wrote Alex de Waal and Julie Flint in the *Guardian*. They foresaw more problems as "fuel to run the water pumps" ran low and "the worst meningitis epidemic in a decade [spread] with lethal speed." As they noted, "it was the ICC prosecutor who set the match to the dry tinder that is Sudan."[39]

In a report to the UN Security Council on April 14, 2009, Secretary General Ban Ki-moon stated that the expulsion of the aid agencies put "well over 1 million people at life-threatening risk." Nina Shea, a religious-freedom expert, wrote that the people of Sudan would "soon run out of food, potable water, and medical services" without the international aid.[40] In short, far from being "pragmatic" or "practical," the actions of the International Criminal Court in Darfur/Sudan resulted in harm to the people living there. How did this happen? Isn't the ICC led by well-intentioned humanitarians?

In reality, the aims of the global governance advocates who run the International Criminal Court are, first and foremost, political and ideological. In general, the global governancers seek to expand global authority over nation-states. In the specific terms of the ICC, they seek to establish the supremacy of global law over national law in the realm of international humanitarian law (the laws of war) and human rights law.

The whole party of global governance—including transnationalists in Western governments, the EU, and leading NGOs—heralded the ICC's arrest warrants for the Sudanese leaders as a historic advance for global law. For example, Amnesty International called the announcement of the warrants "an important signal—both for Darfur and the rest of the world."[41] Human Rights First said that when Bashir was brought to court, "a giant step will have been made toward justice."[42] When confronted with the harmful consequences of the ICC actions for the longsuffering population of Sudan, the NGO friends of the ICC dug in their heels. Human Rights Watch urged their European allies to "play it firm," which meant "defending the indictment tooth-and-nail" and acting "decisively to uphold the warrant."[43]

The NGOs have argued that "justice" must take precedence over all other concerns, including human security, public health, public order, and peace in the region.[44] Perhaps, but it appears just as likely that the policy supporting the warrants is primarily an opportunity to enhance the power and prestige of the International Criminal Court, while any humanitarian concern for real people suffering in Sudan is strictly secondary.*

Current and Future Investigations of the ICC

On September 9, 2009, Luis Moreno-Ocampo held a press conference in which he announced that the ICC prosecutor's office was "collecting information on alleged war crimes" committed by the United States in Afghanistan and "conducting preliminary investigations on possible war crimes" committed "by Israeli forces in Gaza."[45] The *Wall Street Journal* reported: "The prosecutor said forces of the North Atlantic Treaty Organization—which include U.S. servicemen—could potentially become the target of an ICC

---

*As of this writing, Bashir remains free of ICC custody. In another African case, the ICC prosecutor Moreno-Ocampo secured approval from a divided ICC Pre-Trial Chamber (2-1) to begin an investigation of six Kenyan politicians for allegedly inciting post-election violence. This was the first time that the prosecutor launched an ICC case on his own initiative, declaring that "there was a reasonable basis to believe that crimes against humanity had been committed." In his dissenting opinion in the Pre-Trial Chamber, Judge Hans-Peter Kaul stated that he did not believe that the alleged crimes rose to the level of "crimes against humanity" but were more likely common crimes probably best handled by local courts. He worried that the approach taken by the ICC prosecutor in Kenya "would broaden the scope of possible ICC intervention almost indefinitely" and "might infringe on State sovereignty and the action of national courts which should not be in the ambit of the [ICC] Statute." See Dissenting Opinion of Judge Hans-Peter Kaul in Pre-Trial Chamber II, *Situation in the Republic of Kenya,* Decision Pursuant to Article 15 of the Rome Statute on the Authorization of an Investigation into the Situation in the Republic of Kenya, International Criminal Court, ICC-01/09, March 31, 2010. Also see Julian Ku, "A Powerful Dissenting Opinion on the ICC's Decision to Authorize an Investigation into Kenya," *Opinio Juris* blog, April 2, 2010; AFP, "ICC to investigate 2007 post-election violence," France 24 International News, March 31, 2010.

prosecution, as the alleged crimes would have been committed in Afghanistan, which has joined the war-crimes court."[46] The *Guardian* revealed that "US soldiers acting for NATO are being investigated for alleged torture of prisoners and use of excessive force." According to the *Guardian*, the ICC prosecutor's information was coming from NGOs, human rights groups, and the Afghan government, and that the prosecutor was " 'very open' to additional information."[47]

Responding to the *Wall Street Journal* story about the prosecution of U.S. soldiers under NATO command, Kenneth Anderson, a highly respected international law professor at American University, stated, "It is, to say the least, remarkable to me that the ICC prosecutor would even consider such a thing." Professor Anderson questioned the "paucity of legal standards" being used by Moreno-Ocampo, who indicated that "collateral damage," the accidental killing of civilians, constituted a "war crime."[48] Anderson suggested that in ordering this preliminary ICC examination, Moreno-Ocampo was expanding the traditionally accepted laws of war to include practices that the United States has never considered war crimes, such as the "failure" to warn civilians before an air attack—a provision of Protocol 1 that the United States has rejected. Anderson argued, moreover, that Moreno-Ocampo's comments to the press implied that the ICC had authority to second-guess the good-faith judgment of American military commanders in the field, and of their closely consulted JAG military lawyers, on the selection of appropriate targets in Afghanistan and on their sincere efforts to avoid or minimize civilian causalities.[49]

Professor Anderson's cogent analysis of Moreno-Ocampo's prosecutorial overreach is off the mark in only one respect: The ICC prosecutor's comments are not "remarkable," or at least they will not be in the future; they will be routine. This is so because the ultimate purpose of the International Criminal Court is the establishment of global legal authority over all nation-states, and particularly over the United States of America.

Besides the United States, the democratic nation-state of Israel is also in the ICC prosecutor's sights. At the World Economic Forum conference in Davos in February 2009, a reporter from the *Times* of London met with Moreno-Ocampo and learned that "The International Criminal Court is exploring ways to prosecute Israeli commanders over alleged war crimes in Gaza." Moreno-Ocampo said that the Palestinian Authority argued that it is the de facto state in Gaza and asked the ICC to examine alleged Israeli war crimes. "They are quoting jurisprudence.... It's very complicated," the ICC prosecutor told the reporters. The *Times* also reported that the ICC had received "files on alleged crimes" from "Palestinian groups" and was "awaiting further reports from the Arab League and Amnesty International containing evidence gathered in Gaza."[50]

On September 13, 2009, Moreno-Ocampo gave an interview to the influential pan-Arab newspaper *Al-Hayat*, where he suggested a second method of gaining ICC jurisdiction over alleged war crimes in Gaza, besides accepting the request of the Palestinian Authority to take the case. An Israeli army officer who was allegedly involved in authorizing war crimes, Lieutenant Colonel David Benjamin, held dual citizenship in Israel and South Africa. A group of South African lawyers and NGOs asked the ICC to investigate on the grounds that South Africa is a party to the ICC treaty and the citizens of state parties are subject to the jurisdiction of the ICC. Moreno-Ocampo agreed with this legal position and told *Al-Hayat*, "if this Southern African legal adviser [of Israel]★ committed crimes, we have jurisdiction."[51] The next step, Moreno-Ocampo said, was for the ICC prosecutor's office to review the allegations and see if there was a case to proceed with a full investigation. Commenting on the prosecutor's position regarding ICC jurisdiction in this dual citizenship case, Michael Newton, a professor of international law at Vanderbilt University, said that "The implications for the U.S. are potentially very troubling."[52]

★Brackets in the *Al-Hayat* story.

The possibility of a direct confrontation between the ICC and the United States or between the ICC and Israel at some point in the not too distant future is growing. The general ideological and administrative trajectory of the ICC is headed in that direction. Such a showdown may not occur during Luis Moreno-Ocampo's tenure as the first ICC prosecutor, but it could come under the next prosecutor. It is significant that Moreno-Ocampo is asserting the global court's authority to examine war crimes charges against democratic states that have refused to join the treaty: the United States in Afghanistan and Israel in Gaza. He is even using the technicality of the dual citizenship status of an Israeli officer to expand the ICC's reach. In other words, the ICC is establishing precedents that could be employed, if not by Moreno-Ocampo himself, then by a future prosecutor.

The "Crime of Aggression"

In 1998, the Rome Statute of the International Criminal Court added the "crime of aggression" to the court's jurisdiction, along with "war crimes," "crimes against humanity," and "genocide." Defining what exactly constitutes "aggression" and the circumstances in which the ICC would exercise jurisdiction was postponed until a review conference that was held May–June 2010 in Kampala, Uganda.

For weeks prior to the Kampala conference, American diplomats (led by the State Department legal advisor Harold Koh) visited European capitals urging NATO allies not to expand the ICC's jurisdiction to the crime of aggression. The Europeans ignored the American pleas and joined other ICC state parties in a "consensus" establishing the court's jurisdiction and adopting a vague, problematic definition of the "crime of aggression."[53] Labeled as "aggression" are a wide range of military actions, not only full-scale invasions of foreign territory but also blockades, air strikes, and the temporary occupation of foreign lands, which are considered by their "character, gravity and scale" to constitute "manifest" violations of the United Nations Charter.[54] As the Obama administration's ambassador-at-large for war crimes, Stephen J. Rapp, complained to the Kampala conference, these terms—character, gravity, scale, manifest violations—were never clearly defined.[55]

It is entirely possible that the international lawyers and judges of the ICC would label as "crimes of aggression" any military actions other than immediate self-defense from full-scale invasion. Thus, crimes of aggression might be said to include President Kennedy's blockade of Cuba during the 1962 missile crisis, President Clinton's use of airpower in Kosovo in 1999, President Reagan's actions to rescue the American medical students and remove the Marxist government of Grenada in 1983, President Obama's launching of missile strikes against terrorists hiding in Pakistan, Israel's various responses to continuous terrorist attacks by Hamas and Hezbollah, and any future preemptive strike by the United States or Israel to prevent Iran from acquiring nuclear weapons.[56] Harold Koh objected to the "risk of criminalizing lawful uses of force" in adopting the proposed "crime of aggression" provision. He told the ICC delegates that their "flawed" definition of the crime of aggression could conceivably risk prosecution of leaders who planned humanitarian military missions designed to prevent genocide from occurring in the first place.[57]

The Kampala conference established in principle the concept that the ICC prosecutor (with the approval of the ICC Pre-Trial Chamber) could proceed with a case against political and military leaders for the crime of aggression without the approval of the United Nations Security Council, which under the UN Charter has traditionally had primary responsibility for dealing with breaches of international peace and security and issues of aggression. As a practical matter, the U.S. delegation (headed by Stephen Rapp and Harold Koh)★ did succeed in severely limiting any effects that the

---

★The United States attended the Kampala conference as an "observer" along with sixteen other countries that are not members of the ICC.

ICC's "crime of aggression" provision might have on U.S. officials and policies. The ICC provisions on aggression will not apply to citizens of non-ICC states (such as the United States), and even ICC member states could "opt out" of the specific provision covering aggression. Further, the Kampala conference agreed that the amendment covering the crime of aggression would not go into effect until at least 2017, at which point the state parties to the ICC would have to vote again in order for it to be fully implemented.[58]

Nevertheless, the Kampala conference overall was an advance for global governance as it extended *in principle* the supranational judicial authority of the ICC over the traditional international process of the UN Security Council. For the most part, the ICC remains an unaccountable supranational court, which claims authority to try citizens of democratic nation-states for "war crimes," "crimes against humanity," and "genocide" without the consent of those democratic nation-states.

There is no doubt that the International Criminal Court is a major project of the global governance party and is central to its primary agenda: the promotion of global law over national law. The International Criminal Court is, and has been from its inception, an affront to the fundamental principles of democratic self-government. Of course, the ICC is only one instrument in the arsenal of the global governancers. As we have seen, global authority is promoted in a number of other ways: under the banner of "global domestic politics" in which treaties become "international law," through aggressive "lawfare," and by the expansion of "universal jurisdiction." The next chapter examines how these tools are wielded against Israel, a main front in the struggle for a new world.

CHAPTER TWELVE

Will Israel Be Allowed
to Defend Itself?

We have examined how the global governance coalition launched a sustained assault on American domestic practices and policies during Bill Clinton's presidency, and how these transnational progressives aim to transform America domestically through the implementation of UN treaty-made law. The transnational progressive agenda was pushed vigorously at the World Conference against Racism, Racial Discrimination, Xenophobia and Related Intolerance held in Durban, South Africa, in 2001. The Durban conference represented a microcosm of the transnational politics of the future, pitting the forces of global governance against the liberal democratic nation-state, and particularly against Israel.

The World Conference against Racism

Chapter One described the press conference in the fall of 2000 at which an American NGO spokesman explained that the NGOs were turning to the United Nations in "frustration" because they were unable to enact their agenda through the regular process of American democracy. The UN high commissioner for human rights, Mary Robinson, was present at the press conference and said she was honored to receive the "call for action" from the NGOs.[1]* The relationship between the American NGOs (along with their funders) and Commissioner Robinson was supportive and symbiotic. They were all part of the broader "global governance team" that seeks to impose "global human rights norms" on democratic sovereign states. Understanding this alliance helps us interpret the meaning of the UN Durban conference of 2001.

The conventional narrative of the Durban conference runs something like this: "The original idea of the conference was sound. Its originators, including Commissioner Robinson, sought to highlight and combat global problems of racism and xenophobia and promote tolerance and human rights. Unfortunately, this conference was 'hijacked' and turned into an anti-Israeli and anti-Western propaganda extravaganza."

The conventional narrative is partly true, but incomplete. It suggests that there were two main forces at Durban: the well-meaning organizers of the conference and the hijackers. We need a broader and more detailed narrative. If we examine the Durban conference through the lens of the new transnational politics, we see three distinct groups of actors with competing goals. The first bloc, led by well-meaning Western democratic officials, somewhat naïvely hoped that the conference could promote tolerance and combat racial discrimination.

The second group was a "global South," "nonaligned," or Third World alliance of predominantly African and Islamic nations. One wing of this bloc, composed of African nations led by South Africa, sought redress from the West, including financial reparations, for past wrongs such as colonialism, slavery, imperialist exploitation, and racial discrimination. The other wing, made up of Islamic nations united in the Organization of the Islamic Conference, attempted to use the UN forum to delegitimize Israel as a racist "apartheid" state, the moral equivalent of the old white South African regime of P. W. Botha.

---

*For a list of the American NGOs involved, see Chapter One.

The third bloc was the forces of global governance, mostly the UN leadership, Western NGOs, and Western philanthropies. This group sought to expand "global human rights norms" and establish global authority over sovereign states in controversial policy areas. For them, the conference was a continuation of the ideological campaign launched in the early 1990s to promote "global domestic politics," described in Chapter Nine. At Durban they advocated the transnational progressive agenda: support for ethnic, racial, and gender preferences or quotas in employment; minority language rights, meaning enforced bilingualism and multilingualism; multicultural education; gender-awareness education, as defined by radical feminists; restrictions on "hate speech"; migrant rights, which usually means special rights for illegal immigrants; and equality of outcomes based on ethnicity, race, and gender. In addition, the global governancers urged nations that have ratified the UN conventions on civil and political rights (ICCPR) and on race (CERD) to drop all reservations to these treaties; this was a thinly veiled admonition to the United States.

All these measures found their way, in some form, into the final Durban Declaration and Plan of Action. Thus, Reed Brody of Human Rights Watch said the conference "marked a step forward," achieving "critical progress" in "repairing the legacy of slavery and colonialism," in the "protection of migrants," and in antiracism "public awareness campaigns in schools and the media."[2] Because the transnational progressive agenda had advanced, the global governancers called the Durban conference essentially a success— despite the outcry over anti-Semitism, the demonization of the Jewish state, and the walkout by the United States and Israel.

The Demonizing of Israel

In 2001, Tom Lantos of California was the ranking Democrat on the House International Relations Committee. A Holocaust survivor and the founder of the Congressional Human Rights Caucus,

Lantos served as a U.S. delegate to Durban and wrote a long article analyzing the conference, which he had initially viewed with optimism. Like the secretary of state, Colin Powell, he greeted the conference as a "historic opportunity to achieve real progress on the issue of racism."[3]

At the African regional preparatory meeting of the World Conference against Racism in Dakar, Senegal, the delegates endorsed financial reparations for descendants of the victims of Western slavery and colonialism—but not Arab and Islamic slavery—over the objections of the United States, Canada, and European nations. The explicit endorsement of the regional meeting included reparations not only for individuals of African descent living in the West, but also for African nation-states.[4]

At the Asian regional preparatory meeting in Tehran, the Organization of the Islamic Conference (composed of over fifty Muslim nations) seized the initiative and launched a campaign to delegitimize Israel. Before the conference even began, Iranian officials blocked Israeli passport holders and Jewish NGOs from attending. Congressman Lantos noted that the conference organizer, Mary Robinson, "took no action . . . to overcome Iran's bar on granting visas to citizens of Israel."[5] At Tehran, the conference text declared that Israel was implementing "a new kind of apartheid, a crime against humanity" in the West Bank and Gaza, and denounced the "emergence of racist and violent movements based on racist and discriminatory ideas, in particular, the Zionist movement, which is based on racial superiority."[6]

Secretary Powell and Congressman Lantos repeatedly told Commissioner Robinson that the language condemning Israel was a deal breaker for the United States. At the same time, the Americans were willing to compromise on the proposed slavery language in order to "save the conference." They would agree to expressing "deep regret and profound remorse" for U.S. slavery, but not an explicit "apology," which could be legally binding in terms of financial reparations. The U.S. delegation worked assiduously for this compromise.[7]

Robinson's response was a speech to the delegates at the final preparatory meeting in Geneva in which she drew moral equivalence between "the historical wounds of anti-Semitism and the Holocaust on the one hand, and . . . the accumulated wounds of displacement and military occupation" of Palestinians under Israeli authority on the other. As Lantos put it, "Instead of condemning the attempt [by the OIC] to usurp the conference, she legitimized it." Moreover, he asserted, "Robinson's intervention broke all momentum that the U.S. had developed" for a compromise, and "represented the *coup d'grace* [*sic*] on efforts to save the conference from disaster."[8]

Right before the final meeting in Durban, another attempt at "compromise" was put forward by Norway and Canada, to express "concern" about the situation in the Middle East without explicitly mentioning Israel. This effort got nowhere.[9] During the Durban conference, the Europeans did not act as they had during the conference on the International Criminal Court in Rome, where they were leading advocates for the global governance agenda. At Durban, by contrast, they were uncomfortable with parts of the UN-NGO agenda, such as reparations, but they still wanted the conference to "succeed" and the global project to advance. Thus, unlike the United States and Israel, the Europeans did not walk out of the conference, and they approved the final Durban Declaration and Plan of Action despite its anti-Israel and anti-Western language—and with its agenda of race awareness, gender education, multiculturalism, linguistic and migrant rights, and hate-speech restrictions.

Congressman Lantos found the attitude of the Europeans "troubling."[10] He wrote that "our diplomats met stiff resistance as they sought support from our closest democratic allies" in Europe and elsewhere. Some Europeans, Lantos said, were "genuinely angry" at the lack of U.S. support for global initiatives on "climate change, chemical and biological weapons proliferation, and the trade in small arms,"[11] but for others, "the Bush administration's foreign policies provided a convenient excuse for acting on their anti-Israeli proclivities."[12]

Outside the main conference center in Durban, an NGO Forum to represent the voice of global civil society (in UN-speak) was held in conjunction with the World Conference against Racism. The official declaration that emerged from the NGO Forum condemned Israel as a "racist apartheid state," pronounced it guilty of "genocide," and demanded an end to "racist crimes" against the Palestinians.[13] The venerable liberal Jewish American publication *The Forward* reported that the NGO Forum featured "posters displaying Nazi icons and Jewish caricatures, anti-Israel protest marches, organized jeering, incendiary leaflets and anti-Jewish cartoons, in addition to anti-American agitation."[14] Congressman Lantos said, "Jewish leaders and I who were in Durban were shocked at this blatant display of anti-Semitism. For me, having experienced the horrors of the Holocaust first hand, this was the most sickening and unabashed display of hate for Jews I had seen since the Nazi period."[15] Palestinian NGOs, aided by Islamists and other Third World allies, held key positions at the NGO Forum and orchestrated the attack on the State of Israel and the scurrilous anti-Semitic propaganda.

Major elements within the forces of global governance bankrolled the Palestinian and Middle Eastern NGOs that led the assault on Israel at Durban. It shocked some Jewish groups to learn that the Ford Foundation, the European Union, and some European nations (including Sweden, Norway, and the Netherlands) were funding the radical Palestinian NGOs that were engaged in the anti-Semitic campaign.

The Jewish Telegraphic Agency conducted a thorough two-month investigation of the NGO funding sources, involving "interviews with dozens of individuals in seven countries as well as a review of more than 9,000 pages of government and organizational documents." This investigation revealed massive Ford Foundation support for Palestinian radicals. For example, during the two-year period of preliminary meetings and the Durban conference itself, Ford's Cairo office awarded $35 million to 272 Arab and Palestinian organizations.[16]

Reporting on the JTA investigation in *The Forward,* Edwin Black wrote that "Ford officials played an active role in promoting the Durban conference and provided funding for several of the leading anti-Israel groups at the event." Ford was a major funder for the Palestinian NGO Network (a coalition of ninety NGOs) that promoted a resolution at Durban calling "upon the international community to impose a policy of complete and total isolation of Israel as an apartheid state." Speaking from Ramallah, the program director of the Palestinian NGO Network said, "Ford is our biggest funder."[17] Black quotes David Harris, the executive director of the American Jewish Committee, saying, "We are struck by the scores of Palestinian NGOs funded by Ford . . . a number of which have deeply disturbing and troubling records on Israel and Jews."[18] A representative of the Jewish women's organization Hadassah and a delegate to Durban reported, "There was no way to miss the anti-Semitism. The Ford guy would have to be blind. It was the most anti-Semitic and anti-Zionist stuff you ever saw."[19]*

---

*After Edwin Black's report was published by the Jewish Telegraphic Agency in October 2003, the Ford Foundation at first "denied to JTA that any anti-Israeli agitation or anti-Semitic activities took place in Durban." But under pressure from twenty U.S. congressmen led by Jerrold Nadler (D-NY) and the threat of a lawsuit by the American Jewish Congress, "Ford reversed itself." Ford's president, Susan Berresford, apologized and issued revised guidelines to prevent this from happening in the future. The congressmen announced that they were satisfied. Nevertheless, after a new investigation, JTA revealed in 2008 that Ford was still funding NGOs that were attempting to "paint Israel as a racist, apartheid state and isolate the Jewish nation through boycotts, divestment, and sanctions." Michael J. Jordan, "Ford Foundation Still Funding anti-Israel Groups," JTA, July 23, 2008. In mid-April 2011, *The Forward* reported that the Ford Foundation would not renew the grants to the progressive NGOs in Israel in 2013 (they had received $40 million since 2003). The article stated that the director of the Ford Israel Fund would "work in coming years on ensuring that grantees develop alternative

American NGOs Avert Their Eyes

What were the leading Western and American human rights NGOs, who were present at Durban, doing when this was going on? "Shockingly," said Congressman Lantos, "they did almost nothing to denounce the activities of the radicals in their midst. They made no statements protesting the debasement of human rights mechanisms and terms taking place in front of their eyes."[20]

As the full NGO Forum voted to adopt the final declaration condemning Israel as an "apartheid state" that practiced "genocide," Amnesty International, Human Rights Watch, and the Lawyers Committee for Human Rights chose not to vote either for or against it. At a press conference two days later, these same NGOs described the NGO Forum Declaration as representing the "voices of the victims."[21] Speaking for Human Rights Watch, Smita Narula said that the document "gives expression to all voices." The secretary general of Amnesty International, Irene Khan, called it "a collection of the voices of the victims. We don't believe it was appropriate to vote. . . . The angry voices of the victims at this conference have been heard. . . . The angry voices are the failure of governments." The executive director of the Lawyers Committee for Human Rights, Michael Posner,* described the document as "a multiplicity of views, backgrounds, experience from which we come. There is language in it we do not endorse, but let's understand it for what it is."[22]

On the controversy over the blatantly anti-Semitic NGO Forum Declaration, Congressman Lantos commented, "What is perhaps

---

funding sources for the day after the Ford Foundation pulls out." Nathan Guttman, "Ford Foundation, Big Funder of Israeli NGOs, Pulling Out," Forward.com, April 15, 2011.

*Since September 2009, Michael Posner has served in the Obama administration as assistant secretary of state for the Bureau of Democracy, Human Rights, and Labor. The Lawyers Committee for Human Rights is now Human Rights First.

most disturbing about the NGO community's actions is that many of America's top human rights leaders—Reed Brody of Human Rights Watch, Michael Posner of the Lawyers Committee for Human Rights, Wade Henderson of the Leadership Conference on Civil Rights, Gay [McDougall] of the International Human Rights Law Group—participated." Lantos found it "surprising how reluctant they were to attack the anti-Semitic atmosphere and the clear OIC [Muslim nations] effort to derail the conference."[23]

To be sure, some of the American-based NGOs did criticize the NGO Forum Declaration, but rather mildly, after the damage had been done, and while simultaneously continuing to attack Israel's security policies. For example, Reed Brody said that "Israel has committed serious crimes against Palestinian people but it is simply not accurate to use the word genocide and to equate Zionism with racism."[24] Michael Posner remarked that although there had been "serious human rights violations in the West Bank and Gaza," his organization found the "language" of the declaration "inaccurate" and therefore "reject[ed] it." Nevertheless, he agreed with Irene Khan that "there is much of value in this document."[25] Indeed, three weeks before the World Conference against Racism, the executive director of Human Rights Watch, Kenneth Roth, told National Public Radio, "Clearly Israeli racist practices are an appropriate topic" to discuss at Durban.[26]

A representative of the International Association of Jewish Lawyers and Jurists (IAJLJ) stated that Jewish groups were made unwelcome at a crucial meeting of Western NGOs that was deciding how to vote on the NGO Forum Declaration. The IAJLJ representative, Anne Bayefsky, described the situation:

> As we arrived at our meeting the chief Durban representative of Human Rights Watch, advocacy director Reed Brody, publicly announced that as a representative of a Jewish group I was unwelcome and could not attend. The views of a Jewish organization, he explained, would not be objective and the decision on how

to vote had to be taken in our absence. Not a single one of the other international NGOs objected.[27]

Writing in the *Jerusalem Post*, Bayefsky criticized the activities of Human Rights Watch at Durban. Reed Brody responded to Bayefsky on several points, but did not challenge her account of how Human Rights Watch (backed by all the other Western NGOs) insisted on excluding Jewish groups from participating in the strategy meeting that decided how to vote on the NGO Forum Declaration.[28]

Why did the Ford Foundation and leading Western and human rights NGOs act the way they did at the Durban conference? Their supporters claim the motivation was strictly humanitarian, that they are interested in exposing human rights violations whether perpetrated by authoritarian regimes or democratic states. Their critics see a disproportionate emphasis on alleged transgressions by Israel, to the neglect of Palestinian terrorist attacks on the Jewish state. Examined through the lens of the global governance agenda, the NGO actions become clear.

Western NGOs and philanthropies (such as the Ford, Rockefeller, and MacArthur foundations) had much invested in the "success" of the World Conference against Racism. Their main agenda was to use the conference to advance global governance, along with their ideological viewpoint on race, gender, multiculturalism, linguistic rights, migrant rights, and the like. For many (such as Human Rights Watch), this ideology also included "repairing the legacy of slavery and colonialism."[29]

The NGOs were aware that controversies over anti-Semitism and anti-Zionism could discredit the entire Durban conference, which in turn could damage the long-term strategy of the global governance project. But they also realized that speaking out forcefully against the NGO Forum Declaration could have led to a rift with the Third World bloc, with which they had good working relations. Hence their ambiguous response to the virulent anti-Israeli rhetoric. Once the backlash against Durban commenced, the

Western NGOs claimed (inaccurately) to have vigorously opposed the anti-Israeli hate-fest at the time it occurred.*

Political War against Israel, from Durban to Gaza

Around the globe today, the democratic world is engaged in a violent struggle with the forces of radical Islam. At the same time, the liberal democratic nation-state is under a sustained political assault by the party of global governance. In both of these struggles, Israel is on the front lines. Israel is the first line of defense for liberal democratic sovereignty from both the "hard" challenge of radical Islam and the "soft" challenge of global governance.

Islamic and Arab rejectionists—the terrorist organizations like Hamas and Hezbollah, and some nation-states such as Iran—deny the legitimacy of Israel's existence and openly call for its destruction, including a possible nuclear threat. The goal of the radical Islamists is nothing less than the extinction of the Jewish state.

The global governancers, meanwhile, are waging a nonviolent yet coercive political war against the democratic sovereignty of the Israeli nation. The party of global governance does not seek Israel's destruction, but does aspire to subordinate it to global authority. This challenge constitutes a different type of "existential" threat, aimed not at Israel's material existence but at its political existence as an independent democratic sovereign state.

Israel is the most vulnerable of the world's independent democracies, often targeted by the global governancers as a surrogate for the United States or for the independent democratic state generally.

---

*In April 2009, the UN Durban Review Conference (Durban II) was held in Geneva, Switzerland. When it became clear that the Organization of the Islamic Conference would dominate the proceedings, the United States and some other nations decided to boycott the conference. At the same time, leading American NGOs were urging all nations to participate in Durban II. The final document reaffirmed the original Durban statement of 2001 and repeated its key points.

Precedents regarding the laws of war, international human rights law, universal jurisdiction and the like are first established against Israel, then later used against the United States and other liberal democracies. To transnational progressives, Israeli democratic nationalism is an obstacle to the new world they are seeking to create. Israel, says the exemplary transnationalist Strobe Talbott, presents a "chronically vexing" problem, embodying "both the strength and weakness of nationhood itself."[30] Indeed, Israel's vigorous assertion of its national sovereignty (like that of the United States) is a direct affront to the concept of a postnational "shared sovereignty." Thus, a good part of the animus toward Israel among Western globalists is ideological and philosophical.[31]

Since the conclusion of the Durban conference, a number of crucial sectors in the global governance party have waged relentless political war against Israel.[32] These include:

(1) Major Western philanthropies, particularly the Ford Foundation.

(2) Leading Western human rights NGOs, specifically Human Rights Watch, Amnesty International, the Center for Constitutional Rights, and Oxfam.

(3) Elements of the United Nations, at times including the secretary-general's office; the office of the high commissioner for human rights under Mary Robinson, Louise Arbour, and Navi Pillay; and the Human Rights Council, which has a strong Islamic bloc.

(4) The International Criminal Court, including the office of the chief prosecutor, Luis Moreno-Ocampo.

(5) Sectors of the European Union, including the European Commission (with its heavy funding of rejectionist Palestinian NGOs), the EuroMed office (the Barcelona program that also funds rejectionists), the European Council on Foreign Relations, and sometimes the European Parliament.

(6) Some European nation-states, in particular Sweden, Norway, Ireland, and Switzerland.

(7) Transnational progressives throughout the West, particularly in mainstream Protestant churches and church organizations (World Council of Churches, National Council of Churches); "boycott Israel" activists in universities; and post-Zionist "peace" elements within Israel, including B'Tselem, an Israeli NGO heavily funded by the European Commission.

The Israeli democracy does have some international support in this global conflict. First, the Congress of the United States under the leadership of both parties has traditionally been committed to the survival of Israel and has been a major strategic asset for the Jewish state. (Through the years, the American executive branch has been supportive of Israel for the most part, but less so than the legislature.) American public opinion, unlike European opinion, is generally favorable to Israel.[33] There is firm support for Israel in the Jewish community in the United States and elsewhere. In addition, evangelical Christians in the United States are particularly enthusiastic supporters of the Jewish state.

Since the Durban conference, Israel has faced continuous crises: the Second Intifada (Palestinian uprising); the IDF incursion into Jenin, resulting in spurious claims of a "massacre" and calls throughout Europe for sanctions; opposition to the building of a security fence, leading to an advisory ruling against Israel by the International Court of Justice; campaigns to get Western universities and churches to divest funds from Israel; and lawfare initiatives to use "universal jurisdiction" to prosecute Israeli officials, including Ariel Sharon in Belgium and General Moshe Yaalon in Spain. There was also the Second Lebanon War of 2006, the Gaza War of 2008–2009, and the Turkish flotilla incident of 2010.

No doubt new crises and incidents will follow, and the basic pattern of behavior by the major actors will remain the same. First, terrorists attack. Second, Israel responds against the terrorists. Third, the global governancers join the radical Islamist / Third World bloc in bitterly condemning the Israeli response, in UN resolutions, NGO reports, lawsuits against Israeli officials, and calls for divestment, boycotts, and sanctions. We can observe this pattern by examining the Gaza conflict of 2008–2009.

The root of the crisis goes back to September 2005, when Israel completely and unilaterally withdrew from Gaza, leaving routine administration in the hands of the Palestinian Authority. In 2007, the more radical Palestinian faction, Hamas, defeated Fatah in Gaza elections. Civil strife ensued and Hamas seized power in a coup, killing or driving out their Fatah rivals, who remained dominant in the West Bank. Hamas—which has been designated as a terrorist organization by the United States, the European Union, and many Western nations—made heavy use of suicide bombers during its violent campaign against Israel, and launched approximately eight thousand rockets into Israel over an area in which more than one million Israelis lived.

Finally, Israel responded on December 27, 2008, first with an extensive air campaign against Hamas targets in Gaza, followed by a ground incursion into Gaza on January 3, 2009. The Israel Defense Forces withdrew from Gaza on January 18. The entire campaign, called Operation Cast Lead, lasted three weeks. According to Dore Gold, former Israeli ambassador to the United Nations, "The single reason Israel went to war on December 27, 2008, was to finally bring the rain of rocket fire on its civilians to a halt."[34] The defense minister, Ehud Barak, likewise stated:

> Our aim is to force Hamas to stop its hostile activities against Israel and Israelis from Gaza. . . . [W]e shall not allow a situation where our towns, villages and civilians are constantly targeted by Hamas. . . . We have restrained ourselves for a long time but now is the time to do what needs to be done. We are determined to afford our citizens what any citizen anywhere in the world is entitled to—peace, tranquility and freedom from threats.[35]

Almost immediately after the initial Israeli air strikes, Western human rights NGOs began to blast the Israeli response to Hamas terrorism. On the second day of Operation Cast Lead, December 28, Amnesty International accused Israeli forces of "unlawfully" killing "scores of unarmed civilians" and "police personnel who were not directly participating in the hostilities." However, the Hamas policemen were not innocents, but members of the terrorist Izz al-Din al-Qassam Brigade.[36] Oxfam, a British-based NGO (which receives funding from the British government and the Ford Foundation) stated on the same day that the rocket attacks by Hamas on Israeli civilians "cannot justify" Israel's military response. "The international community must not stand aside and allow Israeli leaders to commit massive and disproportionate violence against Gazan civilians in violation of international law," said Oxfam.[37] Very quickly, other NGOs piled on—Human Rights Watch, B'Tselem, Israeli Arab and Palestinian NGOs (funded by the EU, the Ford Foundation, and some European governments). The Jewish state was pilloried for "war crimes," "indiscriminate attacks," "disproportionate force," "targeting civilians," and "crimes against humanity."[38]

Once the fighting ended, the NGOs called for international war crimes investigations. Three such "investigations" were launched, with NGOs playing a major role. The first, commissioned by the Arab League and coordinated by the Palestinian Center for Human Rights, an NGO funded by the EU and some European governments, accused Israel of "genocide." The second investigation, launched by the United Nations secretary general, condemned Israel for "egregious breaches" and "intentionally striking UN property." This mission was led by the former head of Amnesty International and relied heavily on accusations against Israel made by Human Rights Watch.[39] The third investigation was commissioned by the UN Human Rights Council and led to the "Goldstone Report," which proved to be a milestone in the political conflict between the forces of global governance and the Israeli democratic state.

The Goldstone Report

On April 3, 2009, the president of the UN Human Rights Council established a "Fact Finding Mission on the Gaza Conflict," headed by Richard Goldstone, a South African judge. The mission was tasked with investigating "all violations of international human rights law and international humanitarian law [the law of war]" that occurred in Gaza.[40] At the time of his appointment, Judge Goldstone was on the board of Human Rights Watch, resigning only after charges of a conflict of interest were raised.[41] A quintessential transnational progressive, he had been the chief prosecutor on the International Criminal Tribunal for Rwanda and for the former Yugoslavia. On May 25, 2009, in the middle of the Gaza controversy, he received the MacArthur Award for International Justice. In presenting the award, the MacArthur Foundation's president, Jonathan Fanton, stated that Goldstone "has made a crucial contribution to building the international system of justice."[42] Indeed, Goldstone had been influential during the Rome conference to create the International Criminal Court. At a crucial point in the debates, he urged the delegates to move away from the American position favoring a court with limited jurisdiction and instead embrace broader supranational authority for the ICC.[43]

The UN Fact Finding Mission was biased against Israel from the start. All four members of the mission had previously signed open letters alleging "crimes against civilians" in Gaza. For example, three months before she was appointed to the mission, Professor Christine Chinkin had cosigned a public letter to the *Sunday Times* of London declaring that Hamas's rocket strikes on Israeli civilians did not "amount to an armed attack entitling Israel to rely on self-defence" and that Israel's response constituted a "war crime."[44] Nevertheless, Judge Goldstone defended Professor Chinkin's appointment, telling an interviewer on Israel's Channel 1, "I'm absolutely satisfied that she's got a completely open mind and will not exhibit any bias one way or the other."[45]

Several weeks before the creation of the UN Fact Finding Mission, on March 16, Goldstone himself and the two other future members of the mission, Hina Jilani and Desmond Travers, all signed an open letter to the UN secretary general, Ban Ki-moon, saying, "The events in Gaza have shocked us to the core." The letter, organized by Amnesty International, called for an international investigation of "gross violations of international humanitarian law" in Gaza, in order to "establish the truth about crimes perpetuated [*sic*] against civilians on both sides," it said diplomatically—although it was clear to all that Israel was the main target.[46]

The Goldstone mission released a 575-page report on September 15, 2009, charging Israel with "war crimes" and "possible crimes against humanity." The Goldstone Report accused Israel's top political and military leaders of "a deliberate policy of disproportionate force aimed not at the enemy [Hamas] but at . . . the civilian population."[47] The authors of the report were astute enough to include some criticism of Hamas, but it was little in comparison with the overwhelming condemnation of Israel. Moreover, the report did not charge Hamas leaders (unlike Israeli leaders) with a deliberate intent to harm civilians. For example, it said there was no "direct evidence" that Hamas had the "specific intent" to shield their rocket forces by hiding among civilians. Dore Gold noted, however, that "photographic evidence shows clearly that Hamas launched rockets from populated areas."[48] By contrast, the report claimed that Israeli actions in Gaza were "designed to punish, humiliate and terrorize a civilian population," and charged that a "failure to distinguish between combatants and civilians" by Israel was "deliberate."[49]

On October 16, 2009, the UN Human Rights Council endorsed the Goldstone Report with 25 in favor, 6 opposed, 11 abstentions, 5 not voting.[50] On November 5, the full UN General Assembly adopted the report with 114 in favor, 18 against, and 44 abstentions.

The Israelis countered that many accusations of "intentional" human rights violations were taken directly from NGO reports and written by staff members who had not been in Gaza, but relied on

Palestinian "eyewitnesses" who were sometimes Hamas supporters, or often intimidated by the terrorists into giving false witness. They insisted that the IDF did everything it could to minimize civilian causalities, but this was very difficult because "Hamas intentionally placed military camps, weapons depots, and rocket-launching areas right in the heart of civilian population centers."[51] Dore Gold stated that "there was ample evidence to conclude that the mosques [in Gaza] were militarized, and were being used to launch rockets. Mosques were also used to store Kassam and Grad rockets."[52]

Moreover, the IDF warned civilians with phone calls as well as leaflets before major attacks. The Israelis argued that these actions, taken to lessen civilian causalities, were almost unprecedented in the history of warfare.* But Judge Goldstone was not impressed. He declared that the phone calls and leaflets were not good enough because the Israelis "Didn't say when. Didn't say where" the attacks would occur. "If you're going to give warnings, they should be specific," Goldstone retorted.[53]

Strategic Goals of the UN Fact Finding Mission

It is not surprising that the recommendations of the UN Fact Finding Mission (the Goldstone Report) promoted two main strategic goals of the global governance project: expanded authority for the International Criminal Court and broader use of universal jurisdiction against the liberal democratic nation-state. First, the Goldstone Report recommended that the "United Nations Human Rights Council

---

*According to Colonel Richard Kemp, who led UK forces in Afghanistan, "During Operation Cast Lead, the Israeli army did more to safeguard the rights of civilians in a combat zone than any other army in the history of warfare. Israel did so while facing an enemy that deliberately positioned its military capability behind the human shield of the entire civilian population." Quoted by Dore Gold, "The UN Gaza Report: A Substantive Critique," Jerusalem Center for Public Affairs, p. 14.

submit this report to the Prosecutor of the International Criminal Court." Second, it recommended that the UN Security Council "require the Government of Israel" to conduct its own investigation and prosecution of the "serious violations of international humanitarian and international human rights law reported by the Mission."[54] If Israel did not carry out these investigations and prosecutions in good faith and "in conformity with international standards," the issue should be referred "to the Prosecutor of the International Criminal Court."[55]

At the same time, however, the Goldstone Report suggested that Israel would not be likely to operate in good faith, saying, "there are serious doubts about the willingness of Israel to carry out genuine investigations." The report asserted that Israeli military courts have "inherently discriminatory features" and conduct criminal investigations in an "unprofessional way."[56] The implication is that justice is not possible within Israeli democracy and that global overseers are therefore required—despite the traditionally liberal rulings of the Supreme Court of Israel, which regularly incorporates international law into domestic law and vigorously monitors the actions of the Israel Defense Forces.

Declaring an "increasing unwillingness on the part of Israel to open criminal investigations that comply with international standards," the Goldstone Report advocated a "reliance on universal jurisdiction," which it called "a potentially efficient tool for enforcing international humanitarian law and international human rights law."[57] It called upon the nations that belong to the Geneva Convention to "start criminal investigations in national courts, using universal jurisdiction," concerning Israeli actions in Gaza.[58] Thus, the UN report openly encouraged other countries (and, by inference, legal activists) to prosecute Israeli officials under universal jurisdiction statutes if such prosecutions could be justified in their respective legal systems. Indeed, when the former Israeli foreign minister Tzipi Livni planned to visit London for a conference in December 2009, a British arrest warrant was issued for her, citing "war crimes" allegedly committed by Israelis in Gaza—a classic example of lawfare.[59]

With the Goldstone Report, the party of global governance was once again on the offensive, attempting to wield two global legalist instruments—the International Criminal Court and universal jurisdiction—as political weapons to limit the self-government of the democratic nation-state. Today the target is Israel; tomorrow it will be the United States. Thus, the political impact of the assumptions and presuppositions of the Goldstone Report reaches beyond the conflict in the Middle East, bearing on the broader struggle between liberal democracy and global governance.[60]

The transnational progressives who pilloried Israel's antiterrorist policies in Gaza are sophisticated enough to insist that they believe in Israel's right to self-defense. Goldstone told Bill Moyers, "I accept the right of Israel, absolutely, to defend itself."[61] The key question for Goldstone, however, was "whether the manner in which Israel defended itself was in accord with humanitarian law."[62] Likewise, the executive director of Human Rights Watch, Kenneth Roth, stated that "Of course Israel is entitled to defend itself from Hamas' rocket attacks, but when it does so in violation of its duty to spare civilians, and with so massive a civilian toll, public outrage is entirely predictable."[63]

Obviously, Israel's political and military leaders would concur that Israel has a right to defend itself. They would also say that Israel should, and does, adhere to international humanitarian law, or the law of war. The crucial disagreement is over who determines the laws of war. Who decides what is "in conformity to international standards"? Who establishes the rules under which a democratic nation-state can defend itself?

It is clear from the UN's Gaza report, along with the reports of NGOs and statements by UN officials and other elements of the global governance coalition, that the global governancers believe they have the right to determine the rules by which Israel may defend itself. Moreover, the global governancers are saying to Israeli leaders: if you do not follow our interpretation of the rules, we will attempt to have you prosecuted. Israelis notice the double standard. The "international community" rarely if ever seeks to prosecute

Hamas and Hezbollah for war crimes, or attempts to arrest their leaders if they visit London or Brussels.

In the view of Israel's defenders, the forces of global governance have effectively attempted to "criminalize" the Jewish state's antiterrorist campaign.[64] As a practical matter, the supporters of global governance characterize almost all Israeli responses to attacks from Hamas or Hezbollah as "violations" of the laws of war. Thus, while the Arab rejectionists and the global governance party have different strategic goals, they share an interest in diminishing Israeli democratic sovereignty within the new transnational politics of the Middle East.

Europeans and the Goldstone Report

As we have seen, there is a close and symbiotic relationship among the UN Fact Finding Mission, leading human rights NGOs, UN officials, funders of the global governance project in Western philanthropies, the European Union, and some European nation-states. They all share a strategic vision: to advance supranational authority in the Middle East, particularly by limiting Israeli sovereignty.

Nevertheless, European governments were divided in their response to the Goldstone Report. With an ambivalence reminiscent of their response to the Durban conference, many Europeans were uncomfortable with the degree of anti-Israeli bias on display at the UN, yet they were also critical of Israel's actions in Gaza and did not want a complete break with the Islamic/Non-Aligned bloc. Tactically, they did not want to appear too critical of the NGO/"global rule of law" forces, with whom they are usually allied. Hence, most western European countries made the decision to abstain in the UN General Assembly vote on the Goldstone Report.★

★Austria, Belgium, Denmark, Finland, France, Norway, Spain, Sweden, and the United Kingdom abstained. Ireland, Portugal, and Switzerland voted for the Goldstone Report.

At the same time, Italy, Germany, and the Netherlands joined the United States, Canada, Australia, several countries of central and eastern Europe (Poland, Hungary, Czech Republic, Slovakia, Ukraine), and a few Pacific Island states in voting against the Goldstone Report. In some of these nations, such as Canada and Italy, new right-of-center governments were friendlier to Israel than the previous left-of-center governments.[65]

Goldstone's Second Thoughts

In a *Washington Post* article published on April 1, 2011, Judge Goldstone retracted his report's most serious allegations against Israel. He no longer believed that the Israelis had deliberately targeted civilians in Gaza as a matter of policy, and he noted that Israel had "dedicated significant resources" to investigating the actions of its own soldiers in Gaza. "If I had known then what I know now," he wrote, "the Goldstone Report would have been a different document."[66]

But the report of the UN Fact Finding Mission on the Gaza Conflict was not the work of one man. At the heart of the UN mission were the activist NGOs—particularly Amnesty International, Human Rights Watch, B'Tselem, and the Palestinian Center for Human Rights—that first raised accusations of "war crimes" and "human rights violations" by Israel, and then lobbied the UN Human Rights Council and the General Assembly to accept the Goldstone Report.[67] These NGOs, in turn, were strongly backed by their longtime ally Navi Pillay, the UN high commissioner for human rights and a major sponsor of the report within the UN bureaucracy, who had condemned Israel for "egregious violations of human rights" in Gaza in January 2009, before the Goldstone mission even began its investigation.[68]

After Judge Goldstone's disavowal was published, Prime Minister Binyamin Netanyahu of Israel declared, "It's time to throw this [Goldstone] report into the dustbin of history."[69] The global governance party, however, insisted that Israel was still guilty and continued to urge transnational legal action against the Jewish state. In the view of Amnesty International, "Recent Israeli government calls for the United Nations to retract the 2009 report" were "a cynical attempt to avoid accountability for war crimes." Amnesty reiterated its call for the International Criminal Court's prosecutor to "seek a legal determination from the Pre-Trial Chamber on whether an investigation could be launched on the basis of a 2009 declaration by the Palestinian Authority accepting the Court's jurisdiction over crimes committed on the Palestinian territories." Further, Amnesty called once again for "national authorities of other states to exercise universal jurisdiction over war crimes committed during the 2008–2009 Gaza conflict."[70]

Human Rights Watch's executive director, Kenneth Roth, claimed that Goldstone had "not retreated from the report's allegation that Israel engaged in large scale attacks in violation of the laws of war." This Israeli "misconduct," Roth said, "was so widespread and systematic that it clearly reflected Israeli policy." Finally, Roth asserted that Israel had "failed to investigate adequately the policy-level decisions that apparently lie behind the large-scale indiscriminate and unlawful attacks in Gaza."[71]

While Israeli leaders including Netanyahu and President Shimon Peres asked the UN to retract the Goldstone Report, a spokesman for the UN Human Rights Council, Cedric Sapey, insisted that such a measure would require the support of the Fact Finding Mission as a body, along with action by the Human Rights Council and the General Assembly.[72]

Meanwhile, the other three members of the UN Fact Finding Mission (Hina Jilani, Christine Chinkin, and Desmond Travers) disputed Goldstone's retraction, declared that they "firmly stand by" the original conclusion of the report, and denounced what they called "an attempt to delegitimise the findings of this report and to cast doubts on its credibility."[73] In Britain, *The Commentator* website reported that a "consensus" was forming at the UN to continue promoting the Goldstone Report. The British and German foreign ministries indicated that they would not support a retraction; a spokesman for the British Foreign Office asserted that other "credible organisations" had corroborated the original allegations in the report.[74]

Thus, it appears that despite Judge Goldstone's retraction, the UN report that bears his name will continue to be wielded as a transnational legal weapon by both the Islamist-Arab rejectionist bloc and the global governance party against the democratic state of Israel.

Turning Point: Israel's Ideological Counterattack

More than a year and a half before Goldstone's bombshell recantation, as the worldwide media campaign against the IDF's Gaza operation escalated in the summer of 2009, the *Jerusalem Post* reported that Israel's democratic leadership was preparing for political war against adversarial NGOs such as Human Rights Watch and Amnesty International. The *Post* stated that the Israeli Ministry of Foreign Affairs, in coordination with the Prime Minister's Office, was planning to "deal more systematically with this issue," meaning the ideological agenda of NGOs that feign impartiality but are biased against Israel.[75] Ron Dermer, a chief policy advisor to Prime Minister Binyamin Netanyahu, declared emphatically, "We are going to dedicate time and manpower to combating these groups. We are not going to be sitting ducks in a pond for the human rights groups to shoot at us with impunity."[76]

In what the *Jerusalem Post* described as "the opening shot of a battle Jerusalem has decided to wage with NGOs," a spokesman for the Israeli prime minister blasted Human Rights Watch's fundraising in Saudi Arabia.[77] In May 2009, the NGO had held a fundraising dinner with elite Saudis, including the head of the Shura Council, the body that enforces strict Islamic law in the Saudi kingdom. The Middle East director for HRW, Sarah Leah Whitson, solicited the Saudis for funds by emphasizing the organization's "battles" with "pro-Israel pressure groups" that were attempting to "discredit" its Gaza reports.[78] The Israeli Prime Minister's Office commented that "a human rights organization raising money in Saudi Arabia is like a women's rights group asking the Taliban for a donation.... For an organization that claims to offer moral direction, it appears that Human Rights Watch has seriously lost its moral compass."[79]

The decision by the Netanyahu government in the summer of 2009 to launch a vigorous ideological counterattack against the adversarial NGOs was a major historical turning point in the broader struggle between the forces of global governance and the liberal democratic nation-state. Previously, Western democratic leaders viewed the prominent human rights NGOs as essentially "on our side," part of the "Western" or "democratic team." They might be naïve, too single-minded, and a bit difficult at times, but they were genuine humanitarians who operated in good faith and mostly did useful work. This was the attitude of most American administrations, who might quarrel with particular NGO reports but generally regarded their role in world affairs as positive.

Involved in a serious existential struggle, the Israelis are the first liberal democrats to actively counter the adversarial role that the NGOs are playing against the democratic nation-state. After a decade of unsubstantiated charges of "serious violations" of international law—after repeated controversies over Durban, Jenin, the Second Intifada, the security barrier, the Second Lebanon War, and Gaza—Israelis believe that their right to defend themselves in the manner they choose as a democratic self-governing people is under a sustained global attack by NGOs that are funded by Western philanthropies, the European Union, and some European nation-states. Further, it is clear that this NGO project is not some "good faith," evenhanded, humanitarian initiative that admonishes "both sides."

In terms of both quantity and quality, the NGO reports disproportionately target the democratic Israelis in a way that advantages the antidemocratic terrorists of Hamas and Hezbollah. Year after year, both Human Rights Watch and Amnesty International charge Israel with "violations of human rights and international law" more than any other country or non-state entity in the Middle East.[80] While extreme violence—to many observers, genocide—was being perpetrated in Sudan (2000–2004), Human Rights Watch and Amnesty International published fewer than half the number of reports on the horrors of Sudan than they did on alleged "human rights violations" related to the Israeli-Palestinian conflict.[81]

The NGOs present themselves as unbiased moral arbiters who investigate and condemn violations of international humanitarian law and human rights law everywhere in the world. If the moral authority of the NGOs is undermined, if they are shown to be ideologically partisan activists, their brand name would be tarnished and their influence would erode. The Israeli counterattack strikes at the NGOs' "center of gravity," their moral authority. This strategy aims to demystify the human rights NGOs and remove their halo.

Unlike other Western liberal democrats, the Israelis are taking the NGOs seriously. The Netanyahu government is saying (accurately, in my view) that Human Rights Watch, Amnesty International, and some other NGOs are not impartial arbiters who operate in good faith, but partisans who operate in bad faith; who have an ideological agenda at odds with the security of Israel in its war with radical Islamist terror. In the conflict between global governance and liberal democracy, Israeli democratic sovereigntists are identifying as political adversaries those particular groups whose goals are antithetical to the sovereignty of democratic nation-states.

The fundraising among Saudi elites by Human Rights Watch helped fuel a broader condemnation of that NGO. Its own founder, Robert Bernstein, in an opinion article in the *New York Times* in October 2009, criticized HRW's Gaza reports for "helping those who wish to turn Israel into a pariah state" and for basing their accusations on the testimony of Palestinians "whose stories cannot be verified."[82] Soon afterward, Elie Wiesel and other Jewish civic leaders signed a letter accusing Human Rights Watch of playing a "destructive role" in the Arab-Israeli conflict.[83] Then, the *Guardian* reported that "HRW was shaken by accusations that its military expert and collector of war memorabilia, Marc Garlasco, is a Nazi sympathiser after describing an SS jacket as 'so cool' in comments on a blog."[84]

The Israeli counterattack also confronts those forces in Europe, both EU officials and some nation-states, that are funding an array of adversarial NGOs, including western European, Palestinian, Arab-Israeli, and Israeli "peace" NGOs. The Netanyahu government complained to the British, Dutch, and Spanish governments about their funding of Breaking the Silence, an antiwar activist group of Israeli former soldiers and peace advocates, who have loudly charged the IDF with war crimes in Gaza.

The Knesset (Israeli parliament) launched an investigation of European funding of Israeli political activists. Professor Gerald Steinberg, the president of NGO Monitor and a key player in the controversy, argued that the EU and European governments were "major sources of funding for dozens of Israeli and Palestinian organizations claiming to promote human rights and similar moral causes" while pushing agendas that were "more political than moral." The European Commission and fifteen European governments (including Spain, Britain, and France) provided little information about this funding, noted Steinberg, adding:

> The nature and scale of European influence is unique—in no other case do democratic countries use taxpayer money to support opposition groups in other democracies. Imagine the French response to U.S. government financing for radical NGO anti-abortion campaigns in Paris, or for promoting Corsican separatists under the guise of human rights. Would Spain tolerate foreign government funding of NGO campaigns involving the violent Basque conflict?[85]

Steinberg pointed out that allegations in the Goldstone Report were "in some cases copied directly" from twenty European-funded

NGOs, many of which were also involved in the international campaign of boycotts, divestment, and sanctions against Israel. Europeans provided Breaking the Silence with travel funds that were "used to promote its efforts to spread allegations of war crimes around the world," said Steinberg, who decried the use of European taxpayers' money for this kind of "political warfare."[86]

Prime Minister Netanyahu's aide, Ron Dermer, directly confronted the Europeans, attacking their funding of adversarial NGOs that were "working to delegitimize the Jewish state." This funding amounted to "blatant and unacceptable" interference in Israeli democracy, Dermer said. "Just as it would be unacceptable for European governments to support anti-war NGOs in the US, it is unacceptable for the Europeans to support local NGOs opposed to the policies of Israel's democratically-elected government."[87]

The Netanyahu government, the Knesset, and NGO Monitor have pressed the Europeans on two issues: interference in Israeli domestic politics, and the lack of transparency in European funding of controversial NGOs. The European Union's ambassador to Israel responded in an interview in the *Jerusalem Post*. An enthusiastic transnationalist who describes himself as a "committed European with a British passport," Ambassador Andrew Standley told the *Post* that funding for Israeli NGOs did not constitute meddling. "There is a certain perception in Israeli society that what we are financing in Israel and in this region is unique, and that these are programs aimed at influencing public policy in Israel," Standley said. But in reality, "these are global programs," he stressed, and are "just as easily funded in places like China, India, Indonesia and even the US." Standley said the criteria used to fund the NGOs "are global, universal criteria," and that "one can feel comfortable with the kind of support provided here, because it is in the context of a global commitment to universal values and human rights that these actions are being funded." When questioned specifically about the funding of the Israeli radical anti-defense group Peace Now,

Standley answered that "the funding is not provided for a political agenda, but rather in support of a universal objective such as human rights." He emphasized that the EU funded projects of this type not only in Israel "but all over the planet."[88]

Ambassador Standley's response is revealing in two ways. First, he maintained that the EU funds only universally recognized human rights activities and not anti-Israeli boycotts, divestment campaigns, lawfare suits against the IDF, and the like. However, as almost anyone involved with nonprofit organizations knows, funding within NGOs is fungible. The more money the NGO receives, the more projects it can support, and the more likely it is that funds can be shifted around. Surely, Ambassador Standley is aware that EU funding to the adversarial NGOs is helping (however indirectly) the global anti-Israel campaign of boycotts, divestment, sanctions, and lawfare.

Second, Standley's argument reveals the broad philosophical divide between the forces of global governance and the liberal democratic nation-state. Standley blithely declared that "one can feel comfortable" because the EU funds projects that support "universal values and human rights," such as "the rights of women" and "minorities," and does so "all over the planet."[89] But that is precisely the problem. What exactly constitutes "universal values," "human rights," "women's rights," and "minority rights" is bitterly contested within the West and around the globe, as we have seen in the controversies over the International Criminal Court, Additional Protocol I, the laws of war, and the UN CEDAW and CERD treaties.

In Israel and "all over the planet," the European Union is funding one particular version of "universal values," the transnational progressive version. But democratic nation-states including Israel, India, and the United States do not accept the EU's definition of universal human rights as put forth in the ICC and Additional Protocol I of the Geneva Conventions. Democratic sovereigntists "all over the planet" do not accept the supranational interference in domestic politics that is routine within the EU—the "global domestic politics" touted by Joschka Fischer and Robert Cooper. Hence, Ambassador Standley's remarks to the *Jerusalem Post* exemplify the deeper ideological struggle between the global governance party and the democratic nation-state.

CHAPTER THIRTEEN

Assimilation of Immigrants:
Patriotic or Multicultural?

E very day in the news we see stories concerning global migration, multiculturalism, and immigrant assimilation. For
instance, the American Civil Liberties Union signs a formal
alliance with the Mexican government to work together for the
"rights" of illegal immigrants in the United States.[1] An Australian
citizen of Italian descent enters the Italian parliament as a representative of ethnic Italians living abroad. (These dual-citizen deputies
are responsible for the ouster of the Berlusconi government in
Italy.)[2] A scholar at the Brookings Institution publishes a major academic paper arguing that nation-states must accommodate the new
"diaspora consciousness," and particularly the "dual citizenships"
and "multiple allegiances" that come with it.[3]

France bans the female headscarf.[4] Switzerland votes to prohibit
the construction of minarets on mosques.[5] Canada issues a new
citizenship test that emphasizes patriotism and Canadian military
valor.[6] Israel constructs a new fence to stop illegal immigrants for
cultural and economic (not just security) reasons.[7] Italy repatriates
illegal immigrants to Africa amid protests from the United Nations,
human rights groups, the Vatican, and the political opposition at
home.[8] Swedish police and firefighters are frequently attacked by
Muslim youths in certain neighborhoods of Malmö.[9] France explicitly

lists 751 "Sensitive Urban Zones," essentially no-go areas dominated by mostly Muslim immigrant gangs, into which the police rarely venture.[10] Somali Muslim taxi drivers in Minneapolis refuse to serve passengers carrying alcohol.[11]

Jorge Bustamante, the UN special rapporteur on migrant rights, asserts that "xenophobia and racism towards migrants in the United States has worsened since 9/11" and that "the United States has failed to adhere to its international obligations" with respect to migrants.[12] The American Constitution Society publishes a major paper by Catherine Powell, a law professor, advocating that the United States adhere to the UN Migrant Rights Treaty.[13] The Mexican president Vicente Fox declares that he is president of 118 million Mexicans: 100 million in Mexico plus 18 million in the United States, including American citizens.[14] Manuel de la Cruz, a naturalized U.S. citizen living in California, is elected to the Mexican Congress on the anti-American Democratic Revolutionary Party ticket.[15]

Oregon, Utah, and the Los Angeles Unified School District hire Mexican teachers to use Mexican history textbooks to instruct Mexican American students in American public schools.[16] During a protest against immigration reform proposals being debated in Congress, American high school students of Mexican descent hoist the Mexican flag over a school in California, with the American flag hanging upside down beneath it.[17]

Three public charter schools in Chicago are named after Latino war veterans.[18] Sixty-five percent of the top scorers in the U.S. Math Olympiad are children of immigrants.[19]

The preceding news stories about immigrants—some positive, some negative, depending upon one's point of view—all bear on the issue of who accommodates to whom, and on what terms. To probe further, let us pose four interrelated questions:

(1) Should immigrants accommodate to host countries, or vice versa?

(2)   What degree of accommodation should be made, and by whom? Is it a fifty-fifty proposition or something else?

(3)   Who or what decides the terms of the accommodation: host countries, immigrants, negotiations between them, transnational authorities, economic factors?

(4)   On what principles or pragmatic grounds are these decisions made: democratic self-government, global rights, political maneuvering, labor market demands, economic calculus, or a combination of the above?

Two Models of Integration

For most of American history, our leaders have largely agreed that the patriotic attachment of newcomers to the American body politic was vital to the health and indeed the survival of the republic. From George Washington, Thomas Jefferson, and Alexander Hamilton during the founding era, to Theodore Roosevelt, Woodrow Wilson and Louis Brandeis during the Ellis Island period, American leaders advocated the patriotic assimilation of immigrants. Today, however, there are deep disagreements about the integration of immigrants, expressed in controversies over bilingualism, multicultural education, multilingual voting, dual citizenship, illegal immigration, and border enforcement. These disagreements generally divide between two broad frameworks for immigrant assimilation: the democratic sovereigntist model and the global governance–multiculturalist approach.

The Democratic Sovereigntist Vision of Integration. In this framework, the liberal democratic nation-state would fully exercise its sovereign right to determine immigration and assimilation policy, and not be limited by supposed "global norms" that it did not explicitly accept in treaties or domestic law. The philosophical basis of the democratic sovereigntist model is democratic consent, including the moral right of a liberal democratic nation-state to decide its own immigration policies without a veto either by subnational communities or by transnational authorities. It includes the collective right of a nation's citizens to perpetuate their civic culture and way of life.

Democratic sovereigntists favor the patriotic integration of immigrants into the body politic and civic culture of the democratic nation-state. Historically, democratic sovereigntists have frowned on dual citizenship and multiple allegiances. In the United States, this perspective has traditionally been compatible with the existence of vibrant ethnic subcultures, while in France it has traditionally meant complete cultural assimilation and the disappearance of most ethnic customs.

The Global Governance–Multiculturalist Vision of Integration. The forces of global governance argue that migration from the "global South" (the developing world) to the "global North" (the developed world) is both inevitable and beneficial for economic and humanitarian reasons. The migrants or immigrants are said to carry universal human rights along with them, including not only individual rights of human dignity, but also, more controversially, collective rights to maintain native languages and customs, mores and values, even those that are adversarial to the mainstream culture of their new home. In other words, the argument goes, immigrants have the right of social reproduction, meaning the right to perpetuate a way of life as a collective entity.[20]

This multicultural approach to immigration promotes economic integration along with legal and civic rights, but also embraces dual citizenship, diaspora consciousness, and multiple allegiances and loyalties. Crucially, this model limits the political choices and thus the democratic self-government of the host nations. It interferes with the right of social reproduction of the citizens already living in those nations.

The Ampersand vs. the Hyphen

As the debate in Congress over immigration heated up in the spring of 2007, reporters for the *Chicago Tribune* interviewed Jose Luis

Gutierrez, a top aide to the governor of Illinois and head of the state's Office of New Americans. "The nation-state concept is changing," Gutierrez told the *Tribune*. "You don't have to say, 'I am Mexican,' or 'I am American.' You can be a good Mexican citizen and a good American citizen and not have that be a conflict of interest. Sovereignty is flexible."[21]

The *Tribune* article described an emerging transnational politics, noting that "Gutierrez and others say they form a budding new political consciousness among Mexican immigrants, a third 'nation' of sorts that transcends the border."[22] In boldly declaring himself "both Mexican and American," Gutierrez repudiated the traditional concept of the hyphenated American who is proud of his ethnic heritage and customs but whose political loyalty is exclusively to the United States. Instead, Gutierrez introduced us to the ampersand citizen, who is not an Irish-American, Italian-American, or Mexican-American, but rather Irish & American, Italian & American, or Mexican & American, and whose political loyalty is ambivalent.

The binational/multicultural model of integration promoted by Jose Luis Gutierrez is the official state-endorsed model in Illinois. In 2006, the governor's office issued an "Interagency Task Force Report" with recommendations for promoting immigrant integration from Illinois state agencies involved in employment, health, education, children and family services, aging, and human resources. The report was partly funded by the MacArthur and Carnegie foundations. Among the recommendations were:

- Create a new state bureaucracy, the "Office of Language and Cultural Competence," that would "serve to coordinate key language and cultural competence functions."[23]
- "Develop a comprehensive linguistic and cultural competency training for all state staff." Each state agency should provide "services that are culturally and linguistically competent," and create "a service delivery system that is culturally and linguistically sensitive."[24]

- Require the development of a "cultural competency curriculum" that would be mandated for "all state employees" and taught by "cultural competency trainers."[25]
- Emphasize bilingualism (English and Spanish), with large-scale hiring of bilingual employees, a special new "bilingual pay policy," a new statewide "bilingual competency testing process,"[26] "translating all vital documents into Spanish within 3 months,"[27] and continuous "efforts to recruit and hire bilingual staff."[28]
- Recruit bilingual teachers and trainers, including "highly qualified teachers from Spain . . . to teach Bilingual Education classes,"[29] and explore the possibility of "Mexican national social workers coming to Illinois" in order to "train" Illinois state employees on "cultural issues."[30]
- Eliminate "barriers" to bringing in more foreign nurses, in order to increase the number of bilingual nurses.[31]

The emphasis of Illinois's integration policy is on immigrants as clients with a need for social services. The role of the state bureaucracy is to provide these services, including bilingual specialists and a "culturally and linguistically sensitive" delivery system. The default position is multiculturalism. Newcomers are seen less as potential patriotic citizens than as members of distinct subnational "communities" within the United States that speak languages other than English and maintain cultural norms and perspectives different from those of other Americans. These differences (and the grievances associated with them) should, in this view, be accommodated by the American mainstream.

The Illinois model is mirrored in other states that have launched their own immigrant integration projects. The Massachusetts governor's office recommends that state educators "develop a cultural competency curriculum that can be disseminated statewide" and "a bank of professionals who can provide cultural competency training for schools and other public agencies." Massachusetts urges educators to "emphasize multilingual and multi-cultural skills when hiring teachers," in a report illustrated with pictures of immigrant protestors and women in Muslim headscarves.[32]

Massachusetts is promoting "dual immersion," the cutting edge of bilingual education. The idea is that instead of "pushing children to learn English as quickly as possible, programs would aim to build students' literacy in their native language as well as in English."[33] Moreover, *all* children, not just immigrants, would be "immersed" in a foreign language (mostly Spanish) along with English. The Massachusetts task force calls for "increased funding, support and prevalence of dual immersion programs" for all students.[34]

A task force was created in Maryland to promote the maintenance of immigrants' birth languages with funding from the state government. "It is critical that we provide for the preservation of our heritage languages," declared the task force.[35] One of the reasons listed was a central tenet of multiculturalism: to preserve the "core of the identities of children, representing their values, culture, and traditions."[36]

The Division of Language Minority and Migrant Programs at the Indiana Department of Education has claimed that "supporting native language bolsters students' self-esteem." The agency promotes "multilingualism in all learners" and the use of "curricula that reflect the culture, values, interests, and concerns of language minority students." Indiana educators insist that more bilingual staff should be employed and that course material should include native-language "books, magazines, and films," presumably from immigrant children's home countries.[37]

The idea that the integration of immigrants is a "two-way street" is an often repeated cliché. In the Massachusetts task force report, "Integration represents a two-way commitment with the host community and the newcomer populations agreeing to work together to create a more prosperous future."[38] It is "a process in which both newcomers and welcoming communities share responsibilities and benefits."[39] Few would object to the idea that immigrants and the host society both need to make some form of accommodation to each other. In the binational/multicultural model of integration, however, it appears that most of the accommodating would be done by the host community, rather than the newcomers.

The Americanization Model

While state bureaucrats in Illinois and elsewhere implement the multicultural and transnationalist model of integration favored by Jose Luis Gutierrez, another Mexican American in Chicago articulates an entirely different vision. Juan Rangel is the head of the United Neighborhood Organization (UNO), the largest Latino community group in Chicago. To the surprise of many—and against the reigning orthodoxy of school administrators, social studies educators, state bureaucrats, and bilingual advocates—he openly promotes the "assimilation" and "Americanization" of immigrants. Rangel believes that Latinos should not see themselves as a victimized minority. Inspired by the successes of Irish, Italian, German, Jewish, and Polish immigrants during the twentieth century, his organization aims to build on the immigrant experience to produce the latest example of the American success story.[40]

UNO started in 1984 as an adversarial community group of the Saul Alinsky type. Through the years, particularly under Rangel, it has evolved into a major actor in Chicago public affairs, maintaining cordial relations with the mayor and other Chicago and Illinois political leaders. Most significantly, UNO runs eight charter schools that are the antithesis of the multicultural education offered in Chicago's (and most of America's) public schools today. With approximately 3,500 students, UNO's schools represent an effort to replicate the ethos of Americanization that prevailed in the public schools in immigrant neighborhoods during the Ellis Island period.

UNO's curriculum stands in stark contrast to the apologetic multicultural rhetoric and tepid social service language of the various state "integration" projects. For UNO, integration does not mean that vaguely autonomous "newcomer populations" agree to "share responsibilities" with a "host community," as stated in the Massachusetts governor's report, implying a fifty-fifty negotiated arrangement between two distinct communities. Instead, it means immigrants becoming patriotic Americans, pledging loyalty to their adopted country and joining the mainstream of American life, while at the same time remaining proud of and honoring their ethnic heritage.

From the start, UNO's "American Civics Initiative: A School Curriculum for Immigrant Assimilation" affirms the principle of *E pluribus unum* and announces an agenda of "promoting American values, ideals, opportunities and successes."[41] With illustrations of young UNO students reciting the Pledge of Allegiance, the document explains that the Pledge and the National Anthem "powerfully convey commitment and reverence toward the United States." It notes that a promise of opportunity "has driven generations of immigrants to this nation. In return, we have an obligation to pledge our loyalty and demonstrate national unity. In deference to these ideals, UNO students will begin every day by reciting the Pledge of Allegiance. Teachers will explain the protocol when addressing the flag."[42]

Saying that "it is incumbent on schools to impress upon students the significance of . . . national holidays," the UNO curriculum creates lesson plans to commemorate not only the major American holidays such as Memorial Day, Veterans Day, and Thanksgiving, but also Constitution Day (September 17) as a time to emphasize an understanding of America's founding documents, and 9/11 as a day to remember "the American spirit of service and heroism."[43] Under a picture of George Washington with the caption "Leadership," the curriculum explains that "UNO uses the holiday observances in January and February of three of our greatest leaders —George Washington, Abraham Lincoln, and Martin Luther King Jr.—as a backdrop for talking about leadership in the context of civic responsibility and stewardship."[44] There is a section in the curriculum titled "Freedom and Our War Heroes."[45] Three of UNO's schools are named after Latino American war veterans.

Unlike the public schools in Chicago and nationwide that emphasize bilingualism or dual immersion, UNO puts a priority on English learning and uses English immersion for its many Spanish-speaking students. To be sure, UNO students also have an opportunity to develop good Spanish-language skills, which "are usually not taught at home." The curriculum acknowledges that "Spanish is an asset," but it "should never be emphasized at the expense of English. English is the language that unites Americans and mastery of it is what will lead to success for our students."[46]

Patriotic Integration

We could list five different types of assimilation or integration: economic, linguistic, cultural, civic, and patriotic. Economic integration would mean the newcomer is gainfully employed and doing reasonably well materially. Linguistic integration would mean the immigrant has a practical proficiency in the English language. Cultural integration would mean acculturation into American popular cultural and all it entails. Civic integration means the immigrant is assimilated into the American political and legal system, obeys the law, and participates in community or public life in some fashion.

All these forms of integration are necessary, but not sufficient. The type of integration that matters most for the long-term health of American democracy—and the type that was advocated by Washington, Adams, Jefferson, Hamilton, Theodore Roosevelt, Woodrow Wilson, and Louis Brandeis—is political loyalty and emotional attachment to the American republic. George Washington envisioned that immigrants would be "assimilated to our customs, measures, and laws," and thus "soon become one people" with the native-born. Similarly, Abraham Lincoln spoke of immigrants becoming "blood of the blood, and flesh of the flesh of the men who wrote [the] Declaration" of Independence.[47] Commonly known as "Americanization," this can also be called "patriotic integration." It occurs when newcomers essentially adopt America's civic culture and the story of America as their own, when they and their children begin to think of American history as "our" history, not "their" history.

For example, imagine the daughter of Korean immigrants studying American history in the eighth grade. When she is studying the Constitutional Convention of 1787, does she think of this event as part of "their" history—something that white males of European descent did long before any of her ancestors came to America? Or does she think of this narrative as "our" history, as something that "we" Americans did in creating a constitution? If she identifies with the national "we," she has become, as Lincoln anticipated, "blood of the blood and flesh of the flesh" with the Founding Fathers.[48]

In contemporary terms, patriotic integration does not mean giving up all ethnic traditions, customs, cuisine, or birth languages. Multiethnicity and ethnic subcultures (as opposed to adversarial multiculturalism) have always been part of the fabric of society and have enriched American life. Patriotic integration does, however, mean rejection of dual allegiances and ambiguity over one's political loyalty. It does mean a transfer of allegiance from one's birth nation to the United States as sworn in the oath of citizenship, which is formally called the Oath of Renunciation and Allegiance, because it both affirms loyalty to the U.S. Constitution and renounces all prior political allegiances.

In this vein, one could well imagine that a working-class Mexican-born graduate of Chicago's UNO charter schools, who has internalized and identified with the American narrative, is more likely to be "patriotically integrated" than, say, an affluent French or German entrepreneur in the Silicon Valley who has become an American citizen mainly because it is useful for business. This hypothetical European could be an example of civic integration without patriotic integration. He is fluent in English, is well informed on American politics, and votes. On the other hand, he is a dual citizen and votes in Europe as well. Most significantly, he is rather ambiguous about any specific American political loyalty. He likes democracy well enough, but is not particularly attached to the American version, compared with any other. Patriotism embarrasses him. It is somehow bad form. The serious political allegiances that he might maintain are to what he would consider global humanitarian ideals and not to any particular political entity or democratic nation-state.

Barriers to Patriotic Assimilation

The barriers and obstacles to patriotic integration today are technological, ideological, legal, and political. We no longer live in the world of Ellis Island, when immigrants crossed the Atlantic and for the most part did not return to their native lands. As the immigration scholar Gerald Neuman writes, "We live in an age of transnational migrants, enabled by advanced technologies of transportation, communication, finance, and trade to operate simultaneously as partial members of more than one national community."[49] Inexpensive travel and modern communications mean that today's immigrant does not have to make a wrenching break with "the old country," as was necessary during the heyday of mass immigration in the early twentieth century.

At the same time, the ideological outlook of American professionals involved in the day-to-day business of assimilating immigrants (educators, social workers, government bureaucrats, immigration lawyers) is considerably different from that of their counterparts a century ago. Public school teachers and administrators at that time were on the front lines of the Americanization campaign, and the school curriculum was the main engine of patriotic integration. Today, the curriculum is dominated by multiculturalism and diversity, emphasizing the *pluribus* rather than the *unum*. American educators even enlist foreign teachers and foreign curricula to "integrate" newcomers into American society, or into what they perhaps envision as a binational or global society.

In 2007, the *Oregonian* reported that "Oregon is counting on a new tool to educate Spanish-speaking students," specifically, "Mexico's curriculum." The story explained:

Already in place at three Oregon high schools, the programs [aim] to use textbooks, a detailed online Web site, DVDs and CDs provided for free by the Mexican government to teach math, science and even U.S. history to Spanish speakers in Oregon. Conversations are under way between the Oregon Department of Education and Mexico's secretary of public education to align the curriculums of Oregon and Mexico. . . . The innovative move puts Oregon on par with other educators nationwide who have launched similar ventures in Yakima, Wash.; San Diego, Calif.; and Austin, Texas.[50]

Moreover, school districts in Utah, Los Angeles, Houston, and elsewhere are recruiting teachers from Mexico to teach Mexican American students in bilingual curricula. "The Mexican consulate in Los Angeles showered nearly 100,000 textbooks on 1,500 schools in the Los Angeles Unified School District" in 2005, wrote Heather Mac Donald of the Manhattan Institute.[51] The press attaché at the consulate, Mireya Magaña Gálvez, said it was important for young Americans of Mexican descent to know Mexican history. Thus, the textbooks celebrate "Mexican patriotic symbols: the flag, currency, and the national anthem," and ask students to learn about "what happened to your territory [Mexico] when the U.S. invaded."[52] Mac Donald remarks sardonically, "it is hard to see how studying Mexican history from a Mexican perspective helps forge an American identity," particularly when the teaching of American history is inadequate.[53]

Obviously, using Mexican textbooks to teach students the history of, for example, the Mexican War of 1846–48 is not simply a matter of learning Mexican history, but of promoting Mexican nationalism at the expense of American identity. This is far different from the Ellis Island age. One could not imagine Theodore Roosevelt's America importing teachers and textbooks from Italy and Germany to teach history to the children of Italian and German immigrants in our public schools. Yet today, the U.S. Department of Education assists the Mexican government in bringing Mexican teachers to the United States to promote Mexican history and culture among American students.[54] In addition, professional groups such as the National Association of Bilingual Educators and think tanks like the Migration Policy Institute also collaborate with Mexican government officials and academics in fostering both bilingual education and binational integration policies in the United States.[55]

In the United States today, there is a structure of laws and administrative procedures that discourage and, indeed, hinder newcomers from building a strong American identity. These legal and political barriers to patriotic integration have developed gradually since the late 1960s through a combination of Supreme Court decisions, federal bureaucratic policies, congressional action, and executive orders. What we might call the "anti-Americanization infrastructure" includes:

- Permitting and even encouraging voting in foreign languages in American national and state elections.
- Dual citizenship, which permits naturalized American citizens to vote and even hold political office in their birth nations, despite the fact that they have taken an Oath of Allegiance to the U.S. Constitution in which they "absolutely and entirely renounce allegiance" to those nations.
- Executive Order 13166, issued in 2000, which mandates official multilingualism in all federally funded programs.
- Bilingual education that emphasizes retaining birth languages instead of quickly acquiring English.
- Multicultural education that promotes ethnic group identity over American national identity.
- Ethnic group preferences for newly arrived immigrants in affirmative action programs that were originally designed to counter the effects of slavery and segregation of African Americans, but today are used to promote ethnic group proportionalism, "substantive" equality, or "diversity."

All these measures work against the formation of an American national identity in newcomers, as envisioned by American leaders from George Washington to Theodore Roosevelt, and supported today by Latino community leaders like Juan Rangel in Chicago. Instead, they promote an ethnic group consciousness that tends to view the American mainstream in an adversarial way.*

The anti-assimilationist mindset was on display in a controversy that arose while the Senate was debating the immigration bill of 2006. Senator Lamar Alexander (R-TN) introduced an amendment calling for the "patriotic integration of prospective citizens into American common values and traditions, including an understanding of American history and the principles of the Constitution." The *Washington Times* reported that in an internal email, Michelle Waslin, director of immigration policy for the National Council of La Raza, called the Alexander amendment "very problematic" because, "while it doesn't overtly mention assimilation, it is very strong on the patriotism and traditional american [*sic*] values language in a way which is potentially dangerous to our communities." Once the email was leaked, La Raza stated that its position on the Alexander amendment was "unclearly communicated."[56]

How Is Patriotic Integration Working Today?

In a *Washington Post* column, Robert J. Samuelson wrote that assimilation "means more than having them [immigrants] join the

---

*When I promoted the concept of patriotic assimilation at a meeting of the Pew Foundation's Citizenship Policy Project on July 23, 2002, there was strong opposition from several attendees. Diana Aviv, a major figure in American philanthropy (former chair of the National Immigration Forum, current president and CEO of the Independent Sector, a powerful lobbying arm of American foundations and corporate philanthropy), responded, "I'm concerned with patriotic assimilation. I take umbrage at that. This could be offensive to people." Demetrios Papademetriou, president of the Migration Policy Institute (MPI), asserted that "Patriotic assimilation is divisive."

economic mainstream. It also means that they think of themselves primarily as Americans. If the United States simply becomes a collection of self-designated 'minorities,' then the country will have changed for the worse."[57] On this particular issue—whether naturalized citizens choose to identify themselves primarily as Americans or by the nationality of the country in which they were born—the empirical data on patriotic integration does not look good.

Professors Alejandro Portes and Rubén G. Rumbaut published a massive longitudinal study of five thousand children of immigrants from seventy-seven different countries living in the Miami and San Diego areas. Conducted in the 1990s, the study began when the youngsters entered high school as freshmen and tracked their attitudes and abilities when they were seniors, finding that their linguistic assimilation was improved, but their patriotic assimilation weakened. When the young people started high school, over 53 percent identified themselves as Americans or hyphenated Americans, whereas only 28 percent identified with their parents' birth nation (Mexico, China, etc.) and 16 percent listed a pan-ethnic identity (Hispanic, Asian). After four years of American high school, the proportion of students who self-identified as Americans or hyphenated Americans had dropped from 53 percent to 34 percent, while the proportion of students who identified with a foreign nationality (e.g. Mexican, Chinese) rose from 28 percent to 35 percent, and the pan-ethnic designation (Latino, Asian) went up from 16 percent to 27 percent.[58]

In December 2002, the Pew Foundation's Hispanic Center and the Kaiser Family Foundation released a broad survey of Latino/Hispanic attitudes. The Pew report posed the question: "Are Latino newcomers undergoing the melting pot experience, or are they and their offspring maintaining their native cultures and becoming an ethnic group that is different from the mainstream?" The authors of the survey answered, "Both to some extent," although most of the evidence they presented emphasized differences with the American mainstream.

Latinos who are American citizens were asked how they chose to identity themselves. There were three choices: (1) American, (2) Latino or Hispanic, or (3) family national origin (Mexican, Salvadoran, Guatemalan, etc.). The question was posed seven to nine months after the 9/11 attacks, a period of intense patriotism nationwide, yet only 33 percent of those American citizens thought of themselves as Americans first, while 44 percent identified themselves by national origin (Mexicans, Guatemalans, etc.) and 22 percent considered themselves primarily as Latinos or Hispanics. Even among the second generation, those born in the United States of immigrant parents, only 35 percent put their American identity first; 38 percent chose their parents' birth nation, and 24 percent considered themselves primarily as Latinos or Hispanics.

A 2007 Pew study revealed that among American citizens of Hispanic descent, only 14 percent thought of themselves primarily as Americans, whereas 54 percent identified with their birth nation first.[59] In 2009, another Pew study, this one of young Latinos, reported that among the U.S.-born children of immigrants, 41 percent refer to themselves "first by the country that their parents left," and "just 33% of these young second generation Latinos use American first, while 21% refer to themselves first by the terms Hispanic or Latino."[60]

Using census data beginning in 1900, Professor Jacob Vigdor of Duke University created an Immigrant Assimilation Index that compared contemporary immigrants with those of the early twentieth century on a scale of 1 to 100. Professor Vigdor identified three categories of assimilation: economic (home ownership, educational attainment, employment success), cultural (English ability, intermarriage rates), and civic (naturalization, military service). The results of the study, released in 2008, showed assimilation today to be "low by historical standards."[61] Whereas immigrants who came through Ellis Island one hundred years ago averaged 50 on the index for overall assimilation, today's immigrants averaged 28 on the scale. Mexican immigrants scored particularly low on the index compared with immigrants from a hundred years ago, perhaps because they are "closer to their home country" and often plan on returning there.[62]

Traditionally, one of the greatest indicators of assimilation has been intermarriage among ethnic groups, and between immigrants and the native-born of different ethnicities. A major study by Professors Zhenchao Qian and Daniel Lichter, published in the *American Sociological Review* in 2007, found substantial declines in interethnic marriage, representing "significant departures from past trends." The report noted that the rate of intermarriage between immigrants and native-born citizens had been increasing as recently as the 1970s and 1980s, but the trend reversed in the 1990s. One implied cause was an increase in the numbers of low-skilled immigrants. The researchers pointed out that immigrants with higher levels of education were more likely to marry outside their immediate ethnic group than those with less education.[63] In recent years, U.S. immigration policy has favored newcomers with low education and skill levels.

Muslim Integration in the United States

The "comforting media narrative" portrays Muslim Americans as "well-assimilated and willing to leave their religion and culture behind in pursuit of American values and lifestyle," wrote the widely acclaimed Century Foundation journalist Geneive Abdo in 2006. But "the real story of American Muslims," she continued, "is one of accelerating alienation from the mainstream of U.S. life, with Muslims in this country choosing their Islamic identity over their American one."[64]★

★Geneive Abdo, the author of *Mecca and Mainstream: Muslim Life in America after 9/11,* is sympathetic to the assertion of Muslim cultural norms in American life and blames Muslim alienation from the mainstream on American attitudes since 9/11 and on U.S. foreign policy.

Abdo's verdict was supported by data gathered in 2007 when the Pew Research Center conducted the first nationwide survey of attitudes among Muslim Americans, 65 percent of whom were foreign-born. The report began by declaring Muslim Americans to be "largely assimilated, happy with their lives," and "decidedly American in their outlook, values, and attitudes."[65] However, despite the rose-colored introduction, the poll's actual statistics indicated serious impediments to patriotic integration.

According to the Pew survey, only 26 percent of Muslim Americans believed that the U.S.-led war on terror was a sincere effort to reduce terrorism, in stark contrast with a 67 percent favorable response for the general public. The poll noted that only 40 percent of the overall American Muslim population believed that Arabs were behind the 9/11 attacks. Asked about their primary identity, 47 percent of respondents said they considered themselves to be Muslims first and Americans second, while 28 percent thought of themselves as Americans first.[66]★ Among those who identified as Muslims first, 13 percent believed that suicide bombing to defend Islam could sometimes be justified. Among Muslims under age thirty, 26 percent said that suicide bombing could be justified.[67]

An earlier poll of American Muslims by Hamilton College in conjunction with Zogby, in May 2002, found that only about one-third believed that Osama bin Laden was responsible for the attacks of September 11, and barely over half regarded the U.S. campaign against al-Qaeda as justified.[68]

★It has been suggested that this finding is not necessarily problematic for the integration of Muslim immigrants into the civic culture of American liberal democracy, since many Christians (and many serious believers of other religions) would similarly give priority to faith over nationality. I argue that the "Muslim first, American second" response is inherently different from an emphasis on Christian identity and that it *does* constitute a problem for American civic culture, as explained in note 66.

Islamist Influence in the United States

Islamism, or political Islam, is a transnational political ideology that seeks to establish Islamic law as supreme over any national or secular law. In such a regime, Sharia would govern all aspects of life: politics, economics, culture, family life, personal relations, and sexual mores. Islamists place loyalty to the *ummah,* the global Muslim "nation," above any loyalty to the nation-state of which they are citizens. The *ummah* is envisioned not simply as a religious-cultural community, but also as a political entity.

Islamists are antidemocratic in the sense that they do not believe in "government by the people," but in government by "God's laws," specifically Sharia. Some Islamists engage in terrorism but many do not, seeking instead to establish Sharia through propaganda and political means. Nevertheless, as the American Muslim thinker Zeyno Baran remarks, "Islamist ideology is the singular root cause of radicalization, and radicalization . . . is the conveyor belt to terrorism."[69]

As we discussed in Chapter Six, Islamist influence in Europe often results in the creation of parallel societies or quasi-autonomous Muslim communities, sometimes governed by Sharia, within Western societies. Zeyno Baran declares that "Islamism is spreading at an alarming rate" in the United States.[70] Another American Muslim democratic activist, Hedieh Mirahmadi⋆ writes that "Today, the Islamist movement's influence can be felt in a majority of American Muslim communities. Islamist clerics and activists set the tone for weekly sermons, organize the training and selection of clerics, and may even decide what books will be sold in mosques and Islamic centers."[71] As new Muslim immigrants come to the United States, they are integrated into "these existing Islamist structures,"[72] which are heavily financed by Saudi Arabia.

⋆Mirahmadi was prominently cited, with photo, in a *Washington Post* story of March 9, 2011, about congressional hearings on Islamic radicalization.

Anti-Islamist American Muslims point out that most of the average mosque-going Muslims in the United States are not Islamists and are uncomfortable with Islamist propaganda and pressure tactics. But this "silent majority" of American Muslims is unorganized and lacks the media savvy, political skills, resources (Saudi funding), and intensity of the Islamists who dominate Muslim institutions in America.[73] Thus, forging an anti-Islamist American Islam will be extremely difficult.

The Public Opinion Divide

For decades there have been two broad approaches to immigration/assimilation policy in the United States, one preferred by elites and the other favored by a majority of American citizens. The elite position is support for continued or even increasing mass immigration, with the assumption that assimilation occurred naturally in the past and will continue doing so. The popular majority position is to reduce current levels of immigration and insist on patriotic assimilation.

American Elites and Immigration

For the most part, the governing class and the leading institutions of American media, business, labor, religion, politics, and philanthropy have consistently favored large-scale (mostly low-skilled) immigration, the legalization of illegal immigrants, and a panoply of multicultural and bilingual projects in education, voting, employment, ethnic preferences, dual citizenship, and the like. These elites raise myriad objections to serious border and interior enforcement, and mostly assume that immigrant assimilation is proceeding with little if any difficulty.

Roughly speaking, we could include in this category: Big Media (*New York Times, Los Angeles Times, Wall Street Journal,* * and most major television networks); Big Business (U.S. Chamber of Commerce, large corporations such as Tyson Foods and Bank of America); Big Labor (AFL-CIO, Service Employees International Union); Big Religion (leaders of the mainline Protestant churches, Catholic bishops, leaders of Jewish organizations); the political class (presidents of both parties, most congressional leaders, governors, and big-city mayors); and leaders of the major American philanthropies (Ford, Rockefeller, MacArthur, Atlantic Philanthropies, Pew, Gates). As we notice, the elites' position in favor of mass immigration—accompanied by a laissez-faire stance on assimilation and general support for multiculturalism—often cuts across the left and the right of the political spectrum. Thus, the elite consensus includes the *New York Times* along with the *Wall Street Journal,* the SEIU as well as the Chamber of Commerce.

The American elites' approach to immigration appears to be mainly pragmatic rather than ideological, in the globalist sense. To be sure, some elite professionals and institutions are sympathetic to the global governance vision of a humanitarian, "rights-carrying" transnational migration. This group could include NGOs like the ACLU, think tanks such as the Migration Policy Institute, immigration lawyers, and some academics and activists. But for the most part, American elites are more narrowly focused on perceived short-term gains. The elite right (particularly some business interests) want cheap labor immediately. The elite left (thinking a little more long-term) correctly envision low-skilled workers as future left-wing voters—at least as long

---

*To be sure, the *Wall Street Journal* editorial page opposes multiculturalism, bilingual education, and ethnic quotas. The editorialists also favor American sovereignty over global governance. But they have not supported serious border and interior enforcement measures (E -Verify, workplace enforcement), nor have they actively opposed dual citizenship or acknowledged that continuous low-skilled immigration creates circumstances that provide the rationale for multiculturalism and an anti-assimilation infrastructure.

as they remain low-skilled and don't join the middle class, hence the need for a perpetual new infusion of low-income immigrants to offset those who may have advanced economically.

Furthermore, American elites have given little thought to the matter of assimilating immigrants in any serious way. So-called "integration" programs run by state agencies and school systems are conceived in terms of promoting multiculturalism. Thus, the state bureaucrats and public educators tell us that the influx of more immigrants into the United States means that we need more "cultural competence trainers," bilingual specialists, multicultural curricula, and teachers and textbooks from Mexico. This is exactly the opposite of what American elites did during the great wave of immigration one hundred years ago, when they insisted on Americanization.

Elite vs. Popular Opinion

There is an enormous gap between elite and popular opinion in the United States concerning both legal and illegal immigration. In 2002, Harris Interactive conducted a scientific poll on immigration issues for the Chicago Council on Foreign Relations, comparing the opinions of the general public with those of "opinion leaders." Among the approximately four hundred opinion leaders were top executives from Fortune 1000 corporations, labor union presidents, newspaper editors, TV and radio news directors, network newscasters, columnists, religious leaders, university presidents, leading academics, presidents of major interest groups, members of Congress, and high-level members of the administration. The poll found that while 60 percent of the general public regarded the present level of immigration as a "critical threat to vital interests" of the United States, only 14 percent of elites agreed. The public by 55 percent favored reducing legal immigration, but only 18 percent of opinion leaders agreed.

Data from Zogby International in 2009 revealed that rank-and-file church and synagogue goers disagreed with their ministers, priests, and rabbis on immigration policy. While leaders of mainline Protestant churches, Catholic bishops, and Jewish religious leaders have argued for increased immigration and some form of legalization for illegal immigrants rather than strict enforcement, their congregations oppose these policies. Among mainline Protestants, 72 percent believed that legal immigration was "too high"; 64 percent supported enforcing the law causing illegal immigrants to return home, as opposed to 24 percent who favored granting legal status and a pathway to citizenship with conditions for illegal immigrants. Among Catholics, 69 percent believed that legal immigration was "too high"; 64 percent favored enforcing immigration law causing illegal immigrants to leave, while 24 percent supported conditional amnesty. Among Jews, 50 percent believed that legal immigration was "too high" and only 5 percent considered it "too low," with 22 percent deeming it "just right." Enforcement leading to illegal immigrants leaving the United States was supported by 43 percent of Jews, compared with 40 percent who favored legalization with conditions.[74]

While ethnic group spokesmen often promote increased immigration, majorities of Americans of Latino, Asian, and African American descent disagree. In 2010, Zogby found that 56 percent of Latino Americans, 57 percent of Asian Americans, and 68 percent of African Americans believed that legal immigration was "too high." In addition 65 percent of Latinos, 69 percent of Asians, and 81 percent of African Americans believed there were "plenty of American workers" to do unskilled jobs if they were paid enough. Therefore, increasing unskilled immigration was unnecessary.

Zogby also reported that most American small business owners and executives as well as union households opposed the elite position on immigration, and instead supported enforcement that would cause illegal immigrants to return home over conditional legalization that would permit them to obtain citizenship and work in America. Among business executives, 59 percent supported enforcement to encourage illegal immigrants to go home, while 30 percent favored legalization with conditions. Among small business owners, 67 percent supported enforcement, and only 22 percent favored conditional legalization. Among union households, 58 percent favored enforcement, as opposed to 28 percent favoring conditional amnesty.

In August 2009, Gallup found that 50 percent of Americans supported decreasing immigration and only 14 percent favored increasing the number of legal immigrants to the country.★ Rasmussen also reported that 70 percent of Americans believed that increased border control should be the highest priority of immigration reform, whereas only 22 percent prioritized legalizing illegal immigrants. In March 2009, Rasmussen found that 73 percent of the public wanted police officers to check the immigration status of individuals stopped for routine traffic violations. Fully 79 percent of Americans supported using the military on the Mexican border to fight drug violence.[75]

Year in and year out, whether the polls are conducted by Gallup, Harris, Rasmussen, or Zogby, the results are the same. Most Americans disagree with our elites; they favor reducing legal immigration and enforcing laws against illegal immigration. Not surprisingly, therefore, elite-supported "comprehensive immigration reform" failed to pass the Congress in 2006 and 2007. The bills would have legalized and provided a path to citizenship for millions of illegal immigrants, and promised more funds for securing the border but without actually guaranteeing that the border would be secured. Popular opinion was not convinced. The comprehensive immigration bill of 2007 was stopped cold by what Rich Lowry, editor of *National Review,* called a "techno-populist revolt," a large public outcry fueled by twenty-first-century technology. The Senate voted 61 to 34 against cutting off debate (cloture) on the legislation

---

★The same Gallup poll reported that for nine straight years, since 2001, the number of Americans who favored decreasing immigration was considerably higher than those who favored increasing immigration, and almost always higher than the number of Americans who wanted immigration maintained at current levels.

sponsored by Harry Reid (D-NV) and favored by the Bush administration.

The American Public on Immigration and Assimilation

While the American public generally favors reducing legal immigration and enforcing laws against illegal immigration, Americans also believe that immigration for the most part has been good for America.[76] In the public's mind, the upbeat narrative of "a nation of immigrants" is tightly linked to the notion that the newcomers are "Americanized," and thus they renew and strengthen American national identity.

American elites traditionally understood that the perpetuation of democratic self-government in the United States required a robust national identity, or what social scientists call civic nationalism.[77] If twenty-first-century elite opinion reveals that many in the leadership class favor multiculturalism over patriotic assimilation, contemporary public opinion echoes and reaffirms the traditional "Americanization" stance held by America's leaders from the founding period to roughly the middle of the twentieth century.

A Harris poll commissioned by the Bradley Project on American National Identity, released in June 2008, surveyed a cross-section of American citizens (2,421 poll takers) on issues of national identity, assimilation, sovereignty, and civic education.* The poll revealed that the American people are overwhelmingly patriotic, with a strong sense of national identity, but they are very worried about the future of America because they believe that national identity is weakening. For example, 83 percent believe that Americans "share a unique national identity based on a shared set of beliefs, values, and culture," but among this subset, 63 percent believe that the national identity is getting "weaker." Moreover, 89 percent of all respondents view

---

*See Appendix for a more detailed breakdown of selected questions from the Bradley-Harris poll.

the United States as divided along cultural or ethnic lines, and 80 percent are "very concerned" about this division.[78]

When presented with choices such as U.S. Constitution vs. international law, or American citizen vs. global citizen, or national identity vs. ethnic identity, Americans by large margins choose the stronger civic nationalist position over the weaker alternative. For example, among registered voters, if there is a conflict between the U.S. Constitution and international law, 69 percent believe the Constitution should be "the highest legal authority for Americans," while 16 percent say international law. Eighty-five percent of registered voters think of themselves "more as a citizen of the United States" than as "a citizen of the world." Ninety percent believe that "Americanization, including learning English and embracing American culture and values, is important in order for immigrants to successfully fulfill their duties as American citizens"; the same view is held by 90 percent of Latinos and 89 percent of African Americans. Notice that this is a "thicker" definition of assimilation than is usually employed, with the explicit endorsement of "Americanization" rather than simply "integration," and the embrace of American culture, not just "democratic ideals."

American voters, by a majority of 83 percent, believe that our schools should put a higher priority on teaching students "to be proud of being part of the US and about the rights and responsibilities of citizenship," rather than focusing "on each student's ethnic identity to ensure that they feel proud of their own heritage and ethnic group," a priority favored by only 8 percent. Majorities of Latinos (70 percent) and African Americans (54 percent) favor an emphasis on American citizenship over ethnic heritage. Eighty-five percent of registered voters believe that English should be made the official language of the United States, and 71 percent favor ballots being printed only in English. Seventy-five percent believe that immigrants "should be required to give up loyalty to their former country when they become American citizens."

When asked if the United States overall is "better than other nations" or rather "a country like any other . . . no better or no worse than other nations," 66 percent of registered voters say "better," 27 percent say "like others," and 2 percent say "worse." The differences between native-born and naturalized citizens are also noteworthy. On fifteen of sixteen questions, native-born citizens chose the most "patriotic" or "civic nationalist" response in much greater numbers than did naturalized citizens. This empirical evidence belies the often repeated myth that newly naturalized immigrants are somehow more patriotic than American-born citizens.*

The Moral Case for Patriotic Assimilation

At the heart of democratic self-government is first and foremost the moral right of a free people to govern itself—that is to say, government by the consent of the governed. This includes the moral right of a self-governing free people to determine its own immigration policy and the right to decide the conditions for assimilating immigrants. It also means the moral right of a democratic people to perpetuate its institutions and way of life and bequeath them to posterity.

To argue that immigrant populations within a democratic nation-state have the right to perpetuate their own ways of life in an adversarial manner, against the wishes of the majority of the citizens, is to argue that a free people does not have the moral right either to

---

*For example, on U.S. Constitution vs. international law, native-born citizens by 67 percent to 16 percent said the Constitution is superior, whereas among naturalized citizens the response was 37 percent for the Constitution and 29 percent for international law. On whether the United States is "better than other nations," 65 percent of native-born said "better," while only 44 percent of naturalized citizens said the same. On the question of U.S. citizen vs. world citizen, 85 percent of native-born said the former, while among naturalized citizens the response was 54 percent U.S. citizens and 29 percent world citizens.

govern itself or to perpetuate its way of life. On democratic grounds, this is a profoundly immoral position.*

To argue that the "two-way street" of integration involves a fifty-fifty parity between the democratic host nation and the immigrant populations—to argue that the conditions of integration are to be "negotiated" between these two putatively equal "communities"—is to repudiate democratic self-government. It is to say that a self-governing people is not permitted to determine the terms on which it admits and assimilates immigrants, and therefore the terms on which it perpetuates itself.

To argue that economic conditions in less developed countries will essentially dictate the number of immigrants entering the United States, and that little can or should be done about it (as people will enter illegally if they cannot do so legally), is an inherently antidemocratic analysis. It places impersonal forces over free political choice; economic determinism over constitutional democracy. It is a way of thinking at odds with the founding principles of the American regime.

In the first of *The Federalist Papers,* Alexander Hamilton remarked that "it seems to be reserved to the people of this country ... to decide the important question whether societies of men are really capable or not of establishing good government by reflection and choice, or whether they are forever destined to depend ... on accident and force." Hamilton was saying that success in forming good government required that the American people deliberate and decide the important political issues for themselves, rather than have decisions forced upon them or made by happenstance. In *Federalist* No. 1, Hamilton expressed the Founding Fathers' view that

---

*To be sure, if a nation consciously chooses multicultural-style integration, this would clearly be democratic. However, while Western elites have promoted multicultural integration in many countries, it is unproven and unlikely that the general populace in any nation (including Canada, Britain, and Belgium) favors a multicultural approach to immigrant integration.

Americans should not be slaves of forces beyond their control, but instead should determine their own destiny.[79]

Revive the Barbara Jordan Plan

On June 8, 1995, the *New York Times* reported that Barbara Jordan, as chairman of the Commission on Immigration Reform, had delivered an immigration plan to President Bill Clinton at a White House meeting. President Clinton congratulated Jordan and declared that her reform plan was "consistent with" his own views, being "pro-family, pro-work, pro-naturalization."

Barbara Jordan was a civil rights icon. In 1972 she became the first African American woman elected from a southern state to serve in the U.S. Congress. As a Democratic representative from Texas, Jordan gained prominence with a powerful speech supporting the impeachment of President Richard Nixon. In 1976, she was the first African American to give the keynote address at a national party's presidential nominating convention. In short, when Barbara Jordan spoke, politicians and the public listened.

Jordan insisted that immigration must primarily serve the national interest; indeed, her plan was titled "The National Interest." The plan stated that the purpose of its recommendations was to "maximize the many positive opportunities that legal immigration presents to our nation."[80] Like George Washington, Theodore Roosevelt, Woodrow Wilson, and Louis Brandeis, the Jordan Commission report noted that immigration "has costs as well as benefits."[81] And like past American leaders, the Jordan plan explicitly called for the Americanization of immigrants. In a *New York Times* op-ed, "The Americanization Ideal," Jordan wrote:

> Immigration imposes mutual obligations. Those who choose to come here must embrace the common core of American civic culture. We must assist them in learning our common language

... we must renew civic education in the teaching of American history for all Americans. We must vigorously enforce the laws against ... discrimination.[82]

At the heart of the Jordan plan was an immigration policy consistent with effective assimilation. The commission report acknowledged that the two went hand in hand. The level of immigration must be consistent with the nation's ability to assimilate the newcomers. As President Coolidge once declared, "New arrivals should be limited to our capacity to absorb them into the ranks of good citizenship."[83] To achieve this assimilation-immigration balance, in addition to explicitly emphasizing Americanization, the Jordan Commission recommended cutting legal immigration by about one-third, from the projected FY 1996 levels of 725,000 down to 550,000, after a transition period of five to eight years; eliminating low-skilled immigration visas that do not serve the national interest; and strengthening border enforcement to combat illegal immigration.

The main ideas of the Jordan plan were incorporated into legislation proposed by Senator Alan Simpson (R-WY) and Congressman Lamar Smith (R-TX), and originally supported by President Bill Clinton. Unfortunately, Barbara Jordan died in January 1996, and the immigration-assimilation reform legislation lost an invaluable ally and courageous voice. Opposition to the Simpson-Smith bill came from an array of special-interest lobbies among business groups, ethnic spokesmen, and NGOs like the ACLU. Members of Congress from the libertarian right joined some liberals in gutting key provisions of the bill that would have reduced low-skilled immigration and implemented serious border enforcement measures with tamper-proof identification cards. What eventually passed was a watered-down bill that kept immigration at the 1990 level, but restricted social benefits for legal immigrants.

The core principles of Barbara Jordan's plan were essentially the traditional ideas of American leaders from the founding era through the Ellis Island period, until the appearance of multiculturalism in the mid-1960s. An updated Jordan plan would mean—as Barbara Jordan herself proposed and the American people overwhelmingly favor—some reduction in the current level of legal immigration. As the *Washington Post* columnist Robert Samuelson once wrote, "We may face a paradox. To benefit from immigration, we may need a little less of it."[84] The numbers could always be changed later, up or down, depending on the success of patriotic assimilation. A new Jordan plan would also include a greater emphasis on skilled over unskilled immigrants—just as George Washington in his letter to John Adams talked about the need for "useful mechanics" and particular "professions," and Jordan proposed eliminating the unskilled worker visa. Obviously, a new Jordan plan would include truly effective border and interior enforcement with tamper-proof identification.

Moreover, an updated Jordan plan would include a serious Americanization policy. Among other things, this would mean that the U.S. government takes the Oath of Renunciation and Allegiance seriously. When an applicant for American citizenship swears to "absolutely and entirely renounce and abjure all allegiance and fidelity to any foreign prince, potentate, state or sovereignty," the Oath should mean exactly that. Therefore, retaining a previous citizenship, using a foreign passport, and voting or holding office in one's former country should be against American law. As the prominent Supreme Court justice Felix Frankfurter once wrote, retaining political loyalty to the old country after taking an oath to the United States reveals "something less than complete and unswerving allegiance to the United States," and is "in some measure, at least, inconsistent with American citizenship."[85]

For more than two centuries, the transfer of allegiance from the old country to the United States has been a central feature of America's great success in assimilating immigrants. We are not simply "a nation of immigrants," but more accurately "a nation of assimilated immigrants" and descendants of settlers, whose sole political loyalty is, or morally ought to be, to the United States of America.

CHAPTER FOURTEEN

The Suicide of Liberal Democracy?

A "struggle for a new world" has begun. Across a broad range of far-flung, often obscure, but nevertheless vital fronts, the liberal democratic nation-state is locked in an intense ideological and institutional conflict with the forces of global governance. At the center of the coalition supporting liberal democracy stands an independent sovereign American nation-state. Across the trenches, the overarching goal of the global governance party is the subordination of American constitutional democracy to global authority.

As we enter the second decade of the twenty-first century, liberal democracy in general and the American nation-state in particular face three serious opponents: radical Islam, a rising autocratic China, and the forces of global governance. The first two are mostly (although not always publicly) recognized as threats or at least challenges; the third, much less so. It is time to re-imagine the global chessboard of international politics and recognize that the global governance movement is a significant political actor on the world stage, sometimes competing and sometimes cooperating with other political actors: nation-states, transnational coalitions, and multinational alliances.

While two of the most serious threats to America and the liberal democratic nation-state are external, the threat from the global governance movement is internal, coming from the bosom of the democratic world. To be sure, the transnational progressives and transnational pragmatists who are promoting global governance— at the UN, the EU, the ICC, in the postmodern governments of Europe, in the corporate world, the foundations and NGOs, the universities and law schools—see themselves as supporters of democracy. But the effect of their policies would be fundamentally at odds with the basic principles and practices of democratic self-government. As Professor Kenneth Anderson remarked, the global governance project "seeks legitimacy not in democracy and popular sovereignty, but rather in universal principles of human rights," as determined by transnational elites in supranational bodies, unaccountable to any democratic process and constantly evolving from one year to the next.[1]

Advocates of global governance argue that their proposals to "share" or "pool" sovereignty are democratic if the decision to "share" is made by democratic institutions such as national legislatures, elected executives, or representatives of democratic governments. This is nothing more, they insist, than the well-practiced policy of delegating authority, like the U.S. Congress delegating authority to regulatory agencies. But this argument was effectively refuted more than three hundred years ago by John Locke when he explained that if the legislative (the representative democratic body) transfers sovereign authority to an outside power, whether a supranational authority or other nations with which sovereignty is shared, the regime itself has been fundamentally transformed.[2]*

---

*John Locke's exact words that develop this argument are: "The delivery also of the people into the subjection of a foreign power, either by the prince, or by the legislative, is certainly a change of the legislative, and so a dissolution of government: for the end why the people entered into society being to be preserved an entire, free, and independent society, to be governed by its own laws: this is lost, whenever they are given up into the power of another."

It is no longer an independent, self-governing regime, but a subordinate, dependent regime.

A century later, Alexander Hamilton echoed Locke in pointing out that sovereign legislative decision making cannot be delegated away under the American Constitution. Hamilton wrote that a treaty "shall not change the Constitution; which results from this fundamental maxim, that a delegated authority cannot alter the constituting act.... An agent cannot new model his own commission. A treaty, for example, cannot transfer the legislative power to the executive."[3]

As we have seen throughout this book, the global governance agenda—through its particular interpretation of universal human rights, international law, UN treaty monitoring, and the laws of war—would shift power from democracies to supranational institutions and rules, and thus severely restrict democratic decision making in independent states. Through treaty monitoring and the human rights agenda, the forces of global governance claim authority over a wide range of policies long thought to be matters that a free people should decide for itself, including school curricula, textbooks, criminal sentencing, budget priorities, immigration, assimilation, border enforcement, language, employment, health, parental leave, the punishment of children within the family, and the gender and ethnic composition of democratic legislatures. The global governancers also claim authority to make the rules by which democracies are permitted (or not permitted) to defend themselves, without the consent of those democracies.

Thus, the global governance project is hostile to the "democratic" part of liberal democracy. This is not to say that its proponents are overtly hostile to democracy; no doubt most would argue that they are simply seeking new forms of decision making consistent with democracy for an age of global interdependence. They are not "antidemocratic" as the Islamists or the Chinese Communist Party leadership are antidemocratic. It would be more accurate to characterize the global governance project as "postdemocratic." Its advocates are subjectively democratic—they regard themselves as democrats—but their political project is objectively more postdemocratic than democratic in the traditional sense.

The global governance agenda is also antithetical to the "liberal" part of liberal democracy: limited government and individual rights. The concept of "substantive equality" for ascribed groups, as interpreted by UN treaty monitoring committees, directly violates the core values of liberalism. A policy of forcing numerical equality of result for all ethnic and gender groups into every nook and cranny of society would require a degree of coercion incompatible with a free society. With its emphasis on substantive equality and group rights, and its support for restricting speech that offends particular groups, the global governance movement could also be characterized as postliberal.

Likewise, American transnational progressives are not anti-American, but post-American. They are thinking in terms of *after* or *beyond* America: beyond what they would consider the narrow parochial concerns of their own nation, to "the world's interests." In their view, one should be a global citizen as much as an American citizen. They might posit that the American nation-state was relatively benign for its time, but today's reality calls for moving it to a new age of global authority.

If the forces of global governance are successful in establishing some form of global authority and a "global rule of law" as they envision it, liberal democracy will be replaced by postdemocratic governance. However, it is highly unlikely that such a utopian vision would succeed on its own terms, particularly since global governance has little support among rising Asian states (China, India) or in nations such as Russia, Turkey, and Brazil, which are fully prepared to exercise a robust national sovereignty.

On the other hand, it is entirely possible that the transnational progressive ideology of global governance and the material interests of the transnational pragmatists might attain a considerable degree of influence among a critical mass of opinion makers and statesmen in Western democracies (including, particularly, the United States). Perhaps this influence would become the conventional wisdom of mainstream elite opinion, achieving what the Italian Marxist thinker Antonio Gramsci called "ideological hegemony."

If that happens—if the mind of the democrat is captured by the arguments of the globalist—then the result could well be, not the triumph of global governance, but the suicide of liberal democracy, both in the realm of domestic self-government and in the arena of self-defense from undemocratic foes. Thus the global governance project, although unable to achieve success in its own right, would essentially disable and disarm the democratic state both internally and externally. Francis Fukuyama predicted, rather convincingly, that it was hard to imagine a future ideological rival with universal appeal that could successfully defeat liberal democracy, but if liberal democracy drinks from the cup of global governance it will have poisoned itself.

The suicide of liberal democracy would likely happen gradually over a long period of time. Chapter Six analyzed the ongoing slow-motion suicide of the liberal democratic nation-states of western Europe, as they transform themselves into subordinate states within the supranational legal regime of the European Union. Among the chief facilitators of this "suicide" process are the national judges of the various European nations. In the effort to build a global regime, likewise, judges at the highest levels within nation-states will play a crucial role.

At the center of the global governance project is the concept of a "global rule of law" and the presumed judicial supremacy of global legalism. Transnational progressives in the legal profession within democratic states are in the vanguard of the effort to incorporate global rules into domestic policy through "evolving" interpretations of international law and human rights treaties. At the same time, in foreign and defense policy, transnationalist interpretations of the rules of self-defense and the laws of war could have damaging and disabling effects on democratic states such as the United States, India, and Israel.

Global legalism threatens democratic politics on two fronts: in domestic self-government, as international law is "coordinated" with constitutional law; and in national security policy, as the rules by which democracies may defend themselves are increasingly made by the "global community," including nondemocracies.

The Global Governancers' Sales Pitch to America

At the end of the day, the American leadership class is crucial to the success or failure of the global governance project. It is unlikely that American submission to global authority could be imposed by outside forces at the UN, EU, IMF, WTO, ICC, and elsewhere. American submission would have to be voluntary, led by American elites. The actual process of subordination would unfold only gradually, over a long period. It would involve the type of supranational legalism and transnational politics described in this book, in which "disaggregated" elites (often in the legal profession in the United States) join with their political allies outside America's constitutional system to subordinate our democratic sovereignty.

However, the transnational progressive vision of the global rule of law is utopian and essentially unworkable. For this reason, a serious attempt to implement global legalism would more likely lead to the "suicide" of American democracy (with a nation-state unable to govern itself at home or defend itself abroad) than to the establishment of global harmony. In any case, let us now analyze in detail the arguments put forth in favor of the promotion of global governance by influential elements of the American leadership class.

The dream of transnational progressives is for America to lead the way to the brave new world of global governance. America embraces the global governance project as its own; voluntarily agrees to "share" large parts of its sovereignty with others; and demonstrates "leadership" by submitting to a supranational global legal regime. In effect, the American caterpillar is transformed into the global butterfly. The challenge is how to sell this plan to the American people. The transnationalists, both progressive and pragmatist, try to make the case that global governance is consistent with the Founders' ideals. More importantly, they tell us, global governance is in America's interests in the interdependent world of the twenty-first century. What is needed, they say, is effective American leadership to make it happen.

"Global governance is consistent with America's Founding ideals."

A phrase from the first paragraph of the Declaration of Independence appears again and again in the writings of global governance advocates in law school journals and international relations periodicals, and in after-dinner speeches before foreign affairs organizations: "a decent respect to the opinions of mankind." This phrase is repeated as a mantra by legions of American lawyers, academics, and politicians. The implied transnationalist meaning is that the Founders somehow believed that "world opinion" should have a moral veto over American decision making. But this interpretation is both false and disingenuous. When the Founders wrote in 1776 that "a decent respect to the opinions of mankind requires that [we] should declare the causes which compel [us] to the separation," they were telling the world, particularly the European great powers, something like the following:

"We Americans, like you, are cognizant of Enlightenment philosophy, the tenets of religion and morality, and the natural rights of man. We, the leaders of this enterprise, are eighteenth-century gentlemen who believe in the power of Reason and in presenting reasoned arguments. We have 'a decent respect' for your opinions. Therefore, in the Declaration of Independence we are explaining to you both our specific case for American independence from Great Britain, and our general political principles, which are universal. We hope our reasonable argument persuades you. However, if 'world opinion' is opposed to our independence, this will not stop us. With all due respect, our new American republic is based (as we explained in our Declaration) on the 'unalienable' natural rights of man and on the 'consent of the governed,' that is, on the good people of these United States, not on the 'opinions of mankind' in general."

By contrast, Anne-Marie Slaughter advocates a "global decision-making process" in which "all nations must have meaningful representation." She notes that some "global or regional institutions" have implemented "various systems to address the representation issue: weighted voting, different classes of members, and rotating membership of states within the region." Just as the American Founders tried to "ensure that the people of tiny Rhode Island had an equal voice with populous Virginia" through the U.S. Senate, she argues, today "the United States must take the lead in applying this principle in international and regional institutions across the board," including the Security Council of the United Nations. "If we truly believe that all human beings have an equal right to institute governments to protect their rights, then those governments must have the ability to do just that at the global level," Slaughter insists. Applying the principle of "meaningful representation" in global decision making is "the right thing to do" and "also the smart thing to do—serving both our ideals and our interests."[4] In responding to questions at the Foreign Press Center, Slaughter stated that national governments would not have to be democratic in order to be represented in the transnational network of global decision making. Although she ruled out North Korea (too "isolated"), the Islamic Republic of Iran would be eligible. ("But do I think it would be possible for Iran, even now, and certainly if the reformists came to power, to participate in these networks? Absolutely.")[5]

Slaughter's line of reasoning is, to say the least, a misuse of our founding ideals. It is inconceivable that the Founding Fathers would have interpreted "all men are created equal" and "consent of the governed" to include support for something like "meaningful representation" of all the world's peoples in a "global decision-making process," in which the national governments of, say, Hapsburg Austria, Romanov Russia, Hohenzollern Prussia, Bourbon Spain, the Islamic Barbary states, the Ottoman Empire, imperial China, George III's Britain, monarchical or even republican France—or, for that matter, the friendly Dutch Republic—could outvote America's constitutional order on "global problems."

"It is in American interests to promote global governance."

One could remark that while the Founders' ideas are all well and good, policy makers are concerned with contemporary problems and the immediate future. In this vein, the basic "realist" argument for promoting global governance is that it serves American interests in the coming world of global interdependence. Both formally and informally, in public writings and in private discussions, transnationalists push the following argument:

"America may be dominant among world powers today, but it will not always be so. China, in particular, is on the rise and may well equal, or surpass, America and other powers in the next few decades. Therefore, it is in our interests to establish global rules now, while we are the strongest state. We should get China to 'buy into' a system of global authority today, so its elites essentially 'internalize' the concept of global governance and are 'locked in' and practicing it by the time China is the more powerful state in the decades to come. In other words, this means that it is in 'our interests' to cede parts of our sovereignty to global authority now and establish a 'global rule of law.' We should agree to limit our sovereignty for the purpose of getting others, particularly China, to do the same, so these restrictions will be in place when they become stronger and cannot be constrained by force but only by the self-restraint of global law, which they have accepted and internalized."

In support of this general line of argument, Anne-Marie Slaughter declared: "What goes around comes around, and as other nations grow in power, size, and economic weight, their decisions will increasingly affect us. Principles that could constrain us today may well guarantee our freedom tomorrow."[6]

Strobe Talbott, in his book on global governance, quotes President Bill Clinton to the effect that American dominance will be temporary: "We're not going to be cock of the roost forever, you know," and "other countries that didn't have our head start are going to catch up with us at some point."[7] Therefore, Clinton reasoned, "We must build a global social system" and "a world for our grandchildren to live in where America was no longer the sole superpower, for a time when we would have to share the stage."[8]★ Clinton himself was ambiguous about what this meant for democratic sovereignty. But over the past decade, it has become more common to hear the argument that it is in America's interest to provide "leadership" to create global institutions and a "global rule of law" that could restrain national sovereignty and keep both the United States and potential future rivals in check.

The argument that global governance is in America's interests is deeply flawed on both pragmatic and principled grounds. The opening premise of this argument, that an inevitable American decline necessitates the construction of grand strategy on a foundation of defeatism, is a poor psychological place to begin, if one considers national will and citizen morale to be important factors in world politics. More importantly, the theory itself does not make sense even on its own terms, either on logical-historical or on moral-democratic grounds.

Historically in foreign affairs, political leaders have acted opportunistically, changing when circumstances change. Old agreements become obsolete, new arrangements are created. Even if the Chinese

---

★Talbott points out that Clinton was "careful not to broadcast" these beliefs "while in office." As we discussed earlier, the Clinton administration, supported and prodded by the Republican-controlled Congress, forthrightly defended American democratic sovereignty in dealing with the ICC and the UN at several crucial points during the 1990s. After his presidency, Clinton more fully developed his views of global interdependence.

agreed to cede sovereignty to global institutions today, what guarantees would the United States have tomorrow that a more powerful China would not change its mind? *Pace* Anne-Marie Slaughter, American self-subordination to "principles that could constrain us today" (submission to global norms in defense policy) will not "guarantee our freedom tomorrow." Our freedom will never be guaranteed by international agreements and global norms, but only by independent military strength, and most importantly by the will to use it to defend our self-government.

It is naïve to attempt to establish a stable and peaceful international order on the utopian premise that because the United States agreed to subordinate its sovereignty to global authority when it was the leading power, therefore China (or another rising nation) would adhere to the same limits upon becoming the world's next leading power—when the Chinese could justifiably consider those global rules obsolete. It is more likely that China, or another new leading power, would try to fashion a different international system more to its own liking. There is no particular reason to believe that any Chinese "buy-in" to global governance arrangements would be permanent. Once they are strong enough to bypass or refashion the global rules themselves, they could and probably would do so. If history is any guide, they would act as leading powers have always acted, in pursuit of their own interests, and not as the forces of global governance hope they would act.

Moving from the pragmatic-realist grounds to fundamental principles, the argument that "global governance is in our interests and consistent with our values" fails on the moral grounds of the protection of democratic self-government. The *most vital* of the "vital interests" of a liberal democratic nation-state like the United States is the preservation and perpetuation of its democratic self-government, its liberty, and its way of life. The very purpose of American foreign and security policy is to ensure the continued existence of the self-government and freedom of the American people. At the point that American constitutional democracy submits to global authority, our vital interests have been surrendered. To argue that it is "in our interests and consistent with our values" to subordinate American self-government to foreigners outside of our constitutional democracy is an oxymoron. It is to argue, in effect, that committing democratic suicide is "in our interests and consistent with our values."

The Affirmation of Philadelphian or Democratic Sovereignty

Throughout the book, I have emphasized democratic sovereignty as distinct from sovereignty in general: that is to say, Philadelphian sovereignty, not just Westphalian sovereignty. Democratic sovereignty may be an unworkable concept in formal international law, but it is entirely usable in international politics as a universal normative principle that is at the heart of liberal democracy in general and American constitutionalism in particular.

Sovereign states can be undemocratic. At the same time, postsovereign, postnational forms of governance—including both existing entities such as the European Union and proposed global governance entities of the future—have a "democratic deficit," as some of their proponents admit. They have not yet figured out how to ensure democratic accountability and government by the consent of the governed. Postnational regimes have no *demos*, no "people," which is a necessary condition of democratic government. Indeed, in democratic sovereignty, the people themselves are sovereign and exercise their sovereign self-government through the instrument of the liberal democratic nation-state. This institution, in which a particular people rules itself, has provided the only real historical home for liberal democracy in modern times.★ Without democratic sovereignty there is no functioning liberal democracy.

★As noted in Chapter Three, premodern democracies and republics were not liberal. In theory, in the contemporary world, democratic sovereignty and liberal democracy could be housed in city-states (like Singapore or Hong Kong) if they

The American political regime—a sovereign people with a liberal democratic political system housed in an independent nation-state—is the epitome of democratic sovereignty. Therefore, when American political leaders promote "our values" on the world stage, they should affirm the principle of democratic sovereignty.

Encouraging the Recovery of Democratic Sovereignty in Europe

For years the United States has encouraged deeper European integration and strengthening the power of the EU at the expense of the democratic nation-states. This makes little sense on either practical or principled grounds. The more that European defense and foreign policies are decided at the EU level, rather than the nation-state level, the less support the Europeans will offer the Americans.

Individual nation-states that belong to the EU but act as nation-states, for example Britain and Poland, are usually very supportive of U.S. policies. But if the proposed "Common Foreign and Security Policy" is fully established, Britain and Poland and likeminded nations would be constrained by other EU countries and the EU bureaucracy who are less supportive of the United States. A "consensus" or lowest-common-denominator position would be reached that could prevent friendly European nations from helping Americans achieve their objectives. As a practical matter, continued U.S. support for deeper EU political integration is harmful to American interests. Indeed, for many among European elites, one of the main purposes of the EU is to provide a counterweight to American influence and power in world politics.

Despite the implementation of the Lisbon Treaty, the ideological-political battle within the European Union between federalist

---

were liberal and democratic, or in small nations (like Quebec, Catalonia, Flanders) if the decisions were based on consent of the governed, negotiated with the central governments, and mutually agreeable to the different parties involved.

supranationalists and democratic sovereigntists is far from over. New and reoccurring crises over economics, security, and immigration will continue to confront the European project. EU elites will respond to every crisis with calls for deeper political integration: more power for the organs of the EU, less for the nation-states.

But resistance to Brussels could very well grow. Beneath the surface of the Euro-conformity of establishment institutions and their courtiers, the spirit of democratic sovereignty has not been extinguished. The people of what is called "Middle England," the soul of the Tory Party, and not a few Labourites would welcome the full restoration of British parliamentary democracy. Many Gaullists, intellectuals, activists, and other democratic nationalists of the right and the left have always been reluctant to surrender the sovereignty of the French Republic and will continue to seek ways to recapture as much independence and self-government as possible. More and more middle-class Germans realize that their leaders might have made a big mistake in abandoning the formidable Deutschmark for the euro, and the time has perhaps come to return some powers from Brussels to Berlin.[9] A sizable group of people in the Flemish part of Belgium are beginning to envision a new form of self-government free of their French-speaking Walloon neighbors and the stifling overreach of EU institutions.

In short, democratic sovereignty has allies in the heart of postsovereign, transnationalist Europe. The theory of the "disaggregated" state, nation, or other political entity works both ways. While there are transnational progressives among the elites of democratic sovereign states who promote supranational governance, either global or regional, there are also democratic sovereigntists within postmodern European states who seek restoration of sovereign self-government.

The United States has neither practical (realist) nor principled (idealist) grounds on which to object to political attempts to restore democratic sovereignty within the nation-states of the European Union. However, to smooth American acceptance of a resurgence of democratic sovereignty in Europe, it would be necessary for the U.S. foreign policy establishment to break the habit of reflexive support for further European integration. It is no longer useful—if it ever was—for the United States to make "one phone call" to Europe, as Henry Kissinger famously suggested.

A policy of taking democratic sovereignty seriously would mean that the American foreign policy apparatus would not disparage the domestic policies of democratic nation-states, as the Bush administration did in 2003, indulging in its own version of "global domestic policy." As ambassador-at-large for international religious freedom, John Hanford criticized France for enacting legislation that banned Islamic headscarves and other "conspicuous religious items" from public schools. Hanford called the wearing of Islamic headscarves "a basic right that should be protected." A French official responded, "Never have you heard a French diplomat comment on an internal debate in the United States." (Of course, this is not exactly true. French officials have criticized U.S. domestic policy, particularly death penalty laws.)

For the French, the wearing of Islamic headscarves in public schools represented an Islamist political challenge to the legitimacy of the French Republic's secular tradition. For the Americans, it was an issue of religious freedom. The French law was not consistent with American notions of religious pluralism, but it was consistent with French democratic and national traditions, and it was enacted within the workings of a democratic nation-state. Different democratic states often have varied interpretations of human rights, and view the tensions between personal liberty and democratic decision making differently. It might make sense if the U.S. State Department reports on religious liberty focused on the serious violations of religious freedom that occur in undemocratic states such as Iran and Saudi Arabia instead of criticizing legislation enacted in democratic nations. At the same time, the French could condemn major human rights violations in tyrannies instead of American democracy's death penalty jurisprudence.[10]

In the conflict between democratic sovereignty and global governance, the roles played by particular countries will be significant. Besides the activities of the United States, what Britain does with regard to the tension between parliamentary democracy and the European Union will be very important. Many in Britain have called for the "repatriation" of powers from Brussels back to the Parliament in Westminster. We will see if, and to what extent, this comes to pass. The countries of the Anglosphere in general will provide much of the intellectual and activist firepower for both sides in this conflict. The nations of central and eastern Europe, after living for decades without sovereign self-government, harbor more vigorous democratic sovereigntist sentiments than many in western Europe. In the internal EU struggle between the federalist Eurocrats and the nation-states, the many central and eastern Europeans could stand on the side of greater independence for the states.

Israel and India: Friends of Democratic Sovereignty

Israel and India will also be crucial nations to watch in the conflict between democratic sovereigntists and global governancers. Israel, as discussed earlier, is on the front lines of this conflict. Israel is the major target of transnational progressives who seek to expand global authority in determining the laws of war. If international law precedents could be established against Israeli security policies, these precedents could be used later to subordinate U.S. defense policies to global law as defined by the transnationalists. Elements of the global governance party—NGOs, Western philanthropies, funding projects by European governments and the EU—are complicit in the worldwide Islamist campaign to delegitimize Israel as an apartheid state through the "boycotts, divestment, and sanctions" strategy. As this campaign heats up (and it surely will), the reaction of the United States will be crucial: to what extent will it defend Israel?

One of the most important nations to watch in the struggle to preserve and perpetuate democratic sovereignty will be the world's largest democracy. As a rising economic power with over a billion people, India will become a major actor in world politics both in the conventional sense and in the ongoing struggle between global governance and democratic sovereignty. In mainstream foreign-policy-speak, India is usually listed as one of the BRIC nations (Brazil, Russia, India, and China). This concept of the BRICs was originally formulated by Goldman Sachs as shorthand to identify emerging economies for investors, but it is now widely used by statesmen and scholars.

Unfortunately, BRICs is a misleading concept, certainly politically and philosophically, even economically: should the Russian economy be thought of as comparable to the Chinese or Indian markets? Most importantly, democratic India should not be envisioned by American policy makers in the same terms as the autocratic regimes of China and Russia. Unlike the other BRICs, India could become a major American ally—politically, militarily, and ideologically—in addition to providing a substantial democratic counterweight to Chinese ambitions in Asia.

Since the end of the Cold War, India has undergone a strategic-diplomatic shift and gradually developed closer ties to the United States. Considering both nations' concern with radical Islam and a potentially troubling China, leading strategists in both countries are recommending a closer bilateral relationship. At a seminar in Washington, D.C., one of India's premier strategic thinkers, Admiral Raja Menon, called for a resurgent United States with a rising India as a key partner.[11]

Besides possibly forming a major geostrategic alliance with the United States, India, as we have seen, already stands with America and Israel against the global governancers on the key issues of the International Criminal Court and Protocol I. In other words, on the vital question of who determines the rules of self-defense—the independent democratic state or the global community—the Indians, unlike European elites, opt for democratic sovereignty. This ideological convergence of Americans, Indians, and Israelis in favor of democratic self-government over so-called global norms (in which undemocratic states and values are influential) offers democratic sovereigntists an opportunity to seize the moral high ground in the broader war of ideas.

Specifically, this could mean a no-nonsense intellectual defense of the American-Indian-Israeli opposition to the International Criminal Court and Protocol I on the grounds of democratic sovereignty. For example: "We the people of a democratic state will decide the rules by which we defend ourselves and our democracy—not those of you outside of our democratic process, not those who are not part of our sovereign people, not those who are not our fellow citizens and therefore do not share our particular responsibilities and burdens. Some of you outside judges and lawyers don't even practice democratic government in your own countries, yet you claim authority, in the name of 'global norms' (to which we did not give our consent) to tell us how we are permitted to defend ourselves. How dare you claim moral authority over us."

A Zero-Sum Conflict

The clash between global governance and democratic sovereignty is a moral struggle over the first principles of government and politics. The difference between these two visions of political life is irreconcilable. Who governs? Who determines the laws under which we shall live? Will American citizens live under the Constitution of the United States, or under "evolving norms of customary international law?" These are the issues at stake when some State Department official or international lawyer talks abstractly about "redefining sovereignty" or a "new architecture of global governance."

The Founding Fathers created a distinct notion of sovereignty as something located not in a ruler, or in a state, but in "the People of the United States." Alexis de Tocqueville declared, "If there is a single country in the world where one can hope to appreciate the dogma of the sovereignty of the people ... that country is surely America."[12] In the future, will this sovereignty remain in the hands of the American people, or will it be "shared" or "pooled" with other peoples, with officials of transnational organizations, and with international judges who are not part of our constitutional democracy? The answers to these questions will determine whether Americans remain a self-governing people.

Whatever the result, one thing is clear: the conflict between American constitutional democracy and the forces of global governance is a zero-sum struggle. When one side gains; the other side loses. Whichever side ultimately prevails, its opponent will be defeated. There is no "split the difference," no middle ground, no possible compromise. American sovereignty and "shared sovereignty" are incompatible.

The conflict between the authority of the U.S. Constitution and international law, or rather the "evolving norms of the new transnational law," is recognized as zero-sum by democratic sovereigntists and global governancers alike. American transnationalists seek to establish a "global rule of law," which by definition means that national law is subordinate. Otherwise, there would be simply traditional international law based on the voluntary consent of states, a consent that could be withdrawn. Unlike their European allies, American transnational progressives are reluctant to say this directly, so they publicly insist that the Constitution is "controlling," while international and foreign law are simply "persuasive."

Harold Koh, a leading transnational progressive legal scholar and top State Department lawyer, notes that "The transnationalists view domestic courts as having a critical role to play in domesticating international law into U.S. law." According to Koh,

> domestic courts must play a key role in coordinating U.S. domestic constitutional rules with rules of foreign and international law, not simply to promote American aims, but to advance the broader development of a well-functioning international judicial

system. In Justice Blackmun's words, U.S. courts must look beyond narrow U.S. interests to the "mutual interests of all nations in a smoothly functioning international legal regime" and, whenever possible, should "consider if there is a course that furthers, rather than impedes, the development of an ordered international system."[13]

Further, Koh identifies situations in which he believes it "appropriate for the Supreme Court to construe our Constitution in light of foreign and international law." Indeed, Edward Whelan, a legal scholar, argues convincingly that since U.S. courts cannot change international or foreign law, but only interpret American law, Koh's vision for "domesticating international law into U.S. law" would require that U.S. constitutional law be changed to conform to global law, and not vice versa. This logically implies—although it is almost never openly stated, and indeed is publicly denied by most transnationalists—that global law should be superior to American constitutional law.[14]

Harold Koh writes about how transnational law is "downloaded" into American law, saying, "Perhaps the best operational definition of transnational law, using computer-age imagery, is: (1) law that is 'downloaded' from international to domestic law."[15] Of course, in American democracy, the unelected judiciary is not supposed to "download" international law into domestic law through legal interpretation. Laws are supposed to be made by the elected representatives of the people in Congress and signed by the president. The U.S. Supreme Court might, if a case is brought before it, then decide on the constitutionality of those laws, based on the Constitution itself, not on foreign or international law, or on "the opinions of mankind."

The concept of "downloading" international/transnational law into constitutional law is one more example of what we have emphasized throughout this book: the advocates of global governance and transnationalism seek to bypass, transform, and supersede liberal democracy and popular sovereignty. Their success would not establish the global rule of law, but rather the global rule of international lawyers and judges.

Ostensibly, global governancers reject the concept of zero-sum politics and embrace the idea of win-win, as described by Robert Wright in his best-selling book *Nonzero: The Logic of Human Destiny*.[16] In some spheres, such as economics, there are many non-zero-sum benefits. However, in politics generally, and in the political conflict between transnationalists and democratic sovereigntists specifically, neither side really believes in a win-win scenario. Indeed, in day-to-day practice, the global governance coalition regularly excoriates its opponents as "nationalists," "populists," narrow-minded provincialists, and the like. Presumably, this means that they believe (correctly) that if the "nationalists" and "populists" gain ground—for example, when Sweden voted no on the euro—the transnationalists lose ground.

Which Is the Better Regime?

Since the late eighteen century, the United States and other liberal democratic nation-states have evolved as effective and mostly decent political bodies. In the main, there has been a larger degree of democratic accountability and political liberty, as well as economic prosperity, manifested in the liberal democratic nation-state than in any other type of political regime.

The global governancers charge that the sovereign nation-state and "nationalism" are responsible for the horrific wars of the twentieth century, and that the supranational governance of the European Union is needed to prevent future wars. But in making this argument, globalists in general and EU advocates in particular fail to distinguish between democratic states and undemocratic states, or between undemocratic nationalism and democratic nationalism—which is synonymous with a patriotism that is both natural and necessary to the survival of a free society. The Second World War was not caused by modern democratic nation-states or by democratic nationalism. Weimar Germany had no desire to attack the French Republic. The leading statesmen of Western resistance to Nazi Germany—Winston Churchill, Franklin Roosevelt, and Charles de Gaulle—have all been correctly characterized as nationalists.

Contrary to EU public relations, the peace in Europe since 1945 has little to do with the existence of the European Union. Rather, it is primarily the result of two other factors: the fact that Europe consisted of modern democratic nation-states, and the presence of the United States in Europe and in the NATO alliance. Does anyone imagine that if the European Union had never existed, there would have been any possibility of war between, say, Helmut Kohl's Germany and François Mitterrand's France? U.S. involvement in the continent's affairs and in NATO certainly would have prevented any inter-European wars regardless of the existence or nonexistence of the EU, the common agricultural policy (CAP), the European Court of Justice, or any of the other trappings of supranationalism.

Whereas the liberal democratic nation-state can offer a reasonable record of accomplishments, the global governance movement, like other utopian projects in the past, offers us mostly vague theories. In those few instances where supporters of supranational governance have a record—for example, the European Union and the first years of the International Criminal Court—that record is problematic, especially in the area of democratic accountability.

First and foremost, the global governance party has not solved its "democratic deficit" problem, either in theory or in practice. Theoretically, the advocates of global governance offer an array of organizations (transnational courts, financial institutions, international organizations, NGOs, and postmodern states), but they do not square the circle and clearly explain how all this new global governance "architecture" could be made consistent with democracy and liberty, and how, as a practical matter, the new global system could be infused with the necessary political loyalty to sustain and perpetuate itself as a serious transnational legal regime.

At the heart of global governance theory is the idea that there are global problems that countries cannot solve by themselves, but require global solutions. The problems most often listed are world poverty, global economic inequality, climate change, nuclear proliferation, and war. But these issues involve political and moral choices about which people and nations profoundly disagree; they are not technological or ethical "problems" that can be "solved" either through expertise or by some type of imagined global consensus.

No serious mechanism that is democratic has been proposed by the supporters of global governance to "solve" these "problems." What are presented instead are vague proposals for "overlapping jurisdictions" or "new transnational structures." In other words, mostly top-down, nondemocratic decision making, as in the *New York Times* columnist Thomas Friedman's lament that if only the United States were "China for a day," our environmental problems could be properly addressed without any messy democratic process.[17]

As a practical model of how supranational governance could work, the global governancers usually point to the European Union. It is true that the administrative-judicial apparatus of the EU does achieve a form of supranational governance, but it is not democratic or accountable to any democratic people. Too many decisions about fundamental issues of political life are made by unelected EU bureaucrats in Brussels or by judges in Luxembourg. The European Parliament neither initiates legislation nor fulfills the normal functions of a democratic parliament, with a responsible governing majority and an opposition bloc. In practice, EU leaders seek to replace the modern democratic state with the postmodern state, which "shares" its sovereignty with other states and supranational institutions.

Only a small number of theorists and activists today favor world government or some form of world federation. One of the most prominent of these theorists is David Held, who advocates a world-wide democracy with a global parliament.[18] Exactly how all of the world's peoples could become "one people" with common political principles, mutual interests, emotional attachment, and enough trust in each other to form a global democratic political regime is never clearly spelled out.

What would happen if this worldwide global regime ceased to be a democracy and became a form of tyranny, either the "hard" variety ruled by force or the "soft" variation ruled by bureaucracy, as foreseen and feared by Alexis de Tocqueville? Where could political refugees flee?

Political philosophers have long pondered this problem. As noted in Chapter Two, Immanuel Kant himself worried that a single world republic could eventually become a "soulless despotism."[19] Therefore he favored a federation of nations with supranational powers rather than a single world republic. Jürgen Habermas, a Kant scholar and leading global governance theorist, observes, "Kant fears that a world republic, notwithstanding its federal structure, would inevitably lead to social and cultural uniformity. Behind this fear lurks the objection that a global state of nations would develop an inherent, irresistible tendency to degenerate into a 'universal monarchy.'"[20]

In a famous intellectual exchange, two giants of political philosophy, Leo Strauss and Alexandre Kojève, discussed a hypothetical world government in relation to wisdom and philosophy.[21] Kojève saw the emergence of a "universal and homogeneous state" as the fulfillment of History and Progress. Strauss asserted that "the coming of the universal and homogenous state will be the end of philosophy" under a reign of tyranny.[22]

Strauss maintained that "the Chief of the universal and homogeneous state, or the Universal and Final Tyrant will be an unwise man.... To retain his power, he will be forced to suppress every activity which might lead people into doubt of the essential soundness of the universal and homogeneous state: he must suppress philosophy as an attempt to corrupt the young." If a single world tyranny came into place, Strauss noted, the philosopher [and, one might add, the political refugee] would have nowhere to go. As long as there was no universal state, "the philosophers could escape to other countries if life became unbearable in the tyrant's dominions. From the Universal Tyrant however there is no escape."[23]

Of course, the global governancers we have discussed here do not favor a single global government, or any form of tyranny, but rather "governance" through a hybrid of national, transnational, and supranational legal and regulatory regimes. As Habermas put it, the new regime would be "a politically constituted global society that reserves institutions and procedures of global governance for states at both the supra- and transnational levels."[24] That said, problems of overcentralization, conformity, lack of diversity and innovation, and bureaucratic and legalistic heavy-handedness are intrinsic to the global governance project.

Implicit in the vision of global governance is the notion that there are universal norms and standards for policies on a wide range of issues, from human rights (is capital punishment a violation of human rights?) to government budgetary policies (is a country spending enough money on children and minorities?). Obviously, democrats disagree on these issues. Shouldn't democracies decide them? The global governance project emphasizes the positive aspects of universal constitutionalism, in which standardized one-size-fits-all global legal rules are considered superior to the more diversified rules of democratic national constitutions and laws.

Jed Rubenfeld, a liberal law professor at Yale, takes issue with global governance in general, and with the notion of universal constitutionalism in particular, on the grounds that it goes against liberty and true diversity, and impedes the progress that comes through experimentation. While speaking of transnationalists in general, Rubenfeld comments:

Europeans tend to neglect or minimize the damage that universal constitutionalism does to the prospects for variation, experimentation, and radical change opened up by national democracy. So long as democracy is allied with *national* self-government rather than with *world* governance, it remains an experimental ideal, dedicated to the possibility of variation, perhaps radical variation, among peoples with different values and different objectives. Democratic national constitutionalism may be parochial *within* a given nation, but it's cosmopolitan *across* nations. Democratic peoples are permitted, even expected, to take different paths. They're permitted, even expected, to go to hell in their own way.[25]

Why should we exchange the most decent political system the world has ever known, the independent liberal democratic nation-state, for the utopian promise of global governance? Why should we Americans trade away our independence and subordinate our time-tested Constitution? For what, exactly? For "evolving norms of international law"? Certainly, the burden of proof is on the advocates of global governance, not on the supporters of democratic sovereignty, to demonstrate that their alternative is a superior political regime. This, of course, they cannot do.

The Moral Right to Self-Government

The conflict between global governance and the liberal democratic nation-state is a moral conflict, and the side that seizes the moral high ground and holds it will prevail. The fundamental question beneath the struggle is: Do Americans, or other peoples, have the moral right to rule themselves or must they share sovereignty with others?

More than two hundred years ago, the Founders of the American republic had their own answer to this question, and it led to the

American Revolution. Their answer is expressed in the Declaration of Independence and in the Constitution of the United States. Americans declared their independence from Great Britain in 1776 to establish their right to rule themselves. They believed the British were taking away the degree of self-rule they did enjoy in their colonial governments. In the Declaration of Independence, the Second Continental Congress complained to "our British Brethren" of the "Attempts by their Legislature to extend an unwarrantable Jurisdiction over us." The Declaration charged that George III "has combined with others to subject us to a Jurisdiction foreign to our Constitution,★ and unacknowledged by our Laws; giving his Assent to their Acts of pretended Legislation."

The actions by the British Crown that the American colonists protested are exactly what the advocates of global governance are attempting today: to subject Americans to a jurisdiction foreign to our Constitution. To be sure, the global governancers would argue that they are simply pointing out the universal human rights that no government, democratic or otherwise, has the right to violate. After all, the American Declaration of Independence itself refers to "unalienable" natural rights. Moreover, during the mid-twentieth century, America took the lead in promoting the United Nations Universal Declaration of Human Rights. So why shouldn't universal human rights apply to all people in the world, and all violators of these rights be subject to global justice?

The American Founders in the eighteenth century and American democratic sovereigntists in the twenty-first century would respond to the global governancers with a similar line of reasoning: Of course there are fundamental human rights, but the key question is, as always, *who decides?* First, who decides exactly how those rights are

---

★The "Constitution" that Jefferson referred to in 1776 was the limited self-government that the colonists enjoyed under the unwritten British constitution, "the rights of Englishmen."

defined? Second, who decides how to deal with violations of those rights? In the United States, these issues are *decided and defined within our constitutional system*, which includes an explicit Bill of Rights. This constitutional order seeks to ensure individual human rights and provides for the punishment of those who violate specific human rights. As a universal principle, American democratic sovereigntists support the right of any liberal democratic people living in a free society (Australians, Indians, Britons, Canadians, Spaniards, Indonesians, Israelis, etc.) to *decide and define human rights within the context of their own democratic regime*, without necessarily bowing to "global norms" established by nondemocratic transnational bodies.

The advocates of global governance have a different answer to the question of who defines and decides what exactly are human rights. For them, the content of human rights is defined and decided by the growing and evolving body of the "new" international law, and by international and transnational institutions (UN, UNHRC, ICC, European Court of Human Rights, etc.) and communities (international lawyers and judges) associated with that always evolving "law." We have seen how UN treaty monitoring committees have expanded the definition of "human rights" to include political issues that free people should be able to decide for themselves, involving economics, education, budget, immigration, citizenship, and criminal justice, for example. Further, we have seen how supranational judicial bodies like the ICC claim authority to prosecute democratic citizens without the consent of the democracies involved.

After one has stripped away all the sophisticated verbiage—transnational litigation processes, international legal regimes, postnational forms of citizenship, shared or pooled sovereignty, transjudicialism, global civil society, "downloading" international law into U.S. law, "coordinating constitutional rules with rules of foreign and international law," "redefining" sovereignty, transforming the Westphalian system, creating new transnational treaty regimes, global solutions to global problems—what the global governancers are actually saying is that Americans do not have a moral right to rule themselves. This book argues that Americans do have a moral right to rule themselves, as do all other free peoples and those who aspire to attain or restore self-government. It explains why independent self-government in the sovereign liberal democratic nation-state is preferable to all forms of global governance. These are the issues—particularly the moral right of a people to rule itself—on which Philadelphian sovereigntists today, like the American Founders yesterday, should take their stand for the long struggle ahead.

Let us end this book with a visit to Quincy, Massachusetts, on June 30, 1826. Five days before the fiftieth anniversary of the Declaration of Independence, an elderly and frail John Adams receives a group of visitors "in his upstairs library seated in his favorite armchair." The town leaders are organizing a celebration for the anniversary (which would turn out to be the day that both Adams and Thomas Jefferson died), and they ask Quincy's most prominent citizen, known throughout the young republic as "the Atlas of Independence," for a toast to be read to the celebrants. Adams answers in two words: "Independence Forever." Asked if he has anything more to say, he replies, "Not a word."[26]

Indeed, *Independence Forever.*

Appendix

Question 1

When there is a conflict between the U.S. Constitution and International Law, which should be the highest legal authority for Americans? For instance on human rights, economics, environment, trade, family, and other issues.

	Constitution	**International Law**	**Not Sure**
All Respondents	66%	16%	17%
Registered Voters	69%	16%	15%
High School or Less	65%	15%	20%
Some College	63%	19%	18%
4 Yr. or 2 Yr. College Grads	71%	14%	15%
Post-Graduate	63%	25%	12%
Blacks	53%	24%	23%
Latinos	55%	20%	26%
Whites	71%	14%	14%
Republicans	84%	6%	10%
Democrats	56%	24%	20%
Native-Born Citizens	67%	16%	17%
Naturalized Citizens	37%	29%	34%
Conservatives	82%	5%	13%
Moderates	64%	16%	20%
Liberals	48%	33%	19%
Married	76%	11%	13%
Single	56%	22%	21%
Evangelicals	74%	11%	15%

Question 2

Currently, some radical Islamists have said that they are against the U.S. Constitution and that it should be replaced with Islamic law. If someone believes this, do you think that they should be allowed to migrate to the United States?

	Yes	No	Not Sure
All Respondents	8%	86%	6%
Registered Voters	8%	88%	4%
High School or Less	10%	83%	7%
Some College	9%	85%	6%
4 Yr. or 2 Yr. College Grads	5%	91%	4%
Post-Graduate	8%	90%	3%
Blacks	10%	81%	9%
Latinos	14%	74%	12%
Whites	6%	90%	4%
Republicans	6%	91%	3%
Democrats	9%	86%	5%
Native-Born Citizens	8%	87%	5%
Naturalized Citizens	7%	71%	22%
Conservatives	3%	93%	4%
Moderates	7%	87%	6%
Liberals	17%	76%	8%
Married	5%	93%	2%
Single	11%	80%	9%
Evangelicals	7%	89%	4%

Question 3

In the oath that immigrants take when they become American citizens they promise to renounce all loyalty to their former country. Do you agree or disagree that individuals should be required to give up loyalty to their former country when they become American citizens?

	Agree	Disagree	Not Sure
All Respondents	73%	21%	6%
Registered Voters	75%	20%	5%
High School or Less	71%	20%	9%
Some College	71%	23%	6%
4 Yr. or 2 Yr. College Grads	77%	19%	4%
Post-Graduate	73%	23%	3%
Blacks	66%	19%	15%
Latinos	58%	36%	6%
Whites	77%	18%	6%
Republicans	85%	12%	4%
Democrats	63%	29%	8%
Native-Born Citizens	74%	20%	6%
Naturalized Citizens	53%	33%	14%
Conservatives	81%	13%	6%
Moderates	76%	18%	7%
Liberals	57%	37%	6%
Married	79%	17%	5%
Single	67%	25%	8%
Evangelicals	79%	14%	7%

Question 4

Do you think of yourself more as a citizen of the United States? OR a citizen of the world?

	US Citizen	World Citizen	Not Sure
All Respondents	83%	12%	4%
Registered Voters	85%	12%	3%
High School or Less	84%	12%	4%
Some College	81%	14%	5%
4 Yr. or 2 Yr. College Grads	84%	11%	5%
Post-Graduate	80%	18%	2%
Blacks	76%	16%	8%
Latinos	75%	19%	6%
Whites	87%	10%	3%
Republicans	96%	3%	1%
Democrats	80%	16%	4%
Native-Born Citizens	85%	12%	4%
Naturalized Citizens	54%	29%	17%
Conservatives	92%	4%	4%
Moderates	86%	10%	4%
Liberals	66%	29%	5%
Married	90%	7%	3%
Single	77%	18%	6%
Evangelicals	87%	8%	5%

Question 5

Which of the following statements comes closest to your opinion?
(1) Overall the U.S. is better than other nations.
(2) The U.S. is a country like any other, and is no better or worse than other nations.
(3) Overall, the U.S. is worse than other nations.

	US Better	US Like Others	Worse	Not Sure
All Respondents	64%	27%	3%	4%
Registered Voters	66%	27%	2%	4%
High School or Less	64%	25%	3%	8%
Some College	62%	28%	3%	8%
4 Yr. or 2 Yr. College Grads	67%	27%	2%	4%
Post-Graduate	60%	34%	6%	1%
Blacks	51%	32%	2%	15%
Latinos	58%	31%	3%	8%
Whites	68%	25%	2%	4%
Republicans	83%	13%	1%	3%
Democrats	58%	32%	4%	7%
Native-Born Citizens	65%	27%	3%	6%
Naturalized Citizens	44%	27%	8%	21%
Conservatives	81%	14%	1%	4%
Moderates	63%	29%	2%	7%
Liberals	43%	41%	7%	8%
Married	72%	22%	2%	4%
Single	56%	32%	4%	9%
Evangelicals	71%	22%	2%	5%

Acknowledgments

I am grateful to dozens of people who provided advice and support for this book. Those who read crucial sections of the manuscript and offered helpful advice include Bill Schambra, Jeremy Rabkin, Doug Feith, Charles Horner, Jim Ceaser, Ken Weinstein, Max Singer, Meyrav Wurmser, Scooter Libby, Herb London, Irwin Stelzer, Jonathan Delaney, Noah Pickus, Mark Krikorian, Ted Totman, Robert Schulmann, Joseph Rutigliano, Althea Nagai, Juliana Geran Pilon, and a currently serving U.S. State Department official who will remain anonymous.

I benefited greatly from conversations with Jerry and Abigail Martin, Steve Balch, Hillel Fradkin, Eric Brown, Michael Horowitz, Amy Kass, Jim Kurth, Stanley Kurtz, Peter Berkowitz, Ron Dworkin, Bill McClay, Glynn Custred, Jim Kelly, Steve Groves, Brett Schaeffer, Robin Harris, Ken Minogue, Fred Smith, Myron Ebell, Austin Ruse, Steve Camarota, Jeremy Carl, Marguerite Peeters, Nina Shea, Paul Marshall, Marcello Pera, Juan Rangel, Peter Spiro, and Bob Bork. I thank Mary Ellen Bork for coming up with the title of the book. I also had helpful discussions with two now-deceased Hudson Institute colleagues whose foreign policy views differed widely: the French intellectual Laurent Murawiec and the retired General William Odom. I am especially grateful to the Hudson Institute's past and present leadership—Wally Stern, Allan Tessler, Herb London, and the current CEO, Ken Weinstein—for fostering a collegial and intellectually open atmosphere. Hudson is a wonderful place to work. I have learned much from my colleagues in discussions both formal and informal. The administrative staff and board are extraordinarily helpful.

I would like to thank my brother, Dick Fonte, who gave me very cogent advice and moral support as I proceeded through the book. Tom Klingenstein provided strong support, both financial and intellectual, reading the entire manuscript and offering comprehensive analysis. I am greatly indebted to my friend Chuck Bahmueller, who has discussed the themes of this book with me for years, and who edited each chapter as I went along. John O'Sullivan has earned my gratitude for writing his generous foreword, for publishing my first article in *National Review* sixteen years ago, and for enthusiastically promoting my theories on global governance to a wide international audience.

I'm appreciative of the editorial leadership at several periodicals where my early ideas on transnationalism and global governance have been published and discussed. These include Rich Lowry and Kathryn Lopez at *National Review;* Alan Luxenberg, Walter McDougall, David Eisenhower, and Jim Kurth, all associated with *Orbis* and the Foreign Policy Research Institute; Paul Saunders of the *National Interest* and the Center for the National Interest (formerly the Nixon Center); and Charles Kesler of the *Claremont Review of Books* and the Claremont Institute. I also benefited from presenting papers and engaging in discussions at the University of California, Berkeley, sponsored by the Intercollegiate Studies Institute, and at the University of Virginia, Charlottesville, sponsored by the Jack Miller Center for Teaching American Founding Principles and History.

I was fortunate to have a diligent group of research assistants and interns to help me in preparing this book. They include Aaron Menenberg, Tina Sula, Ryan Arant, Elizabeth Starkey, Ryan Gough, Justin Nicholson, Antonio Sosa Rumbos, Leigh Maltby, Harley Metcalfe IV, and Erich Hartman.

Several foundations have generously supported my work on this project: the Sarah Scaife Foundation, the Lynde and Harry Bradley Foundation, the Fred Maytag Family Foundation, the Stuart Family Foundation, the Castle Rock Foundation, the F. M. Kirby Foundation, and the Klingenstein Fund. Especially helpful in navigating this world have been Dan Schmidt, Mike Hartmann, Michael Gleba, Bill Byrnes, John Jackson, Truman Anderson, and Robert Pickus.

Encounter Books provided me with an extraordinary editor, Carol Staswick, to whom I am greatly indebted. I am also thankful to Encounter's publisher, Roger Kimball, and to Heather Ohle and Emily Pollack of his staff for their strong support. I have a terrific agent, Susan Rabiner, who initially contacted me about writing a book on global governance several years ago. Susan (and her marketing specialist, Helena Schwarz) have believed in this project from the beginning and have offered wise counsel as it has progressed.

Finally and most importantly, I am deeply grateful to my wife, Susan, who has provided love and support throughout the years. This book is dedicated to her with profound appreciation and admiration.

Notes

Introduction

[1] John G. Ruggie, F. Douglas Gibson Lecture in Political Economy, Queen's University, Kingston, Ontario, November 20, 2000. Italics in the original.

Chapter 1: Durban, 2001: A Microcosm of Transnational Politics

[1] Anthony Goodman, "UN Conference 2001 against Racism: Rights Activists Ask UN to Target Racism in U.S.," Reuters, October 27, 2000, http://www.icare.to/archiveoctober2000.html

[2] "A Call to Action to the United Nations," http://www.globalrights.org/site/DocServer/Call-to-Action_-_Final.pdf?docID=210

[3] Ibid.

[4] Ibid.

[5] Goodman, "UN Conference 2001 against Racism."

[6] The Rockefeller Foundation, Form 990PF–2000, p. 151.

[7] The Center on Philanthropy at Indiana University, 550 West North Street #301, Indianapolis, IN 46202.

[8] "Report of the US Leadership Meetings on the World Conference against Racism," convened by Gay J. McDougall, executive director, International Human Rights Law Group, with support from the Ford Foundation, Charles Stewart Mott Foundation, in partnership with the Leadership Conference on Civil Rights, Leadership Conference Education Fund, National Council of Churches USA, Southern Education Foundation, inter alia. In the author's possession.

[9] Goodman, "UN Conference 2001 against Racism."

[10] "A Call to Action to the United Nations."

[11] Karen Iley, "Critics Say U.S. Racial Justice Not a Reality," Reuters, August 6, 2001.

[12] Elizabeth Olson, "U.S. Reports Progress in Fighting Bias; Rights Groups Are Critical," *New York Times*, August 7, 2001.

[13] "U.S. 'Race Relations' Under UN Scrutiny," *New American*, September 10, 2001, http://www.questia.com/PM.qst?a=o&d=5002417329

Chapter 2: A Perennial War of Ideas

[1] Immanuel Kant, "Perpetual Peace: A Philosophical Sketch," in *Kant's Political Writings*, ed. Hans Reiss (Cambridge, UK: Cambridge University Press, 1970).

[2] Emery Reves, *The Anatomy of Peace* (1945; Dallas, Tex.: Dallas Symphony Association, 1994).

[3] Emery Reves, "An Open Letter to the American People," from *The Anatomy of Peace,* available at http://archive1. globalsolutions.org/wfi/documents/OpenLetter.pdf

[4] Ibid.

[5] Albert Einstein, "Towards a World Government (1946)," in *Out of My Later Years* (New York: Kensington Publishing, 1984), p. 138.

[6] The transcript appeared in the Democratic World Federalists' quarterly, *Toward Democratic World Federation,* Autumn 1999, http://www.dwfed.org/pp_cronkite.html

[7] Anne-Marie Slaughter, *A New World Order* (Princeton, N.J.: Princeton University Press, 2004), p. 9.

[8] Ibid., pp. 13–14.

[9] Ibid., p. 4.

[10] Strobe Talbott, "The Birth of the Global Nation," *Time,* July 20, 1992.

[11] Strobe Talbott, *The Great Experiment: The Story of Ancient Empires, Modern States, and the Quest for a Global Nation* (New York: Simon & Schuster, 2009).

[12] Ibid., p. 126.

[13] Ibid., p. 6.

[14] Ibid., p. 45.

[15] Ibid., p. 63.

[16] Ibid., p. 9.

[17] Ibid., p. 24.

[18] Ibid., p. 37.

[19] Ibid., p. 38.

[20] Ibid., p. 38.

[21] Ibid., p. 43.

[22] Ibid., p. 40.

[23] David Gelernter, "Americanism—and Its Enemies," *Commentary,* January 2005.

[24] Michael Novak, *On Two Wings: Humble Faith and Common Sense at the American Founding* (San Francisco: Encounter Books, 2002), p. 8.

[25] Ibid., p. 38. The address was anthologized in the Dutch Republic and elsewhere in Europe.

[26] Talbott, *The Great Experiment,* p. 10.

[27] Ibid., p. 103.

[28] Thomas Hobbes, *Leviathan: or, the Matter, Forme and Power of a Commonwealth, Ecclesiasticall and Civill,* ed. Alfred Rayney Waller (1651; Cambridge, 1904; repr. University of Michigan Press, 1961).

[29] Talbott, *The Great Experiment,* p. 100.

[30] Kant, "Perpetual Peace" (see n. 1).

[31] Talbott, *The Great Experiment,* p. 418, n. 23.

[32] Ibid., p. 102.

[33] Immanuel Kant, "Perpetual Peace: A Philosophical Sketch," available at http://www.mnstate.edu/gracyk/courses/web%20publishing/KantOnPeace.htm

[34] Immanuel Kant, "Idea for a Universal History from a Cosmopolitan Point of View," in *Philosophy of Technology: The Technological Condition—An Anthology,* ed. Robert C. Scharff and Val Dusek (Oxford: Blackwell), pp. 38–44.

[35] Ibid.

[36] Transcript at http://www.founding.com/founders_library/pageID.2270/default.asp

[37] Jeremy A. Rabkin, *Law Without Nations? Why Constitutional Government Requires Sovereign States* (Princeton, N.J.: Princeton University Press, 2007), p. 87.

[38] Ibid., p. 86.

[39] Ibid., p. 87.

[40] Ibid., p. 88.

[41] Ibid., p. 89.

[42] John Locke, *Of Civil Government*, Bk. 2, chap. 19, sec. 217.

[43] Marc F. Plattner, *Democracy Without Borders? Global Challenges to Liberal Democracy* (Lanham, Md.: Rowman & Littlefield, 2008), p. 121.

[44] Ibid., p. 128.

[45] Plattner also points out that Locke, unlike Kant, did not believe that the "inconveniences of the state of nature" would drive the "separate commonwealths into uniting to form a common body politic." Ibid., p. 120.

[46] Forrest McDonald, *Novus Ordo Seclorum: The Intellectual Origins of the Constitution* (Lawrence, Kans.: University Press of Kansas, 1985), p. 67. Practically every other scholar of the founding era also emphasizes the importance of Plutarch's *Lives.*

[47] Carl J. Richard, *The Founders and the Classics: Greece, Rome, and the American Enlightenment* (Cambridge, Mass.: Harvard University Press, 1995).

[48] Ibid., p. 57.

[49] Ibid., p. 86.

[50] Ibid., p. 90.

[51] Ibid., p. 93.

[52] Ron Chernow, *Alexander Hamilton* (New York: Penguin, 2004), p. 398.

[53] Richard, *The Founders and the Classics*, p. 84.

[54] Bernard Bailyn, "The Origins of American Politics," in *The American Scene: Varieties of American History*, ed. Robert D. Marcus and David Burner (New York: Appleton-Century-Crofts, 1971), vol. 1, p. 126.

[55] Ibid., p. 132.

[56] Ibid., p. 127.

[57] Bernard Bailyn, *The Ideological Origins of the American Revolution* (Cambridge, Mass.: Harvard University Press, 1992), pp. 35–45.

[58] Ibid., pp. 53–54.

[59] Gordon S. Wood, "The Intellectual Origins of the American Revolution," *Phi Kappa Phi Journal,* available at http://spot.colorado.edu/~mcguire/wood.htm

[60] Bailyn, *The Ideological Origins of the American Revolution,* p. 44.

[61] Ibid., p. 56.

[62] McDonald, *Novus Ordo Seclorum,* p. viii.

[63] Ibid., p. 235.

[64] Ibid., p. 67.

[65] Charles S. Hyneman and Donald S. Lutz, "The Relative Influence of European Writers on Late Eighteenth-Century American Political Thought," *American Political Science Review,* vol. 78, no. 1 (March 1984), pp. 189–97.

[66] Ibid., p. 192.

[67] Ibid., p. 189.

[68] Jeremy Rabkin, *The Case for Sovereignty: Why the World Should Welcome American Independence* (Washington, D.C.: American Enterprise Institute, 2004), pp. 26–27.

[69] Rabkin, *Law Without Nations?* (see n. 38), p. 71.

[70] Quoted in ibid., pp. 79–80. A different translation of Vattel's *Le droit des gens* may be found at the Liberty Fund's Online Library of Liberty.

Chapter 3: Civic Nationalism and American Liberal Democracy

[1] James W. Ceaser, *Liberal Democracy and Political Science* (Baltimore: Johns Hopkins University Press, 1990), p. 8.

[2] Marc F. Plattner, *Democracy Without Borders? Global Challenges to Liberal Democracy* (Lanham, Md.: Rowman & Littlefield, 2008), p. 10.

[3] Ibid., pp. 78–79.

[4] Fareed Zakaria, "The Rise of Illiberal Democracy," *Foreign Affairs,* November 1997.

[5] Natan Sharansky, with Shira Wolosky Weiss, *Defending Identity: Its Indispensable Role in Protecting Democracy* (New York: PublicAffairs, 2008), p. 2.

[6] Ibid., p. 6.

[7] Ibid., p. 231.

[8] Ibid., p. 16.

[9] Ibid., pp. 135–36.

[10] Roger Scruton, "In Defence of the Nation," in *Debates in Contemporary Political Philosophy: An Anthology,* ed. Derek Matravers and Jonathan E. Pike (New York: Routledge, 2003), pp. 282–83.

[11] Ibid., p. 280.

[12] Ibid., p. 280.

[13] Ibid., p. 281.

[14] Ibid., p. 281.

[15] Ibid., pp. 281–82.

[16] Roger Scruton, "In Defence of the Nation," in *Philosopher on Dover Beach: Essays* (South Bend, Ind.: St. Augustine's Press, 1999), pp. 323–24.

[17] Sharansky, *Defending Identity*, p. 7.

[18] Scruton, *In Defence of the Nation*, p. 319.

[19] James Madison, "The Federalist No. 51," February 1788, in *The Federalist Papers*, ed. Clinton Rossiter (New York: New American Library of World Literature, 1961), pp. 320–25.

[20] Bernard Bailyn, *The Ideological Origins of the American Revolution* (Cambridge, Mass.: Harvard University Press, 1992), p. 345.

[21] James Madison, "The Federalist No. 55," February 1788, in *The Federalist Papers*, ed. Rossiter, pp. 341–46.

[22] Ceaser, *Liberal Democracy and Political Science*, p. 27.

[23] Ibid., pp. 36–37, 42.

[24] Alexis de Tocqueville, *Democracy in America*, ed. Harvey C. Mansfield and Delba Winthrop (Chicago: University of Chicago Press, 2000), pp. 274, 295.

[25] Ceaser, *Liberal Democracy and Political Science*, p. 144.

[26] Tocqueville, *Democracy in America*, pp. 280–81.

[27] Charles Kesler, "The Crisis of American National Identity," Lehrman Lectures on Restoring America's National Identity, Heritage Foundation Lecture no. 906, November 8, 2005.

[28] George Washington, "Farewell Address," http://gwpapers.virginia.edu/documents/farewell/transcript.html

[29] John Adams, *A Defence of the Constitutions of Government of the United States of America*, 1787, available at the Liberty Fund's Online Library of Liberty.

[30] Immanuel Kant, "Perpetual Peace: A Philosophical Sketch," in *Kant's Political Writings*, ed. Hans Reiss (Cambridge, UK: Cambridge University Press, 1970), pp. 112–13.

[31] James Madison, "The Federalist No. 49," February 1788, in *The Federalist Papers*, ed. Rossiter, pp. 313–17.

[32] Ibid.

[33] Walter Berns, *Making Patriots* (Chicago: University of Chicago Press, 2001), p. 76.

[34] James Madison, "The Federalist No. 14," November 1787, in *The Federalist Papers*, ed. Rossiter, pp. 99–105.

[35] John Jay, "The Federalist No. 2," *Independent Journal*, October 1787, in *The Federalist Papers*, ed. Rossiter, pp. 37–41.

[36] Washington, "Farewell Address."

[37] Abraham Lincoln, "The Perpetuation of Our Political Institutions," Address before the Young Men's Lyceum of Springfield, Illinois, January 27, 1838, in *The Collected Works of Abraham Lincoln*, ed. Roy P. Basler (New Brunswick, N.J.: Rutgers University Press, 1953), vol. 1, p. 112, available at http://www.lincolnstudies.com/address-before-the-young-mens-lyceum-of-springfield-illinois.

Basler quotes the final clause as "and to tear the character [charter?] of his own, and his children's liberty," the bracketed word suggesting that he suspected the wording of his primary printed source to be erroneous. Like many others who quote this passage—including the walls of Lincoln Hall at the University of Illinois—I have concluded that "tear the charter of . . . liberty" is much more likely to be what Lincoln actually said.

[38] Washington, "Farewell Address."

[39] Abraham Lincoln, "Second Inaugural Address," Washington, D.C., March 1865, http://www.ourdocuments.gov/doc.php?flash=old&doc=38

[40] Washington, "Farewell Address."

[41] Abraham Lincoln, "Address to the New Jersey State Senate," Trenton, N.J., February 1861.

[42] Matthew Spalding and Patrick J. Garrity, *A Sacred Union of Citizens: George Washington's Farewell Address and the American Character* (London: Rowman & Littlefield, 1996), p. 52.

[43] Don Higginbotham, *George Washington: Uniting a Nation* (London: Rowman & Littlefield, 2005), p. 79.

[44] Washington, "Farewell Address."

[45] Thomas Jefferson, *Notes on the State of Virginia*, ed. Frank Shuffelton (New York: Penguin Classics, 1999), Query 14.

[46] Henry Barnard, *The American Journal of Education*, vol. 15 (New York: F. C. Brownell, 1865), p. 12.

[47] Noah Webster, *On the Education of Youth in America*, 1788.

[48] George Washington, "Address to the Members of the Volunteer Association and Other Inhabitants," December 2, 1783.

[49] George Washington, "Letter to the Vice President," November 15, 1794, available at http://www.founding.com/founders_library/pageID.2223/default.asp

[50] Jefferson, *Notes on the State of Virginia*, p. 91. Also in Thomas G. West, *Vindicating the Founders: Race, Sex, Class, and Justice in the Origins of America* (Lanham, Md.: Rowman & Littlefield, 1997), pp. 153–54.

[51] Alexander Hamilton, "The Examination, No. 7," 1802.

[52] Frank George Franklin, *The Legislative History of Naturalization in the United States* (Chicago: University of Chicago Press, 1906), p. 101.

[53] President Abraham Lincoln, "Speech at Chicago, Illinois," July 10, 1858, http://teachingamericanhistory.org/library/index.asp?document=153. See also John J. Miller, *The Unmaking of Americans: How Multiculturalism Has Undermined America's Assimilation Ethic* (New York: Free Press, 1998), p. 29.

[54] U.S. Department of Labor, Bureau of Naturalization, "Our Nation," *Federal Textbook on Citizenship Training* (Washington, D.C.: USGPO, 1931), p. 236.

[55] Theodore Roosevelt, "True Americanism" *The Forum*, April 1894, http://teachingamericanhistory.org/library/index.asp?document=6728

[56] Woodrow Wilson, "Address to Several Thousand Foreign-Born Citizens after Naturalization Ceremonies," Philadelphia, May 10, 1915, in *President Wilson's State Papers and Addresses*, ed. Albert Shaw (New York: George H. Doran Co., 1918), pp. 114–18, available online.

[57] Louis D. Brandeis, "True Americanism," July 5, 1915, http://www.law.louisville. edu/library/collections/brandeis/node/224

Chapter 4: Liberalism under Assault

[1] Allan David Bloom, *The Closing of the American Mind* (New York: Simon & Schuster, 1987), p. 159.

[2] Francis Fukuyama, *The End of History and the Last Man* (New York: Maxwell Macmillan International, 1992).

[3] John Dewey, *Liberalism and Social Action* (New York: G. P. Putnam, 1935), p. 17.

[4] Charles Merriam, *A History of American Political Theories* (New York: Macmillan, 1920), p. 307.

[5] Richard Hofstadter, *The Age of Reform: From Bryan to FDR* (New York: Alfred A. Knopf, 1955).

[6] James Piereson, *Camelot and the Cultural Revolution: How the Assassination of John F. Kennedy Shattered American Liberalism* (New York: Encounter Books, 2007), p. 6.

[7] Chester Bowles, "We Are All Liberals Now," *New York Times Magazine*, April 19, 1959.

[8] John Dewey, *The Middle Works, 1899–1924*, vol. 13, ed. Jo Ann Boydston, intro. Ralph Ross (Carbondale: Southern Illinois University Press, 1976), p. 332.

[9] Charles A. Beard, *An Economic Interpretation of the Constitution of the United States* (New York: Macmillan, 1921).

[10] Carl Becker, *Declaration of Independence: A Study in the History of Political Ideas* (New York: Alfred A. Knopf, 1942).

[11] John Patrick Diggins explains how liberal and progressive historians embraced a qualified but more or less positive vision of America's past shortly before America's entry into World War II. *On Hallowed Ground: Abraham Lincoln and the Foundations of American History* (New Haven: Yale University Press, 2000).

[12] Arthur M. Schlesinger Jr., *The Disuniting of America: Reflections on a Multicultural Society* (New York: W. W. Norton, 1998), pp. 164–65.

[13] Conrad Black, *Franklin Delano Roosevelt: Champion of Freedom* (New York: PublicAffairs, 2003), p. 944.

[14] Richard Dauer, *A North-South Mind in an East-West World: Chester Bowles and the Making of United States Cold War Foreign Policy, 1951–1969* (Westport, Conn.: Praeger, 2005), p. 14.

[15] Steven Gillon, *Politics and Vision* (New York: Oxford University Press, 1987), p. 18.

16 Arthur M. Schlesinger Jr., *The Vital Center: The Politics of Freedom* (Boston: Houghton Mifflin, 1949).

17 1964 Civil Rights Act, Title VII, sec. 703(j).

18 110 Congressional Record 14329 (June 18, 1964).

19 110 Congressional Record 7420 (April 9, 1964).

20 Amy Gutmann, "Introduction," in *Multiculturalism and the Politics of Recognition*, an essay by Charles Taylor with commentary by Amy Gutmann (ed.), Steven C. Rockefeller, Michael Walzer, and Susan Wolf (Princeton, N.J.: Princeton University Press, 1992), pp. 3–24.

21 Amy Gutmann, "Democratic Citizenship," reply to Martha Nussbaum in "Patriotism or Cosmopolitanism?" *Boston Review* 19:5 (October/November 1994), reprinted in *For Love of Country: Debating the Limits of Patriotism*, ed. Joshua Cohen (Boston: Beacon Press, 1996), pp. 66–71.

22 See Nathan Glazer, *We Are All Multiculturalists Now* (Cambridge, Mass.: Harvard University Press, 1997); and John Fonte, "E pluribus plures," *National Review*, May 5, 1997.

23 Will Kymlicka, "The Rights of Minority Cultures," *Political Theory* 20:1 (February 1992), p. 145.

24 Ibid., p. 140.

25 James A. Banks, "Transforming the Mainstream Curriculum," *Educational Leadership* 51:8, *Educating for Diversity* (May 1994), pp. 4–8.

26 Gilbert T. Sewall, *History Textbooks at the New Century* (American Textbook Council, 2000).

27 Quoted in *Education for Democracy* (Albert Shanker Institute, 2003), p. 20. The institute is endowed by the American Federation of Teachers.

28 See Terry H. Anderson, *The Pursuit of Fairness: A History of Affirmative Action* (New York: Oxford University Press, 2004), p. 173.

29 Fred Lynch, *The Diversity Machine: The Drive to Change the "White Male Workplace"* (New Brunswick, N.J.: Transaction Publishers, 2002), p. 325.

30 Ward Connerly, *Creating Equal: My Fight Against Race Preferences* (San Francisco: Encounter Books, 2000), p. 228.

31 See Donald L. Horowitz, *Ethnic Groups in Conflict* (Berkeley: University of California Press, 1985); Cynthia H. Enloe, *Police, Military, and Ethnicity: Foundations of State Power* (New Brunswick, N.J.: Transaction Books, 1980); Myron Weiner, "The Pursuit of Ethnic Inequalities Through Preferential Policies: A Comparative Public Policy Perspective," in *From Independence to Statehood*, ed. Robert B. Goldman and A. Jeyaratnam Wilson (London: Francis Pinter, 1984); and Thomas Sowell, *Preferential Policies: An International Perspective* (New York: William Morrow & Co., 1990).

32 Donald Horowitz, *Ethnic Groups in Conflict*, p. 667.

33 For an insider's look at the radical movement in the U.S. from leading founders of the New Left who became political conservatives, see: Peter Collier and

David Horowitz, *Destructive Generation: Second Thoughts About the Sixties* (New York: Summit Books, 1989); and David Horowitz, *Radical Son: A Generational Odyssey* (New York: Free Press, 1997).

34 Catharine A. MacKinnon, *Toward a Feminist Theory of the State* (Cambridge, Mass.: Harvard University Press, 1989), p. 172.

35 Carol Gilligan, *In a Different Voice: Psychological Theory and Women's Development* (Cambridge, Mass.: Harvard University Press, 1982).

36 139 Congressional Record 8097 (April 21, 1993).

37 139 Congressional Record 8023 (April 21, 1993).

38 Sally Goldfarb, testimony at the House Judiciary Committee hearing on Crimes of Violence Motivated by Gender, November 16, 1993.

39 Cathy Young, "Act Stirs Up Debate on Crime and Gender," *Insight*, November 29, 1993, pp. 12–16.

40 Alan Charles Kors, "Thought Reform 101," *Reason*, March 2000.

41 Ibid.

42 Herbert Marcuse, "Repressive Tolerance," in *A Critique of Pure Tolerance*, by Robert Paul Wolff, Barrington Moore Jr., and Herbert Marcuse (Boston: Beacon Press, 1969), pp. 85–123.

43 Ariel Alexovich, "A Call to End Hate Speech," The Caucus blog, *New York Times*, February 1, 2008.

Chapter 5: The Rise of Transnationalism

1 T. Alexander Aleinikoff, "Citizenship: Down But Not Out," *Opinio Juris* blog, May 12, 2008, http://opiniojuris.org/author/t-alexander-aleinikoff/

2 John G. Ruggie, F. Douglas Gibson Lecture in Political Economy, Queen's University, Kingston, Ontario, November 20, 2000. Italics in the original.

3 Harold Koh, "International Law as Part of Our Law," *American Journal of International Law* 98:1 (January 2004), p. 53.

4 Joyce Oldham Appleby, Lynn Avery Hunt, and Margaret C. Jacob, *Telling the Truth about History* (New York: W. W. Norton, 1995), pp. 291–92.

5 Linda K. Kerber, "The Meanings of Citizenship," *Journal of American History* 84:3 (December 1997), pp. 833–54.

6 Thomas Bender, "No Borders: Beyond the Nation-State," *Chronicle of Higher Education*, April 7, 2006.

7 Ibid.

8 *La Pietra Report: Project on Internationalizing the Study of American History*, 2000, http://www.oah.org/activities/lapietra/index.html

9 James W. Ceaser, *Liberal Democracy and Political Science* (Baltimore: Johns Hopkins University Press, 1990), p. 97.

10 Ibid.

11 Quoted by Kerber, "The Meanings of Citizenship."

[12] Benjamin Barber, "Democracy and Terror in the Era of Jihad vs. McWorld," in *Worlds in Collision: Terror and the Future of Global Order*, ed. Ken Booth and Tim Dunne (New York: Palgrave Macmillan, 2002), p. 256.

[13] Linda S. Bosniak, "Citizenship Denationalized," *Indiana Journal of Global Legal Studies* 7 (Spring 2000), pp. 447–509.

[14] Ibid.

[15] Ibid.

[16] Ibid.

[17] Michael Sandel, "After the Nation-State: Reinventing Democracy," *New Perspectives Quarterly*, Fall 1992, pp. 4–13.

[18] T. Alexander Aleinikoff and Douglas B. Klusmeyer, eds., *From Migrants to Citizens: Membership in a Changing World* (Washington, D.C.: Carnegie Endowment, 2000); T. Alexander Aleinikoff and Douglas B. Klusmeyer, eds., *Citizenship Today: Global Perspectives and Practices* (Washington, D.C.: Brookings Institution Press, 2001).

[19] David B. Rivkin Jr. and Lee A. Casey, "The Rocky Shoals of International Law," *National Interest*, Winter 2000–01.

[20] Ibid.

[21] Curtis A. Bradley and Jack L. Goldsmith, "Customary International Law as Federal Common Law: A Critique of the Modern Position," *Harvard Law Review* 110:4 (February 1997), pp. 838–39.

[22] Ibid., p. 839.

[23] Paul B. Stephan, "International Governance and American Democracy," University of Virginia School of Law, Public Law Working Paper no. 00-9 (May 2000), p. 13.

[24] Bradley and Goldsmith, "Customary International Law as Federal Common Law," p. 840.

[25] Stephan, "International Governance and American Democracy," p. 2.

[26] Ibid., pp. 8, 9, 14.

[27] Amnesty International, "Universal Jurisdiction: Questions and Answers," December 2001, IOR 53/020/2001.

[28] Henry Kissinger, "The Pitfalls of Universal Jurisdiction," *Foreign Affairs*, July/August 2001.

[29] Harold Hongju Koh, "Transnational Public Law Litigation," *Yale Law Journal* 100 (1991), p. 2366.

[30] Robert Bork, *Coercing Virtue: The Worldwide Rule of Judges* (Washington, D.C.: American Enterprise Institute, 2003), p. 24.

[31] Ibid., p. 25.

[32] *Roper v. Simmons*, at http://supreme.justia.com/us/543/03-633/case.html

[33] Dissenting opinion at http://www.law.cornell.edu/supct/html/03-633.ZD1.html

[34] Ibid.

[35] Ibid.

[36] Ken I. Kersch, "Multilateralism Comes to the Courts," *National Affairs* 154 (Winter 2004).

[37] Ginsburg's concurring opinion at http://www.law.cornell.edu/supct/html/02-241.ZC.html

[38] Kersch, "Multilateralism Comes to the Courts."

[39] Ibid.

[40] Kennedy's opinion at http://www.law.cornell.edu/supct/html/02-102.ZO.html

[41] Breyer's dissent at http://www.law.cornell.edu/supct/html/historics/USSC_CR_0521_0898_ZD2.html

[42] Breyer's dissent at http://www.law.cornell.edu/supct/html/98-9741.ZD.html

[43] Transcript available at http://www.wcl/american/edu/secle/founders/2005/050113.cfm.

[44] Ibid.

[45] Ibid.

[46] Ibid.

[47] Ibid.

[48] Ibid.

[49] Ibid.

[50] Harold Koh, "Why Transnational Law Matters," *Penn State International Law Review* 24 (2006), p. 753.

[51] Ibid., pp. 749–50.

[52] Ibid., p. 752.

[53] Harold Koh, "On America's Double Standard," *American Prospect,* September 20, 2004.

[54] Koh, "International Law as Part of Our Law" (see n. 3), pp. 53–54.

[55] Anne-Marie Slaughter, "The Real New World Order," *Foreign Affairs,* September/October 1997, pp. 183–97.

[56] Ibid., p. 184.

[57] Anne-Marie Slaughter, *A New World Order* (Princeton, N.J.: Princeton University Press, 2004), pp. 75–76, 261.

[58] Slaughter, "The Real New World Order," p. 196.

[59] Peter J. Spiro, "Disaggregating U.S. Interests in International Law," *Law and Contemporary Problems* 67 (Autumn 2004), pp. 195–219.

[60] Ibid., p. 217.

[61] Ibid., pp. 201, 218.

[62] Ibid., p. 201.

[63] Ibid., pp. 218–19.

[64] Advertisement in *Foreign Affairs,* March/April 2008, between pp. 34 and 35.

Chapter 6: The European Union: A Model of Global Governance

1 On Charles de Gaulle, see Christopher Booker and Richard North, *The Great Deception: Can the European Union Survive?* (London: Continuum Books, 2005), p. 132. On Thatcher, see *The Collected Speeches of Margaret Thatcher*, ed. Robin Harris (New York: HarperCollins, 1997), p. 325.

2 Joschka Fischer, "From Confederacy to Federation: Thoughts on the Finality of European Integration," speech at Humboldt University in Berlin, May 12, 2000.

3 *Encyclopedia of the European Union*, ed. Desmond Dinan (Boulder, Col.: Lynne Rienner Pub., 2000), p. 106.

4 Robert Cooper, *The Breaking of Nations: Order and Chaos in the Twenty-First Century* (New York: Atlantic Monthly Press, 2003), p. 26.

5 Ibid., p. 27.

6 Ibid., p. 54.

7 Alec Stone Sweet and Thomas Brunell, "Constructing a Supranational Constitution: Dispute Resolution and Governance in the European Community," *American Political Science Review* 92 (1998), pp. 63–81.

8 Joseph H. H. Weiler, "A Quiet Revolution: The European Court and Its Interlocutors," *Comparative Political Studies* 26 (1994), pp. 510–34.

9 Stone Sweet and Brunell, "Constructing a Supranational Constitution," p. 65.

10 Ibid., p. 66.

11 Walter Mattli and Anne-Marie Slaughter, "The Role of National Courts in the Process of European Integration: Accounting for Judicial Preferences and Constraints," in *The European Court and the National Courts—Doctrine and Jurisprudence*, ed. Anne-Marie Slaughter, Alec Stone Sweet, and Joseph H. H. Weiler (Oxford: Hart Publishing, 1998), p. 269.

12 Eric Stein, "Lawyers, Judges, and the Making of a Transnational Constitution," *American Journal of International Law* 75 (1981), p. 5.

13 Case 26/62 NV *Algemene Transporten Expeditie Onderneming van Gend en Loos v. Nederlandse Administratie der Belastingen* [1963] ECR 1.

14 Case 6/64 *Flaminio Costa v. ENEL* [1964] ECR 585, 593.

15 Stein, "Lawyers, Judges, and the Making of a Transnational Constitution," p. 11.

16 Case 6/64 *Flaminio Costa v. ENEL* [1964] ECR 593, 594.

17 Booker and North, *The Great Deception* (see n. 1), p. 155.

18 Karen Alter, "Explaining National Court Acceptance of European Court Jurisprudence: A Critical Evaluation of Theories of Legal Integration," in *The European Court and the National Courts—Doctrine and Jurisprudence*, pp. 236–37.

19 Ibid., pp. 237–38.

20 Ibid., p. 238.

21 Ibid., p. 239.

[22] Ibid., p. 241.

[23] Anne-Marie Burley and Walter Mattli, "Europe Before the Court: A Political Theory of Legal Integration," *International Organization* 47 (Winter 1993), pp. 41–76.

[24] Alter, "Explaining National Court Acceptance of European Court Jurisprudence," p. 241.

[25] Mattli and Slaughter, "The Role of National Courts in the Process of European Integration," pp. 258–59.

[26] Ibid., p. 264.

[27] Ibid., pp. 254–55.

[28] Ibid., p. 257.

[29] Anne-Marie Slaughter, "The Real New World Order," *Foreign Affairs*, September/October 1997, pp. 183–97.

[30] Mattli and Slaughter, "The Role of National Courts in the Process of European Integration," p. 255.

[31] Alter, "Explaining National Court Acceptance of European Court Jurisprudence," p. 240.

[32] Ibid., pp. 240–41.

[33] *Brasserie du Pêcheur SA v. Federal Republic of Germany* and *The Queen v. Secretary of State for Transport, ex parte Factortame Ltd and Others*, C1996/145/01; author conversation with John O'Sullivan at the Hudson Institute in Washington, D.C., on October 30, 2007; and P. P. Craig, "Report on the United Kingdom," in *The European Court and the National Courts—Doctrine and Jurisprudence*, ed. Anne-Marie Slaughter, Alec Stone Sweet, and Joseph H. H. Weiler (Oxford: Hart Publishing, 1998), pp. 200–3.

[34] P. P. Craig, "Report on the United Kingdom," in *The European Court and the National Courts—Doctrine and Jurisprudence*, pp. 200–3.

[35] Author conversation with John O'Sullivan (see n. 33).

[36] *Encyclopedia of the European Union*, ed. Desmond Dinan.

[37] Booker and North, *The Great Deception*, pp. 355–56.

[38] Charlemagne, "Snoring while a superstate emerges?" *Economist*, May 10, 2003.

[39] Conversation with Angelos Pangratis, deputy head of the Delegation of the European Union to the United States, on October 8, 2010, at a Cato Institute conference in Washington, D.C.

[40] Booker and North, *The Great Deception*, p. 66.

[41] Ibid., p. 72.

[42] Ibid., p. 106.

[43] *The Collected Speeches of Margaret Thatcher*, ed. Robin Harris (New York: HarperCollins, 1997), p. 319.

[44] Margaret Thatcher, *The Downing Street Years* (London: HarperCollins, 1993), p. 743.

[45] Joschka Fischer, "From Confederacy to Federation" (see n. 2).

[46] "Laeken Declaration of 15 December 2001 on the Future of the European Union," *European Navigator*, http://ena.lu/

[47] *Europa* (EU website), http://europa.eu/lisbon_treaty/glance/index_en.htm

[48] Reform Treaty, Protocol on the Role of National Parliaments in the European Union (Lisbon Treaty), C 306/148–149, *Official Journal of the European Union*, http://eur-lex.europa.eu/JOHtml.do?uri=OJ:C:2007:306:SOM:EN:HTML

[49] Lisbon Treaty, C 306/151–152.

[50] Robert Rohrschneider, "The Democracy Deficit and Mass Support for an EU-Wide Government," *American Journal of Political Science* 46:2 (2002), pp. 463–75.

[51] Lauren McLaren, "Explaining Mass-Level Euroskepticism: Identity, Interests, and Institutional Distrust," paper presented to the American Political Science Association, Washington, D.C., September 1, 2005.

[52] Geoffrey Van Orden, "The Stealth Constitution," *Wall Street Journal*, May 7, 2007.

[53] Amitai Etzioni, "Closing the Community Deficit in the EU," Center for European Policy Studies, Policy Brief no. 169, September 9, 2008, p. 1.

[54] Ibid., p. 2.

[55] *Eurobarometer 73: Public Opinion in the European Union, First Results*, Fieldwork May 2010, coordinated by the Directorate-General Communication, European Commission (Brussels: TNS Opinion & Social, August 2010), pp. 15–16.

[56] Some scholars, such as Arend Lijphart, speak of "consocial democracy" as distinct from liberal (majoritarian) democracy. In consocial democracy, the political system is based more on one's membership in a particular group (ethnic, linguistic, religious) than on individual citizenship. Political representation and government jobs are divided among these groups, which are sometimes afforded veto power over majority decision making. The Netherlands and Belgium have exhibited characteristics of consocial democracy, with formal political structures based on religious, linguistic, and ethnic differences. See particularly Arend Lijphart, *Democracy in Plural Societies: A Comparative Exploration* (New Haven and London: Yale University Press, 1977).

[57] "Sharia Law in UK Is 'Unavoidable,'" BBC News, February 7, 2008.

[58] Steve Doughty and Michael Seamark, "Sharia Law Row: Archbishop Is in Shock as He Faces Demands to Quit and Criticism from Lord Carey," *Daily Mail*, February 9, 2008.

[59] Joshua Rozenberg, "Sharia law is spreading as authority wanes," *Telegraph*, November 29, 2006.

[60] Steve Doughty, "Sharia law SHOULD be used in Britain, says UK's top judge," *Daily Mail*, July 2008.

[61] Ian Traynor, "'I don't hate Muslims. I hate Islam,' says Holland's rising political star," *Guardian*, February 17, 2008.

[62] See Eugene Volokh, "Geert Wilders Acquitted," *The Volokh Conspiracy,* June 23, 2011, http://volokh.com/2011/06/23/geert-wilders-acquitted/; and Nina Shea, "Putting the Wilders Win in Context," *National Review Online,* June 24, 2011.

[63] Margaret Talbot, "The Agitator," *New Yorker,* June 5, 2006.

[64] Bruce Crumley, "Is Brigitte Bardot Bashing Islam?" *Time,* April 15, 2008.

[65] *Jyllands-Posten,* September 30, 2005.

[66] Paul Marshall, "The Mohammed Cartoons," *Weekly Standard,* February 13, 2006.

[67] Ibid.

[68] Lars Hedegaard, "New NATO Chief Tiptoeing through Turkeystan," *International Free Press Society,* April 6, 2009.

[69] Owen Bowcott, "Arrest extremist marchers, police told," *Guardian,* February 6, 2006.

[70] Marshall, "The Mohammed Cartoons."

[71] David Rennie, "EU commissioner urges European press code on religion," *Telegraph,* February 9, 2006.

[72] "EU Parliament President Borrell on events following publication of cartoons," February 7, 2006, *European Union @ United Nations,* http://www.eu-un.europa.eu/articles/en/article_5668_en.htm

[73] "Ihsanoğlu calls for EU laws banning blasphemy," *Hurriyet Daily News and Economic Review,* February 14, 2006.

[74] Paul Marshall and Nina Shea, *Silenced: How Apostasy and Blasphemy Codes Are Choking Freedom Worldwide* (Oxford University Press, forthcoming October 2011).

[75] "Free speech advocate guilty of racism," *Copenhagen Post,* May 3, 2011.

[76] Alyssa A. Lappen, "Though Europe Rots, We Must Defend the West," *Pajamas Media,* January 18, 2011.

[77] Robert Cooper, *The Breaking of Nations: Order and Chaos in the Twenty-First Century* (New York: Atlantic Monthly Press, 2003), p. 171.

[78] Ibid., p. 151.

[79] Ibid., p. 142.

[80] *Encyclopedia of the European Union,* ed. Dinan, p. 349.

[81] Harold Koh, "International Law as Part of Our Law," *American Journal of International Law* 98:1 (January 2004), pp. 53–54.

[82] Ed Whelan, "Koh's Written Answers to Senator Lugar's Questions," Bench Memos, *National Review Online,* April 29, 2009.

[83] Bundesverfassungsgericht (German Federal Constitutional Court), Decisions: Headnotes to the judgment of the Second Senate of 30 June 2009, http://www.bundesverfassungsgericht.de/entscheidungen/es20090630_2bve0002 08en.html

[84] Peter J. Spiro, "Disaggregating U.S. Interests in International Law," *Law and Contemporary Problems* 67:4 (Autumn 2004), pp. 195–219.

Chapter 7: Ideas, Institutions, and Interests . . .

[1] Walter Russell Mead, "Nuking Westphalia: Obama's Deep Convictions Point to War with Iran," *American Interest Online*, July 16, 2010.

[2] Kenneth Anderson, "Squaring the Circle? Reconciling Sovereignty and Global Governance Through Global Government Networks," *Harvard Law Review* 118 (February 2005), pp. 1255–1312.

[3] Kenneth Anderson, "After Seattle: Public International Organizations, Non-Governmental Organizations (NGOs), and Democratic Sovereignty in an Era of Globalization: An Essay on Contested Legitimacy," unpublished monograph, p. 160.

[4] UN General Assembly, 21st Session, International Covenant on Economic, Social and Cultural Rights, December 16, 1996, A/RES/2200A (XXI), http://www2.ohchr.org/english/law/cescr.htm

[5] UN General Assembly, 61st Plenary Meeting, Convention on the Rights of the Child, November 20, 1989, A/RES/44/25, http://www.un.org/documents/ga/res/44/a44r025.htm

[6] For example, a survey of 543 universities and colleges conducted by the American Association of Colleges and Universities (AAC&U) a decade ago reported that 54 percent of these institutions had "diversity" requirements in place and 63 percent either had or were in the process of developing diversity curricular requirements for their students. See Debra Humphreys, "National Survey Finds Diversity Requirements Common Around the Country," *Diversity Digest*, Fall 2000, http://www.diversityweb.org/Digest/F00/survey.html. In contrast, a survey of the top fifty universities and colleges (based on the *US News and World Report* ratings) found that "American survey history requirements for history majors have all but disappeared at the top fifty universities and are present at slightly more than 10 percent of leading public universities." Glenn Ricketts, Peter W. Wood, Stephen H. Balch, and Ashley Thorne, *The Vanishing West, 1964–2010: The Disappearance of Western Civilization from the American Undergraduate Curriculum*, Report of the National Association of Scholars (Princeton, N.J., 2011).

[7] American Bar Association, Central and Eastern European Law Initiative, *The CEDAW Assessment Tool: An Assessment Tool Based on the Convention to Eliminate All Forms of Discrimination Against Women*, January 2002.

[8] "The Non-Governmental Order," *Economist*, December 11, 1999, pp. 20–21.

[9] Commission on Global Governance, *Our Global Neighborhood* (Oxford, UK: Oxford University Press, 1995), chap. 2.

[10] "UN Not Delivering Support Needed for Reform—Annan," *New York Times*, April 21, 2005.

[11] Jeremy Rabkin, *The Case for Sovereignty: Why the World Should Welcome American Independence* (Washington, D.C.: American Enterprise Institute, 2004), p. 139.

[12] Ernst-Ulrich Petermann, *The GATT/WTO Dispute Settlement System* (London: Kluwer International, 1997); noted in Rabkin, *The Case for Sovereignty,* pp. 157, 240.

[13] "Lamy Calls for Strengthened System of Global Governance," speech by Director-General Pascal Lamy to the Diplomatic Club of Geneva, March 10, 2010, transcript at *WTO News,* http://www.wto.org/english/news_e/sppl_e/sppl149_e.htm

[14] Rabkin, *The Case for Sovereignty,* p. 158.

[15] Ibid., pp. 158–59.

[16] Claude Barfield, "Securing American Sovereignty: A Review of the United States' Relationship with the WTO," testimony before the Senate Committee on Homeland Security and Governmental Affairs, Subcommittee on Federal Financial Management, Government Information, and International Security, July 15, 2005, transcript at the American Enterprise Institute, http://www.aei.org/speech/22847

[17] Jed Rubenfeld, "The Two World Orders," *Wilson Quarterly,* Autumn 2003, p. 35.

[18] David Jochanan Rothkopf, *Superclass: The Global Power Elite and the World They Are Making* (New York: Farrar, Straus & Giroux, 2008).

[19] Jeff Seabright, Vice President, Environment & Water Resources, The Coca-Cola Company, "Water Sustainability and Corporate Responsibility," speech at the Global Water Futures Workshop, Center for Strategic & International Studies and Sandia National Laboratory, Washington, D.C., February 9, 2005.

[20] Quoted by Robert Bly in *The Sibling Society,* as cited at http://www.commondreams.org/view/2009/08/25-1

[21] Samuel Huntington, "Dead Souls: The Denationalization of the American Elite," *National Interest,* Spring 2004.

[22] Chrystia Freeland, "The Rise of the New Global Elite," *Atlantic,* January/February 2011.

[23] David Rivkin and Lee Casey, "Europe in the Balance," *Policy Review,* June/July 2001, pp. 41–53.

[24] "Reforming the Commission," European Commission white paper, April 2000, http://ec.europa.eu/reform/refdoc/index_en.htm

[25] Peter Mandelson, "We Need Greater Global Governance," *Wall Street Journal,* June 19, 2009.

[26] Intervention of H. E. Mr. Herman Van Rompuy, New President of EU Council, Brussels, November 19, 2009, transcript at *European Union @ United Nations,* http://www.europa-eu-un.org/articles/en/article_9245_en.htm

[27] See Jonathan Weisman, Alistair MacDonald, and Carrick Mollenkamp, "Obama Hits Resistance at G-20," *Wall Street Journal,* April 2, 2009; Mark Landler and

David E. Sanger, "World Leaders Pledge $1.1 Trillion for Crisis," *New York Times,* April 3, 2009.

28 Elena Moya, "Financial Stability Board: How it will work," *Guardian,* April 4, 2009.

29 Mark Landler and David E. Sanger, "World Leaders Pledge $1.1 Trillion for Crisis," *New York Times,* April 3, 2009.

30 Jim Kelly, "Financial Stability Board Portends Economic Global Governance," Global Governance Watch, April 21, 2009, http://www.globalgovernancewatch. org/spotlight_on_sovereignty/recent.asp?id=77&css=p

31 Theodore Bromund, "The G-20 Summit: Mistakes and Missed Opportunities," Heritage Foundation WebMemo no. 2393, April 10, 2009.

32 Gideon Rachman, "Europe's plot to take over the world," *Financial Times,* October 5, 2009. The title is tongue-in-cheek, but the analysis is cogent and penetrating.

33 Ibid.

34 Javier Solana, "Old Thinking and Alliances Endanger the G20," *Japan Times,* September 12, 2010, http://search.japantimes.co.jp/print/eo20100912a2.htm

35 Anne-Marie Slaughter, "The Real New World Order," *Foreign Affairs,* September/October 1997, pp. 183–97.

36 Peter J. Spiro, "Disaggregating U.S. Interests in International Law," *Law and Contemporary Problems* 67:4 (Autumn 2004), pp. 195–219.

37 Ibid., pp. 204–5.

38 See, for example, "Britain: Reject Immunity for U.S. Troops," Human Rights Watch, June 8, 2004, http://www.hrw.org/en/news/2004/06/08/britain-reject-immunity-us-troops

39 Honor Mahony, "German president resigns after military comments," *EUobserver.com,* May 31, 2010, http://euobserver.com/9/30174?

40 Yoram Hazony, "Israel through European Eyes," *Jerusalem Letters,* July 14, 2010.

Chapter 8: Rethinking World Politics

1 John Maynard Keynes, *General Theory of Employment Interest and Money* (New Delhi: Atlantic Publishers, 2006), p. 351.

2 The term comes from Jürgen Habermas, *The Divided West* (Malden, Mass.: Polity Press, 2006).

3 Carl von Clausewitz, *On War,* ed. and transl. Michael Howard and Peter Paret (Princeton, N.J.: Princeton University Press, 1976), pp. 595–97. After the Vietnam War, Clausewitz's theories became central to U.S. military doctrine; see, for example, Harry G. Summers Jr., *On Strategy: A Critical Analysis of the Vietnam War* (New York: Dell, 1984).

[4] Jeane J. Kirkpatrick, from the symposium "American Power—for What?" *Commentary,* January 1, 2000.

[5] Harold Koh, "Transnational Legal Process After September 11," *Berkeley Journal of International Law* 22 (2004), pp. 337–54.

[6] Peter J. Spiro, "Disaggregating U.S. Interests in International Law," *Law and Contemporary Problems* 67:4 (Autumn 2004), pp. 195–219.

[7] Mark Malloch Brown, speech at Pace University, May 22, 2005.

[8] Lloyd Axworthy, *Navigating a New World: Canada's Global Future* (Toronto: Vintage Canada, 2004), Prologue.

[9] James R. Edwards Jr., "Mexico Shows Its Colors—and They Aren't Red, White, and Blue," *American Outlook,* December 19, 2003.

[10] James C. Bennett, "An Anglosphere Primer," paper presented to the Foreign Policy Research Institute, 2002, p. 1, http://explorersfoundation.org/archive/anglosphere_primer.pdf

[11] Ibid., p. 2.

[12] Daniel Hannan, "The borders of the Anglosphere?" *Telegraph,* news blog, April 16, 2008.

[13] Christopher Hitchens, "An Anglosphere Future," *City Journal,* Autumn 2007, p. 3.

[14] See John O'Sullivan, "Long-Term Allies: The Special Relationship Endures," *National Review Online,* July 30, 2007; and John O'Sullivan, "A British-led Anglosphere in world politics?" *Telegraph,* December 29, 2007.

[15] George Washington, "First Inaugural Address," April 30, 1789.

[16] Thomas Hobbes and Alfred Rayney Waller, *Leviathan: or, the Matter, Forme and Power of a Commonwealth, Ecclesiasticall and Civill* (Michigan: University Press, 1904).

[17] Clausewitz, *On War,* p. 596.

[18] Francis Fukuyama, *America at the Crossroads: Democracy, Power, and the Neoconservative Legacy* (New Haven: Yale University Press, 2006), p. 10.

[19] Ibid., p. 156.

[20] Ibid., p. 192.

[21] Ibid., p. 193.

[22] Robert Kagan, *Of Paradise and Power: America and Europe in the New World Order* (New York: Alfred A. Knopf, 2003), p. 1.

[23] Ibid. Kagan first outlined these ideas in "Power and Weakness," *Policy Review,* June/July 2002.

[24] Robert Kagan, "The September 12 Paradigm," *Foreign Affairs,* September/October 2008.

[25] Richard Haass, "Sovereignty and globalisation," op-ed, Council on Foreign Relations website, February 17, 2006; and "State sovereignty must be altered in globalized era," editorial, *Taipei Times,* February 21, 2006.

[26] Stewart M. Patrick, "Don't Tread on Me: July 4th and U.S. Sovereignty," The Internationalist blog, Council on Foreign Relations, July 1, 2011.

Chapter 9: Global Domestic Politics

[1] Fischer used the term *"Weltinnenpolitik,"* which translates to "world domestic politics" or "global domestic policy," in a speech to the Bundestag on November 16, 2001, which may be found at http://www.uni-kassel.de/fb5/frieden/themen/Aussenpolitik/reden.html

[2] Jürgen Habermas, "Toward a Cosmopolitan Europe," *Journal of Democracy* 14:4 (October 2003), pp. 86–100.

[3] Robert Cooper, *The Breaking of Nations: Order and Chaos in the Twenty-First Century* (New York: Atlantic Monthly Press, 2003), p. 27.

[4] Elizabeth Olson, "Good Friends Join Enemies to Criticize U.S. on Rights," *New York Times,* March 28, 1999.

[5] Ibid.

[6] Claire Nullis, "Activist Criticizes U.S. Prison Conditions," Associated Press, April 13, 1999, available at http://www.mail-archive.com/nativenews@mlists.net/msg02311.html

[7] Human Rights Watch and American Civil Liberties Union, *Human Rights Violations in the United States: A Report on U.S. Compliance with the International Covenant on Civil and Political Rights* (New York: Human Rights Watch, 1993).

[8] Ibid., p. 3.

[9] Ibid., p. 7.

[10] Ibid., p. 5.

[11] Ibid., p. 42.

[12] Ibid., p. 42.

[13] Ibid., p. 48.

[14] Ibid., p. 7.

[15] Ibid., p. 144.

[16] Ibid., p. 6.

[17] Ibid., p. 74.

[18] Ibid., p. 71.

[19] Ibid., pp. 54–73.

[20] Ibid., pp. 15–36.

[21] Ibid., p. 15.

[22] Ibid., pp. 25–28.

[23] Ibid., p. 149.

[24] Ibid., pp. 152–54.

[25] Ibid., p. 154.

[26] Ibid., pp. 169–70.

[27] Ibid., pp. 1–3.

28 Rita Maran, "International Human Rights in the U.S.: A Critique," *Social Justice* 26:1 (1999), p. 62.

29 UN Economic and Social Council, Commission on Human Rights, 51st Session, *Implementation of the Programme of Action for the Second Decade to Combat Racism and Racial Discrimination* (Glélé Report), January 16, 1995, E/CN.4/1995/78/Add.1, p. 11, http://www1.umn.edu/humanrts/commission/country51/78add1.htm

30 Glélé Report, pp. 40–44.

31 Ibid., p. 11.

32 Ibid., p. 3.

33 Ibid., p. 22.

34 Ibid., p. 6.

35 Ibid., p. 3.

36 Ibid., p. 30.

37 Ibid., p. 32.

38 Maran, "International Human Rights in the U.S.: A Critique," p. 62.

39 Ibid., p. 63.

40 Ibid., pp. 59–60.

41 Ibid., p. 70.

42 Ibid., p. 60.

43 Report of the Special Rapporteur on extrajudicial, summary or arbitrary executions, Mr. Bacre Waly Ndiaya, submitted pursuant to Commission resolution 1997/61, E/CN.4/1998/68/Add.3.

44 Maran, "International Human Rights in the U.S.: A Critique," p. 60.

45 Joseph Biden and Barbara Boxer, "Senate Needs to Ratify the Treaty for the Rights of Women," *San Francisco Chronicle*, June 13, 2002.

46 Lynn Woolsey, testimony before the Senate Foreign Relations Committee, June 13, 2002.

47 Carolyn Maloney, testimony before the Senate Foreign Relations Committee, June 13, 2002; Connie Morella, testimony before the Senate Foreign Relations Committee, June 13, 2002.

48 Harold Koh, testimony before the Senate Foreign Relations Committee, June 13, 2002, http://www.law.yale.edu/documents/pdf/News_&_Events/KohTestimony.pdf

49 Joseph Biden, testimony before the Senate Foreign Relations Committee, June 13, 2002.

50 Human Rights Watch, "Statement in Support of U.S. Senate Ratification of the Convention on the Elimination of All Forms of Discrimination against Women (CEDAW) to the Senate Foreign Relations Committee," June 13, 2002.

51 Harold Koh, testimony before the Senate Foreign Relations Committee, June 13, 2002.

[52] Ibid.

[53] UN General Assembly, 63rd Session, Supp. no. 38, *Report of the Committee on the Elimination of Discrimination against Women, 40th (14 January–1 February 2008) and 41st (30 June–18 July 2008) Sessions,* A/63/38, pp. 150–51, http://daccess-dds-ny.un.org/doc/UNDOC/GEN/N08/458/40/PDF/N0845840. pdf?OpenElement

[54] Ibid., pp. 145–46.

[55] Ibid., p. 147.

[56] UN Committee on the Elimination of Discrimination against Women, 16th Session, *Concluding Observations: Denmark,* August 12, 1997, A/52/38/Rev.1, paras. 248–74, http://www.un.org/documents/ga/docs/52/plenary/a52-38rev1. htm

[57] UN Committee on the Elimination of Discrimination against Women, 27th Session, *Combined Third and Fourth Period Reports: Belgium,* June 10, 2002, CEDAW/C/SR.559 & 560.

[58] UN Committee on the Elimination of Discrimination against Women, 39th Session, *Concluding Comments: Singapore,* August 10, 2007, CEDAW/C/SGP/CO/3, p. 4.

[59] UN Committee on the Elimination of Discrimination against Women, 40th Session, *Concluding Comments: France,* April 8, 2008, CEDAW/C/FRA/CO/6, p. 4.

[60] Ibid., p. 5.

[61] UN Committee on the Rights of the Child, 31st Session, Convention on the Rights of the Child, *Consideration of Reports Submitted by States Parties under Article 44 of the Convention: Concluding Observations: United Kingdom of Great Britain and Northern Ireland,* October 9, 2002, CRC/C/15/Add.188, pp. 8–9.

[62] Ibid., p. 4.

[63] Ibid., p. 12.

[64] Ibid., pp. 2–3.

[65] UN Committee on the Elimination of Discrimination against Women, 17th Session, *Concluding Comments: Israel,* July 25, 1997, A/52/38/Rev.1, http://www.un.org/womenwatch/daw/cedaw/cedaw25years/content/english/CONCLUDING_COMMENTS/Israel/Israel-CO-1-2.pdf

[66] UN Committee on the Elimination of Discrimination against Women, *Concluding Observations: Australia,* July 18, 1997, A/52/38/Rev.1, Part II, paras. 365–408, http://www1.umn.edu/humanrts/cedaw/cedaw-australia_52_38.htm

[67] UN Committee on the Elimination of Discrimination against Women, *Concluding Comments: Australia,* February 3, 2006, CEDAW/C/AUL/CO/5, http://www.unhcr.org/refworld/docid/441183430.html

[68] UN Committee on the Elimination of Discrimination against Women, 30th Session, Pre-Session Working Group, *List of Issues and Questions with Regard to the Consideration of Periodic Reports: Germany,* January 12–30, 2004,

CEDAW/PSWG/2004/I/CRP.1/Add.3, http://www.un.org/womenwatch/daw/cedaw/cedaw30/GermanyCRPA3-E.PDF

[69] UN press release, "Committee on Elimination of Discrimination against Women Begins Consideration of Report on Ireland," June 21, 1999, WOM/1142, http://www.un.org/News/Press/docs/1999/19990621.wom1142.html

[70] UN Committee on the Elimination of Racial Discrimination, 59th Session, *Concluding Observations: United States of America,* August 14, 2001, A/56/18, paras. 380–407, http://www.unhcr.org/refworld/pdfid/3f52f3ad2.pdf

[71] UN International Covenant on Civil and Political Rights, 87th Session, *Consideration of Reports Submitted by States Parties under Article 40 of the Covenant,* July 10–28, 2006, CCPR/C/USA/CO/3.

[72] UN International Covenant on Civil and Political Rights, 53rd Session, *Consideration of Reports Submitted by States Parties under Article 40 of the Covenant,* October 3, 1995, CCPR/C/79/Add.50.

[73] UN Committee on the Elimination of Discrimination against Women, 16th Session, *Concluding Comments: Slovenia,* January 13–31, 1997, A/52/38/Rev.1, http://www.un.org/womenwatch/daw/cedaw/cedaw25years/content/english/CONCLUDING_COMMENTS/Slovenia/Slovenia-CO-1.pdf

[74] UN press release, "Norway Called 'Haven for Gender Equality,' as Women's Anti-Discrimination Committee Examines Reports on Compliance with Convention," January 20, 2003, WOM/1377, http://www.un.org/News/Press/docs/2003/wom1377.doc.htm

[75] Nicola Clark, "Getting Women into Boardrooms by Law," *New York Times,* January 28, 2010.

[76] Mona Lena Krook, "Candidate Gender Quotas: A Framework for Analysis," *European Journal of Political Research* 46:3 (April 2007), pp. 367–94.

[77] For example: Drude Dahlerup, "Comparative Studies of Electoral Gender Quotas"; Suzanne Lafont, "One Step Forward, Two Steps Back: Women in the Post-Communist States"; Maria Jose Lubertino, "Pioneering Quotas: The Argentine Experience and Beyond"; Robert G. Moser, "The Effects of Electoral Systems on Women's Representation in Post-Communist States"; Pippa Norris and Ronald Inglehart, "Cultural Obstacles to Equal Representation"; Swedish Presidency of the Council of the European Union, "Beijing + 15: The Platform for Action and the European Union"; and Par Zetterberg, "Do Gender Quotas Foster Women's Political Engagement?"

[78] Drude Dahlerup and Lenita Freidenvall, "Quotas as a 'Fast Track' to Equal Political Representation for Women," a paper presented at the IPSA World Congress, Durban, South Africa, June 29 to July 4, 2003, and in an updated version at the APSA Annual Meeting, Philadelphia, August 28–31, 2003.

[79] American Bar Association, Central and Eastern European Law Initiative, *The CEDAW Assessment Tool: An Assessment Tool Based on the Convention to Eliminate All Forms of Discrimination Against Women,* January 2002, p. 2.

[80] Ibid., p. 16.

[81] Ibid., p. 82.

[82] Ibid., p. 84.

[83] Ibid., p. 85.

[84] Ibid., pp. 87–88.

[85] Catherine Powell, *Human Rights at Home: A Domestic Policy Blueprint for the New Administration,* American Constitution Society for Law and Policy, October 2008, http://www.acslaw.org/files/Powell%20full%20combined.pdf

[86] Ibid., pp. 2–3.

[87] Ibid., p. 25.

[88] Ibid., pp. 23–27.

Chapter 10: Who Decides the Rules of War?

[1] For an excellent overview of the modern law of war, see Kenneth Anderson, "Who Owns the Rules of War?" *New York Times Magazine,* April 24, 2003, reposted on Kenneth Anderson's Law of War and Just War Theory Blog, July 21, 2006.

[2] W. Hays Parks, "Air War and the Law of War," *Air Force Law Review* 32:1 (1990), p. 164.

[3] Ibid.

[4] Article 44(3) of Protocol I states: "In order to promote the protection of the civilian population from the effects of hostilities, combatants are obligated to distinguish themselves from the civilian population while they are engaged in an attack or in a military operation preparatory to an attack. Recognizing, however, that there are situations in armed conflicts where, owing to the nature of the hostilities, an armed combatant cannot so distinguish himself, he shall retain his status as a combatant, provided that, in such situations, he carries his arms openly: (a) during each military engagement, and (b) during such time as he is visible to the adversary while he is engaged in a military deployment preceding the launching of an attack in which he is to participate."

[5] Interviews with Douglas J. Feith, August 4 and 9, 2010.

[6] See Judith Miller, "Reagan Shelving Treaty to Revise Law on Captives: Ratification Is Dropped," *New York Times,* February 15, 1987; Memorandum from Assistant Secretary of Defense Richard Perle to Secretary of Defense Caspar Weinberger with handwritten comments by Under Secretary of Defense Fred C. Iklé, February 26, 1987 (in possession of the author). Other opponents within the administration included Perle, Weinberger, Iklé, Attorney General Edwin Meese, Secretary of State George P. Shultz, State Department legal adviser Abraham D. Sofaer, and the Joint Chiefs of Staff and their JAG lawyers. Interviews with Douglas J. Feith, August 4 and 9, 2010.

[7] Douglas J. Feith, "Law in the Service of Terror—The Strange Case of the Additional Protocol," *National Interest,* Fall 1985, pp. 36, 47.

[8] Parks, "Air War and the Law of War," p. 218.

[9] Ibid., p. 219.

[10] Ibid.

[11] Ibid., pp. 223–24.

[12] Ibid., p. 147.

[13] Ibid., pp. 148–49.

[14] Ibid., pp. 157–58.

[15] Ibid., p. 222.

[16] Ibid., p. 216.

[17] Ibid.

[18] Memorandum from Secretary of Defense Caspar Weinberger to Secretary of State George Shultz, on the subject of the 1977 Protocols Additional to the Geneva Conventions of 1949 on War Victims, July 2, 1985 (in the author's possession).

[19] Memorandum from Secretary of State George P. Shultz to the President, on the subject of the 1977 Protocols Additional to the Geneva Conventions of 1949 on the Protection of War Victims, March 21, 1986 (in the author's possession).

[20] Ronald Reagan, "Message to the Senate Transmitting a Protocol to the 1949 Geneva Conventions," January 29, 1987.

[21] "Denied: A Shield for Terrorists," editorial, *New York Times*, February 17, 1987, p. A22.

[22] "Hijacking the Geneva Conventions," editorial, *Washington Post*, February 18, 1987, p. A18.

[23] "NATO/Federal Republic of Yugoslavia: 'Collateral Damage' or Unlawful Killings? Violations of the Laws of War by NATO during Operation Allied Force," Amnesty International, June 5, 2000, p. 2.

[24] Ibid., p. 24.

[25] Ibid., p. 6.

[26] Executive Summary, "Under Orders: War Crimes in Kosovo," Human Rights Watch, 2001, p. 1.

[27] "Civilian Deaths in the NATO Air Campaign," Human Rights Watch, February 1, 2000, p. 3.

[28] "Under Orders: War Crimes in Kosovo," p. 441.

[29] "Civilian Deaths in the NATO Air Campaign," p. 3.

[30] "NATO/Federal Republic of Yugoslavia," p. 15.

[31] Ibid., p. 15; "Under Orders: War Crimes in Kosovo," p. 443.

[32] Colonel Charles J. Dunlap Jr., USAF, "Law and Military Interventions: Preserving Humanitarian Values in 21st Century Conflicts," Carr Center for Human Rights Policy, JFK School of Government, Harvard University, November 29, 2001, p. 34.

[33] "Under Orders: War Crimes in Kosovo," p. 440.

34 "Civilian Deaths in the NATO Air Campaign," p. 8.

35 "NATO/Federal Republic of Yugoslavia," p. 26.

36 "Human Rights in the USA: World Leader in High Tech Repression," Amnesty International, September 21, 1998.

37 Amnesty International USA, *Rights for All: Human Rights Concerns in the U.S.A.,* October 1998.

38 "On 50th Anniversary, U.S. Lags on Human Rights Issues," Human Rights Watch, December 9, 1998.

39 Parks, "Air War and the Law of War" (see n. 2), pp. 147–49.

40 Dunlap, "Law and Military Interventions." Robert S. Dudney wrote in 2010 that "Major General Charles J. Dunlap, Jr., former USAF deputy judge advocate general, has warned about 'lawfare,' defined as 'the use of law as a weapon of war' by foes who exploit 'real, perceived, or even orchestrated incidents of law of war violations' to undermine superior military power." Dudney, "Warfare vs. Lawfare," *Air Force Magazine,* June 2010. See also Major General Charles Dunlap Jr., Deputy Judge Advocate General, "Lawfare amid Warfare," *Washington Times,* August 3, 2007.

41 Dunlap, "Law and Military Interventions," p. 36.

42 Ibid., p. 34.

43 ICTY, *Final Report to the Prosecutor by the Committee Established to Review the NATO Bombing Campaign Against the Federal Republic of Yugoslavia,* p. 1, http://www.ess.uwe.ac.uk/Kosovo/Kosovo-International_Law18.htm

44 Ibid., pp. 2–4.

45 Ibid., p. 14.

46 Ibid., p. 27.

47 Ibid., p. 28.

48 Ibid., p. 34.

49 "Cluster Bombs in Afghanistan," Human Rights Watch Backgrounder, October 2001.

50 Katie Vandever, "Cluster Bomb Ban Passed over U.S. Objections," IPS (Inter Press Service), May 28, 2008.

51 "Fatally Flawed: Cluster Bombs and Their Use by the United States in Afghanistan," Human Rights Watch, December 18, 2002, p. 16.

52 "Welcome to Europe, Mr. Ashcroft: Why Don't the French Trust American Justice?" editorial, *Wall Street Journal,* December 14, 2001.

53 Human Rights Watch press releases: "Off Target: The Conduct of the War and Civilian Casualties in Iraq," December, 11, 2003; "U.S.: Hundreds of Civilian Deaths in Iraq Were Preventable," December 12, 2003; "Afghanistan: U.S. Military Should Investigate Civilian Deaths," December 13, 2003.

54 "U.S.: Hundreds of Civilian Deaths in Iraq were Preventable."

55 "Afghanistan: U.S. Military Should Investigate Civilian Deaths."

56 Parks, "Air War and the Law of War," pp. 156–57.

[57] "Rights Group Supports Belgium's Universal Jurisdiction Law," Human Rights Watch, November 16, 2000.

[58] Glenn Frankel, "Belgian War Crimes Law Undone by Its Global Reach," *Washington Post,* September 30, 2003.

[59] Ibid.

[60] Ibid.

[61] *Amnesty International Report 2005: The State of the World's Human Rights* (May 24, 2005), Foreword, p. 5.

[62] The Siberian prison camps were famously described by Alexander Solzhenitsyn in *The Gulag Archipelago.*

[63] Jim Lobe, "Give Rumsfeld the Pinochet Treatment, Says US Amnesty Chief," IPS (Inter Press Service), May 25, 2005.

[64] Ibid. See also, "Amnesty's 'Gulag,' " editorial, *Wall Street Journal,* May 26, 2005.

[65] Michael Ratner and the Center for Constitutional Rights, "The Trial of Donald Rumsfeld," *Amnesty International Magazine,* Winter 2008.

[66] For information on the role of the Center for Constitutional Rights, see Ratner, "The Trial of Donald Rumsfeld"; Adam Zogorin, "Exclusive: Charges Sought against Rumsfeld over Prison Abuse," *Time,* November 10, 2006; Cesar Chelala, "Rumsfeld Prosecution Could Set Precedent," *Japan Times,* February 17, 2009; and the website of FIDH (International Federation for Human Rights), October 26, 2007.

[67] Marguerite Feitlowitz, "The Pinochet Prosecution: Gains, Losses, Lessons," *Crimes of War,* May 2000, http://crimesofwar.org/expert/pin-marguerite2.html

[68] Marlise Simons, "Spanish Court Weighs Inquiry on Torture for 6 Bush-Era Officials," *New York Times,* March 28, 2009. Gonzalo Boyé, the lead lawyer for the Spanish activists who filed the complaint, told the *New Yorker* that a British international lawyer, Philippe Sands, "played a very big role in my thinking." Jane Mayer, "The Bush Six," *New Yorker,* April 13, 2009. Indeed, Philippe Sands was an important figure in the development of the Spanish complaint. In his book *Torture Team: Rumsfeld's Memo and the Betrayal of American Values* (New York: Palgrave Macmillan, 2008), Sands accused American lawyers in the Bush administration of violating international law by developing the legal justification for torture. This accusation was picked up by the Spanish complainants. See Jeremy Rabkin and Mario Loyola, "The New Spanish Inquisition: Judge Garzón launches a crusade," *Weekly Standard,* April 13, 2009.

Sands specifically cited Douglas Feith, under secretary of defense for policy (on the basis of an interview with Feith) as framing the main arguments for the Bush administration that the Geneva Conventions did not apply to all enemy combatants captured in Afghanistan. In a letter to Representative Jerrold Nadler (D-NY) on August 12, 2008, Feith again challenged Sands to release the transcript of the Sands-Feith interview. Feith wrote, "Mr. Sands seems to be calculating that no one will actually read the transcript with enough care to see that it exposes the fundamental flaws in his book. It shows that Mr. Sands was, at best, careless or ignorant. Actually, the transcript suggests that he was dishonest." Feith testified that he had argued that the Geneva Conventions did apply to Taliban prisoners and that al-Queda detainees were entitled to humane treatment. Feith's rebuttal of Sands is clear from the transcript of their interview, published as "The Tale of the Tape: The Transcript," *Vanity Fair*, Web exclusive, July 25, 2003, http://www.vanityfair.com/politics/features/2008/07/feith_transcript200807?

69 Bruce Falconer, "Nobody Expects the Spanish Prosecution," *Mother Jones*, June 24, 2009.

70 Victoria Burnett and Marlise Simons, "Proposal Would Rein in Spain's Judges," *New York Times*, May 21, 2009.

71 Paul Haven, "Spanish AG Says No to Bush Era Torture Probe," *Miami Herald*, April 16, 2009.

72 Scott Horton, "Prosecution of Bush Six Back On," *Daily Beast*, April 29, 2009.

73 Juan José, "Garzon Goes After Another Pinochet," *Opinio Juris* blog, December 4, 2009.

74 Robert Marquand, "Spanish Judge Opens Guantanamo Investigation," *Christian Science Monitor*, April 30, 2009.

75 See Graham Keeley, "Judge Baltasar Garzón in court on Santander bribe allegations," *Times* (London), April 16, 2010; Santiago Pérez, "Spain Judge Faces Charges over Probe," *Wall Street Journal*, April 8, 2010; Lisa Abend, "Crusading Judge Faces His Own Trial in Spain," *Time*, April 7, 2010; Vicky Short, "Judge Baltasar Garzón Suspended for Investigating Franco's Crimes," World Socialist Web Site, May 29, 2010.

76 "Spain: Charges against Baltasar Garzón are outrageous," Amnesty International, April 22, 2010.

77 "Spanish judge Garzon suspended," Al Jazeera, May 14, 2010; "European Union: Protest Sanctions against Judge Garzón," Human Rights Watch, April 22, 2010.

78 Abend, "Crusading Judge Faces His Own Trial in Spain."

79 "Injustice in Spain," editorial, *New York Times*, April 9, 2010.

80 "Spanish Judge Garzón looks to move to the ICC," Radio Netherlands Worldwide, May 11, 2010.

81 Anita Brooks, "Baltasar Garzón vowed to see Spain's fascists in court. But not this way," *Independent*, April 8, 2010.

82 "Balthasar Garzon wins permission to work at the International Criminal Court," *Telegraph*, May 18, 2010.

83 Ryan Powers, "UN Rapporteur on Torture: Obama's Pledge Not to Pursue Torture Prosecutions of CIA Agents Is Not Legal," *Think Progress*, April 19, 2009.

[84] Glenn Greenwald, "Transcript: Interview with UN torture official Manfred Nowak," *Salon,* April 25, 2009.

[85] Reuters, "U.S. Use of Drones Queried by U.N.," *New York Times,* October 27, 2009; Scott Shane, "C.I.A. to Expand Use of Drones in Pakistan," *New York Times,* December 4, 2009; "US warned on deadly drone attacks," BBC News, October 28, 2009; "US Drone Strikes May Break International Law: UN," Agence France-Presse, October 28, 2009. Most news reports noted that the Obama administration greatly increased the number of drone strikes compared with the Bush administration.

[86] "U.S. Use of Drones Queried by U.N."

[87] "US Drone Strikes May Break International Law: UN."

[88] Jane Mayer, "The Predator War," *New Yorker,* October 26, 2009.

[89] Amy Goodman, "UN Special Rapporteur on Extrajudicial Killings, Philip Alston: Record AfPak Drone Attacks under Obama May Violate International Law," *Democracy Now,* October 28, 2009.

[90] Mike Reicher, "Affordable? U.N. Puts a Questioning Eye on New York's Housing," City Room blog, *New York Times,* October 23, 2009.

Chapter 11: The International Criminal Court

[1] Fanny Benedetti and John L. Washburn, "Drafting the International Criminal Court Treaty: Two Years to Rome and an Afterword on the Rome Diplomatic Conference," *Global Governance* 5 (1999), p. 26.

[2] M. Cherif Bassiouni, *The Legislative History of the International Criminal Court* (Ardsley, N.Y.: Transnational Publishers, 2005), vol. 1, p. 90.

[3] William Lietzau, "International Criminal Law after Rome: Concerns from a U.S. Military Perspective," *Law and Contemporary Problems* 119:64 (Winter 2001), pp. 119–40.

[4] Benedetti and Washburn, "Drafting the International Criminal Court Treaty," p. 27.

[5] Freedom House annual listing from 2010. Nine countries listed as "not free" are part of the ICC: Afghanistan, Cambodia, Chad, Congo, Democratic Republic of the Congo, Gabon, Guinea, Jordan, and Tajikistan. Thirty-three countries listed as only "partly free" are members of the ICC, including, among others, Venezuela, Zambia, Tanzania, Sierra Leone, Senegal, Nigeria, Paraguay, Central African Republic, and Bolivia. Seven fully free societies are not members of the ICC: the United States, India, Israel, Indonesia, Ukraine, El Salvador, and Jamaica. These figures were found by cross-referencing the following websites: http://www.icc-cpi.int/Menus/ASP/states+parties/ and http://www.freedom-house.org/template.cfm?page=363&year=2010

[6] John R. Bolton, "The Risks and Weaknesses of the International Criminal Court from America's Perspective," *Law and Contemporary Problems* 167 (Winter 2001), p. 169.

[7] Lee A. Casey and David B. Rivkin Jr., "The International Criminal Court vs. the American People," Heritage Foundation Backgrounder no. 1249, February 5, 1999.

[8] Source: Freedom House ratings and CIA World Population statistics, http://www.freedomhouse.org/template.cfm?page=351&ana_page=362&year=2010 and https://www.cia.gov/library/publications/the-world-factbook/index.html

[9] Bartram S. Brown, "Unilateralism, Multilateralism, and the International Criminal Court," in *Multilateralism and US Foreign Policy: Ambivalent Engagement,* ed. Stewart Patrick and Shepard Forman (Boulder, Col.: Lynne Rienner Publishers, 2002), p. 330.

[10] Marlies Glasius, *The International Criminal Court: A Global Civil Society Achievement* (London: Routledge, 2006), p. 42.

[11] Ibid., p. 46.

[12] Ibid., p. 43.

[13] Benedetti and Washburn, "Drafting the International Criminal Court Treaty," pp. 9–10.

[14] Ibid., p. 29.

[15] Ibid., p. 36.

[16] Ibid., p. 30.

[17] Glasius, *The International Criminal Court,* p. 25.

[18] David J. Scheffer, "The United States and the International Criminal Court," *American Journal of International Law* 93:1 (January 1999), p. 20.

[19] Ibid., p. 18.

[20] Ibid., p. 12.

[21] Ibid., p. 13.

[22] Eric K. Leonard, *The Onset of Global Governance: International Relations Theory and the International Criminal Court* (Hampshire, UK: Ashgate Publishing, 2005), p. 153.

[23] Ibid., p. 154.

[24] "Stop Threatening International Court, U.S. Officials Told," Human Rights Watch, July 23, 1998.

[25] Lawrence Weschler, "Clinton grows a spine," *Salon,* January 5, 2001. Republican Senators Helms (NC) and Gramm (MN) and Democratic Senators Biden (DE) and Feinstein (CA) all congratulated Ambassador Scheffer for defending American interests during the ICC negotiations.

[26] Glasius, *The International Criminal Court,* p. 44.

[27] Leonard, *The Onset of Global Governance,* p. 135.

[28] Ibid., p. 134.

[29] Brown, "Unilateralism, Multilateralism, and the International Criminal Court," p. 331.

[30] Glasius, *The International Criminal Court,* p. 53.

[31] Address by Senator Jesse Helms, Chairman, U.S. Senate Committee on Foreign Relations, before the United Nations Security Council, January 20, 2000, http://sovereignty.net/center/helms.htm

[32] Jesse Helms, speech on the Senate floor on the subject of National Defense Authorization Act for Fiscal Year 2002, *Congressional Record* S10042, October 2, 2001.

[33] John R. Bolton, "American Justice and the International Criminal Court," remarks to the American Enterprise Institute, November 3, 2003. See also Bolton, "The United States and the International Criminal Court," remarks to the Federalist Society, November 4, 2002.

[34] Markus Benzing, "U.S. Bilateral Non-Surrender Agreements and Article 98 of the Statute of the International Criminal Court: An Exercise in the Law of Treaties," in *Max Planck Yearbook of United Nations Law*, vol. 8, ed. Armin von Bogdandy and Rudiger Wolfrum (Leiden: Martinus Nijhoff Publishers, 2004), p. 190.

[35] Ibid., p. 192.

[36] David B. Rivkin Jr. and Lee A. Casey, "Darfur's Last Hope," *Washington Times*, February 3, 2005.

[37] John R. Bolton, "Goo-Goo Court Boosts Darfur Butchers," *New York Post*, August 6, 2009.

[38] Andrew Natsios, "A Disaster in the Making," *Making Sense of Sudan*, Social Science Research Council blogs, July 12, 2008.

[39] Julie Flint and Alex de Waal, "To put justice before peace spells disaster for Sudan," *Guardian*, March 6, 2009.

[40] Nina Shea, "Remember Darfur?" *National Review Online*, May 4, 2009.

[41] "ICC Issues Arrest Warrant for Sudanese President al-Bashir," Amnesty International, March 4, 2009.

[42] "The ICC Pre-Trial Chamber's Decision: Why Was Genocide Not Included?" Human Rights First, March 4, 2009.

[43] "Playing It Firm, Fair, and Smart: The EU and the ICC Indictment of Bashir," Human Rights Watch, March 19, 2009.

[44] See ibid.; and Sara Darehshori and Elizabeth Evenson, "Justice and Its Overstated Costs," *European Voice,* reprinted by Human Rights Watch, March 6, 2009.

[45] Ellie Rose, "War Crimes Inquiry into NATO Troops and Taliban Insurgents," *Guardian*, September 10, 2009.

[46] Joe Lauria, "Court Orders Probe of Afghan Attacks," *Wall Street Journal*, September 10, 2009.

[47] Rose, "War Crimes Inquiry into NATO Troops and Taliban Insurgents."

[48] Kenneth Anderson, "ICC's Ocampo Indicates Probe Underway into NATO Actions in Afghanistan," *Opinio Juris* blog, September 10, 2009.

[49] Ibid.

[50] Catherine Philp and James Hider, "Prosecutor looks at ways to put Israeli officers on trial for Gaza 'war crimes,'" *Times* (London), February 2, 2009.

[51] Raghida Dergham, "Interview with Luis Moreno Ocampo," *Al-Hayat,* September 13, 2009, http://www.daralhayat.com/portalarticlendah/56391

[52] Dan Ephron, "ICC Prosecutor May Charge Israel with War Crimes," Wealth of Nations blog, *Newsweek,* September 21, 2009.

[53] Jeremy Rabkin, "Aggression Outlawed! Magical Thinking at the International Criminal Court," *Weekly Standard,* August 23, 2010.

[54] International Criminal Court Resolution RC/Res. 6, "The Crime of Aggression," Annex 1, Article 8.1 (June 11, 2010), http://www.icc-cpi.int/iccdocs/asp_docs/Resolutions/RC-Res.6-ENG.pdf

[55] Stephen J. Rapp, U.S. Ambassador-at-Large for War Crimes, statement at the Review Conference of the International Criminal Court, Kampala, Uganda, June 1, 2010, pp. 7–10.

[56] See Rabkin, "Aggression Outlawed!"

[57] Harold Hongju Koh, Legal Adviser, U.S. State Department, statement at the Review Conference of the International Criminal Court, Kampala, Uganda, June 4, 2010, pp. 2–3.

[58] For overviews of the Kampala conference, see Brett D. Schaefer, "The Kampala Aftermath: The U.S. Should Remain Wary of the ICC," Heritage Foundation Backgrounder no. 2448, August 9, 2010; Rabkin, "Aggression Outlawed!"; and the ICC website devoted to the review, http://www.kampala.icc-cpi.info

Chapter 12: Will Israel Be Allowed to Defend Itself?

[1] Reuters, "UN Conference 2001 against Racism: Rights Activists Ask U.N. to Target Racism in U.S.," under Headlines, October 27, 2000, http://www.icare.to/archiveoctober2000.html

[2] "Anti-Racism Summit Ends on Hopeful Note," Human Rights Watch, September 9, 2001.

[3] Tom Lantos, "The Durban Debacle: An Insider's View of the UN World Conference against Racism," *Fletcher Forum of World Affairs,* Winter/Spring 2002, p. 39.

[4] Ibid., p. 38.

[5] Ibid., p. 35.

[6] Ibid., p. 36.

[7] Ibid., pp. 37–43.

[8] Ibid., pp. 43–44.

[9] Ibid., pp. 45–48.

[10] Ibid., p. 40.

[11] Ibid., p. 49.

[12] Ibid., p. 40.

[13] Ibid., p. 46. See the official document at http://www.iacenter.org/wcar/durban_forum041709/

[14] Edwin Black, "Ford Foundation Aided Groups Behind Biased Durban Parley," *Jewish Daily Forward*, October 17, 2003.

[15] Lantos, "The Durban Debacle," p. 46.

[16] Black, "Ford Foundation Aided Groups Behind Biased Durban Parley."

[17] Ibid.

[18] Ibid.

[19] David Twersky, "Gates of Redemption," *New York Sun*, November 20, 2003.

[20] Lantos, "The Durban Debacle," p. 50.

[21] Anne Bayefsky, "Human Rights Watch Coverup," *Jerusalem Post*, April 13, 2004, http://www.ngo-monitor.org/article.php?operation=print&id=908

[22] Durban Watch: Durban I: Durban Photos, "International NGO News Conference after the NGO Forum," *Eye on the UN* website, Hudson Institute, 2005, http://www.eyeontheun.org/view.asp?l=16&p=71

[23] Lantos, "The Durban Debacle," p. 46.

[24] "Israel branded 'racist' by rights forum," CNN.com, September 2, 2001.

[25] David Matas, *Aftershock: Anti-Zionism and Anti-Semitism* (Toronto: Dundum Press, 2005). Also, David Matas, "Durban Conference: Civil Society Smashed Up," B'nai Brith Canada, http://www.zionism-israel.com/issues/Durban_anti_semitism.html

[26] Bayefsky, "Human Rights Watch Coverup."

[27] Ibid.

[28] Ibid.; Reed Brody response published by NGO Monitor, April 25, 2004, http://www.ngo-monitor.org/article.php?id=561

[29] "Anti-Racism Summit Ends on Hopeful Note" (see n. 2)

[30] Strobe Talbott, *The Great Experiment: The Story of Ancient Empires, Modern States, and the Quest for a Global Nation* (New York: Simon & Schuster, 2009), p. 40.

[31] Yoram Hazony makes this point in examining the different worldviews of European elites and Israelis, in "Israel Through European Eyes," *Jerusalem Letters*, July 14, 2010. In addition, there are, of course, myriad reasons (besides ideology) for the transnationalist attitude towards Israel, including: a willingness to appease radical Islamists within Western (particularly European) nations; desire for accommodation with Islamic states in foreign policy; genuine belief that the Palestinians represent the "underdog" and the Israelis the "oppressor"; instinctive support for the non-Western "other" in a "liberationist" struggle against a Western nation; fear of losing oil supplies; as well as anti-Semitism.

[32] See Dore Gold, *The Challenge to Israel's Legitimacy: Trends and Implications*, Jerusalem Center for Public Affairs, 2010; Ehud Rosen, *Mapping the Organizational Sources of the Global Delegitimization Campaign against Israel in the UK*, Jerusalem Center for Public Affairs, 2010; Gerald Steinberg, *Selective Human*

Rights—NGOs and the Delegitimization of Israel, Jerusalem Center for Public Affairs, no date given.

[33] "Support for Israel in U.S. at 63%, Near Record High," Gallup, February 24, 2010, http://www.gallup.com/poll/126155/support-israel-near-record-high.aspx

[34] Dore Gold, *The UN Gaza Report: A Substantive Critique,* An Expanded Text of Ambassador Dore Gold's Presentation During an Exchange with Justice Richard Goldstone at Brandeis University on November 5, 2009 (Jerusalem Center for Public Affairs, 2009), p. 4.

[35] Ehud Barak, "Text: Statement from Israel's Defense Minister," *New York Times,* January 3, 2009.

[36] "The NGO Front in the Gaza War: The Durban Strategy Continues," NGO Monitor, February 12, 2009, p. 21.

[37] Ibid., p. 28.

[38] Ibid.; and Anne Herzberg, "NGOs dominate Gaza fact-finding commissions," *Jerusalem Post,* June 8, 2009.

[39] Herzberg, "NGOs dominate Gaza fact-finding commissions."

[40] UN General Assembly, Human Rights Council, 12th Session, *Human Rights in Palestine and Other Occupied Arab Territories,* Report of the United Nations Fact Finding Mission on the Gaza Conflict (Goldstone Report), September 25, 2009, A/HRC/12/48, p. 13.

[41] "The Goldstone 'Fact Finding' Mission and the Role of Political NGOs," NGO Monitor, September 7, 2009.

[42] Conferral of the MacArthur Award for International Justice, Remarks by Jonathan Fanton, The Hague, Netherlands, May 25, 2009, at the MacArthur Foundation website, http://www.macfound.org/site/c.lkLXJ8MQKrH/b.5187019

[43] Marlies Glasius, *The International Criminal Court: A Global Civil Society Achievement* (London: Routledge, 2006), pp. 52–53.

[44] Christine Chinkin et al., "Israel's bombardment of Gaza is not self-defence—it's a war crime," *Sunday Times* (London), January 11, 2009. See also "The Goldstone 'Fact Finding' Mission and the Role of Political NGOs."

[45] A partial transcript of the Channel 1 interview with Goldstone was published by Hillel Neuer (with a link to the video) in "Goldstone defends Christine Chinkin from bias charge," *View from Geneva,* UN Watch blog, July 13, 2009, http://blog.unwatch.org/?p=416

[46] Mary Robinson, Richard Goldstone, et al., "Gaza Investigators Call for War Crimes Inquiry," Amnesty International Australia, March 16, 2009. See also, Herzberg, "NGOs dominate Gaza fact-finding commissions."

[47] Goldstone Report, p. 407.

[48] See Gold, *The UN Gaza Report: A Substantive Critique,* pp. 14–15 (includes photographs).

[49] Goldstone Report, p. 525; Gold, pp. 407–8.

50 Neil MacFarquhar, "U.N. Council Endorses Gaza Report," *New York Times*, October 16, 2009.

51 Gold, *The UN Gaza Report: A Substantive Critique*, p. 5.

52 Ibid., p. 12.

53 Bill Moyers, "Transcript of Interview with Richard Goldstone," *Bill Moyers Journal*, October 23, 2009.

54 Goldstone Report, p. 423.

55 Ibid., p. 424.

56 Ibid., pp. 393–94.

57 Ibid., p. 399.

58 Ibid., p. 427.

59 The warrant against Livni was instigated by pro-Palestinian lawyers under Britain's universal jurisdiction statute, which permits private persons to bring war crimes charges. Livni cancelled her trip; the warrant was withdrawn; and the Labour government discussed changing the law, but did not act. In the summer of 2010, the new Cameron-Clegg coalition government announced that it would introduce legislation to amend the universal jurisdiction law by requiring the consent of the director of public prosecutions (not simply private individuals) before an arrest warrant for war crimes is issued. See Ian Black, "Tzipi Livni arrest warrant prompts Israeli government travel 'ban,'" *Guardian*, December 15, 2009; James Hider, "Hamas using English law to demand arrest of Israeli leaders for war crimes," *Sunday Times* (London), December 21, 2009; Ze'ev Segal, "A chance to change universal jurisdiction," *Haaretz*, July 26, 2010; Michael Mansfield, "Government's move to curb universal jurisdiction sends wrong message," *Guardian*, July 27, 2010; Marcus Dysch, "Doubts over universal jurisdiction 'solution,'" *Jewish Chronicle Online*, July 29, 2010, http://www.thejc.com/print/36315

60 Peter Berkowitz argues that the Goldstone mission itself was an attempt to radically alter international law (and the liberal tradition generally) by giving primacy to international (i.e., transnational) institutions over nation-states in determining lawful conduct in war. Berkowitz also suggests that "there is a danger that the spread of practices among international bodies and an accumulation of precedents concerning international law will weigh down the United States" in its conflict with terrorists—particularly since there are "powerful trends in American universities and law schools" to support this transfer of power from the national to the transnational. Peter Berkowitz, "The Goldstone Report and International Law," *Policy Review*, August/September 2010.

61 Moyers, "Transcript of Interview with Richard Goldstone."

62 Amy Bracken, "At Brandeis, Goldstone Defends UN War Crimes Report," *Christian Science Monitor*, November 6, 2009.

63 Kenneth Roth, "The Incendiary IDF," Human Rights Watch, January 22, 2009.

[64] For instance, see Gerald M. Steinberg, "The War against Israel," *Wall Street Journal*, June 7, 2010, posted at http://www.ngo-monitor.org/article/the_war_against_israel; also, NGO Monitor, June 2009 Digest (vol. 7, no. 10), http://www.ngo-monitor.org/digest_info.php?id=2497

[65] Germany usually does not vote against Israel for historical reasons, although it has cut off arms sales at various times. It is also true that Merkel is friendlier to Israel than the previous Schröder government.

[66] Richard Goldstone, "Reconsidering the Goldstone Report on Israel and War Crimes," *Washington Post*, April 1, 2011.

[67] "Goldstone's Reversal Highlights NGO Deceit," NGO Monitor, April 5, 2011; and "NGOs vs. Goldstone," NGO Monitor, April 11, 2011.

[68] Anne Bayefsky, "The United Nations and the Goldstone Report—Where Does It Go from Here?" FoxNews.com, April 5, 2011.

[69] Tovah Lazaroff and Yaakov Katz, "PM: Throw Goldstone Report into dustbin of history," *Jerusalem Post*, April 2, 2011.

[70] "United Nations Must Reject Israeli Campaign to Avoid Accountability for Gaza War Crimes," Amnesty International Public Statement, April 5, 2011, http://www.globalresearch.ca/index.php?context=va&aid=24167

[71] Kenneth Roth, "Gaza: the stain remains on Israel's war record," *Guardian*, April 5, 2011.

[72] See Tovah Lazaroff, "Peres asks UN to shelve Goldstone Report," *Jerusalem Post*, April 8, 2011; and JTA News Service, "UN Human Rights Council: Goldstone Report Stands," *Baltimore Jewish Times*, April 5, 2011.

[73] Hina Jilani, Christine Chinkin, and Desmond Travers, "Goldstone report: Statement issued by members of UN mission on Gaza war," *Guardian*, April 14, 2011.

[74] See "Britain pledges continued support for the Goldstone report against Israel even as Goldstone retracts allegations," *The Commentator* blog, April 4, 2011; and "Consensus forming that Goldstone report set to continue passage through UN despite Goldstone's retraction, diplomats, officials suggest," *The Commentator* blog, April 9, 2011.

[75] Herb Keinon, "PMO slams 'biased' human rights NGOs," *Jerusalem Post*, July 15, 2009.

[76] Adam Horowitz and Philip Weiss, "Israel vs. Human Rights," *Nation*, September 30, 2009.

[77] Keinon, "PMO slams 'biased' human rights NGOs."

[78] See Jeffrey Goldberg, "Fundraising Corruption at Human Rights Watch," Voices, *Atlantic*, July 15, 2009; and David Bernstein, "Human Rights Watch Goes to Saudi Arabia: Seeking Saudi Money to Counterbalance 'Pro-Israel Pressure Groups,'" *Wall Street Journal*, July 15, 2009.

[79] Keinon, "PMO slams 'biased' human rights NGOs."

[80] For example, in 2004, Human Rights Watch issued over 400 documents charging human rights abuses in the Middle East. More accusations were issued against Israel (145 documents) than any other country in the area (Egypt was second, with 91, Iran was third, with 44). In 2005, HRW charged Israel with violations of international humanitarian and human rights law 39 times. In contrast, other Middle Eastern countries and non-state entities were cited much less often: Egypt (4 times), Syria (twice), Palestinian Authority (twice), and Morocco (once). In 2006, fully 52 percent (255 out of 489) of Amnesty International's reports on alleged human rights abuses around the world consisted of charges against Israel. In second place, around 24 percent (128) of all Amnesty reports were directed against the United States. The remaining 106 publications were divided among 28 countries, including leading human rights violators such as Sudan, North Korea, Cuba, Zimbabwe, and Syria. See *Watching the Watchers: The Politics and Credibility of Non-Governmental Organizations in the Arab-Israeli Conflict* (NGO Monitor, 2008), pp. 38–39.

[81] Ibid., p. 32.

[82] Robert L. Bernstein, "Rights Watchdog, Lost in the Mideast," *New York Times,* October 19, 2009.

[83] Elie Wiesel et al., "Call for NGO review," Letters, *Guardian,* October 29, 2009.

[84] Chris McGreal, "Israel 'personally attacking human rights group' after Gaza war criticism," *Guardian,* November 13, 2009.

[85] Gerald M. Steinberg, "Manipulating the Marketplace of Ideas," NGO Monitor, November 27, 2009.

[86] Ibid. See also "Foreign Government Funding for Israeli NGOs: Selections 2006–2010," NGO Monitor, http://www.ngo-monitor.org/data/images/File/European_Funding_chart_English.pdf

[87] Herb Keinon, "Israel aims to outlaw foreign government funding for local NGOs that 'delegitimize the state,'" *Jerusalem Post,* July 31, 2009.

[88] Herb Keinon, "'European funding of Israeli NGOs isn't meddling': EU envoy to Post Euro," *Jerusalem Post,* December 30, 2009.

[89] Ibid.

Chapter 13: Assimilation of Immigrants

[1] See, "ACLU–San Diego and Mexico's Human Rights Commission Announce Agreement to Protect Migrants' Human Rights on Border," press release, ACLU–San Diego Foundation, April 28, 2008.

[2] Michael Fullilove, "The world must adapt to diasporas," *Financial Times,* February 15, 2008.

[3] Michael Fullilove, "Diasporas and the International System," Lowy Institute for International Policy (Sydney, Australia), February 2008.

[4] "Muslim Leader Says France Has Right to Prohibit Head Scarves," *New York Times,* December 31, 2003.

[5] Nick Cumming-Bruce and Steven Erlanger, "Swiss Ban Building of Minarets on Mosques," *New York Times,* November 29, 2009.

[6] Laura Stone, "Citizenship guide to focus on military history, symbolism," Canwest News Service, November 10, 2009.

[7] Tani Goldstein, "PM: Infiltrators pull us towards Third World," YNet News, January 21, 2010.

[8] See "Pope Benedict XVI urges Italy to respect migrants," BBC News, January 10, 2010; and Andrea Holzer, "Italy's hard line on illegal immigration," *l'Occidentale,* May 20, 2009.

[9] See, for example, Soeren Kern, "Sweden's Political Landscape: In Muslim Neighborhoods, Firemen and Emergency Workers Refuse to Enter without Police Protection," September 30, 2010, http://www.hudson-ny.org/1573/sweden-political-landscape; also, "Brandmän i Rosengård tvingas skaffa hjälmar" [Firefighters in Rosengård Are Forced to Buy Helmets], *Aftonbladet,* September 8, 2009, http://www.aftonbladet.se/nyheter/article5758228.ab; and "Ambulans-personalen måste skyddas av polis," *Aftonbladet,* September 8, 2004, http://www.aftonbladet.se/vss/nyheter/story/0,2789,529910,00.html

[10] Daniel Pipes, "The 751 No-Go Zones of France," *Daniel Pipes Blog,* January 16, 2010.

[11] Kari Lydersen, "Some Muslim Cabbies Refuse Fares Carrying Alcohol," *Washington Times,* October 26, 2006.

[12] UN Human Rights Council, 7th Session, agenda item 3, *Promotion and Protection of All Human Rights, Civil, Political, Economic, Social and Cultural Rights, Including the Right to Development,* Report of the Special Rapporteur on the human rights of migrants, Jorge Bustamante, Addendum, "Mission to the United States of America," March 5, 2008, A/HRC/7/12/Add.2, pp. 2–3.

[13] Catherine Powell, *Human Rights at Home: A Domestic Policy Blueprint for the New Administration* (American Constitution Society for Law and Policy, October 2008), p. 5, http://www.acslaw.org/files/Powell%20full%20combined.pdf

[14] Mexico: Plan Nacional de Desarrollo 2001–2006, sec. 3.2, p. 19.

[15] Francisco Robles Nava, "Triunfa el PRD en Zacatecas, " *La Opinión* (Mexico), July 5, 2004; Jorge Morales Alamada, "Immigrantes trabajaran con nuevos gobiernos estatales mexicanos," *La Opinión,* July 7, 2004; Alfredo Valadez Rodriguez, "First 'migrantes legislators' take possession in Zacatecas," *La Jornada,* September 10, 2004. On the Popular Democratic Revolutionary Party, see Partido de la Revolución Democratica (PRD), Sección Estadis Unidos and Ideologia Politica del PRD en la Exterior. The PRD California website contained celebratory pictures of both Che Guevara and V. I. Lenin. Accessed via the PRD website on July 11, 2003, and July 1, 2004, respectively.

[16] See Esmeralda Bermudez, "Mexican lesson plans crossing the border," *Oregonian,* September 19, 2007; Heather Mac Donald, "Mexico's Undiplomatic Diplomats," in *The Immigration Solution: A Better Plan Than Today's,* by Heather

Mac Donald, Victor Davis Hanson, and Steven Malanga (Chicago: Ivan R. Dee, 2007), pp. 143–44; first published in *City Journal,* Autumn 2005.

[17] See "MUSD School Officials Clarify Misrepresentation of Montebello High School," press release, Montebello Unified School District, May 5, 2010, http://www.montebello.k12.ca.us/musd_flag_incident_press_release.html; and "In Pictures at *Whittier Daily News,* 3/27: Student Protest," http://lang.whittierdailynews.com/socal/gallery2/?folder=news/032806_SV_walk1

[18] Dan Mihalopoulos and Azam Ahmed, "A Rising Force in Hispanic Chicago," *Chicago Tribune,* June 22, 2009.

[19] Stuart Anderson, "The Multiplier Effect," *International Educator,* Summer 2004, p. 18.

[20] On the concept of social reproduction see Michael Walzer's commentary in *Multiculturalism and the Politics of Recognition,* an essay by Charles Taylor with commentary by Amy Gutmann (ed.), Steven C. Rockefeller, Michael Walzer, Susan Wolf (Princeton, N.J.: Princeton University Press, 1992), particularly pp. 99–103 passim.

[21] Antonio Olivo and Oscar Avila, "Influence on both sides of the border," *Chicago Tribune,* April 6, 2007.

[22] Ibid.

[23] The Office of New Americans and the immigrant integration project was launched by Governor Blagojevich and reinforced as official state policy by his successor, Governor Patrick Quinn. State of Illinois, New Americans Interagency Task Force, Office of Governor Rod R. Blagojevich, *Immigrant Integration: Improving Policy for Education, Health and Human Services for Illinois' Immigrants and Refugees* (December 2006), p. 22.

[24] Ibid., p. 16.

[25] Ibid., p. 16.

[26] Ibid., pp. 8, 15.

[27] Ibid., p. 22.

[28] Ibid., p. 27.

[29] Ibid., p. 31.

[30] Ibid., p. 25.

[31] Ibid., p. 28.

[32] State of Massachusetts, Governor's Advisory Council for Refugees, Office of Governor Deval Patrick, *Massachusetts New Americans Agenda* (October 1, 2009), p. 20. Hereafter, "Massachusetts Task Force."

[33] Sarah Karp, "A makeover for bilingual ed?" *Catalyst Chicago,* December 2007.

[34] Massachusetts Task Force, p. 21.

[35] Maryland Department of Education, *Report of the Task Force on the Preservation of Heritage Language Skills in Maryland* (2008), p. 1.

[36] Ibid., p. 3. The report also suggested that the maintenance of native languages by immigrants would be good for global business in Maryland.

[37] Indiana Department of Education, Language Minority and Migrant Programs, *Best Practices: The Use of Native Language during Instructional and Non-Instructional Time,* updated 2005.

[38] Massachusetts Task Force, p. 7.

[39] Ibid., p. 5.

[40] Interview with Juan Rangel, April 25, 2011. See also, "UNO's American Civics Initiative: A School Curriculum for Immigrant Assimilation," available from United Neighborhood Organization, p. 3.

[41] Ibid., pp. 3–4.

[42] Ibid., pp. 5–6.

[43] Ibid., pp. 9–10.

[44] Ibid., p. 14.

[45] Ibid., p. 10.

[46] Ibid., p. 17.

[47] President Abraham Lincoln, "Speech at Chicago, Illinois," July 10, 1858, http://teachingamericanhistory.org/library/index.asp?document=153

[48] This concept of patriotic integration is what the prominent immigration scholar Lawrence H. Fuchs described when he wrote about Japanese American students at McKinley High School in Honolulu speaking of "our Pilgrim forefathers" and "reciting the Gettysburg Address by heart." See Fuchs, *The American Kaleidoscope: Race, Ethnicity, and the Civic Culture* (Hanover, N.H.: Wesleyan University Press, 1990), p. 225.

[49] Gerald L. Neuman, "Amnesty should be a matter for regret, not a bonus for those who persevere" (response to Joseph H. Carens, "The Case for Amnesty"), *Boston Review,* May/June 2009.

[50] "Mexican Lesson Plans Crossing the Border," *Oregonian,* September 19, 2007.

[51] Mac Donald, "Mexico's Undiplomatic Diplomats" (see n. 16), pp. 143–44.

[52] Ibid., pp. 144–45.

[53] Ibid., p. 148.

[54] Ibid., pp. 147–48.

[55] Ibid., p. 145. From the Migration Policy Institute, see, for example: Aaron Terrazas and Michael Fix, "The Binational Option: Meeting the Instructional Needs of Limited English Proficient Students," November 2009; Laureen Laglagaron, "Protection through Integration: The Mexican Government's Efforts to Aid Migrants in the United States," January 2010; "Mexican Government Uses Innovative Strategies to Help Its Migrants Integrate into the United States," January 21, 2010; "Promoting Success on Both Sides of the Border: Binational Approaches to US Immigrant Integration," a discussion between MPI scholars and a Mexican government official, January 28, 2010.

[56] "An Image Problem," editorial, *Washington Times,* April 3–4, 2006.

[57] Robert J. Samuelson, "Can America Assimilate?" *Washington Post,* April 6, 2001.

[58] Alejandro Portes and Rubén G. Rumbaut, *Legacies: The Story of the Immigrant Second Generation* (Berkeley: University of California Press, 2001), pp. 154–57.

[59] Roger Waldinger, "Between Here and There: How Attached Are Latino Immigrants to Their Native Country?" Pew Hispanic Center Survey, October 25, 2007, p. 14.

[60] "Between Two Worlds: How Young Latinos Come of Age in America," Pew Hispanic Center Survey, 2009, p. 3.

[61] Jacob L. Vigdor, "Measuring Immigrant Assimilation in the United States," Manhattan Institute for Policy Research, Civic Report no. 53, May 2008, Executive Summary.

[62] Eunice Moscoso, "Slowdown Found in Assimilation of Immigrants," *Deseret News*, May 13, 2008.

[63] Jeff Grabmeier, "Immigration Slows Rate of Racial and Ethnic Intermarriages," *Ohio State University Research News*, 2007.

[64] Geneive Abdo, "America's Muslim Aren't as Assimilated as You Think," *Washington Post*, August 27, 2006.

[65] "Muslim Americans: Middle Class and Mostly Mainstream," Pew Research Center, May 22, 2007.

[66] The Christian attitude toward politics is informed by the biblical admonition "Render therefore unto Caesar the things which are Caesar's, and unto God the things that are God's" (Matthew 22:21), and by St. Augustine's idea of the City of God and the City of Man as separate realms. Even when the Church was at its most powerful politically during the Middle Ages, Christian theologians recognized temporal authority (*regnum*) as distinct from spiritual authority (*sacerdotium*), and not always subordinate to it. By contrast, Islam traditionally has no concept of an autonomous sphere of political authority for earthly affairs, separate from religious authority for matters of the soul.

  The Muslim notion of the *ummah*, which could be translated as the global Muslim "nation," is broadly understood to have political as well as religious and cultural dimensions. There is no equivalent to the *ummah* in Christianity today. Someone who says he is a Christian first and an American second is most likely expressing a spiritual attachment to God over any earthly attachments, not declaring a political loyalty to "Christendom" or a global "Christian community" over the American nation-state. He is saying that he believes in a moral authority and moral law higher than the state—not in some organized entity that trumps the democratic state. On the other hand, a "Muslim first, American second" stance, understood in relation to the *ummah*, complicates the matter of political allegiance. For instance, a sizable segment of the American Muslim population does not support any war against fellow Muslims (as revealed in the Zogby poll of May 2002 cited in the text). America has fought wars with various other Christian nations—Britain, France, Mexico and Spain, Germany and Italy—and rarely do American Christians argue that war should never be waged against fellow Christians because they are Christian. During the conflict over Kosovo in the 1990s, few Christian leaders complained that American forces were assisting Muslims against the Christians of Serbia.

Thus, the analogy between Muslim and Christian preferential identity is limited and superficial.

[67] "Muslim Americans: Middle Class and Mostly Mainstream"; Jennifer Harper, "Young U.S. Muslims Back Suicide Attacks," *Washington Times*, May 23, 2007.

[68] Hamilton College Muslim American Poll, in collaboration with Zogby International, May 30, 2002, http://www.hamilton.edu/news/MuslimAmerica/MuslimAmerica.pdf

[69] Zeyno Baran, "Introduction and Overview," *The Other Muslims: Moderate and Secular,* ed. Zeyno Baran (New York: Palgrave Macmillan, 2010), p. 3.

[70] Ibid., p. 4.

[71] Hedieh Mirahmadi, "Navigating Islam in America," in *The Other Muslims,* p. 24.

[72] Ibid., p. 26.

[73] Ibid., pp. 24–32.

[74] Steven A. Camarota, "Religious Leaders vs. Members: An Examination of Contrasting Views on Immigration," Center for Immigration Studies, December 2009, p. 2.

[75] "79% Support U.S. Troops on the Border to Fight Drug Violence," Rasmussen Reports Poll, March 16, 2009.

[76] "Americans Return to Tougher Immigration Stance," Gallup Poll, August 5, 2009.

[77] See Noah Pickus, *True Faith and Allegiance: Immigration and American Civic Nationalism* (Princeton, N.J.: Princeton University Press, 2005).

[78] "E Pluribus Unum: A Study of Americans' Views on National Identity," prepared for the Bradley Project on National Identity, Harris Interactive, May 13, 2008.

[79] Alexander Hamilton, "The Federalist No. 1," in *The Federalist Papers,* ed. Clinton Rossiter (New York: New American Library, 1961), pp. 33–37.

[80] U.S. Commission on Immigration Reform, *The National Interest,* 1995, p. 3.

[81] Ibid., p. 1.

[82] Barbara Jordan, "The Americanization Ideal," *New York Times,* September 11, 1995.

[83] President Calvin Coolidge, "First Annual Message to Congress," December 6, 1923, available at the American Presidency Project, http://www.presidency.ucsb.edu/ws/index.php?pid=29564#axzz1Kbux2Og3

[84] Robert J. Samuelson, "Can America Assimilate?" *Washington Post,* April 6, 2001.

[85] *Perez v. Brownell,* 356 U.S. 44 (1958), p. 8.

Chapter 14: The Suicide of Liberal Democracy?

[1] See notes 2 and 3 to Chapter 7 above.

[2] John Locke, *Of Civil Government,* Bk. 2, chap. 19, sec. 217.

[3] Hamilton statement quoted by Jeremy Rabkin, *Why Sovereignty Matters* (Washington, D.C.: AEI Press, 1998), p. 11; from "Camillus," in *Works of Alexander Hamilton,* ed. Henry Cabot Lodge (G. P. Putnam's Sons, 1885), vol. 5, p. 30.

[4] Anne-Marie Slaughter, *The Idea That Is America: Keeping Faith with Our Values in a Dangerous World* (New York: Basic Books, 2007), pp. 103–4.

[5] Anne-Marie Slaughter, "A New World Order," Foreign Press Center Briefing, April 12, 2004, Washington, D.C., p. 7, http://2002-2009-fpc.state.gov/31320.htm

[6] Slaughter, *The Idea That Is America,* pp. 104–5.

[7] Strobe Talbott, *The Great Experiment: The Story of Ancient Empires, Modern States, and the Quest for a Global Nation* (New York: Simon & Schuster, 2009), p. 330.

[8] Ibid., p. 329.

[9] See Nicholas Kulish, "German Identity, Long Dormant, Reasserts Itself," *New York Times,* September 10, 2010.

[10] See, Christopher Marquis, "U.S. Chides France on Effort to Ban Religious Garb in Schools," *New York Times,* December 19, 2003; and "US concern over French scarf ban," BBC News, December 19, 2003.

[11] Admiral Raja Menon spoke at the Hudson Institute on June 23, 2010; I was present. Menon discussed his book, written with Rajiv Kumar, *The Long View from Delhi: To Define the Indian Grand Strategy for Foreign Policy* (New Delhi: Academic Foundation / Indian Council for Research on International Economic Relations, 2010). See also, Pratap Bhanu Mehta, "India eyes an American special relationship," *Financial Times,* July 28, 2010; Evan A. Feigenbaum, "India's Rise, America's Interest," *Foreign Affairs,* March/April 2010; and Sadanand Dhume, "It's Time to Re-Align India," *Wall Street Journal,* April 21, 2011.

[12] Alexis de Tocqueville, *Democracy in America,* transl., ed., and intro. Harvey C. Mansfield and Delba Winthrop (Chicago: University of Chicago Press, 2002), vol. 1, part I, chap. 4, "On the Principle of the Sovereignty of the People in America," p. 53.

[13] Harold Hongju Koh, "International Law as Part of Our Law," *American Journal of International Law* 98:1 (January 2004), pp. 53–54.

[14] Ed Whelan, "Obama Supreme Court Candidate Harold Koh—Part 1," Bench Memos, *National Review Online,* September 24, 2008.

[15] Harold Hongju Koh, "Why Transnational Law Matters," *Penn State International Law Review* 24 (2006), pp. 745–46.

[16] Robert Wright, *Nonzero: The Logic of Human Destiny* (New York: Vintage Books, 2000).

[17] Thomas Friedman, in an MSNBC *Meet the Press* interview on September 7, 2008, transcript at http://www.msnbc.msn.com/id/26590488/

[18] David Held has argued extensively for global governance. See *Globalization/Anti-Globalization: Beyond the Great Divide* (2007), *Models of Democracy* (2006), *Global Covenant* (2004), *Global Transformations: Politics, Economics and Culture* (1999), and *Democracy and the Global Order: From the Modern State to Cosmopolitan Governance* (1995).

[19] Immanuel Kant, "Perpetual Peace: A Philosophical Sketch," in *Kant's Political Writings*, ed. Hans Reiss (Cambridge, UK: Cambridge University Press, 1970).

[20] Jürgen Habermas, "Does the Constitutionalization of International Law Still Have a Chance?" in *The Divided West*, ed. and transl. Ciaran Cronin (Cambridge: Polity Press, 2006), p. 128.

[21] Leo Strauss, *On Tyranny*, revised and extended edition including the Strauss-Kojève correspondence, ed. Victor Gourevitch and Michael S. Roth (1991; Chicago and London: University of Chicago Press, 2000).

[22] Ibid., p. 211.

[23] Ibid.

[24] Habermas, *The Divided West*, p. 135.

[25] Jed Rubenfeld, "The Two World Orders," *Wilson Quarterly*, Autumn 2003, p. 35.

[26] David McCullough, *John Adams* (New York: Simon & Schuster, 2001), p. 645.

Index

Abbot, Abiel, 18

Abdo, Geneive, 326

Abduction from the Seraglio (Mozart), 29

Abu-Jamal, Mumia, 210

Adams, John, 27, 28, 340; on education, 50–51, 55; "independence forever," 369

Adams, John Quincy, 43

Addison, Joseph, 29, 56

Adler, Mortimer, 13

Adorno, Theodore, 86

Afghanistan, 241–42, 249; "war crimes" in, 273–74, 408

AFL-CIO, 330

African American Human Rights Foundation, 207

Albert Shanker Institute, 78

Aleinikoff, T. Alexander, 93–94

Alexander the Great, 11, 16, 93, 159

Algeria, 250

Alien Tort Statute, 107–8

Alito, Samuel, 114

Alston, Philip, 249, 250–51

Alter, Karen, 135–38

America at the Crossroads (Fukuyama), 194–95

American Association of University Women, 88

American Bar Association (ABA), 108; on CEDAW, 164, 219, 222–24; on Garzón, 248

American Civil Liberties Union (ACLU), 4, 209; and ICCPR, 203–7; on immigration, 309, 339

American Constitution Society, 224, 310

American Founders: and Bible, 18–19; and classics, 26–28, 31, 37; Declaration of Independence, 347–48, 366–67; foreign influences, 112–13; on human nature, 45–47, 71; on immigrants, 57–59; on law of nations, 32–34, 101; on liberty, 28–30; and Locke, 24–26; on mores & culture, 47–51; on natural rights, 64–65; on patriotism, 51–56; Whig influence, 28–31

American Friends Service Committee, 5, 164, 209

American Historical Association, 68, 97

American Jewish Congress, 285*n*

American Service-Members' Protection Act, 266–67, 269, 270

American Society for International Law, 218

Americans for Democratic Action, 70

Amnesty International, 164; on Afghan & Iraq wars, 241; and Durban conference, 5, 286; on Garzón, 248; on Guantanamo Bay, 244; and ICC, 256, 258, 263–64, 272, 275; vs. Israel, 275, 290, 293,

425

Amnesty International (cont.)
295, 300–2, 304; on Kosovo War,
233–39; on Sudan/Darfur, 272,
304; and universal jurisdiction,
106, 244–45; on U.S. issues, 202,
207, 209
Anatomy of Peace (Reves), 13
Anderson, Kenneth, 161, 162, 342;
on democracy, 193; on ICC over-
reach, 274
Anglosphere, 189–91, 356
Annan, Kofi, 164, 166
Anthony, Susan B., 43
Anti-Defamation League, 207
Appardurai, Arjun, 98–99
Appleby, Joyce, 95–96
Arab-American Anti-Discrimination
Committee, 4, 207
Arab American Institute, 4
Arab League, 275, 293
Arbour, Louise, 154, 290
Argentina, 63, 245; and ICC, 256,
258, 269
Aristotle, 16, 47, 124; on education,
51; and Founders, 26, 31, 48
Ashoka, 16
Association for the Dignity of Prison-
ers, 246
Atlantic Philanthropies, 165
Attlee, Clement, 144
Augustine, St., 421
Aurillac, Michel, 135–36
Australia: gender equity in, 216; on
Goldstone Report, 300; immi-
grants to, 217; on Protocol I, 228,
231
Austria, 123, 299*n*
Aviv, Diana, 323*n*
Axworthy, Lloyd, 188, 191, 258

Babylonian empire, 16, 17, 18
Bailyn, Bernard, 28–30, 46

Ban Ki-moon, 272, 295
Bank of America, 330
Banks, James, 75–76
Barak, Ehud, 292
Baran, Zeyno, 328
Barber, Benjamin, 99
Bardot, Brigitte, 152–53
Barfield, Claude, 168
Barnett, Thomas P. M., 197*n*
Bashir, Omar al-, 271–72, 273*n*
Bassiouni, Cherif, 259, 264
Bayefsky, Anne, 287–88
BBC, 191
Beard, Charles, 65, 68
Beck, Glenn, 92
Becker, Carl, 68
Belgium: as "consocial democracy,"
394; Flemish separatism in, 354;
on Goldstone Report, 299*n;* opin-
ion on EU, 148; as postdemocra-
tic, 243; and Treaty of Rome, 121;
universal jurisdiction law, 243–44;
women's status in, 213, 220
Belz, Herman, 77*n*
Bender, Thomas, 97, 98
Benedetti, Fanny, 253, 259
Benedict XVI, Pope, 152
Benjamin, David, 275
Bennett, James C., 189
Berkowitz, Peter, 415
Berns, Walter, 52
Bernstein, Robert, 304
Berresford, Susan, 285*n*
Berry, Mary Frances, 4
Bible, 16–19; in American founding,
18–19, 25, 30, 31
Biden, Joseph, 88, 267*n;* on CEDAW,
210–11; on ICC, 410
bin Laden, Osama, 327
"Birth of the Global Nation, The"
(Talbott), 15
Bismarck, Otto von, 179

Black, Conrad, 189
Black, Edwin, 285
Black's Law Dictionary, 106
Blackstone, William, 29–32
Blair, Tony, 151, 172
Bloom, Allan, 63
Blunkett, David, 151
Bobbitt, Philip, 197*n*
Boeing, 82, 83, 170
Bolingbroke, Henry St. John, Viscount (Lord), 29, 30, 31
Bolton, John, 267–68, 271
Bork, Robert, 108
Borrell, Josep, 154
Bos, Adriaan, 258, 263, 264
Bosnia, 268
Bosniak, Linda S., 99–100
Botha, P. W., 280
Boutros-Ghali, Boutros, 166
Bowles, Chester, 67, 70
Boyé, Gonzalo, 246, 247, 407
Bradley, Curtis, 103, 104
Bradley Project on American National Identity, 334–36
Brandeis, Louis, 57, 60–61, 311
Brazil, 84, 344; and BRICs, 357; and ICC, 270
Breaking the Silence, 305–6
Breyer, Stephen, 110–14
BRIC nations, 357
Britain. *See* Great Britain
Brody, Reed: at Durban, 281, 287–88; on Garzón, 248; on universal jurisdiction, 246
Bromund, Ted, 173
Brookings Institution, 309
Brown v. Board of Education, 204–5
Brunell, Thomas, 131–32
Brutus, 26–27, 37
B'Tselem, 291, 293, 300
Bukovsky, Vladimir, 164*n*
Bulgaria, 123

Burke, Edmund, xiii–xiv, 42
Burkina Faso, 255
Burley, Anne-Marie. *See* Slaughter, Anne-Marie (Burley)
Burma, 191
Bush, George H. W., 77, 203; border policy, 208; "war crimes" charges, 243
Bush, George W., & administration: on French headscarf ban, 355; on ICC, 263, 267–71; immigration policy, 334; and Mexico, 188; "war crimes" charges, 246
Bustamante, Jorge, 310

Caddell, Patrick, 160*n*
Caesar, Julius, 27–28, 31
Caldwell, Christopher, 151
Calhoun, John C., 75
California, 83, 84, 223
Camelot and the Cultural Revolution (Piereson), 66
Cameron, David, 149*n*, 415
Canada, 106, 188; citizenship test, 309; and Durban conference, 282, 283; Francophone community in, 75; on Goldstone Report, 300; and ICC, 176, 256, 257–58, 260, 269; and NGOs, 165
capital punishment, 105, 202; Supreme Court on, 108–10; UN report on, 204, 209–10
Carnegie Endowment for International Peace, 89, 100, 165–66, 313
Carter, Jimmy, 210
Casey, Lee A., 101–2, 105, 171; on ICC, 255
Castaneda, Jorge, 188–89
Catalonia, 353
Cathala, Bruno, 270
Catiline, 27
Cato (the Younger), 27, 29, 31, 37

Cato (Addison), 29, 56
Cato's Letters (Trenchard & Gordon), 29, 31
Ceaser, James W., 35, 47–48, 98
CEDAW Assessment Tool, The (ABA), 222–24
Center for Constitutional Rights, 9, 207, 245, 290
Central African Republic, 270
Central Intelligence Agency (CIA), 169, 248–49
Chad, 254
Chang, Nancy, 9
Charlemagne, 11, 16
Charles Stewart Mott Foundation, 5, 89, 165–66
Chayes, Abram, 263
Cheney, Lynne V., 77
Chernow, Ron, 27
Chicago, 310, 316–18
children's rights. *See* UN Convention on the Rights of the Child
Chile, 169, 245–46
China, 16, 177; as BRIC nation, 357; as challenger, 180–82, 185, 341, 349–51; Communist Party of, 343; efficiency of, 363; and G20, 174; on Human Rights Council, 250; and ICC, 260, 265; as sovereigntist, 191, 344; and universal jurisdiction, 247
Chinkin, Christine, 294, 301
Chirac, Jacques, 110
Christianity, 42, 48, 327*n;* on church/state, 421–22; and Israel, 291; *see also* Bible
Churchill, Winston, 41, 362
Cicero, 26–28, 31
Cincinnatus, 27
CIO-PAC, 70
citizenship: in antiquity, 37; and assimilation, 57–61; and civic

education, 49–56; and divided loyalty, 75, 259, 312–14, 334–35, 340; dual, 309, 311–12, 319–20, 322, 329, 330*n;* equality of, 36, 38–39, 43, 73, 149; global, 99–100, 119, 163, 335, 344; and group identity, 73–75, 96, 313–16; oath of, 319, 322, 340; responsibilities of, 39, 42–43, 46–47; and Sharia, 149–51; transnational, 94, 96–98, 163
"Citizenship Denationalized" (Bosniak), 99–100
Citizenship Today: Global Perspectives and Practices, 100
Civil Rights Act (1964), 71–72, 80
civil rights movement, 45, 71–73; and "disparate impact," 80–81; *see also* diversity agenda
Civil War, 44, 45, 54
Clark, Wesley, 240
Clausewitz, Carl von, 186, 193
Cleveland, Grover, 66
Cleveland, Sarah, 225
Clinton, Bill, & administration, 8, 160*n,* 350; border policy, 208; and human rights, 201–9; and ICC, 260–63; on immigration, 338, 339; and Kosovo, 233, 236, 277
Clinton, Hillary, xi, 160*n,* 267*n*
Closing of the American Mind, The (Bloom), 63
Coca-Cola, 170
Coercing Virtue (Bork), 108
Cold War, 186; end of, xv, 93, 101–2, 129, 166; idealist view of, 180; and moral equivalence, 79; progressives in, 69–71; and realpolitik, 179
Colgate-Palmolive, 170
Collier, Peter, 388–89
Colmes, Alan, 92
Colombia, 238

Colorado State Board of Education, 76
Commager, Henry Steele, 69
Commentaries on the Laws of England (Blackstone), 29
Commission on Immigration Reform (Jordan Commission), 338–39
communism, 40, 63, 64, 185; Chinese, 182, 343; liberal conflict on, 69–71; and Marcuse, 90; quotas in, 214
Conde-Pumpido, Condido, 247
Congo, Democratic Republic of the, 254, 270
Connerly, Ward, 83–84
Conquest, Robert, 189
Continental Congress, 32, 50, 367
Coolidge, Calvin, 339
Coomaraswamy, Radhika, 202
Cooper, Robert, 181, 191; on EU, 129–30, 155–56; on global domestic politics, 201, 221, 307–8; on postmodern states, 130, 155, 177
Cooper, Samuel, 18–19
corporate transnationalists, 169–70
Costa v. ENEL, 128, 133–34
Costco, 83
Council for Basic Education, 77, 78
Council of Europe, 127
Council of the European Union, 124, 127
Council on Foreign Relations, 197, 238
Court of Justice of the European Union. *See* European Court of Justice
courts, 94–95, 104–18, 156–58, 160, 359–60; Garzón prosecutions, 246–47; and UN treaties, 222, 225; Sharia, 150; *see also* European Court of Justice; International Criminal Court; U.S. Supreme Court

Cox, Larry, 225
Creating Equal (Connerly), 83
critical theory, 85–92, 225; on human rights, 205–6
Cronkite, Walter, 13–14
Cross, Christopher T., 77, 78
Cuba, 250; missile crisis, 277
customary international law: "new" vs. traditional, 101–6; Protocol I, 229*n*, 231, 234–35, 239, 242; state consent in, 103–4, 234; and universal jurisdiction, 106–8; *see also* international law; law of nations
Cyprus, 123
Czech Republic, 123, 129*n*, 300

Dahlerup, Drude, 220
Danish Free Speech Society, 154–55
Dante, 19, 21, 159; *De Monarchia,* 12
Darfur, 270–73
Dawkins, Richard, 13
Declaration of Independence, 32, 43–44; celebration of, 369; "deconstruction" of, 68; equality in, 37; and immigrants, 59; vs. "Interdependence," 99; and Locke, 24; national unity in, 76; on "unwarrantable Jurisdiction," 367
Defending Identity (Sharansky), 39–42
de Gaulle, Charles, 41, 122–23, 362
de la Cruz, Manuel, 310
Delors, Jacques, 122, 167
Del Ponte, Carla, 239–40, 248
Democracy in America (Tocqueville), 47–48
Democracy Without Borders? (Plattner), 25
Democratic Party, 193; and New Deal, 66; in Cold War, 70
Democratic Republic of the Congo, 254, 270
Demosthenes, 26, 27, 37

Denmark, 122, 123; free speech in, xxii, 153–55; on Goldstone Report, 299*n;* women's status in, 213
Dermer, Ron, 302, 306
de Waal, Alex, 271–72
Dewey, John, 64–65, 68
Dewey, Thomas, 70
Dickenson, John, 28
Dicker, Richard, 262–63, 264
Diggins, John Patrick, 77*n*
Dirksen, Everett M., 71–72
disaggregated nation-states, 116–18, 175–76; in EU integration, 139–40; and philanthropies, 165–66
"Disaggregating U.S. Interests in International Law" (Spiro), 117–18
Disuniting of America, The (Schlesinger), 79
diversity agenda, 79–85; coercion in, 85, 344; at corporations, 82–83; in courts, 81–82; and immigrants, 322, 324–26; and "mobility ladders," 84; and "substantive equality," 8–9, 322; voters on, 83–84; and "white privilege," 89–90; *see also* multiculturalism
Diversity Machine, The (Lynch), 83
Dobbs, Lou, 92
Dorsen, Norman, 113
Douglas, William O., 13
Douglass, Frederick, 43
Draghi, Mario, 174
Dubinsky, David, 70
Dunlap, Charles, 235, 238, 406
Durban conference. *See* UN World Conference against Racism, Racial Discrimination, Xenophobia and Related Intolerance
Dworkin, Ronald, 75

Ebell, Myron, 162*n*
Eddie Bauer, 83
Edgar, Bob, 4
Edley, Christopher, Jr., 225
education: bilingual, 314–15, 322; critical theory in, 85–92; of immigrants, 310, 313–18, 320–22, 339; multicultural, 74–79, 310, 320–24, 335; patriotic, 50–52, 55–56, 68, 335; and race, 204–5; in "transnational" citizenship, 96–98, 163; women in, 204–5
Educational Disabilities Act, 205
Egypt (ancient), 16–18
Egypt (modern), 182, 259, 417
Einstein, Albert, 13, 159
El Salvador, 255
End of the Nation-State, The (Ohmae), 169
England. *See* Great Britain
Enlightenment, 35; in American founding, 24, 25, 31, 347; Kant, 12, 19–20; Locke, 20, 24–26; resistance to, 63–64
Enloe, Cynthia, 84
Equal Employment Opportunity Commission, 81
Estonia, 123
Etzioni, Amitai, 148
Eurobarometer, 148–49
EuroMed program, 290
European Central Bank, 128, 146*n*
European Coal and Steel Community, 121, 144
European Commission, 122–27, 171; initiating legislation, 124–26, 146; on Israel, 290, 291; on Muhammad cartoons, 154; on national courts, 133
European Common Market, 121–22
European Communities Act, 141–42

European Community, 122–23; "constitutionalization" of, 130–42; Court of Justice, 127–28; *see also* Treaty of Rome

European Council, 126–27, 172

European Council on Foreign Relations, 290

European Court of Human Rights, 110

European Court of Justice (ECJ) (Court of Justice of the European Union), 125, 127–36, 168; acquiescence to, 136–42, 177; *Costa v. ENEL*, 128, 133–34; *Factortame*, 141–42; *Francovich v. Italy*, 128; incrementalism of, 140, 157–58; vs. national legislatures, 138–40; *Van Gend & Loos*, 127–28, 132–35, 139

European Economic Community, 122

European Monetary Union, 128

European Parliament, 124–26, 162*n*; on Afghan war, 241; on Israel, 290; limitations of, 126, 145–47, 363; on Muhammad cartoons, 154; on USA Patriot Act, 241

European People's Party, 162*n*

European Union, xiv–xv, 11, 16, 95; beginning of, 121–23; on capital punishment, 108; Charter of Fundamental Freedoms, 129; Common Agricultural Policy, xv; Common Foreign and Security Policy, 353; constitution, 123, 127, 145; "democratic deficit" in, 131*n*, 145–49, 171, 352, 362, 363; External Action Service, 129; and G20, 170–75; and ICC, 256, 257, 269; incrementalism of, 121–23, 140, 155–58; institutions of, 124–29; Laeken Declaration, 123, 145; Lisbon Treaty, 145–49; Maastricht Treaty, 142–45; on Muhammad cartoons, 154; "Muslim community" in, 159–61; and national suicide, 345; opposition to 147–49, 353–54; Palestinian NGO funding, 284, 293, 305–8; as peacekeeping, 121, 361; as "postmodern state," 129–30; and self-interest, 137–39; Single European Act, 122, 127; speech restrictions in, 149, 151–55; subsidiarity in, 143–44, 146–47; and U.S., 353

Factortame case, 139, 141–42, 147

Fallaci, Oriana, 152

Fanton, Jonathan, 294

fascism, 63, 64, 185, 214

Fatah, 292

Federalist Papers, The, 24, 26, 49, 101; on Europe, 111–12; on human nature, 45–46; on patriotism, 51–52; on representative democracy, 38; on self-determination, 337–38

Federalist Party, 47, 66

Federal Textbook on Citizenship Training, 59–60

Feinstein, Dianne, 160*n*, 410

Feith, Douglas J., 229–30, 407–8

feminism, 87–88, 89

Filartiga v. Pena-Irala, 107–8

Financial Stability Board (G20), 172–74

Finland, 123, 202; on Goldstone Report, 299*n*; and ICC, 256, 258, 270

Finn, Chester, 77

Fischer, Joschka: on capital punishment, 202; on democratic deficit, 123, 145; on "global domestic

Fischer, Joschka (cont.)
politics," 201, 221, 307–8
Fitna (film), 151
Fitzpatrick, James F., 4
Flanders, 353
Flanigan, Tim, 245
Flint, Julie, 271–72
Folsom, Burton, Jr., 77*n*
Force of Reason, The (Fallaci), 152
Ford Foundation: and diversity
agenda, 89, 90; and Durban con-
ference, 5, 284–85, 288; and ICC,
257; and Israel, 290, 293; and
NGOs, 165–66
Foreign Affairs, 106, 116, 119, 196
Forward, The, 284–85
Foundation for Individual Rights in
Education, 91
Founders and the Classics, The
(Richard), 26–27
Fox, Vicente, 188, 310
Fox-Genovese, Elizabeth, 77*n*
France, 11; assimilation in, 312; on
death penalty, 355; Estates-Gen-
eral, 214; EU constitution vote,
123, 127, 147; on Goldstone
Report, 299*n;* headscarf ban, 309,
355; and ICC, 260, 270; Muslims
in, 152–53, 309–10; nuclear capac-
ity, 177; opposition to EC/EU,
144–45, 354; on Protocol I, 228,
233, 239; Secret Army Organiza-
tion, 63–64; and Treaty of Rome,
121; and universal jurisdiction,
245; *Vabre* case, 135–36; women's
status, 213–14, 220
Franco, Francisco, 63
Francovich v. Italy, 128
Frankfurter, Felix, 340
Frankfurt School, 86, 90, 225
Frattini, Franco, 154
Freedom House, 254

freedom of speech, 7, 35, 43, 66–67,
185; and critical theory, 86; and
diversity agenda, 83; in English Bill
of Rights, 38; in EU, 149, 151–55;
First Amendment, 8, 91, 209; and
"hate speech," 8, 91, 154–55, 281,
283; and "Islamophobia," 151–55;
and race, 209; as "repressive tolerance," 90–91; UN restrictions on,
8–9, 209, 217, 344
Freeland, Chrystia, 170
Freidenvall, Lenita, 220
Freud, Sigmund, 86
Friedman, Thomas, 363
*From Migrants to Citizens: Membership
in a Changing World*, 100
Fukuyama, Francis, xvi, 64, 88, 102,
180, 345; on "horizontal accountability," 194–96

G20, xix, 172–75
Gagnon, Paul, 77*n*
Galbraith, John Kenneth, 69
Gallup poll, 333
Gálvez, Mireya Magaña, 321
Garlasco, Marc, 305
Garrity, Patrick, 53, 55
Garzón, Baltasar, 245–48
Gates, Bill, Sr., 83
Gaza, 282, 287; Goldstone mission
on, 294, 302; NGOs on, 302–5;
war in, 273, 275, 291–93
Gender Equity in Education Act, 88
General Agreement on Tariffs and
Trade (GATT), 167, 168
Geneva Conventions (1949), 227,
230, 234, 237, 257, 407–8
Geneva Conventions: Additional
Protocol I, 191, 227–37, 239–40;
civilian endangerment by, 228,
230, 232, 237; and customary
international law, 234, 239, 242;

and ICC, 257, 274; on irregular combatants, 228–29, 232–33, 237, 249; Joint Chiefs on, 229–32, 242; opposition to, 307, 357–58; property vs. life in, 230–31, 237; and Red Cross, 227–28, 230, 239, 242; U.S. media on, 232–33; and Yugoslavia, 233–37, 239–40

Geneva Protocol (1925), 227

George, Erika, 9

George III, 18, 19

Georgetown Law Center, 93, 163

German Federal Constitutional Court, 157

German Federation of Republican Lawyers, 245

Germany, 63, 165; on capital punishment, 202; euro adoption, 177, 354; and European Court of Justice, 138; Euroskepticism in, 157, 354; and gender equity, 217, 219–20; and ICC, 256, 258, 269; on Israel, 300, 301–2, 416; Nazi, 64, 69, 178, 362; as postmodern state, 177–78; and Treaty of Rome, 121; and universal jurisdiction, 245

Gilligan, Carol, 87–88

Gillon, Steven, 70

Ginsburg, Ruth Bader, 110, 114

Giscard d'Estaing, Valéry, 123, 126

Glasius, Marlies, 257, 263

Glasser, Ira, 4

Glélé-Ahanhanzo, Maurice, 207–9

Gold, Dore, 292, 296

Goldman Sachs, 357

Goldsmith, Jack, 103, 104, 244

Goldstone, Richard, 294–96, 298; second thoughts of, 300–2

Goldstone Report. *See* UN Fact Finding Mission on the Gaza Conflict

Gonzales, Alberto, 244, 245

Goodman, Amy, 249

Goodman, Ryan, 225

Gordon, Thomas, 29, 31

Govan, Thomas P., 27

Gramm, Phil, 410

Gramsci, Antonio, 86, 345

Great Britain (United Kingdom), 11; as ally, 353; balanced constitution, 29; Bill of Rights, 38, 190; children's rights in, 215–16; common law, 30, 189–90; on EC/EU, 122–23, 144, 145, 354, 356; *Factortame* case, 139, 141–42, 147; and Falklands, 64, 141; Foreign Office, 191; Glorious Revolution, 38, 142; on Goldstone Report, 299*n*, 301–2; and ICC, 260; and Israel, 297, 305; on Lisbon Treaty, 129*n*, 147–48; Merchant Shipping Act, 141; Muslim protests in, 154; nuclear capacity of, 177; and Oxfam, 293; and Pinochet, 245–46; on Protocol I, 228; Racial and Religious Hatred Act, 151; Sharia in, 150–51; on universal jurisdiction, 415; Whig tradition, 28–30; women's status in, 212–13, 220

Great Experiment, The (Talbott), 15–16, 19–21

Greece (ancient), 11, 25–27, 37

Greece (modern), 122, 148, 149, 177*n*

Greenpeace, 164

Griggs v. Duke Power Company, 81

Grossman, Claudio, 111

Grotius, Hugo, 22, 32–34, 101

Grutter v. Bollinger, 82, 110

Guantanamo Bay, 244, 246–47

Guardian, 191, 271, 274, 305

Guatemala, 220

Guenther, Richard, 60

Gulf War (1991), 205, 241, 243

Gutierrez, Jose Luis, 312–13, 316
Gutmann, Amy, 74–75

Haass, Richard, 197
Habermas, Jürgen, 183, 365; on global domestic politics, 201, 221; on Kant, 364
Hague Convention, The (1907), 227
Hall, Christopher Keith, 264
Hallstein, Walter, 123
Hamas, 277, 289, 292–99, 304
Hamilton, Alexander, 24; on classical models, 26–27; on delegated authority, 343; on immigration, 57–58, 60–61, 311; progressives on, 66; realism of, 46; on representative democracy, 38; on self-determination, 337–38
Hanford, John, 355
Hannan, Daniel, 189, 190
Hannity, Sean, 92
Hapsburgs, xvi, 11, 16, 36, 63
Harrington, James, 29
Harris, David, 285
Harris Interactive, 331, 334
Hartz, Louis, 69
Havel, Vaclav, 164n
Hazony, Yoram, 178, 413
Hedegaard, Lars, 154–55
Held, David, 364
Helms, Jesse, 262–63, 266–67, 410
Henderson, Wade, 4–5, 7, 225, 287
Henry, Patrick, 46
Hernandez, Antonia, 4
Hezbollah, 277, 289, 299, 304
Higham, John, 41
Himmelfarb, Gertrude, 77n
Hitchens, Christopher, 190
Hitler, Adolf, 178
Hobbes, Thomas, 19–20, 182, 195
Hofstadter, Richard, 66, 69, 71
Hohenzollerns, 63

Holy Roman Empire, 11, 12, 159
Hong Kong, 352n
Horkheimer, Max, 86
Horner, Christopher, 162n
Horowitz, David, 388–89
Horowitz, Donald, 84, 85
Houston schools, 321
Hugo, Victor, 12
human rights: and capital punishment, 105, 202, 204, 209–10; in customary international law, 102–3; and expediency, 182; policy preferences as, 205–7, 217–20, 343; "serial absolutism" of, 161–62; and "substantive equality," 212–15, 344; and "systemic racism," 105; transnational progressives on, 160–62; in U.S., 201–10, 224–26, 250; see also international humanitarian law
"Human Rights at Home" (Powell), 224–25
Human Rights First, 256, 272, 286n
Human Rights Foundation, 164n
Human Rights Watch (HRW), 4, 161, 164; on Afghan & Iraq wars, 241–42; on CEDAW, 211; on CERD treaty, 9; and death penalty, 209; at Durban, 9, 286–88; on Garzón prosecutions, 246, 248; and Goldstone, 294; and ICC, 256, 258, 262–64; on Israel, 290, 293, 298, 300–5, 417; on Kosovo war, 233–39; Saudi funding of, 302–3; on Sudan, 272, 304; on universal jurisdiction, 243; on U.S. "violations," 176, 203–9
Hume, David, 30, 31
Humphrey, Hubert, 70, 71–72
Hungary, 123, 300
Huntington, Samuel, 170
Hussein, Saddam, 176, 241

Hutchens, Robert Maynard, 13
Huxley, Julian, 16
Hyneman, Charles, 31

Ideological Origins of the American Revolution, The (Bailyn), 28
Illinois, 313–14
Immigrant Assimilation Index, 325–26
immigrants: assimilation of, 316–18, 334–35, 338–40, 373–75; divided loyalty, 310, 313, 320–23, 340; education of, 313–18, 320–22, 339; and ethnicity, 322, 324–26; "human rights" of, 204, 206, 217, 312; intermarriage of, 325–26; "language rights" of, 204, 281, 313–15; Muslim, 149–50, 184, 309–10, 326–29; naturalization, 58–61; Oath of Renunciation and Allegiance, 319, 322, 340; patriotic integration, 316–26; as social-service clients, 313–14
immigration, 309–40; and bilingual education, 314–15; border control, 204, 208, 217, 329, 332–33, 339–40; and democratic sovereignty, 311–12; and economic determinism, 337; and Ellis Island, 311, 316, 320, 321, 325, 339; illegal, 217, 281, 309, 331–34, 339; Jordan Commission on, 338–40; and multiculturalism, 73–79, 312–16, 320–23, 339–40; public opinion on, 329–36; Simpson-Smith bill, 339; unrestricted, 204, 206
In a Different Voice (Gilligan), 88
India, 12, 16; as ally, 357–58; and Anglosphere, 190; and ICC, 191, 253, 254, 255, 260, 265, 357–58; on Protocol I, 234, 307, 357–58; rise of, 180, 344; Supreme Court of, 110, 111

Indiana, 315
Indonesia, 191, 234, 255
Institute for Global Policy, 264
International Association of Jewish Lawyers and Jurists, 287–88
International Commission of Jurists, 243
International Committee of the Red Cross (ICRC), 164; on Afghan war, 241; on prisoners of war, 227; and Protocol I, 227–28, 239, 242
"international community," xxii, 16, 186, 191; and EU, 155; and Financial Stability Board, 173; and Israel, 293, 298–99; "shaming" by, 222
International Court of Justice, 101, 104, 166; on Israeli security fence, 291
International Covenant on Civil and Political Rights (ICCPR), 108–9, 203–7; "reservations" to, 206–7, 222, 281
International Covenant on Economic, Social and Cultural Rights, 161
International Criminal Court, 11, 14, 95, 166; on Afghan war, 273–74, 276; on "collateral damage," 274; on "complementarity," 254; on "crime of aggression," 276–78; establishment of, 253–69; EU support for, 171, 256, 257; on Garzón, 248; in Goldstone Report, 296–98, 301; on Israel & Gaza, 273, 275–76, 290; and Like-Minded Group, 256–60, 263–64, 269–70; and NGOs, 165, 256–60, 263–66; and non-surrender agreements, 268–69, 270; and Protocol I, 257, 274; resistance to, 191, 196, 254–56, 260–63, 357–58; and

International Criminal Court (cont.)
Saddam Hussein, 176; and Security Council, 272, 277–78; unaccountability of, 254–56, 264–68, 278, 362; and UN peacekeeping missions, 176; U.S. response to, 253, 260–63, 266–69; *see also* Rome Statute

International Criminal Tribunal for Rwanda, 270, 294

International Criminal Tribunal for the Former Yugoslavia, 101, 239–40

International Federation for Human Rights, 243, 245, 258

international humanitarian law, 227–33; and Goldstone Report, 294–301; and Gulf War, 241; and ICC, 254, 257, 272; and Kosovo War, 233–37; and NGOs, 234–38, 304; and Yugoslavia tribunal, 239–40

International Human Rights Law Group, 4, 5, 209, 287

International Labor Organization, 166

international law: and "disaggregated" states, 116–18; and EC/EU, 131–33; "evolving norms" of, 93, 94–95, 171, 183, 358–59; and human rights, 102–3, 160–61; Koh on, 114–16, 156–57; practitioners of, 163–64; and universal jurisdiction, 106–8, 242–44, 291; *see also* customary international law; law of nations

International Law Commission, 257, 262

International Monetary Fund (IMF), 165, 166, 168–69; at G20, 174

International Telephone and Telegraph, 169

Iran, 40, 348, 355; and CEDAW, 211; and Israel, 282, 289; and nuclear weapons, xxii, 277

Iraq, 238, 241–42, 276

Ireland, 122, 148; and ICC, 270; and Israel, 291, 299*n;* on Lisbon Treaty, 123, 147; women's status in, 217

Islam & Muslims, 40; caliphate aims, 181, 182; and demographics, 184; and diversity agenda, 80; at Durban (OIC), 280, 282, 287, 289*n;* in Europe, 149–55, 309–10, 328, 355; and Muhammad cartoons, xxii, 153–55; *ummah,* 181, 328, 421–22; UN presence, 290; in U.S., 329–29

Islamic Center of Geneva, 152

Islamism, 181–82, 341, 343; appeasement of, 413; dominance of, 329; in Europe, 328, 355; and Israel, 284, 289, 292, 302, 304, 356; and Russia/China, 185; Saudi funding of, 328–29; Sharia, 150–51, 181, 182, 184, 328; and speech restrictions, 151–55; terrorism by, 180, 184, 186, 328; in U.S., 328–29

Israel (ancient), 16–19, 31

Israel (modern), 12, 17–18; as "apartheid state," 105, 282, 284, 285, 286, 356; civilian protection, 296; and divestment campaigns, 285*n,* 291–92, 306–7, 356; and Durban conference, 279, 281–89; and Ford Foundation, 284–85; as front-line state, 192, 278, 289–93, 356; Gaza War, 273, 275, 291–303; "gender sensitization" in, 216; "genocide" charge, 284, 286, 287, 293; and Goldstone Report, 294–

302; and ICC / "war crimes," 255, 260, 265, 273, 275–76, 305; illegal immigrants to, 309; and Jenin "massacre," 291, 303; lawfare against, 291, 297, 307; and Lebanon, 291, 303; and NGOs, 166, 302–8; on Protocol I, 229, 234; security fence, 291, 303; terrorism in, 29, 291–93, 300–4; and universal jurisdiction, 243–44, 247, 291; U.S. support for, 291; as "vexing" problem, 17, 290

Israel Defense Forces (IDF), 296, 297, 302, 305

Italy: Africans in, 309; on capital punishment, 202; city-states of, 12; *Costa v. ENEL,* 128, 133–34; dual citizenship in, 309; and Fallaci, 152; *Francovich v. Italy,* 128; on Goldstone Report, 300; and Treaty of Rome, 121

Izz al-Din al-Qassam Brigade, 293

Jackson, Andrew, 66
Jackson, Jesse, 4
Japan, 40, 69, 191
Jay, John, 26, 52
Jefferson, Thomas, 28, 369; on Caesar, 27; on education, 56; on immigrants, 57–58, 311; and Locke, 24; progressives on, 66
Jerusalem Post, 288, 302, 306
Jewish Telegraphic Agency, 284–85
Jilani, Hina, 295, 301
Johnson, Lyndon, 160*n*
Joint Chiefs of Staff of the Armed Forces, 229–32, 242
Jordan, Barbara, 338–40
Juste, Carsten, 153
Jyllands-Posten, 153–54

Kagan, Donald, 77*n*
Kagan, Robert, 194, 195–96
Kaiser Family Foundation, 324–25
Kant, Immanuel, 12, 19–24, 34, 51, 183; and Europe, 195; on republicanism, 21–23; on "soulless despotism," 21, 364
Kaul, Hans-Peter, 273*n*
Kelly, Jim, 173
Kemp, Richard, 296*n*
Kennedy, Anthony, 108–10, 114
Kennedy, John F., 160*n*, 277
Kenya, 273*n*
Kerber, Linda, 96–97, 98
Kersch, Ken, 110
Kesler, Charles, 49
Keynes, John Maynard, 180
Khan, Irene, 286, 287
King, Martin Luther, 43, 317
King, Rodney, 208
Kirkpatrick, Jeane, 187
Kirsch, Philippe, 258–60, 263–64, 269
Kissinger, Henry, 20, 106–7; on "one phone call," 355; realpolitik of, 179, 180
Klor de Alva, Jorge, 75
Knesset, 305, 306
Knight v. Florida, 111
Koh, Harold, 95, 114–15, 119, 224; on CEDAW, 211; confirmation hearings, 156–57; on "domesticating" international law, 359–60; on *Filartiga,* 107–8; and ICC Kampala conference, 276, 277; on "transnational norm entrepreneurs," 264
Kohl, Helmut, 362
Köhler, Horst, 177–78
Kojève, Alexandre, 364
Kokott, Juliane, 138

Kors, Alan, 89–90
Kosovo War, 233–38, 241, 277, 422
Kunstler, William, 245
Kuwait, 154
Kyl, Jon, 194*n*
Kymlicka, Will, 75
Kyoto protocols, ix

Laeken Declaration on the Future of the European Union, 123, 145
Lafont, Suzanne, 214*n*
Lamm, Carolyn, 248
Lamy, Pascal, 167, 174
landmines, 161, 165, 258
Lantos, Tom, 281–84, 286–87
La Raza, National Council of, 4, 91
Latvia, 123
lawfare, 238–51; on Afghan & Iraq wars, 241–42; vs. Israel, 291, 297, 307; and Pinochet, 245–46; and universal jurisdiction, 242–48, 291; and Yugoslavia, 239–40
law of armed conflict (LOAC). *See* international humanitarian law
law of nations, xxiii, 101–4, 242–43; Founders on, 32–34, 101; Kant on, 22, 34; *see also* international law
law of war. *See* international humanitarian law
Lawrence v. Texas, 110–11
Law Without Nations (Rabkin), 23
Lawyers Committee for Human Rights, 4; on ICC, 256, 258, 264; and Israel, 286–87; *see also* Human Rights First
Leadership Conference on Civil and Human Rights, 4, 287
Lebanon, 291, 303
Lee, Richard Henry, 46
Lenin, Vladimir, 89
Lennon, John, 40

Leonard, Eric, 263
Lerner, Robert, 77, 78
Liberal Democracy and Political Science (Ceaser), 47
liberalism, 35–36, 38–39, 165, 344; and civil rights movement, 71–73; and critical theory, 85–92; and diversity agenda, 79–85; in Europe, 149–50, 154–55; on individual merit, 214–15; and multiculturalism, 73–79; and national identity, 41–44; and progressivism, 64–71
Libya, 154, 250
Lichter, Daniel, 326
Lijphart, Arend, 394
Lincoln, Abraham, 43, 66; Gettysburg Address, 44, 52, 53, 55; honoring of, 317; on immigrants, 59, 318–19; on natural rights, 65; on patriotism, 53–55, 101; on religion, 54; on sovereignty, xx, 23
Lindseth, Peter, 130–31*n*
Lipset, Seymour Martin, 69
Lisbon Treaty, 123–29, 143–49, 353; and "democratic deficit," 145–47; and financial crisis, 172; Irish vote on, 123, 147; public opinion on, 147–49, 157; subsidiarity in, 143, 146–47
Lithuania, 123
Livni, Tzipi, 297, 415
Locke, John, 20, 144, 183; and Founders, 24–26, 30–33; on popular sovereignty, 25, 38; on transferring sovereignty, 342–43
Lockheed Martin, 170
"Locksley Hall" (Tennyson), 12
Lodge, Henry Cabot, 266
Los Angeles Unified School District, 310, 321
Lowry, Rich, 333

Lutz, Donald, 31, 32
Luxembourg, 121, 148
Lynch, Fred, 83

Maastricht Treaty (Treaty on European Union), 123, 127; "competences" in, 142–43; objections to, 123, 157; subsidiarity in, 143
MacArthur Foundation: diversity agenda, 89; and Durban conference, 5, 288; Goldstone award, 294; and ICC, 257; on immigrants, 313; and NGOs, 165–66
Mac Donald, Heather, 321
Machiavelli, Niccolò, 19–20, 179
MacKinnon, Catharine, 87, 88
Madison, James, 24, 26, 38; on education, 56; on European law, 111–12; on human nature, 45–46; on immigrants, 57; on patriotism, 51–52
Magna Carta, 38, 189
Mahmood, Khalid, 151
Maistre, Joseph de, 63
Maksoud, Hala, 4
Malaysia, 84, 234
Malinowski, Thomas, 225
Malloch Brown, Mark, 188, 191
Maloney, Carolyn, 211
Malta, 123
Mandelson, Peter, 172
Mann, Thomas, 13
Marcuse, Herbert, 86, 90–91
Marshall, John, 46
Marshall, Paul, 154
Marshall Plan, 119
Marx, Karl, 124
Marxism, xvi, 71, 180; "cultural," 86–89, 92; Colombian guerrillas, 238; Gramsci, 345; in Grenada, 277; *see also* communism
Maryland, 76–77, 315

Mason, George, 46
Massachusetts, 314–15
Massimino, Elisa, 225
Mathews, Jessica T., 100
Matthews, Chris, 160*n*
Mattli, Walter, 132, 137–40
Mayer, Jane, 249
McDonald, Forrest, 26, 30, 77*n*
McDougall, Gay, 225, 287
McDougall, Walter, 77*n*
McKinley, William, 66
McLaren, Lauren, 148
McLeish, Archibald, 69
Mead, Walter Russell, xiv–xv, 159
Meese, Edwin, 81
Mellon Foundation, 89
Mendès-France, Pierre, 144–45
Menon, Raja, 357
Meritor Savings Bank v. Vinson, 87
Merkel, Angela, 149*n*, 416
Merriam, Charles, 65
Metternich, Klemens, Prince von, 63
Mexican American Legal Defense and Educational Fund, 4, 207
Mexico, 188; binational policies, 321–22; border violence, 333; and dual allegiance, 310, 313, 320–23; and U.S. border policy, 207–8, 309, 310
Meyer, Cord, 13
Michigan, 82, 83
Microsoft, 82, 83
Migration Policy Institute, 322, 323*n*, 330
Miller, Zell, 266
Milosevic, Slobodan, 233
Milton, John, 29, 31
Mink, Patsy, 88
Mirahmadi, Hedieh, 328
Mitterrand, François, 362
Mongol empire, 16
Monnet, Jean, 121, 137, 155, 156

Montesquieu, 47; and Founders, 25, 29–32; on mores, 48–49; on patriotism, 52

Morella, Connie, 211

Moreno-Ocampo, Luis, 248, 265, 269–71; on Israel, 273, 275–76, 290; on U.S., 273–74

Mott Foundation, Charles Stewart, 5, 89, 165–55

Movement against Racism and for Friendship between Peoples, 152

Moyers, Bill, 298

Muhammad, 16; cartoons of, xxii, 153–54

multiculturalism, 60, 73–79, 95–96; and "diversity," 79–85, 322; elite support for, 330–31; failure of, 149n; and Muslim immigration, 149–51

multinational corporations, 169–70

Murguia, Janet, 91–92

Murrow, Edward R., 69

Muslims. *See* Islam

NAACP Legal Defense Fund, 209

Nadler, Jerrold, 285n

Nagai, Althea, 77, 78

Napoleon Bonaparte, 11

Narula, Smita, 286

Nation, 70

National Association of Bilingual Educators, 322

National Coalition to Abolish the Death Penalty, 209

National Council for the Social Studies, 75

National Council of Churches, 4, 291

National Council of La Raza, 4, 91

National Farmers Union, 70

National History Standards, 77–79, 96

national identity, 39–43; American, 42, 43–47, 186–87; and corporate elites, 169–70; education for, 48–51; and emotional attachment, 51–56; in EU, 48, 53; and immigrants, 59–61, 318–26; and liberal internationalists, 119–20; and multiculturalism, 73–75, 79, 92, 163, 321–27; and "postnational" citizenship, 95–101, 119; progressives on, 68–69; public opinion on, 334–36; *see also* patriotism

"National Interest, The" (Jordan plan), 338–39

nationalism: authoritarian, 181–82; benefits of, 41; danger of, 178, 361–62; democratic, 181, 183, 240, 290, 334; ethnic, 45, 59; and EU, 137, 151; Mexican, 320–22

National Organization of Women, 4

national security, 195–96, 226, 345–46; and Anglosphere, 190; and ICC, 266–69, 276–77; and lawfare, 238–50; and multinational corporations, 169; and Protocol I, 227–42

NATO: and European peace, 362; and "war crimes," 233–35, 239–40, 273–74

Natsios, Andrew, 271

naturalization, 58–61; Oath of Renunciation and Allegiance, 319, 322, 340; *see also* citizenship; immigration

natural rights, 26, 30, 33, 48; in Declaration of Independence, 43, 347, 348, 367; and progressivism, 64–65

Nazir-Ali, Michael, 150

Nazis, 40, 64, 362; and empire, 178; and Nuremberg trials, 102

Ndiaye, Bacre Waly, 209–10
Nebraska, 83
Netanyahu, Binyamin, 243–44, 300–3, 305, 306
Netherlands, 11; as "consocial democracy," 394; EU constitution vote, 123, 127, 147; gender quotas in, 220; and ICC, 256, 257–58; and Israel, 300, 305; and Palestinian NGOs, 284; and Treaty of Rome, 121; *Van Gend & Loos*, 127–28, 132–33, 139; Wilders prosecution, 151–52
Neuman, Gerald, 320
New Deal, 66–68
New Republic, 70
Newton, Michael, 275
New York State, 75, 76
New York Times: on Garzón, 248; on immigration, 330; on Protocol I, 232–33
New York University: Center for Global Affairs, 119–20, 163
NGO Monitor, 305–6
Niebuhr, Reinhold, 70, 71
Nietzsche, Friedrich, 179
nonaligned nations, 228, 280, 299
nongovernmental organizations (NGOs): and CERD, 3–4, 8–9, 281; at Durban, 3–9, 165–66, 281, 283–89; and ICC, 165, 256–60, 263–66, 272–73; on immigration, 339; Israeli investigation of, 302–7; on landmines, 165, 258; lawfare by, 238–42; networking by, 164–65; Palestinian, 284–85, 290, 293; on Sudan, 272–73; and UN, 207, 211, 221; on U.S. human rights, 202–10; and World Bank, 165; *see also* Amnesty International; Human Rights Watch

Nonzero: The Logic of Human Destiny (Wright), 361
North Korea, 191, 348
Northwest Ordinance, 50
Norway: on capital punishment, 202; gender quotas in, 220; and ICC, 256, 258; on Israel & Palestinians, 283, 284, 291, 299*n;* and Muhammad cartoons, 154; and NGOs, 165
Notes on the State of Virginia (Jefferson), 58
Novak, Michael, 18–19
Nowak, Manfred, 248–49
Nuremberg trials, 102

Obama, Barack, & administration, 193; and ICC, 270, 276–77; and war on terror, 248–49, 277
O'Connor, Sandra Day, 82, 110, 113–14
Ohmae, Kenichi, 169
On Two Wings (Novak), 18
Open Europe, 148
Open Society Institute, 165
Oregon, 310, 320–21
Organization of American Historians, 96, 97
Organization of the Islamic Conference (OIC), xxii, 280, 282, 287, 298*n*
Oslo Freedom Forum, 164*n*
O'Sullivan, John, 189
Ottawa Landmines Conference, 258
Ottomans, 16, 349
Our Global Neighborhood (UN), 166
Oxfam, 164, 290, 293

Pace, William R., 264
Pakistan, 234, 249, 277
Palestine Liberation Organization, 205

Palestinian Authority, 275, 292, 301
Palestinian Center for Human Rights, 293, 300
Palestinian NGO Network, 285
Palestinians: at Durban, 283, 284–85, 288; *see also* Gaza
Paraguay, 107
Parallel Lives of Noble Greeks and Romans (Plutarch), 26, 31
Parents Against Police Brutality, 209
Parks, W. Hays, 228, 230–31, 237, 242
Parrington, Vernon, 65
Patrick, Stewart M., 197
patriotism (civic nationalism), 39–45, 51–56; education for, 52, 55–56; of immigrants, 57–61, 318–26; moral case for, 336–38; and multinational corporations, 169; *see also* national identity
Peace Now (NGO), 306–7
Peres, Shimon, 301
Permanent Court of International Justice, 103
Pew Foundation, 323n, 324–25
Pew Research Center, 327
Philadelphian sovereignty, xx–xxi, 36–38, 352–53, 369
philanthropy (foundations): at Durban, 5–6, 284–85, 288; and ICC, 257; on immigration, 329–30; on Israel, 290, 293; and multiculturalism, 89–90, 313, 323n; transnationalism of, 95, 162, 165–66
Philippines, 191, 220, 234
Phillips, Nicholas Addison, Lord, 150
Piereson, James, 66
Pietra Report, La, 97
Pillay, Navi, 290, 300
Pilon, Roger, 162n
Pinochet, Augusto, 245–46

Plattner, Marc, 25, 37, 38
Pledge of Allegiance, 119, 317
Plutarch, 26, 31, 32
Poland, 123, 129n; as ally, 353; and CEDAW, 219; on Goldstone Report, 300
Portes, Alejandro, 324
Portugal, 122, 219–20, 299n
Posner, Michael, 4, 286–87
"postmodern states," 129–30, 176–78; and ICC, 256–60, 264
Powell, Catherine, 224–26, 310
Powell, Colin, 243, 282
Powell, Lewis, 81, 82
Printz v. United States, 111
Progressive Citizens of America, 70
Progressive Party, 71
progressives, 64–71; on civil rights, 69; on human rights, 183; managerialism of, 65; and national narrative, 68–69; and Popular Front, 70–71; *see also* transnational progressives
Protocol I. *See* Geneva Conventions: Additional Protocol I
Publius Valerius Publicola, 26
Pufendorf, Samuel, 22, 31, 32–34, 101

Qaeda, al-, 408
Qahtani, Mohammed al-, 245
Qian, Zhenchao, 326
Quebec, 353

Rabkin, Jeremy, 32; on Kant, 23–24; on WTO, 168
Rachman, Gideon, 173–74
racial issues, 6–9; critical theory on, 85–86, in diversity agenda, 80–85; in education, 204–5; and free speech, 209, 217; in policing, 203; and proportional representation, 8–9, 80–81, 208–9, 322; and repa-

rations, 6–7; structural racism, 6, 85–86, 105, 208–9; UN rapporteur on, 207–9; *see also* diversity agenda; UN Convention on the Elimination of All Forms of Racial Discrimination
Rage and the Pride, The (Fallaci), 152
Rainbow PUSH Coalition, 4
Rangel, Juan, 316–18, 323
Rapp, Stephen J., 277
Rasmussen, Anders Fogh, 153
Rasmussen poll, 333
Ratner, Michael, 245
Ravitch, Diane, 77, 78
Rawls, John, 75
Reagan, Ronald, & administration, 192; border policy, 208; and Grenada, 277; on group preferences, 81; on Protocol I, 229–33
realpolitik, 19–20, 179–81
Red Cross. *See* International Committee of the Red Cross
Reflections on the Revolution in Europe (Caldwell), 151
Reflections on the Revolution in France (Burke), xiii
Regents of the University of California v. Bakke, 81
Rehnquist, William, 109
Reid, Harry, 334
religion: in American founding, 18–19, 25, 30, 31; and diversity agenda, 80; in national identity, 40–42, 48, 54; vs. state, 421–22; *see also* Islam
"Repressive Tolerance" (Marcuse), 90–91
Republican Party, 66, 70, 193–94
Reuther, Walter, 70
Reves, Emery, 13
Revilla, Emiliano, 246
Reynolds, William Bradford, 81

Rice, Condoleezza, 270
Richard, Carl, 26–28
Riesman, David, 69
Rivkin, David, Jr., 101–2, 105, 171; on ICC, 255
Roberts, Andrew, 189
Roberts, John, 114
Roberts, Owen, 13
Robinson, Mary, 111, 290; at Durban, 3–5, 279–80, 282–83
Rockefeller Foundation, 5, 89, 165–66, 288
Rohrschneider, Robert, 148
Rolnik, Raquel, 250–51
Roman Empire, 11, 16
Romania, 123, 269
Romanovs, 63, 349
Rome (ancient), 11–12, 26–28, 31
Rome Statute of the International Criminal Court, 253–54, 257–66; amendments proposed, 253; Article 98, 268–69; on "crime of aggression," 276; and Goldstone, 294; ratification of, 267; *see also* International Criminal Court
Roosevelt, Eleanor, 70
Roosevelt, Franklin D., 119, 192; and New Deal, 66–67; as patriot, 41, 69, 101, 160*n*, 362; and Supreme Court, 140
Roosevelt, Theodore, 66; on immigrants, 57, 59–61, 311
Roper v. Simmons, 108–9, 112
Rose, Flemming, 153
Rosen, Jeffrey, 110
Roth, Kenneth, 4, 236; on Afghan & Iraq wars, 242; on Israel, 287, 298, 301; on Saddam Hussein trial, 176
Rothkopf, David, 169
Rousseau, Jean-Jacques, 45, 46
Rubenfeld, Jed, 168–69, 365–66
Rubin, Nancy, 202

Ruggie, John, xix–xx, 94
Rumbaut, Rubén G., 324
Rumsfeld, Donald, 244, 245
Rushdie, Salman, 151
Russell, Bertrand, 13
Russia, 177, 344; as BRIC nation, 357; as challenger, 180–82, 185; czarist, 63; on UN Human Rights Council, 250

Sagan, Carl, 13
Samuelson, Robert J., 323–24, 340
Sanchez, Ricardo, 244, 245
Sandel, Michael, 100
Sands, Philippe, 407–8
Sapey, Cedric, 301
Sarkozy, Nicolas, 149n, 153
Satanic Verses (Rushdie), 151
Saudi Arabia, 40, 154, 355; funding of HRW, 302–3; funding of Islamists, 328–29; on UN Human Rights Council, 250
Scalia, Antonin, 109–13, 114
Scheffer, David, 260–63, 265
Schlesinger, Arthur, Jr., 69–71; on multiculturalism, 76, 77n, 79
Schlesinger, Arthur, Sr., 68
Schulz, William, 244–45
Schuman, Robert, 121
Schuman Declaration, 174
Schumer, Charles, 160n
Schwarzkopf, Norman, 243
Scotland, 215
Scruton, Roger, 41–43, 45
Seabright, Jeff, 170
September 11 (9/11) attacks, 152, 170, 180; lawfare after, 240–42, 245; and Muslim alienation, 326n, 327; and patriotism, 317, 325; and "xenophobia," 310
Service Employees International Union (SEIU), 330

Sewall, Gilbert T., 77n, 78
Shanker, Albert, 77
Shapiro, Ilya, 162n
Sharansky, Natan, 39–41, 42
Sharia (Islamic law), 181, 182; in Europe, 150–51, 328; in U.S., 328–29
Sharon, Ariel, 243–44, 291
Shea, Nina, 272
Shultz, George, 231–32
Sidney, Algernon, 29, 31
Sifton, John, 242
Simpson, Alan, 339
Singapore, 191, 213–14, 234, 352n
Singh, Manmohan, 190
Single European Act, 122, 127, 142
Skin Deep (film), 90
Slaughter, Anne-Marie (Burley), 14, 132; on "disaggregated" states, 116–17, 139–40, 181; on ECJ, 137–39; on ICC, 263; on "meaningful representation," 348, 349–50
Slovakia, 123, 300
Slovenia, 123, 218
Smith, Adam, 30
Smith, Fred, 162n
Smith, Lamar, 339
Smith, William French, 81
Snowe, Olympia, 88
Solana, Javier, 154, 174
Somalia, 215
SOS Racisme, 152
Soustelle, Jacques, 144
Souter, David, 114
South Africa, 280; and ICC, 256, 258, 270
South Korea, 191, 270
Soviet Union, xvi, 44n, 64; and Cold War, 179–80; fall of, 93; liberal conflict over, 69–70; on Protocol I, 228–29

Sowell, Thomas, 84
Spain, 11, 122; Civil War, 247; gender quotas / CEDAW, 219–20; and Israel, 299*n*, 305; and universal jurisdiction, 245–48
Spalding, Matthew, 53, 55
Spirit of the Laws (Montesquieu), 29
Spiro, Peter, ix, 117–18, 158, 175–76, 181
Sri Lanka, 190, 234
Standley, Andrew, 306–8
Starbucks, 83
Stein, Eric, 135
Steinberg, Gerald, 305–6
Stephan, Paul B., 104–5
Stevens, John Paul, 114
Stone Sweet, Alec, 131–32
Strauss, Leo, 364–65
Strauss-Kahn, Dominique, 174
Sudan, 154, 250; and ICC, 270, 271–73; NGOs on, 304
Sweden, 123; on Afghan war, 241; currency, 361; gender quotas, 220; and ICC, 256, 258; on Israel, 291, 299*n*; Muslim violence in, 309; and Palestinian NGOs, 284; and Protocol I, 228; and universal jurisdiction, 245
Switzerland, 152; on Israel, 291, 299*n*; minaret ban, 309; and Protocol I, 228
Syria, 154, 250

Taft, William Howard, 66
Tajikistan, 254
Talbott, Strobe, 15–17, 191, 350; on Israel, 16–17, 290; on Kant vs. Hobbes, 19–21, 195
Taylor, Charles, 75
Tenet, George, 244
Tennyson, Alfred, Lord, 12
terrorism, 180, 184, 186, 328; in Israel, 29, 291–93, 303–4; Lockerbie, 238*n;* and Protocol I, 228–29, 232–33, 327; *see also* Hamas; September 11
Thailand, 191, 234
Thatcher, Margaret, 64, 122, 145; and *Factortame* (ECJ), 141–42, 147
Thernstrom, Stephan, 77*n*
Thirty Years War, 36
Thomas, Clarence, 109, 114
Thurmond, Strom, 70
Tocqueville, Alexis de, 47–48, 80, 358–59, 364
Toynbee, Arnold, 13
transjudicialism, 14, 116–18, 368
transnational pragmatists, 162–63, 187, 194; corporate, 162, 169–70; on democracy, 342, 347; on financial regulation, 172–75; hawkish, 196–97; influence of, 344–45
transnational progressives, 64, 160–69, 184, 193, 342; in Anglosphere, 190–91; in churches, 291; and democracy, 342; at Durban, 279, 281; in foundations, 165–66; Goldstone as, 294; and Israel, 290–91, 298, 356; lawyers as, 163–64, 345; in NGOs, 164–65, 237, 248; on "pooling" sovereignty, 176–77; as post-American, 344; in universities, 163, 251; as utopian, 346–47; in WTO, 167–69
Travers, Desmond, 295, 301
Treaty of Rome (European Community Treaty), 121–22, 126, 142; "constitutionalization" of, 130–35; ECJ in, 127; opposition to, 144–45
Treaty of Westphalia, 36, 129
Treaty on European Union. *See* Maastricht Treaty
Trenchard, John, 29

Truman, Harry, 69, 160*n*; anticommunism of, 70–71, 79; Marshall Plan, 119
Truman Doctrine, 69
Turkey, 233, 234, 344
Turner, Frederick Jackson, 65
Tyson Foods, 330

Uganda, 270
Ukraine, 300
Union for Democratic Action, 70
United Kingdom. *See* Great Britain
United Methodist Church, 207
United Nations (UN), xix, 94, 102, 104, 129; and Balkans, 239–40, 268; Charter of, 13, 277; on CIA interrogations, 248–49; Commission on Global Governance, 166; on drone strikes, 249–50; Goldstone mission, 293–302; and ICC, 253, 257–58, 262, 268; and Israel, 166, 290, 293; on Muhammad cartoons, 154; and NGOs, 164, 165; treaty monitoring committees, 211–22, 368; *see also* UN Security Council
UN Commission on Human Rights, 202–3, 207–10, 250
UN Convention against Torture, 245, 248
UN Convention on the Elimination of All Forms of Discrimination against Women (CEDAW), 210–14; ABA on, 164, 219, 222–24; on child care, 217, 218, 220, 224; on "comparable worth," 219; monitoring committees, 211–20; resistance to, 210, 307; and "substantive equality," 212–15, 219–20; in U.S., 110, 210, 219, 222–25
UN Convention on the Elimination of All Forms of Racial Discrimina-

tion (CERD), 3–4, 5; "reservations" on, 8, 217, 222, 281, 307; on substantive equality, 8–9
UN Convention on the Rights of the Child, 108–9, 161, 215–16; U.S. on, 222, 225–26
UN Durban Review Conference (Durban II), 289*n*
UN Fact Finding Mission on the Gaza Conflict (Goldstone mission), 293–302; bias in, 294–95; European ambivalence on, 299–300; Report on, 295–99; Goldstone's disavowal, 300–2; and NGOs, 295, 298, 299, 300–1; recommendations of, 296–97
UN Human Rights Council, 249–50; vs. Israel, 290, 293, 295–97, 300, 301; undemocratic members of, 250
UN Migrant Rights Treaty, 310
UN Security Council, 185, 348; on Darfur, 270, 272; in Goldstone Report, 297; and ICC, 257, 258, 262, 268, 277–78; and Yugoslavia tribunal, 239
UN World Conference against Racism, Racial Discrimination, Xenophobia and Related Intolerance (Durban, 2001), 3–9; anti-Israel/anti-Semitic bias, 281–89; Europeans at, 283; NGOs at, 3–9, 165–66, 281, 284–89; NGO Forum Declaration, 286–88; non-aligned nations at, 280; Palestinians at, 284–85; on reparations, 282, 283; transnational progressives at, 279, 281; walkout from, 281, 283
United Neighborhood Organization (UNO), 316–18, 319
United States: "Americanization" movement, 57–61; capital punish-

ment in, 108–11, 202, 204, 209–
10, 355; church/state, 205; civil
rights movement, 45, 71–73, 80–
81; as creedal nation, 44–45; in
Cold War, 179–80; constraints on,
177, 187–89, 194–96; diversity
agenda in, 79–85; ethnic subcultures in, 312, 319; federalism in,
47, 49, 111, 216, 217; free speech
in, 8, 66, 91, 205, 209, 217; and
G20, 174; on Goldstone Report,
300; human rights in, 201–25,
244–51; on ICC, 253, 260–63,
266–69; and ICCPR, 281; Iraq
War, 241–42; and Israel, 291;
language minorities in, 204; Mexicans in, 309, 310, 313–14; "mobility ladders" in, 84; as multinational
state, 76–79; Naturalization Act,
58–59; New Deal, 66–68; non-
surrender agreements, 268–69;
patriotism in, 51–56; progressivism
in, 64–71; racial issues / CERD, 3–
6, 8–9, 105, 203, 204–5, 208–9,
281; religion in, 48, 49–50, 54;
"systemic inequality" in, 88, 203,
205–6, 225; Tocqueville on, 47–
48; UN investigations of, 207–10,
248–51; war on terror, 205, 248–
50, 327; women's status / CEDAW,
203–4, 210–11, 219, 222–25; as
"xenophobic," 310; *see also* American Founders
Universal Declaration of Universal
Human Rights, 6, 102, 236, 367
universal jurisdiction, 106–8, 242–
50, 291, 415; and Goldstone
Report, 296–98
University of California, 81
University of Michigan Law School,
82, 110
University of Nebraska, 89–90

University of Virginia, 56
USA Patriot Act, 241
U.S. Border Patrol, 204, 208, 217
U.S. Chamber of Commerce, 330
U.S. Commission on Civil Rights, 4
U.S. Congress, 34, 120; Alien Tort
Statute, 107; American Service-
Members' Protection Act, 266–67,
270; Civil Rights Act, 71–72;
enabling legislation, 115; Gender
Equity in Education Act, 88; and
ICC, 262–63, 269, 270; on immi-
gration, 310, 333–34, 339; and
Israel support, 291; Naturalization
Act, 58–59; Nethercutt amend-
ment, 269, 270; and New Deal,
67–68; on terror financing, 205;
USA Patriot Act, 241; Violence
Against Women Act, 88; Voting
Rights Act, 72; *see also* U.S. House
of Representatives; U.S. Senate
U.S. Constitution, 37–38, 46, 49–50;
Bill of Rights, 176, 190, 368; and
capital punishment, 204; as "controlling," 118, 157–58, 359; equal
protection clause, 225; First
Amendment, 8, 91, 209, 217; and
foreign law, 109–18; and ICC, 255,
266; and international treaties, 8,
206–7; national unity in, 76; in
naturalization oath, 58–59; popular
attachment to, 335, 336*n;* subordination of, 94–95, 156–58; and
"world opinion," 347–48
U.S. Court of Appeals for the Second
Circuit, 107
U.S. Department of Defense, 232,
246
U.S. Department of Justice, 205,
244–46; Civil Rights Division, 81
U.S. Department of State, 358; on
CERD, 8; on "crime of aggres-

U.S. Department of State (cont.) aggression," 276–78; officials of, 14, 95, 116, 157, 224–25; on religious liberty, 355; treaty reservations, 8, 229

U.S. House of Representatives, 267; race in, 208

U.S. Immigration and Naturalization Service, 208

U.S. Math Olympiad, 310

U.S. Senate: CEDAW ratification, 110, 210; CERD ratification, 8; on civil rights, 71–72; and ICC, 262–63, 266–67; on immigration law, 323, 333–34; "meaningful representation" in, 348; on National History Standards, 77

U.S. Supreme Court, 114; *Bakke*, 81; *Brown v. Board of Education*, 204–5; foreign law at, 108–13, 157, 360; *Griggs v. Duke Power Company*, 81; *Grutter v. Bollinger*, 82, 110; on illegal aliens, 204; *Knight v. Florida*, 111; *Lawrence v. Texas*, 110–11; *Meritor* (sexual harassment), 87; *Printz v. United States*, 111; on race, 204–5; on right of appeal, 204; and Roosevelt, 140; *Roper v. Simmons*, 108–9, 112; *Zobrest*, 205

Utah, 310, 321

Vabre case, 135

Van Gend & Loos, 127–28, 132–35, 139

Van Orden, Geoffrey, 148

Van Rompuy, Herman, 172

Vasquez, Hugh, 90

Vatican, 309

Vattel, Emmerich de, 22, 32–34, 101

Venezuela, 255

Vietnam, 191, 250

Vietnam War, 73, 231, 386

Vigdor, Jacob, 325

Violence Against Women Act (1994), 88

Vital Center, The (Schlesinger), 71

Voltaire, 29

Voting Rights Act (1965), 72

Wales, 215

Wallace, Henry, 70–71, 79

Wall Street Journal, 330

war crimes charges: in Afghanistan, 273–74, 276; in Balkans, 233–36, 239–40; in Colombia, 238; in Darfur, 270–72; in Gulf War, 243; and ICC, 254, 257, 270–78; and Israel (Gaza), 273, 275–76, 293–301, 305; and NATO, 233–35, 239–40, 273–74; universal jurisdiction for, 106, 243–48; vs. U.S., 243, 245–47, 403

war on terror, 248–50, 327

Washburn, John L., 253, 259

Washburn, Wilcomb, 77*n*

Washington, George, 27–29, 46; on education, 55–56, 163; honoring of, 317; on immigrants, 57, 311, 318, 340; on liberty, 192; on patriotism, 53–56; on religion & morality, 49–50, 54

Washington Post, 300, 323, 340; on Protocol I, 232–33

Washington State, 83

Weatherford, Jack, 16

Webster, Noah, 56

Weiler, Joseph, 131

Weinberger, Caspar, 230, 231–32

Weiner, Myron, 84

Wells, H. G., 13, 159

Westphalian sovereignty, xx, 36–37, 129, 352

Weyerhaeuser, 83

Whelan, Edward, 360

Whigs, 26, 28–30, 66
Whitson, Sarah Leah, 302–3
Wiesel, Elie, 164*n*, 304–5
Wilders, Geert, 151–52
Williams, Rowan, 150
Wilson, Edmund O., 13
Wilson, Woodrow, 74, 180; on immigrants, 57, 59–60, 311
Windschuttle, Keith, 189
Wolfensohn, James, 165
women's status, xi; quotas for, 220, 223; and "substantive equality," 212–15, 222–25; in UK, 212–13; and UN monitors, 216–20; in U.S., 203–4; *see also* UN Convention on the Elimination of All Forms of Discrimination against Women
Woolsey, Lynn, 210
World Bank, 165, 168, 169
World Council of Churches, 207, 291
World Economic Forum, 169, 275
World Federalist Association, 13
World Federalist Movement, 257, 264

world government, 12–14, 363–64
World Health Organization, 166
World Trade Organization, 165, 166–69
World War I, 63, 68
World War II: and EU idea, 121; and GATT, 167; and international law, 102; nationalism in, 41, 178, 361–62; progressives on, 68–69
Wright, Robert, 361
Wu, Harry, 164*n*
Wu, Yolanda S., 4

Yaalon, Moshe, 291
Yale Law School, 114, 119, 163
Yoo, John, 244
Yugoslavia, 233–37, 239–40
Yzaguirre, Raul, 4

Zakaria, Fareed, 39
zero-sum outcomes, xxii–xxiii, 184, 266, 358–61
Zobrest v. Catalina Foothills School District, 205
Zogby, James, 4
Zogby International, 327, 331–33